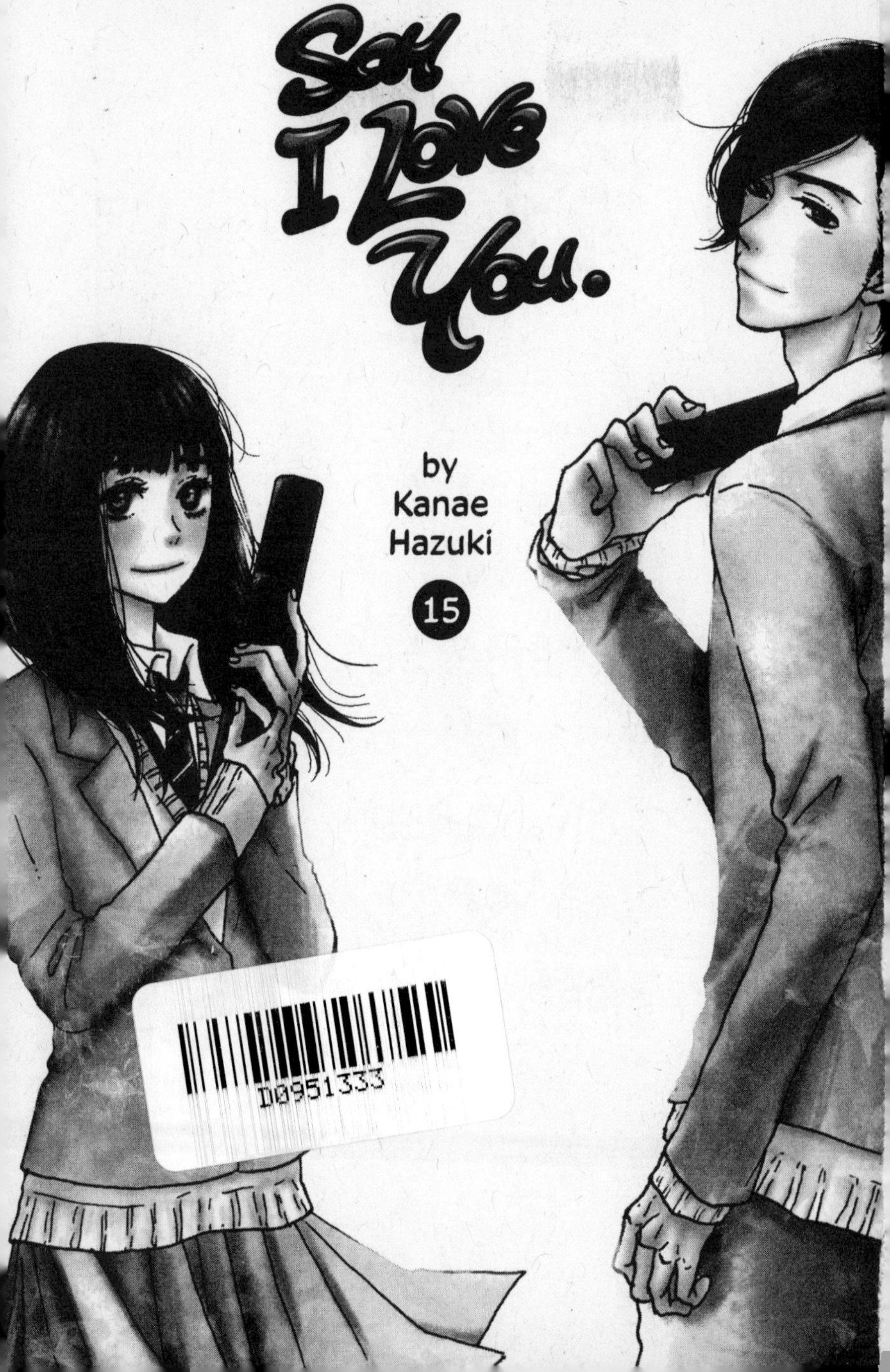
Say I Love You.
by
Kanae
Hazuki
15

Kanae Hazuki
presents

Say I Love You.

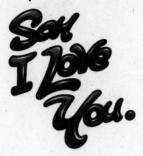

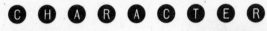

CHARACTER

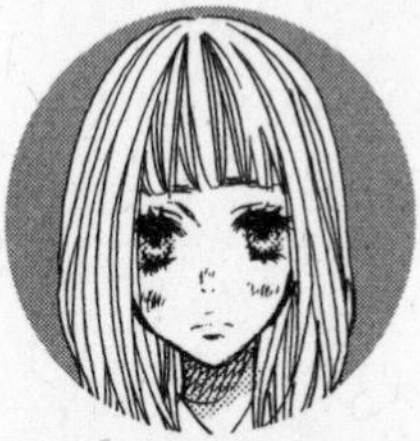

Mei Tachibana

A girl who hasn't had a single friend, let alone a boyfriend, in sixteen years and has lived her life trusting no one. She finds herself attracted to Yamato, who, for some reason, just won't leave her alone, and they start dating.

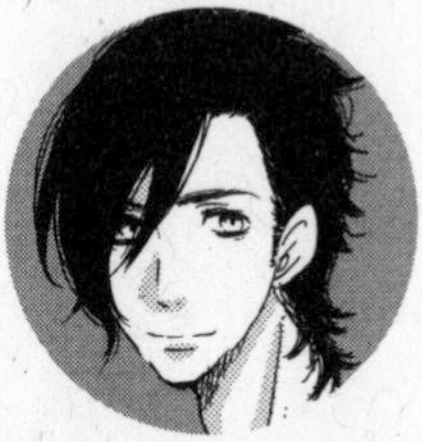

Yamato Kurosawa

The most popular boy at Mei's school. He has the love of many girls, yet for some reason, he is obsessed with Mei, the brooding weirdo girl from another class.

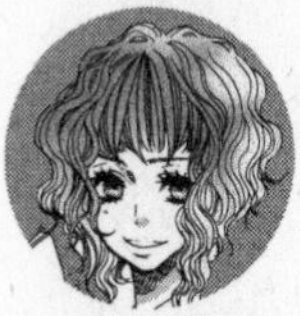

Megumi

A popular amateur model. She had her sights set on Yamato, but he rejected her. She set off on her own for Paris, to advance her modeling career.

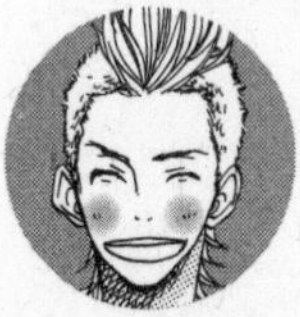

Kai

Yamato's classmate from middle school. For his own reasons, he started high school a year late. He dated the model Rin after she told him she loves him, but they've broken up?!

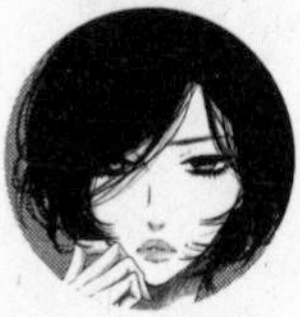

Rin Aoi

A first-year student at Mei's school, who is currently modeling under the name RIN. She fell in love with Kai at first sight, and they dated, but it didn't work out...

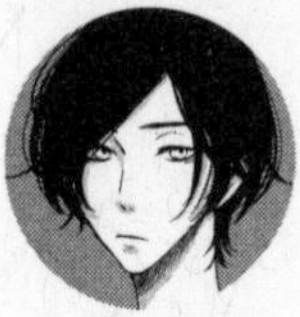

Ren Aoi

Rin's twin brother. The complete opposite of his social sister, he is rather unfriendly, but has a kind side. He introduced Mei to a preschool where she could volunteer.

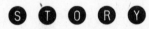

STORY

Mei Tachibana spent sixteen years without a single friend or boyfriend, but now she's starting the third year of her relationship with Yamato Kurosawa, the most popular boy in her school. Now third-years in high school, they each begin walking the path to their desired careers—a preschool teacher for Mei and a photographer for Yamato. Meanwhile, Megumi went to Paris over summer vacation, where she became the girlfriend of a French photographer. Kai started dating Rin after the amateur model confessed her love to him, but the relationship didn't work out and the two separated. All the while, Ren's feelings for Mei grow stronger...?!

Say "I love you".

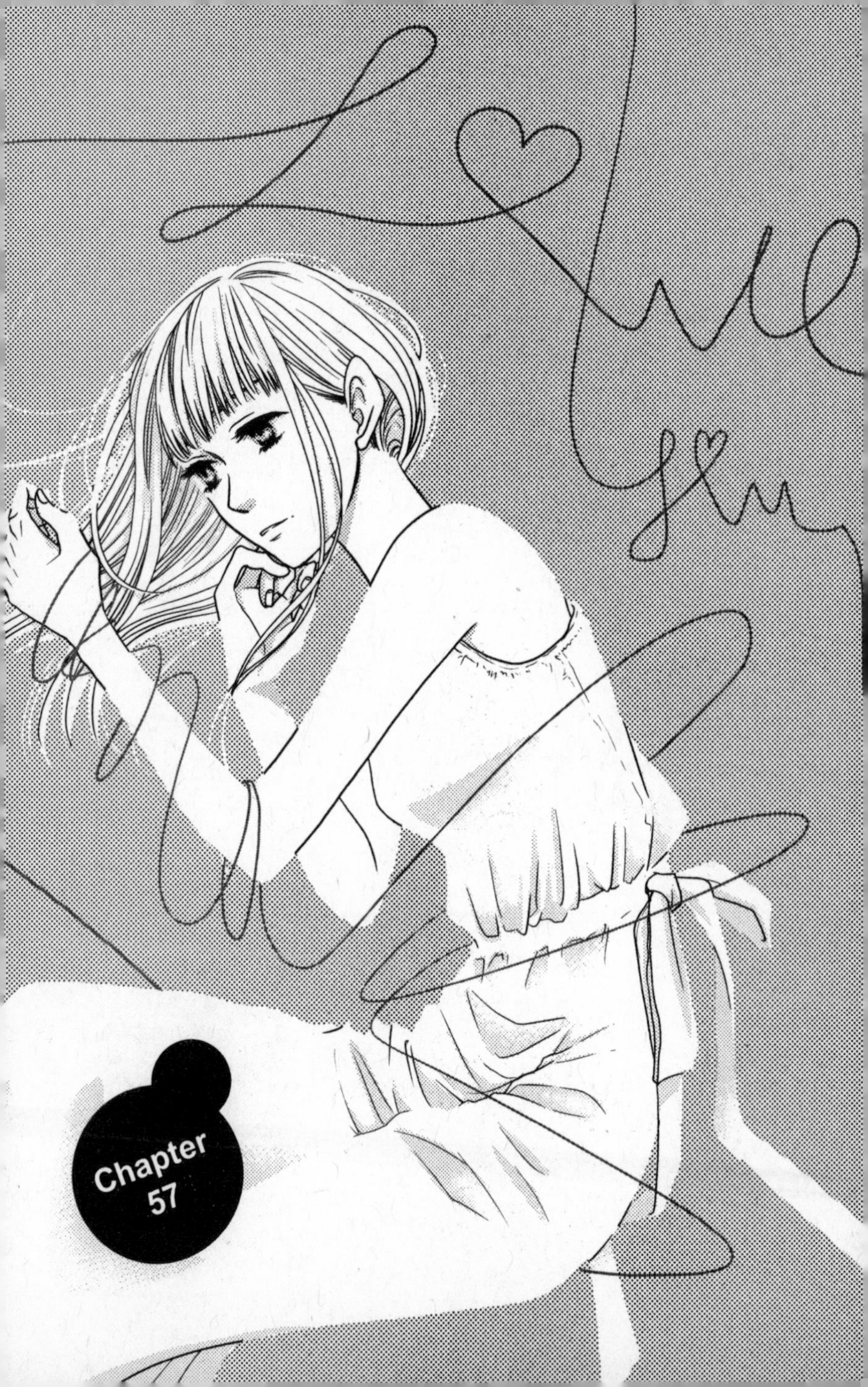
Chapter
57

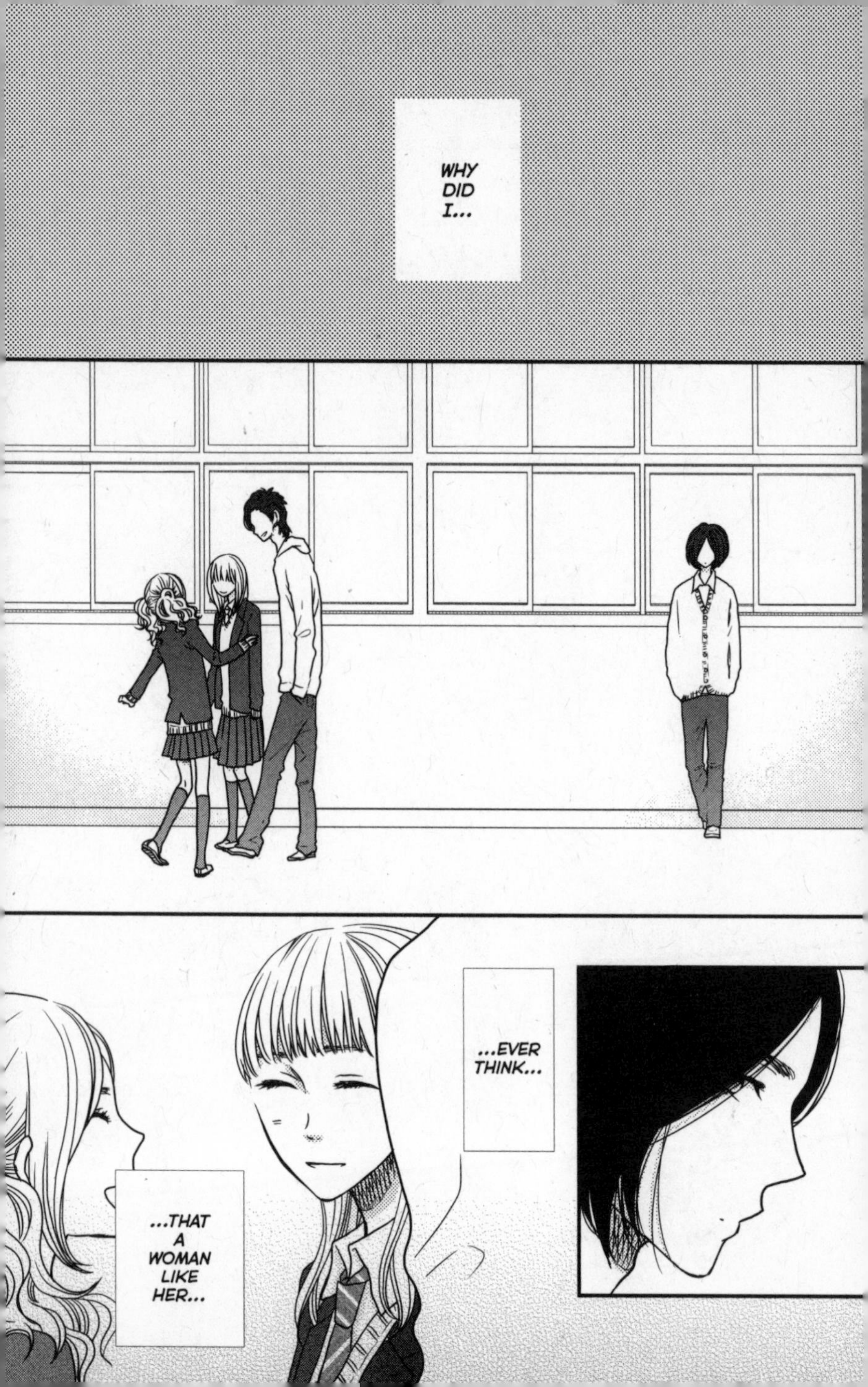
WHY DID I...
...EVER THINK...
...THAT A WOMAN LIKE HER...

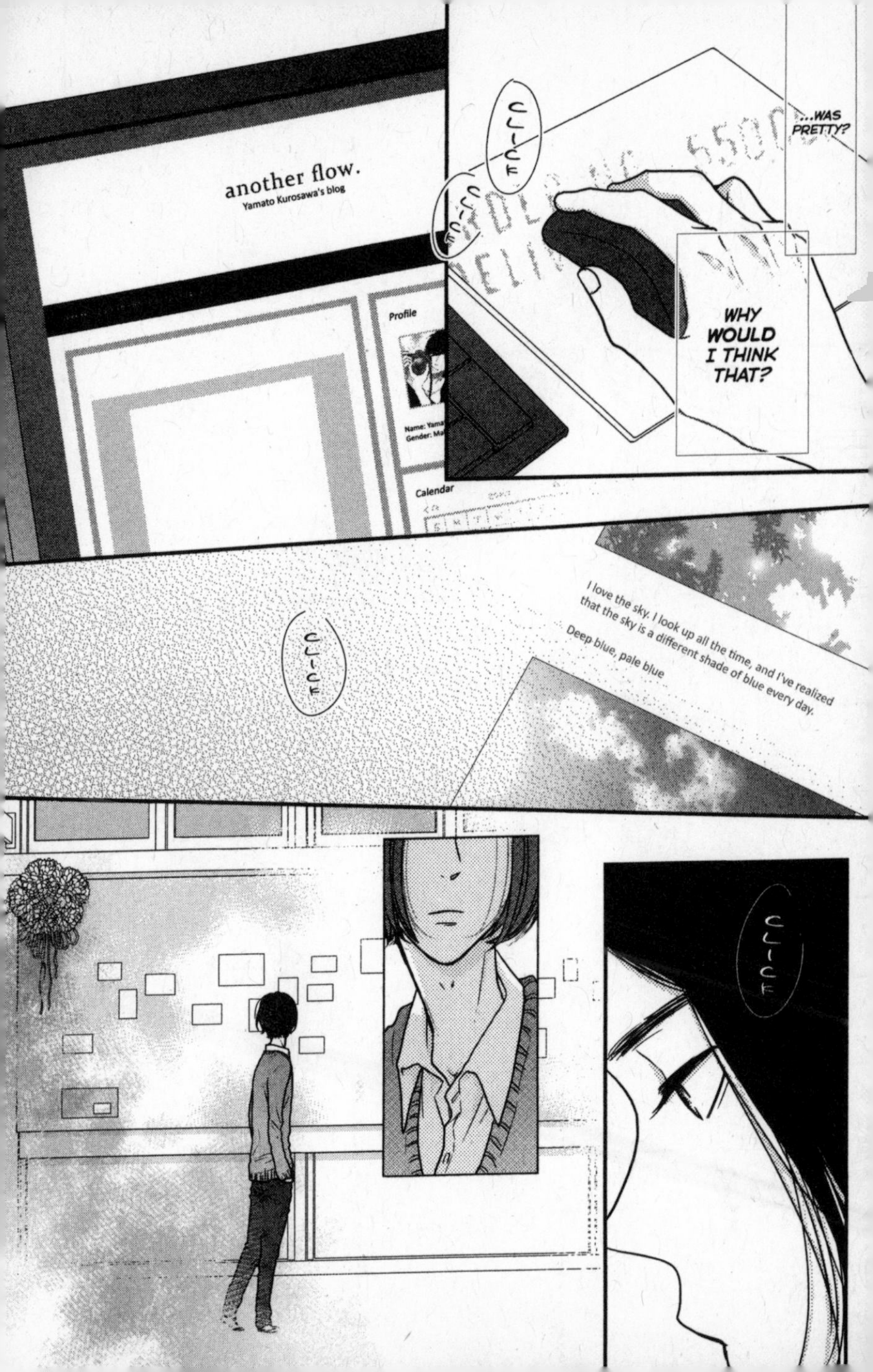

...WAS PRETTY?
CLICK
CLICK
WHY WOULD I THINK THAT?
another flow.
Yamato Kurosawa's blog
Profile
Calendar
I love the sky. I look up all the time, and I've realized that the sky is a different shade of blue every day.
Deep blue, pale blue
CLICK
CLICK

I CAN'T BELIEVE HE'S COMFORTABLE SHOWING PICTURES OF HIS GIRLFRIEND TO THE WHOLE WORLD.

BUT EVEN AS I ASK MYSELF THAT...

Yamato Kurosawa

I started a photo...
http://www.picb...

...I SIT HERE STARING AT PIC-TURES OF HER...

...AND MY EYES WON'T LET ME LIE TO MYSELF.

The backlighting makes her hair look brown. It was so pretty.

Comment

Comment   Twitter   Like

Read Comments

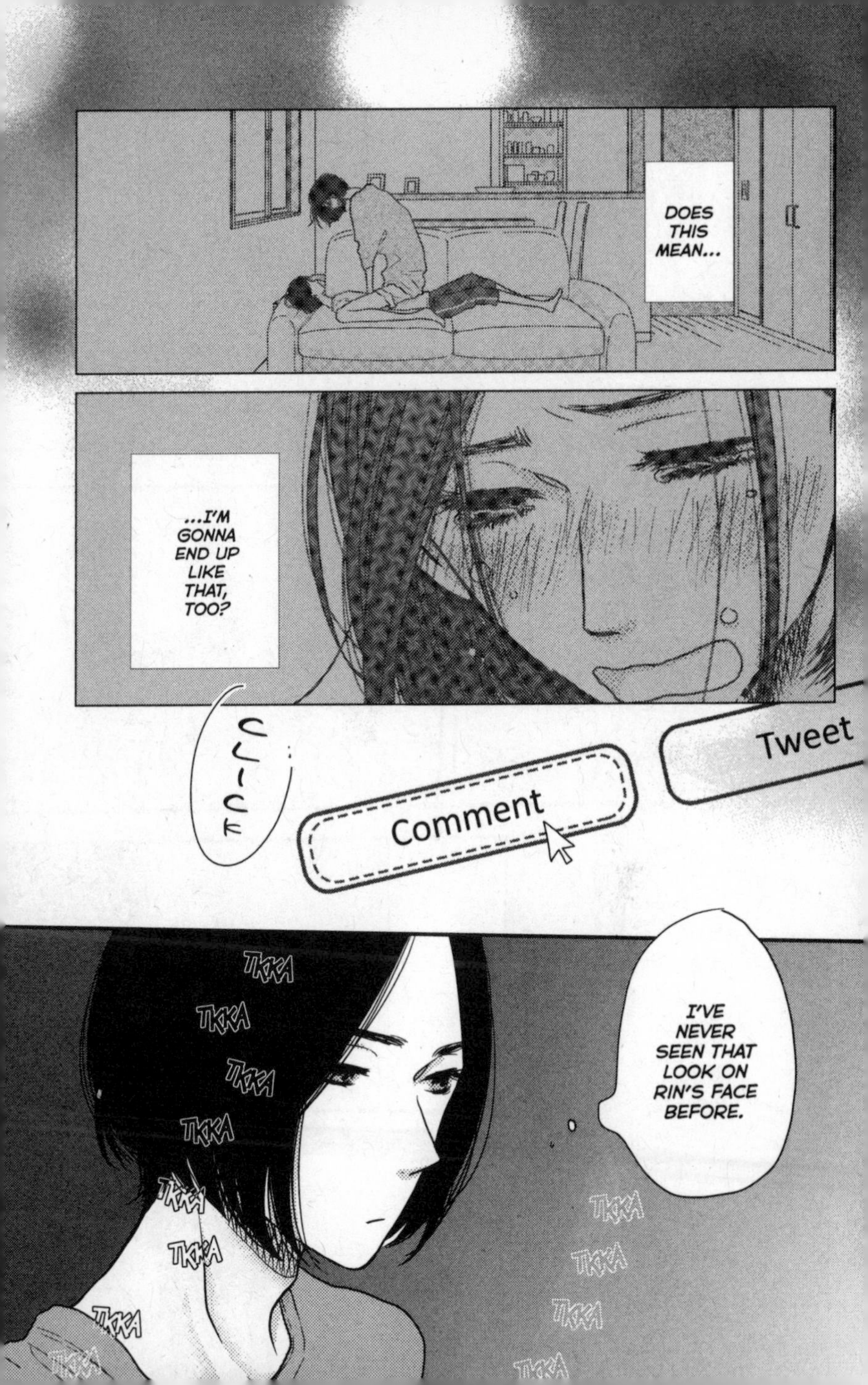
DOES THIS MEAN...
...I'M GONNA END UP LIKE THAT, TOO?
Tweet
Comment
CLICK
I'VE NEVER SEEN THAT LOOK ON RIN'S FACE BEFORE.
TKKA
TKKA
TKKA
TKKA
TKKA
TKKA
TKKA
TKKA
TKKA
TKKA
TKKA
TKKA

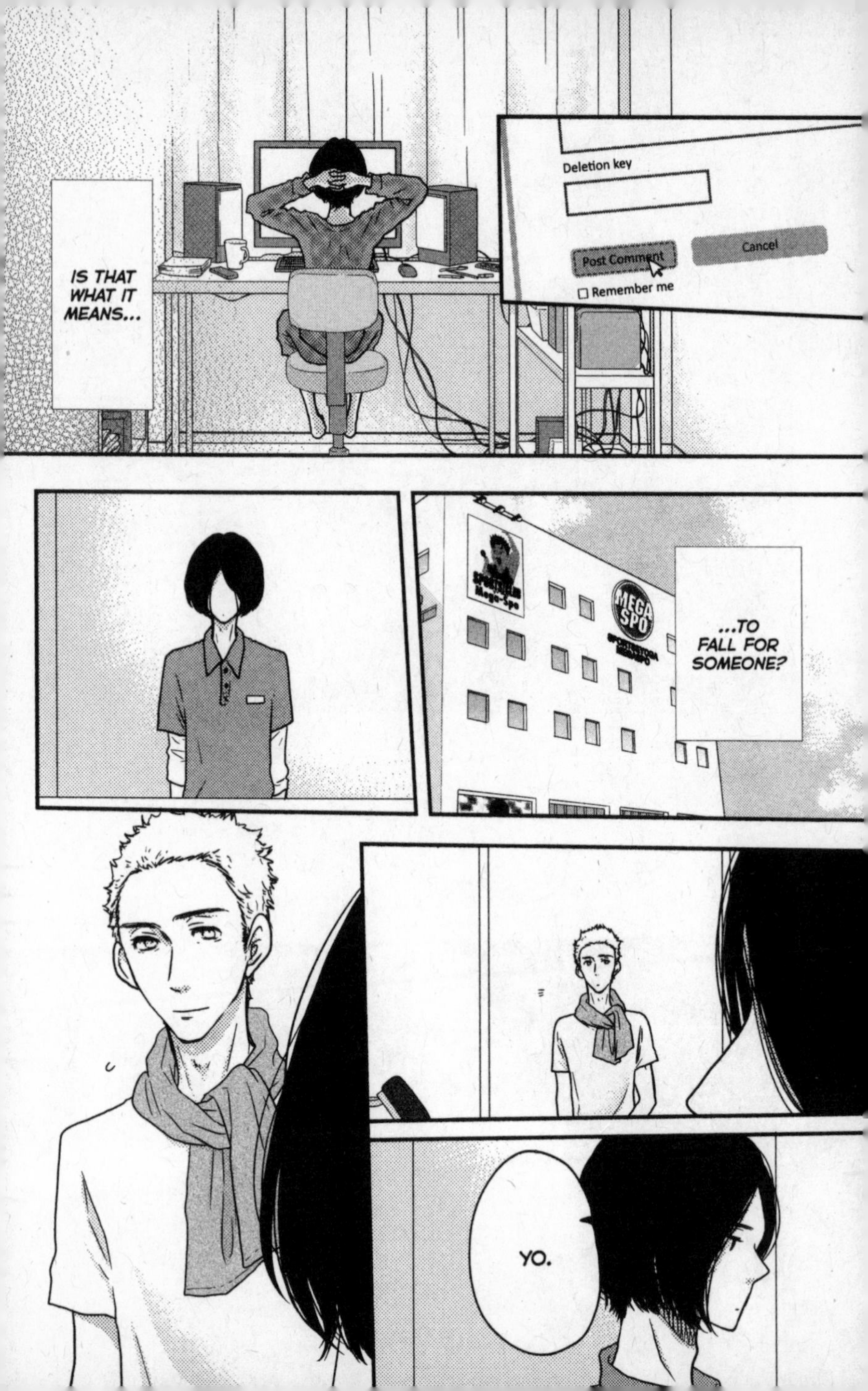
Deletion key
Post Comment
Cancel
Remember me
IS THAT WHAT IT MEANS...
MEGA SPO
...TO FALL FOR SOMEONE?
YO.

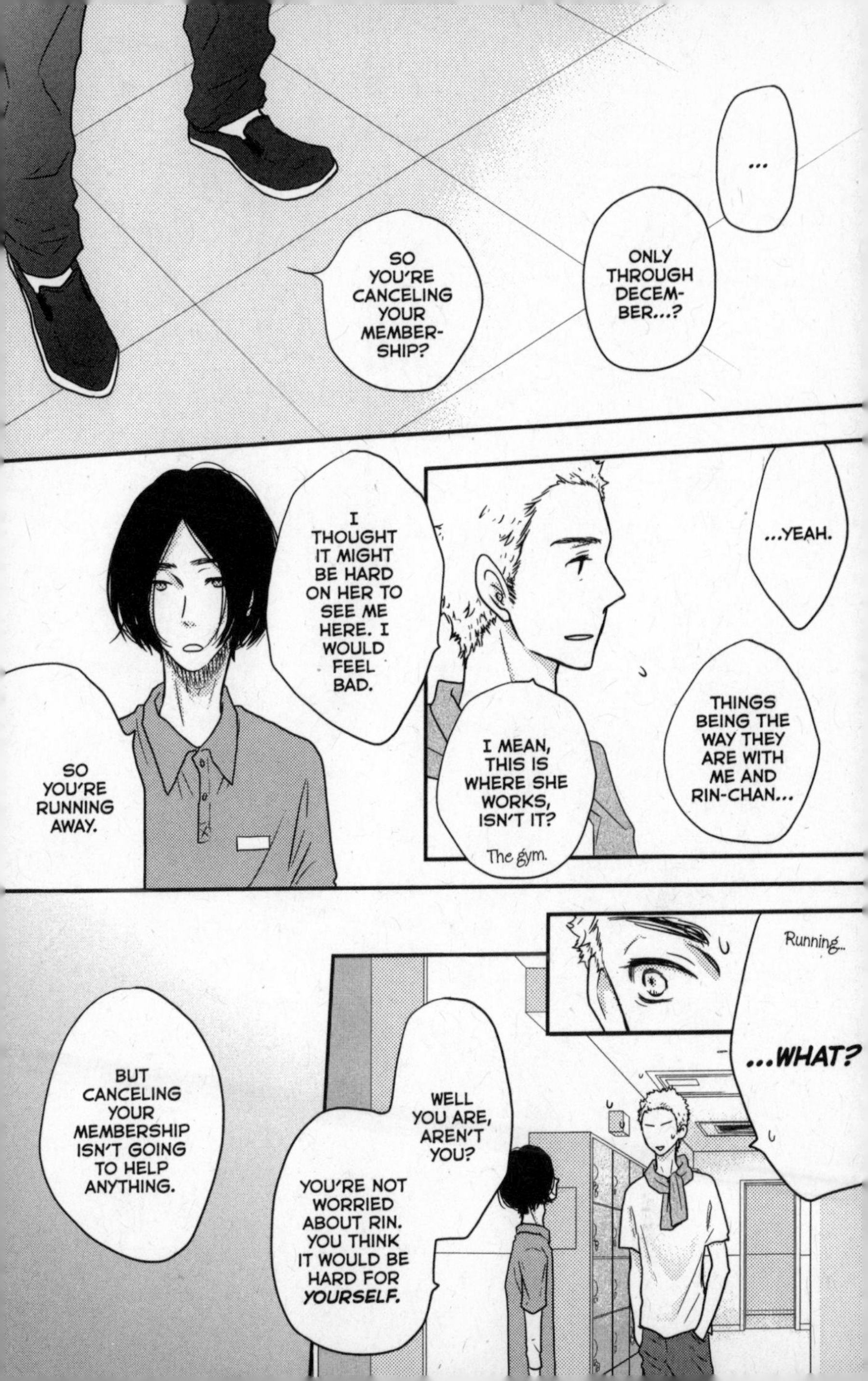
...
ONLY THROUGH DECEMBER...?
SO YOU'RE CANCELING YOUR MEMBERSHIP?
...YEAH.
THINGS BEING THE WAY THEY ARE WITH ME AND RIN-CHAN...
I MEAN, THIS IS WHERE SHE WORKS, ISN'T IT?
The gym.
I THOUGHT IT MIGHT BE HARD ON HER TO SEE ME HERE. I WOULD FEEL BAD.
SO YOU'RE RUNNING AWAY.
Running...
...WHAT?
WELL YOU ARE, AREN'T YOU?
YOU'RE NOT WORRIED ABOUT RIN. YOU THINK IT WOULD BE HARD FOR *YOURSELF*.
BUT CANCELING YOUR MEMBERSHIP ISN'T GOING TO HELP ANYTHING.

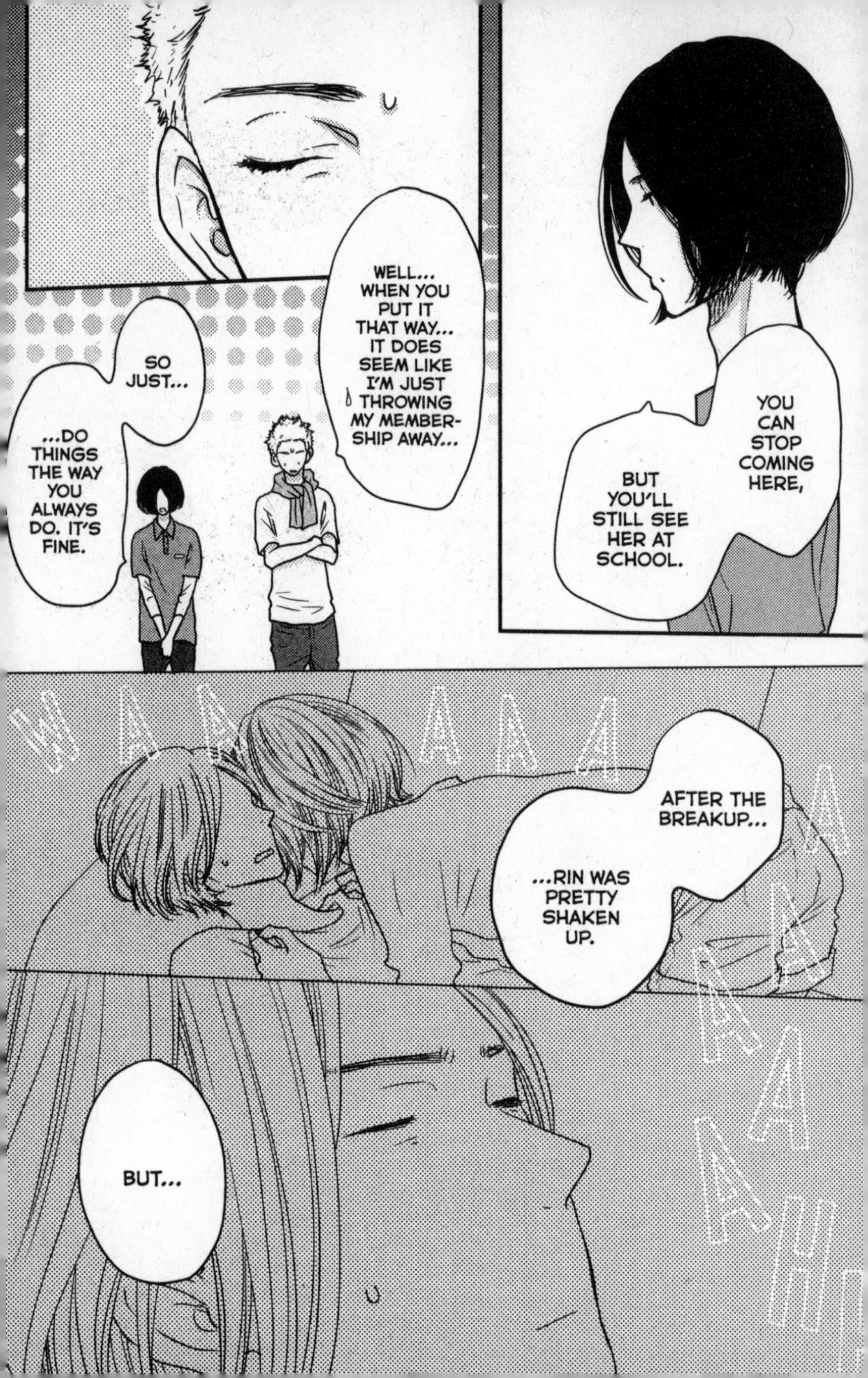
YOU CAN STOP COMING HERE,
BUT YOU'LL STILL SEE HER AT SCHOOL.
WELL... WHEN YOU PUT IT THAT WAY... IT DOES SEEM LIKE I'M JUST THROWING MY MEMBERSHIP AWAY...
SO JUST...
...DO THINGS THE WAY YOU ALWAYS DO. IT'S FINE.
AFTER THE BREAKUP...
...RIN WAS PRETTY SHAKEN UP.
BUT...

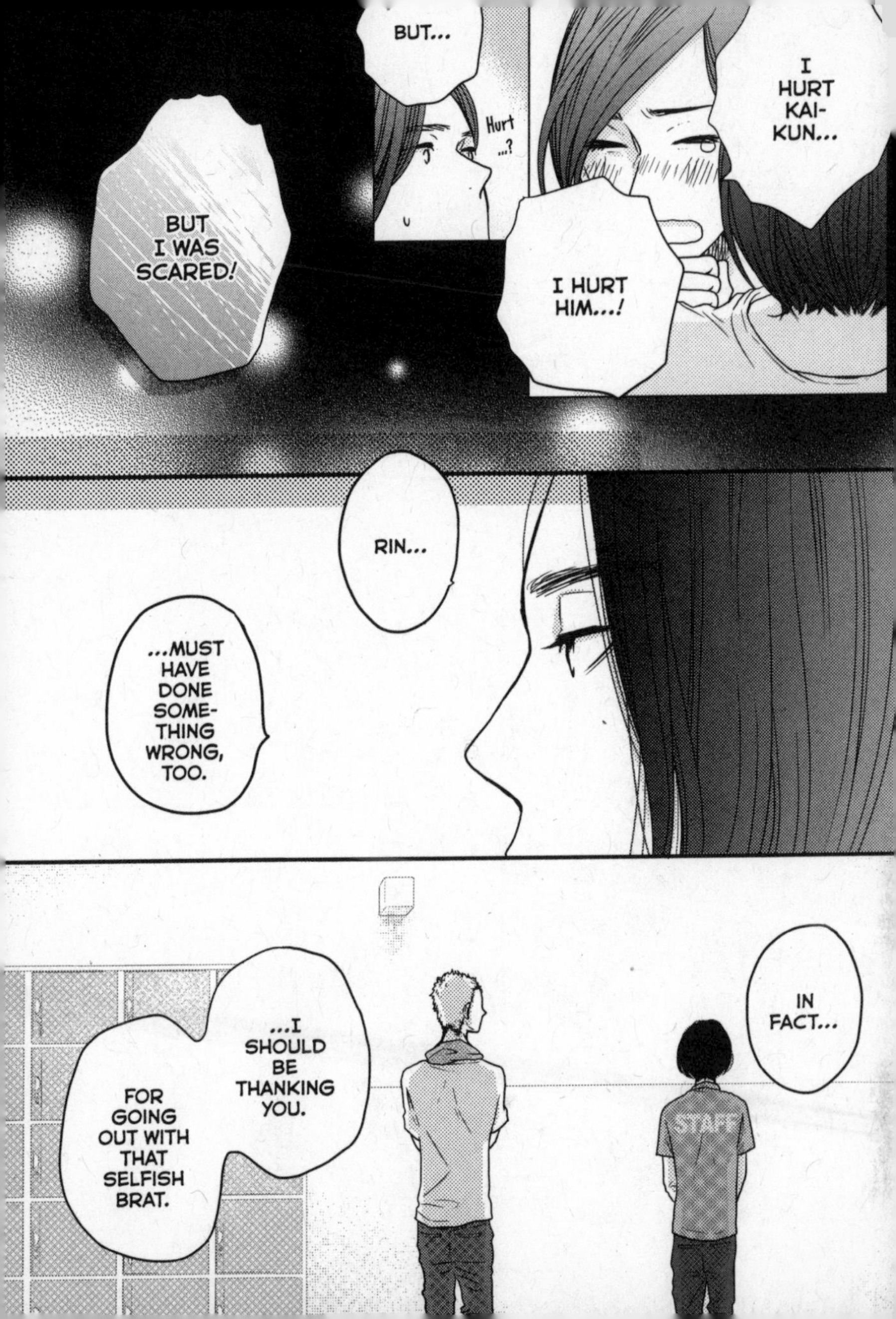
I HURT KAI-KUN...
I HURT HIM...!
BUT...
Hurt ...?
BUT I WAS SCARED!
RIN...
...MUST HAVE DONE SOMETHING WRONG, TOO.
IN FACT...
...I SHOULD BE THANKING YOU.
FOR GOING OUT WITH THAT SELFISH BRAT.
STAFF

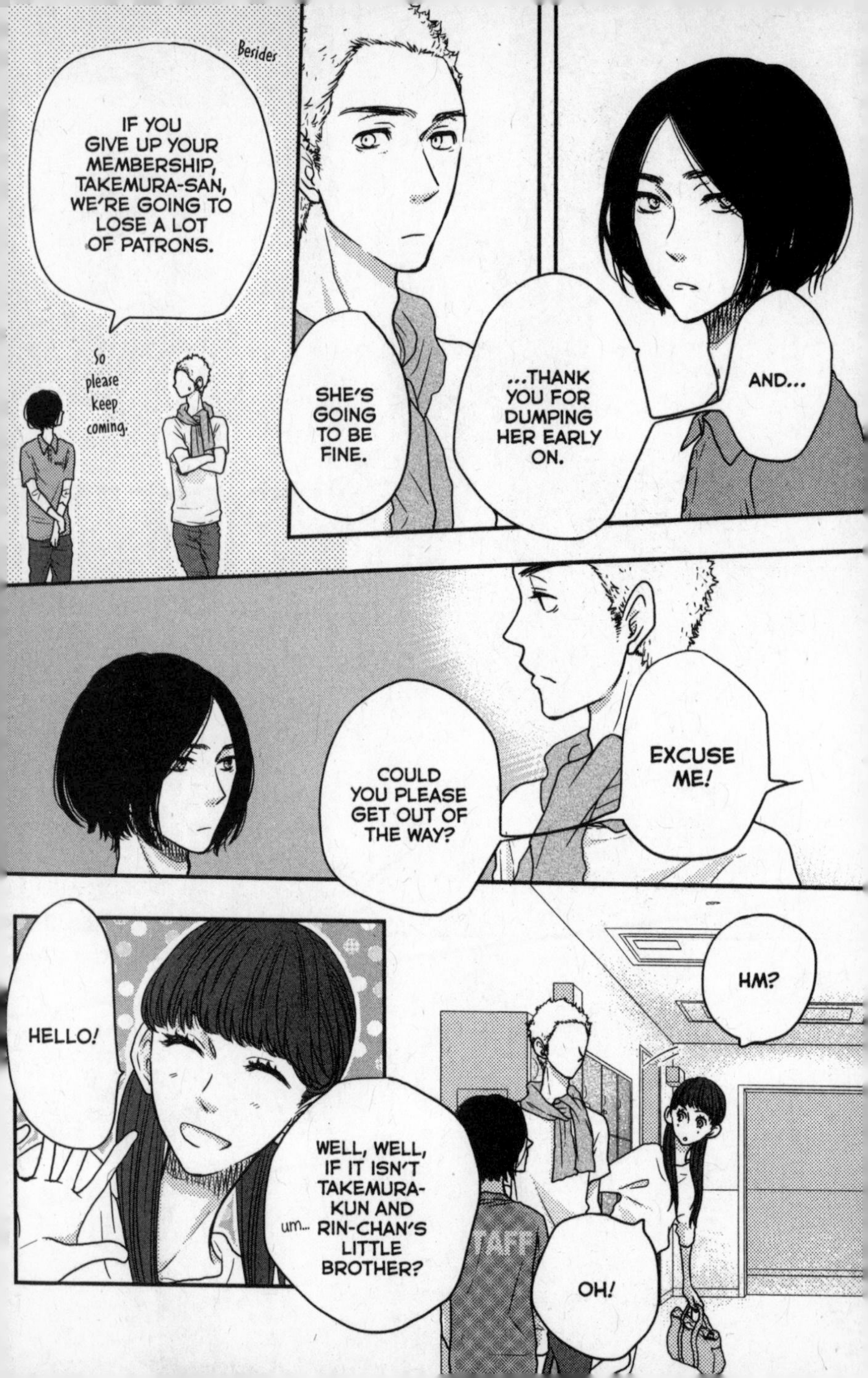
AND...
...THANK YOU FOR DUMPING HER EARLY ON.
SHE'S GOING TO BE FINE.
Besides
IF YOU GIVE UP YOUR MEMBERSHIP, TAKEMURA-SAN, WE'RE GOING TO LOSE A LOT OF PATRONS.
So please keep coming.
EXCUSE ME!
COULD YOU PLEASE GET OUT OF THE WAY?
HM?
OH!
HELLO!
WELL, WELL, IF IT ISN'T TAKEMURA-KUN AND um... RIN-CHAN'S LITTLE BROTHER?
STAFF

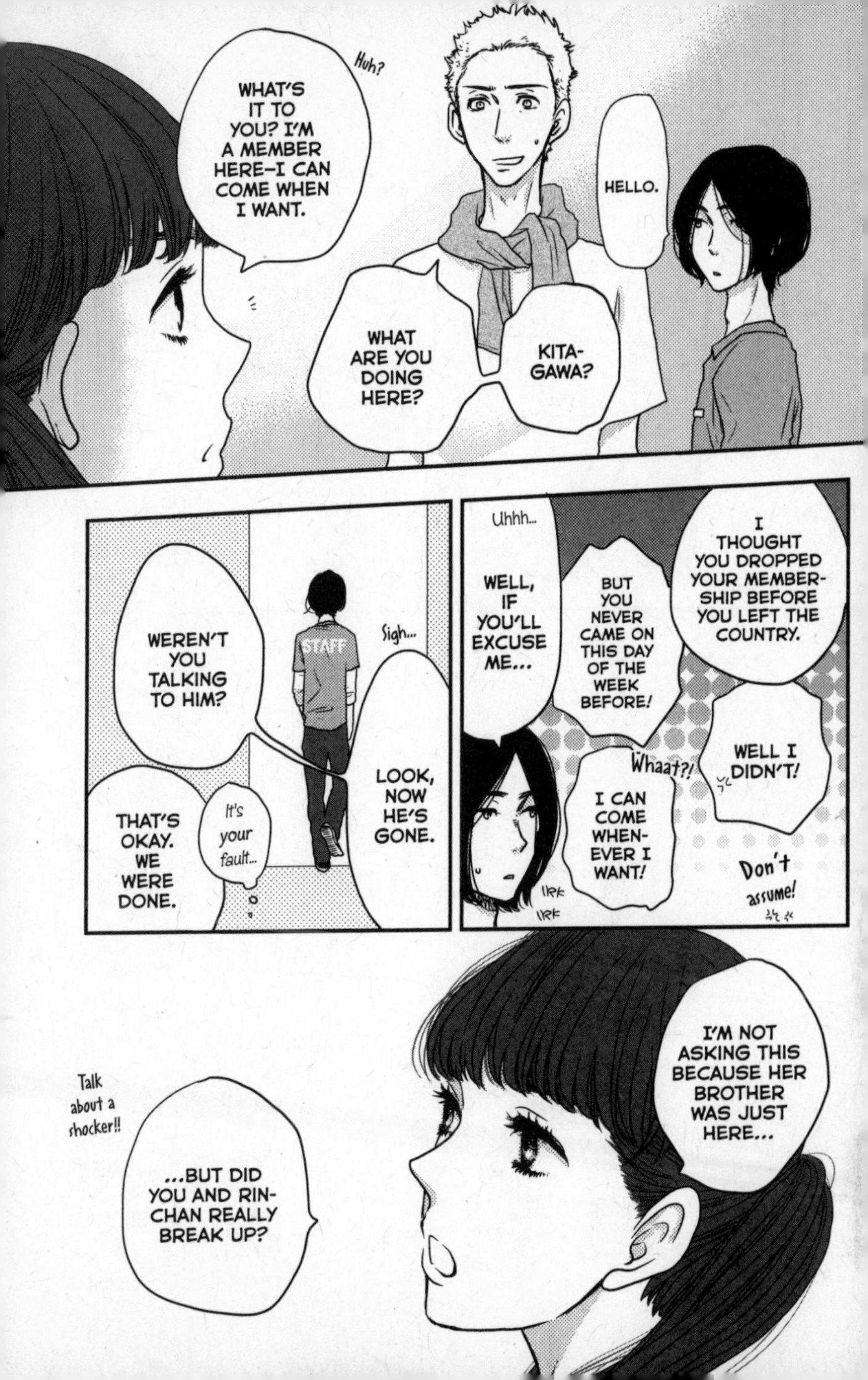
HELLO.
KITA-GAWA?
WHAT ARE YOU DOING HERE?
Huh?
WHAT'S IT TO YOU? I'M A MEMBER HERE—I CAN COME WHEN I WANT.
I THOUGHT YOU DROPPED YOUR MEMBER-SHIP BEFORE YOU LEFT THE COUNTRY.
BUT YOU NEVER CAME ON THIS DAY OF THE WEEK BEFORE!
Uhhh...
WELL, IF YOU'LL EXCUSE ME...
WELL I DIDN'T!
Whaat?!
I CAN COME WHEN-EVER I WANT!
Don't assume!
IRK IRK
Sigh...
LOOK, NOW HE'S GONE.
WEREN'T YOU TALKING TO HIM?
It's your fault...
THAT'S OKAY. WE WERE DONE.
I'M NOT ASKING THIS BECAUSE HER BROTHER WAS JUST HERE...
...BUT DID YOU AND RIN-CHAN REALLY BREAK UP?
Talk about a shocker!!

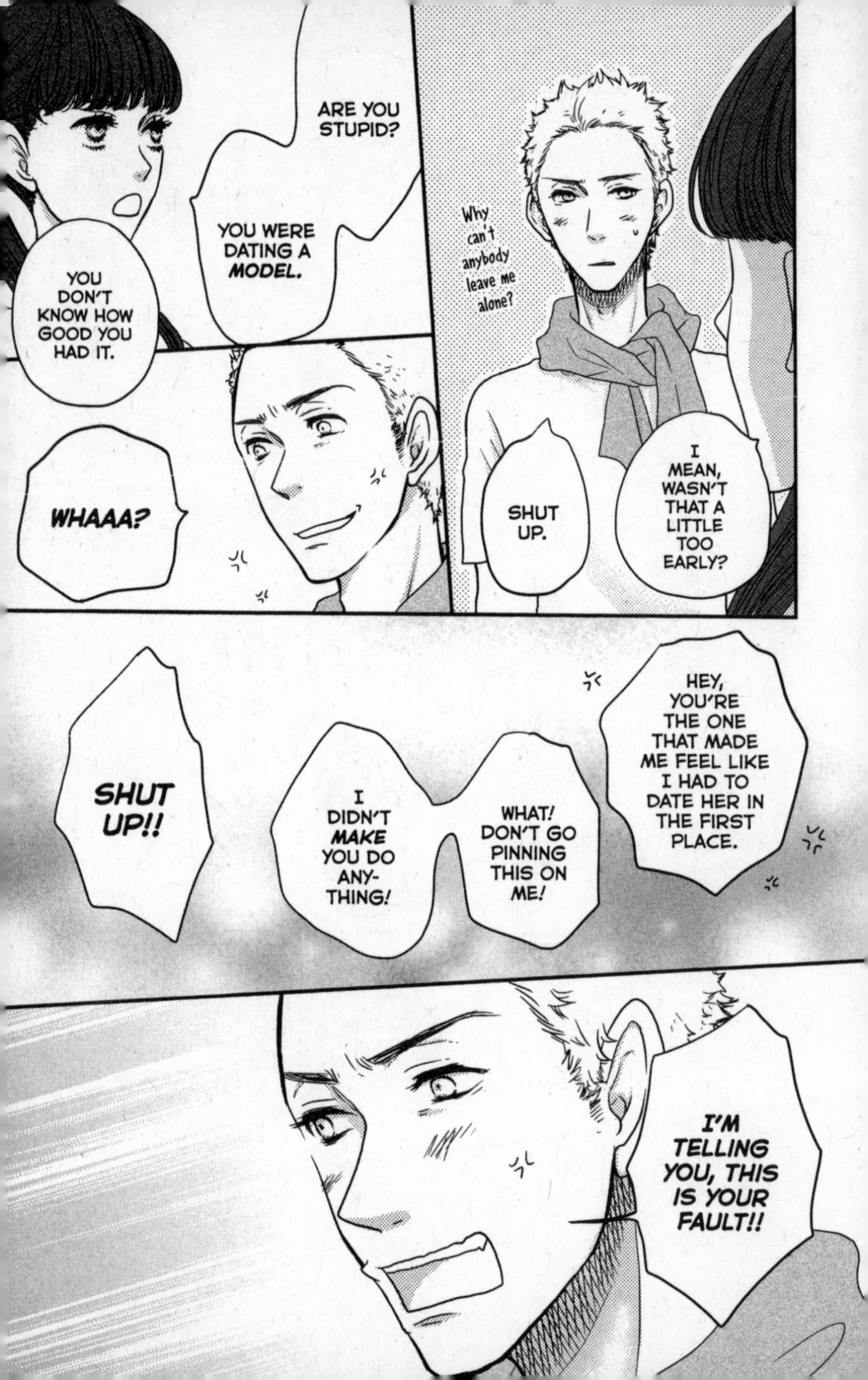
I MEAN, WASN'T THAT A LITTLE TOO EARLY?
SHUT UP.
Why can't anybody leave me alone?
ARE YOU STUPID?
YOU WERE DATING A *MODEL.*
YOU DON'T KNOW HOW GOOD YOU HAD IT.
WHAAA?
HEY, YOU'RE THE ONE THAT MADE ME FEEL LIKE I HAD TO DATE HER IN THE FIRST PLACE.
WHAT! DON'T GO PINNING THIS ON *ME!*
I DIDN'T *MAKE* YOU DO ANY-THING!
SHUT UP!!
I'M TELLING YOU, THIS IS YOUR FAULT!!

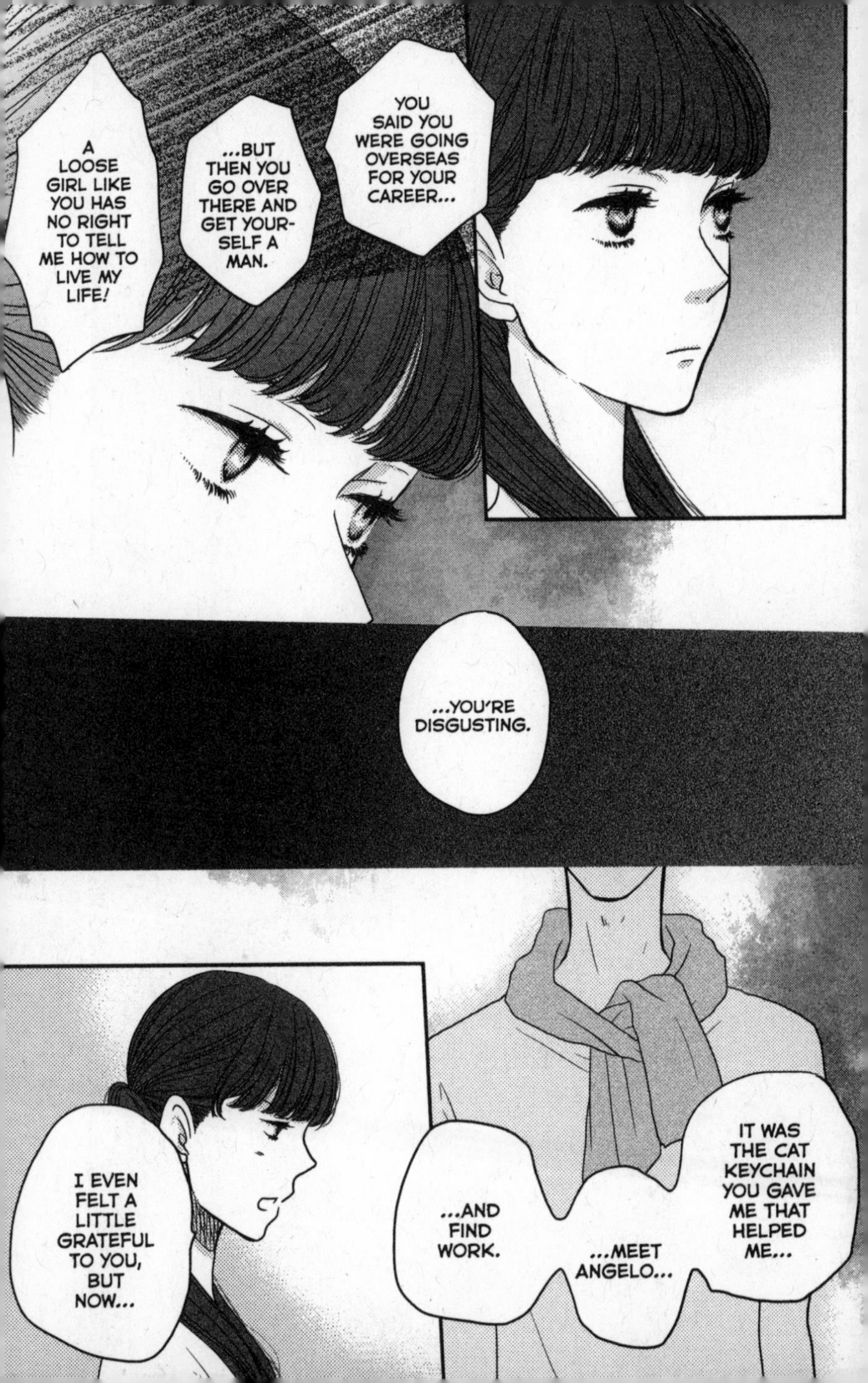
YOU SAID YOU WERE GOING OVERSEAS FOR YOUR CAREER...
...BUT THEN YOU GO OVER THERE AND GET YOURSELF A MAN.
A LOOSE GIRL LIKE YOU HAS NO RIGHT TO TELL ME HOW TO LIVE MY LIFE!
...YOU'RE DISGUSTING.
IT WAS THE CAT KEYCHAIN YOU GAVE ME THAT HELPED ME...
...MEET ANGELO...
...AND FIND WORK.
I EVEN FELT A LITTLE GRATEFUL TO YOU, BUT NOW...

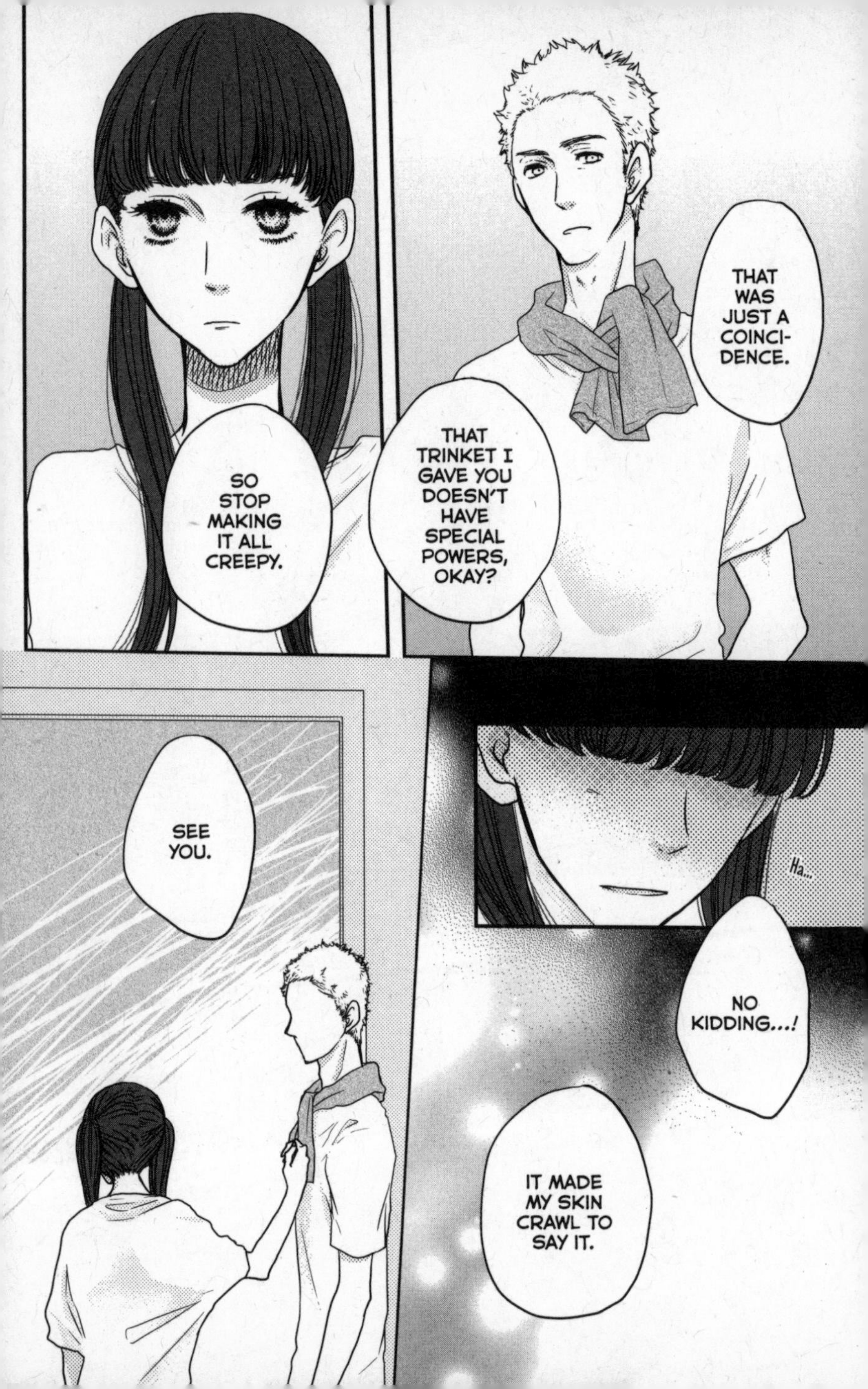
THAT WAS JUST A COINCIDENCE.
THAT TRINKET I GAVE YOU DOESN'T HAVE SPECIAL POWERS, OKAY?
SO STOP MAKING IT ALL CREEPY.
Ha..
NO KIDDING...!
IT MADE MY SKIN CRAWL TO SAY IT.
SEE YOU.

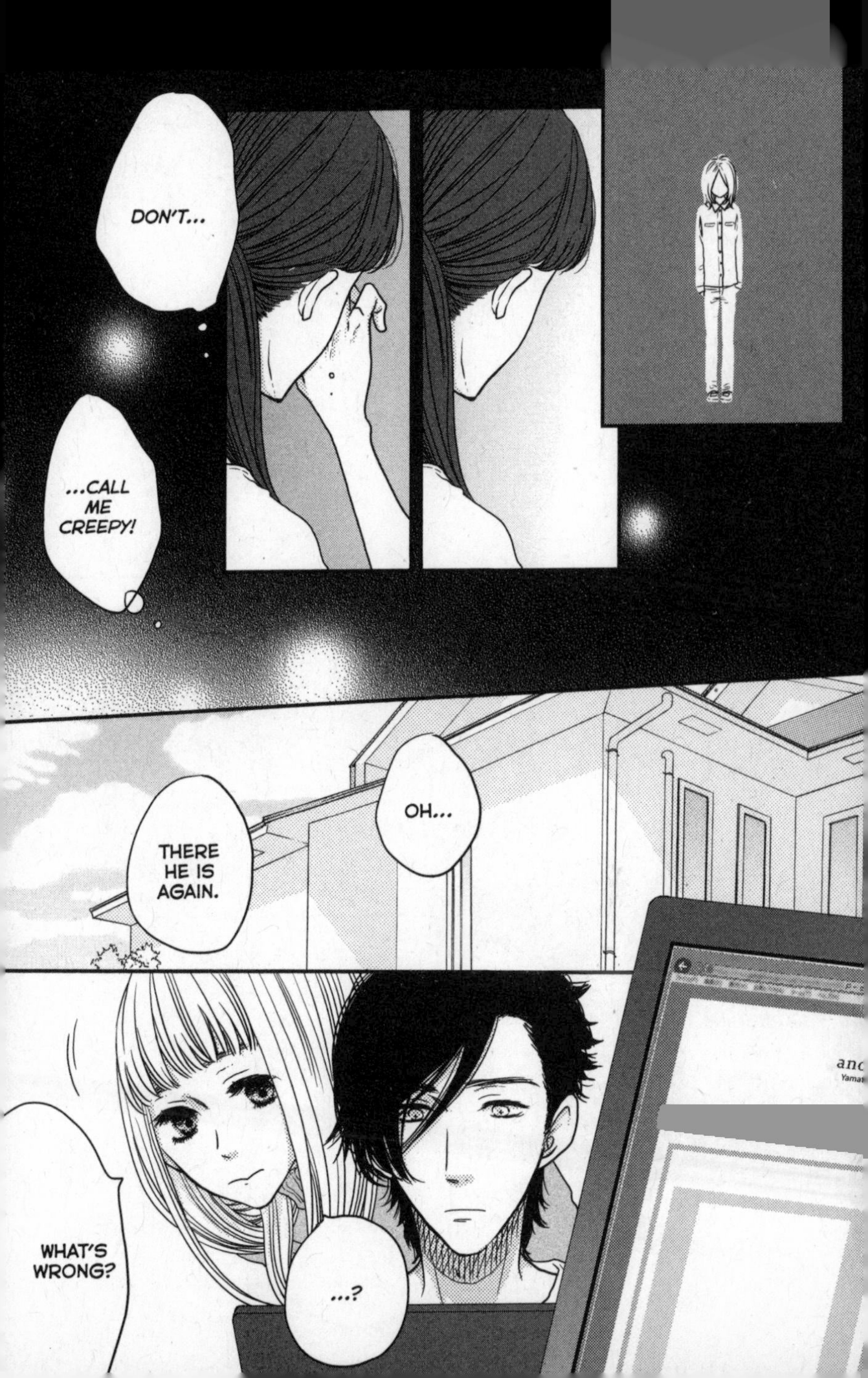
DON'T...
...CALL ME CREEPY!
OH...
THERE HE IS AGAIN.
WHAT'S WRONG?
...?

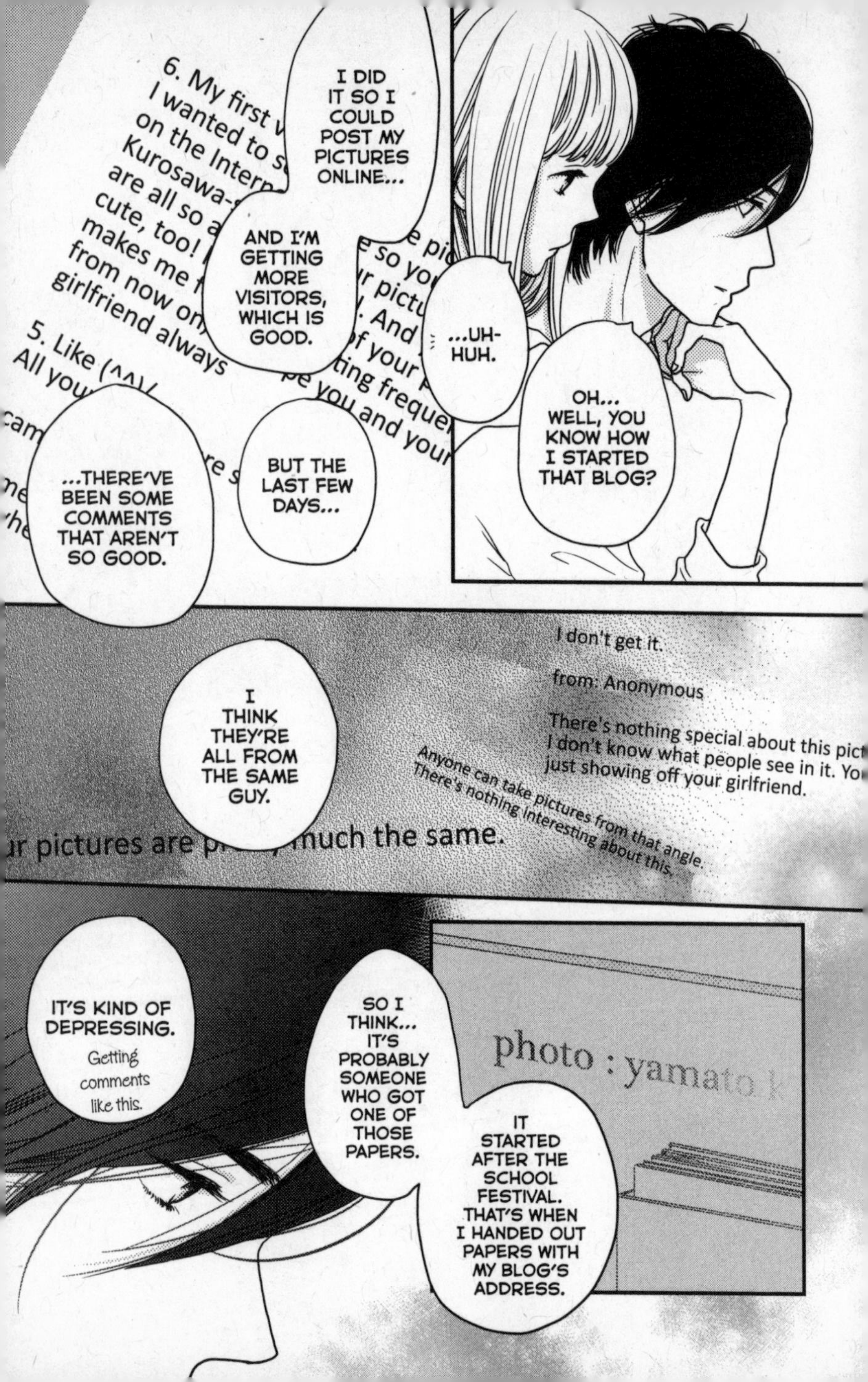
OH... WELL, YOU KNOW HOW I STARTED THAT BLOG?
...UH-HUH.
I DID IT SO I COULD POST MY PICTURES ONLINE...
AND I'M GETTING MORE VISITORS, WHICH IS GOOD.
BUT THE LAST FEW DAYS...
...THERE'VE BEEN SOME COMMENTS THAT AREN'T SO GOOD.
I don't get it.
from: Anonymous
There's nothing special about this pic
I don't know what people see in it. Yo
just showing off your girlfriend.
Anyone can take pictures from that angle.
There's nothing interesting about this.
I THINK THEY'RE ALL FROM THE SAME GUY.
photo : yamato k
IT STARTED AFTER THE SCHOOL FESTIVAL. THAT'S WHEN I HANDED OUT PAPERS WITH MY BLOG'S ADDRESS.
SO I THINK... IT'S PROBABLY SOMEONE WHO GOT ONE OF THOSE PAPERS.
IT'S KIND OF DEPRESSING.
Getting comments like this.

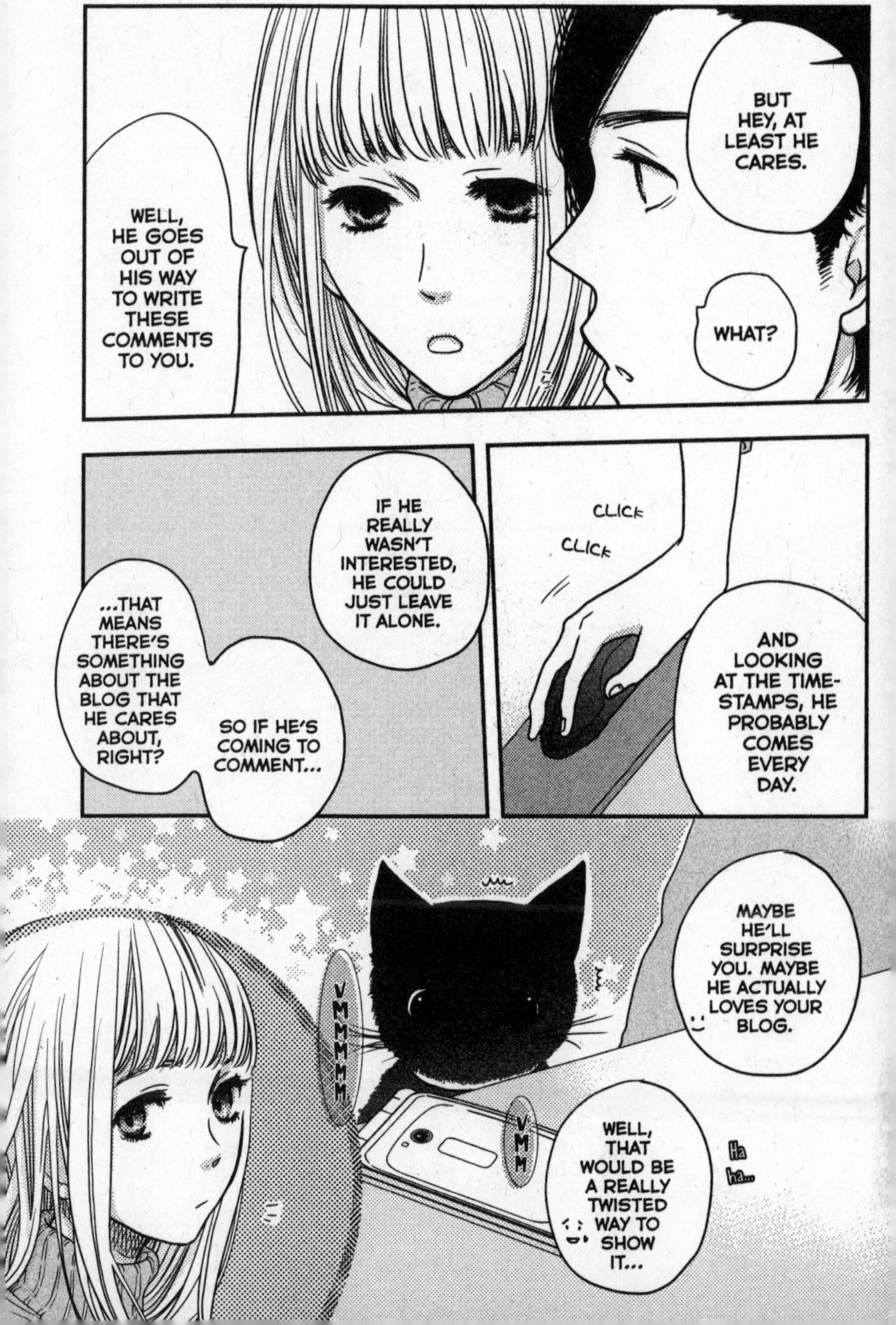
BUT HEY, AT LEAST HE CARES.
WHAT?
WELL, HE GOES OUT OF HIS WAY TO WRITE THESE COMMENTS TO YOU.
CLICK
CLICK
AND LOOKING AT THE TIME-STAMPS, HE PROBABLY COMES EVERY DAY.
IF HE REALLY WASN'T INTERESTED, HE COULD JUST LEAVE IT ALONE.
SO IF HE'S COMING TO COMMENT...
...THAT MEANS THERE'S SOMETHING ABOUT THE BLOG THAT HE CARES ABOUT, RIGHT?
MAYBE HE'LL SURPRISE YOU. MAYBE HE ACTUALLY LOVES YOUR BLOG.
Ha ha...
WELL, THAT WOULD BE A REALLY TWISTED WAY TO SHOW IT...
VMM
VMMMMM

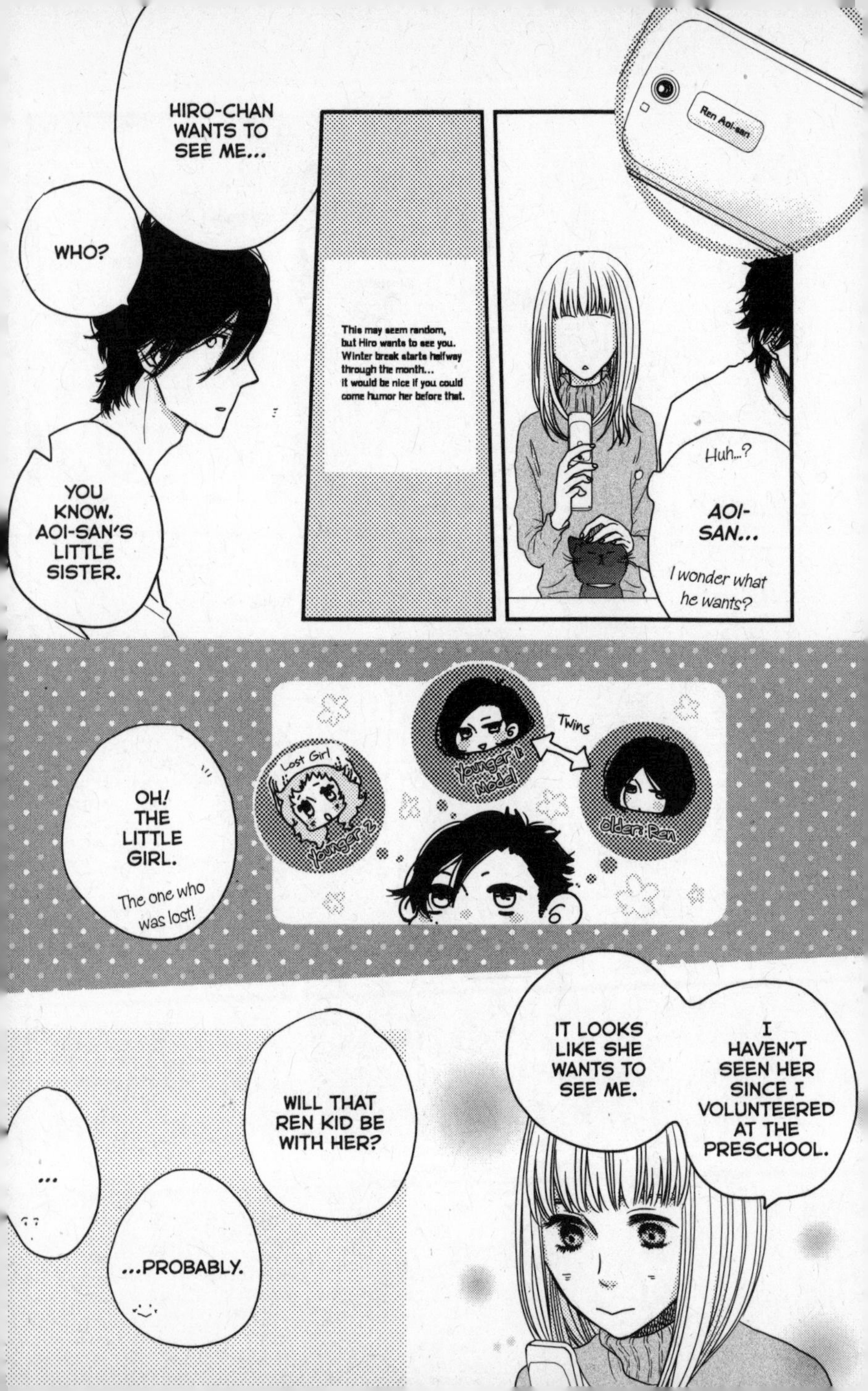
Ren Aoi-san
Huh...?
AOI-SAN...
I wonder what he wants?
This may seem random, but Hiro wants to see you. Winter break starts halfway through the month... It would be nice if you could come humor her before that.
HIRO-CHAN WANTS TO SEE ME...
WHO?
YOU KNOW. AOI-SAN'S LITTLE SISTER.
Twins
Younger 1: Model
Older: Ren
Lost Girl
Younger 2
OH! THE LITTLE GIRL.
The one who was lost!
I HAVEN'T SEEN HER SINCE I VOLUNTEERED AT THE PRESCHOOL.
IT LOOKS LIKE SHE WANTS TO SEE ME.
WILL THAT REN KID BE WITH HER?
...
...PROBABLY.

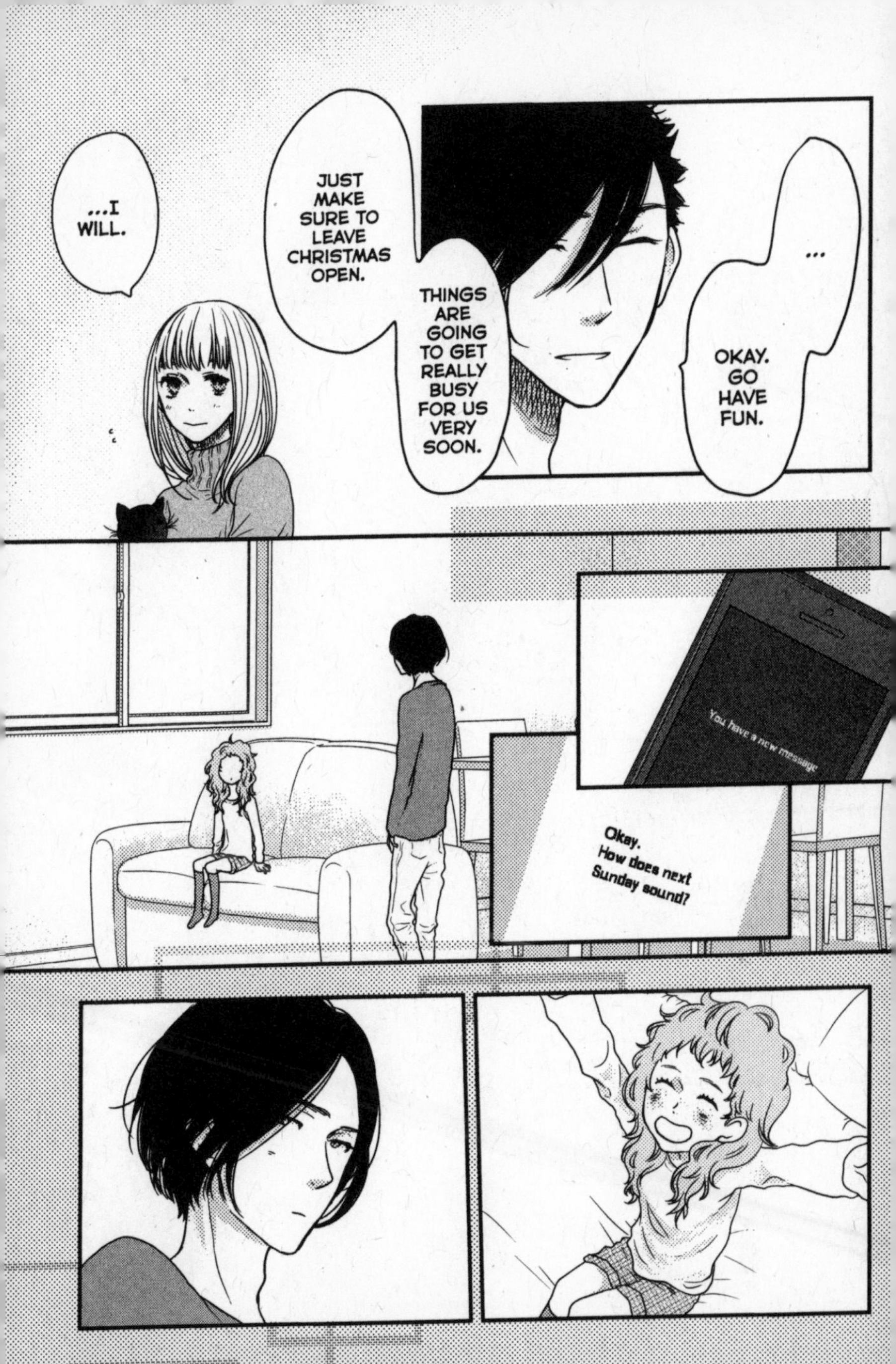
...
OKAY. GO HAVE FUN.
JUST MAKE SURE TO LEAVE CHRISTMAS OPEN.
THINGS ARE GOING TO GET REALLY BUSY FOR US VERY SOON.
...I WILL.
You have a new message
Okay. How does next Sunday sound?

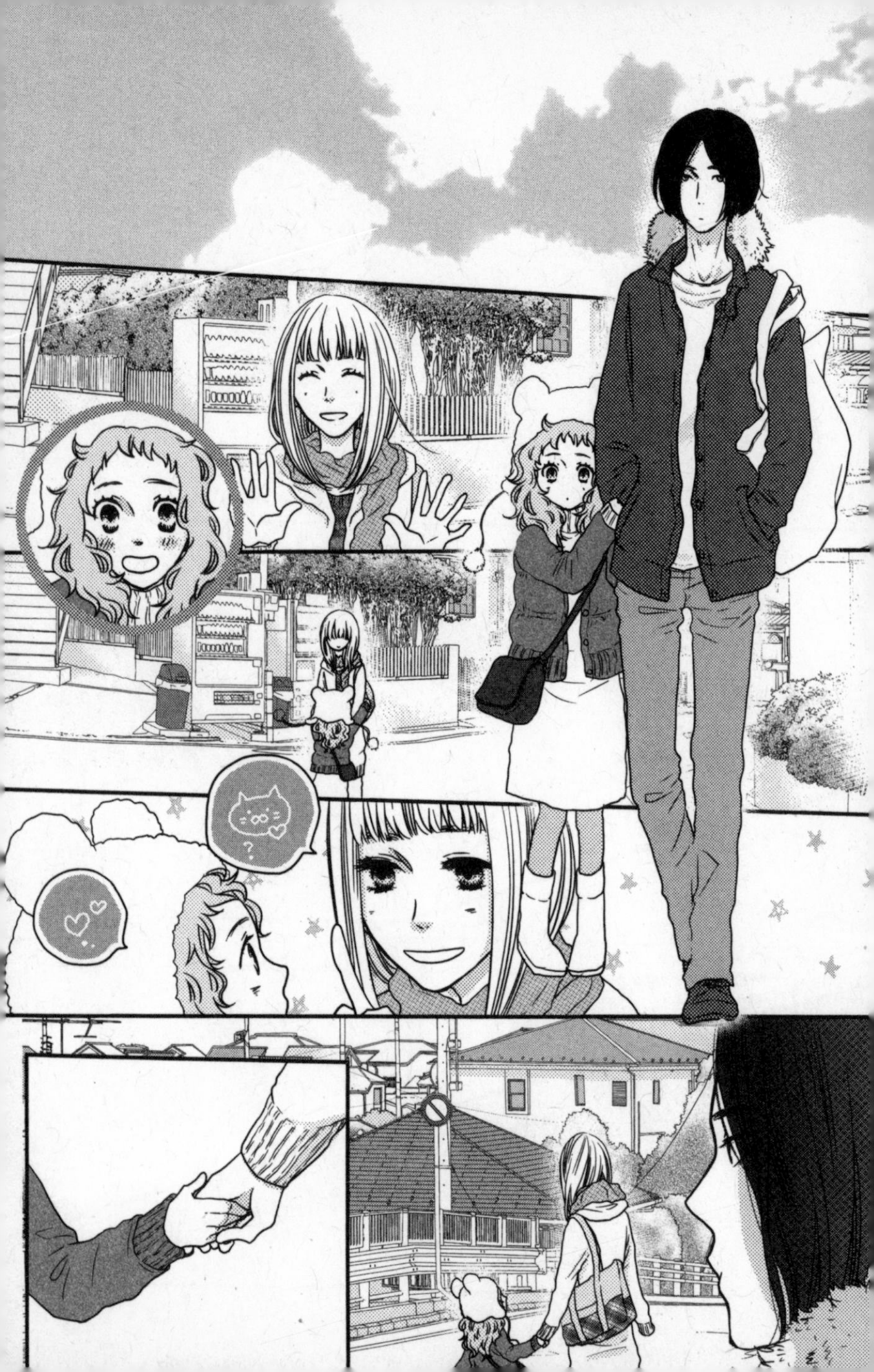

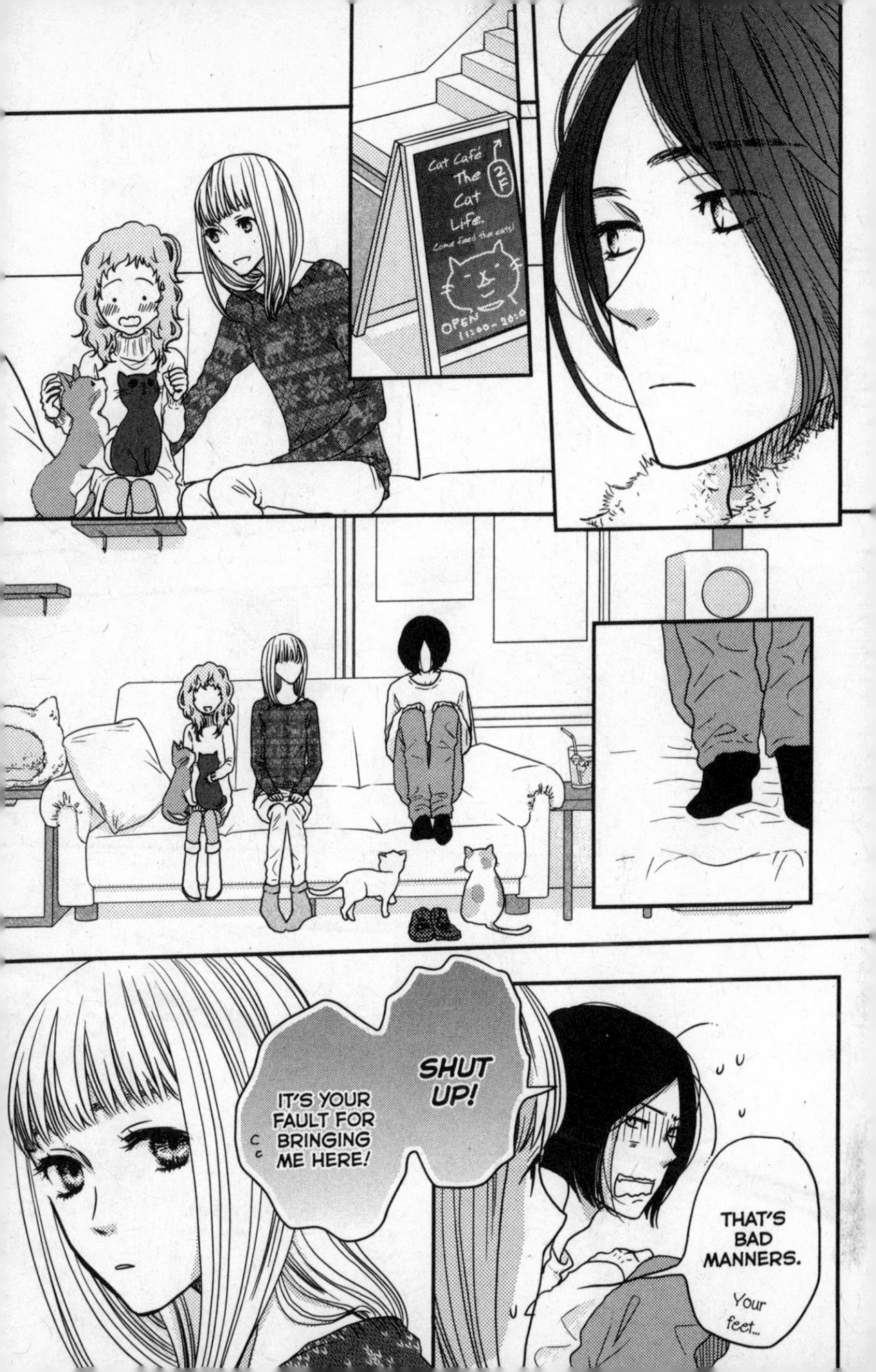
Cat Café
The Cat Life.
2F
Come feed the cats!
OPEN 11:00-20:0
THAT'S BAD MANNERS.
Your feet...
SHUT UP!
IT'S YOUR FAULT FOR BRINGING ME HERE!

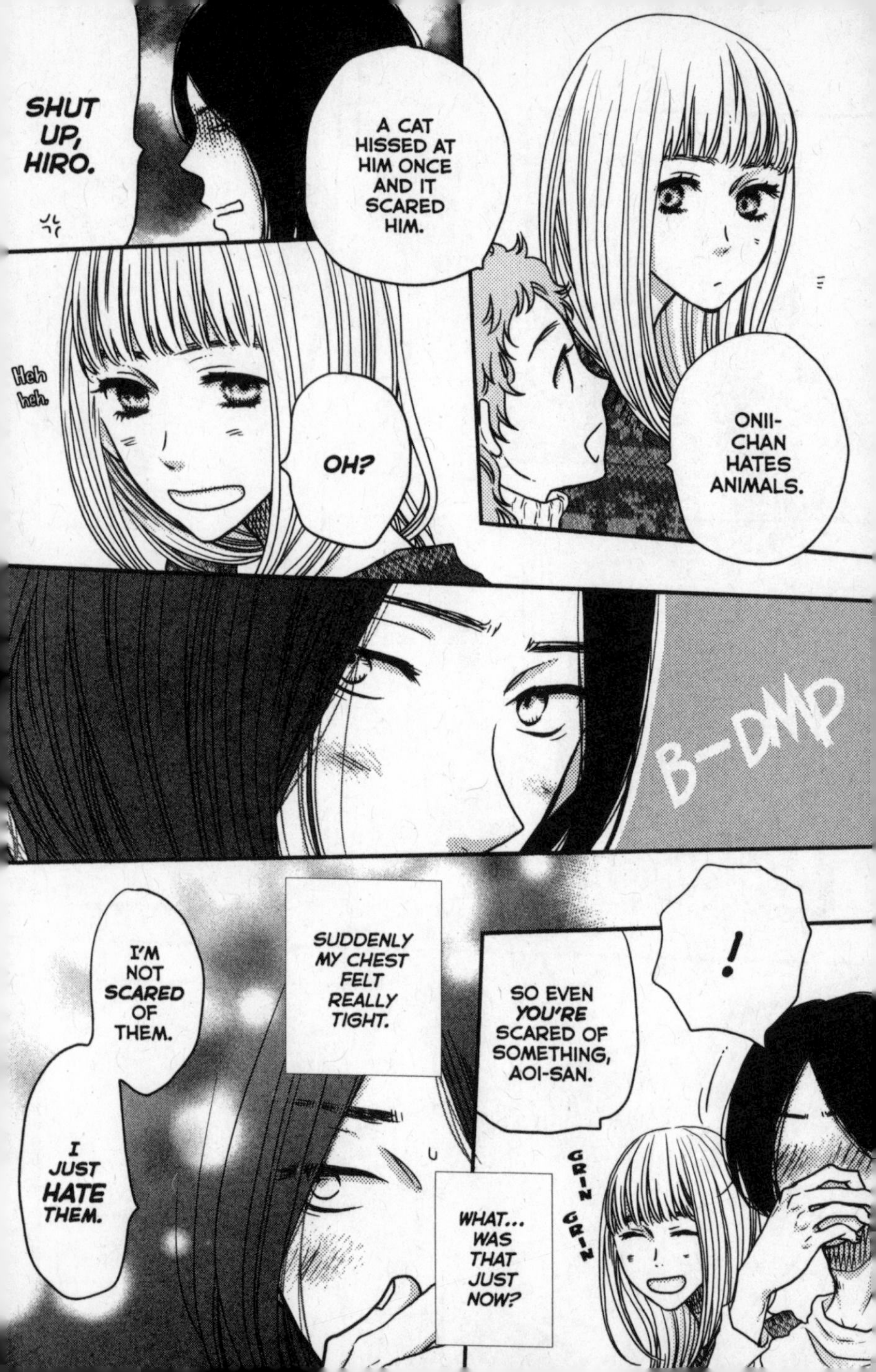
ONII-CHAN HATES ANIMALS.
A CAT HISSED AT HIM ONCE AND IT SCARED HIM.
SHUT UP, HIRO.
OH?
Heh heh.
B--DMP
!
SO EVEN YOU'RE SCARED OF SOMETHING, AOI-SAN.
GRIN GRIN
SUDDENLY MY CHEST FELT REALLY TIGHT.
I'M NOT SCARED OF THEM.
I JUST HATE THEM.
WHAT... WAS THAT JUST NOW?

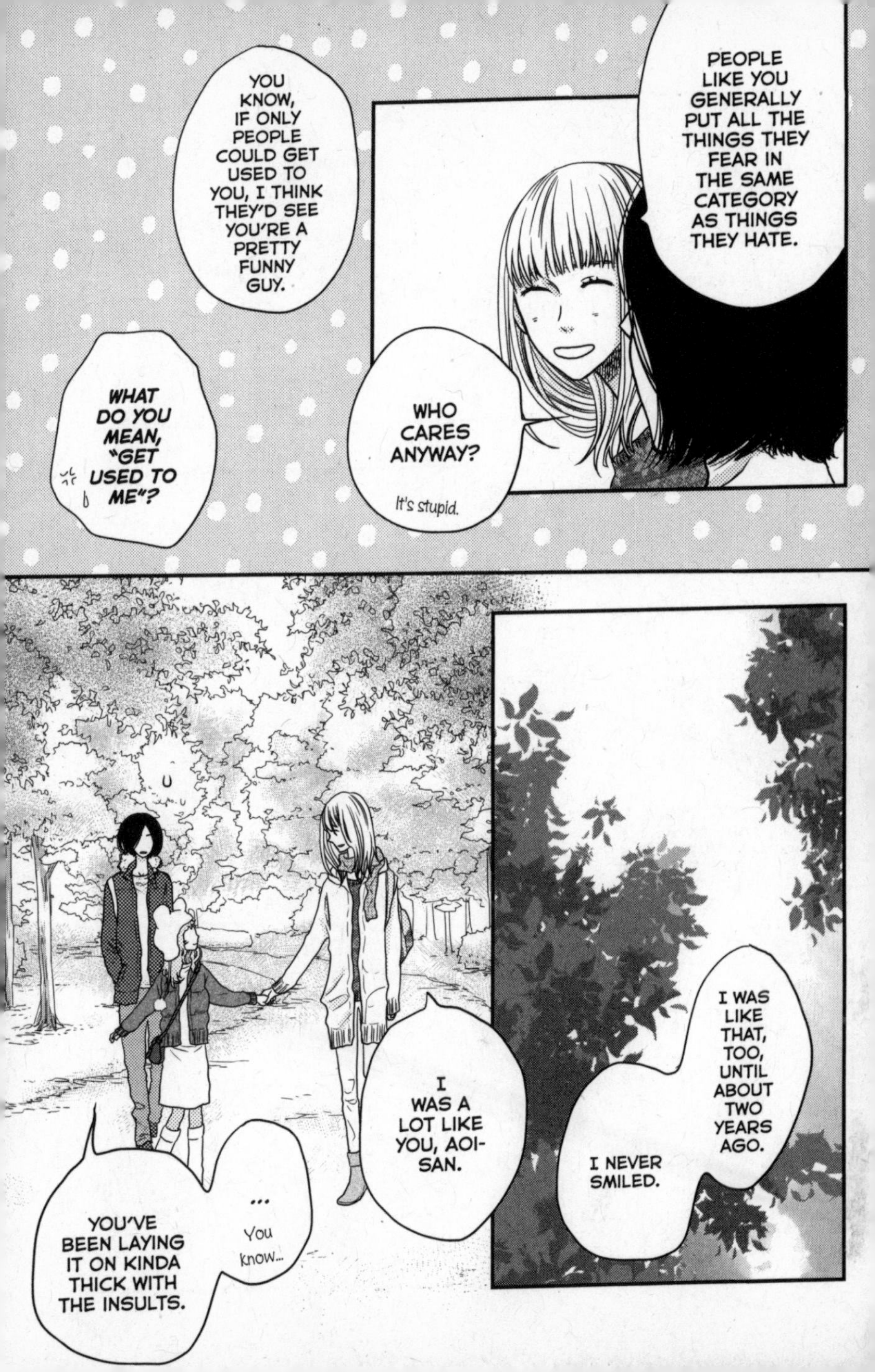
PEOPLE LIKE YOU GENERALLY PUT ALL THE THINGS THEY FEAR IN THE SAME CATEGORY AS THINGS THEY HATE.
WHO CARES ANYWAY?
It's stupid.
YOU KNOW, IF ONLY PEOPLE COULD GET USED TO YOU, I THINK THEY'D SEE YOU'RE A PRETTY FUNNY GUY.
WHAT DO YOU MEAN, "GET USED TO ME"?
I WAS LIKE THAT, TOO, UNTIL ABOUT TWO YEARS AGO.
I NEVER SMILED.
I WAS A LOT LIKE YOU, AOI-SAN.
...
You know...
YOU'VE BEEN LAYING IT ON KINDA THICK WITH THE INSULTS.

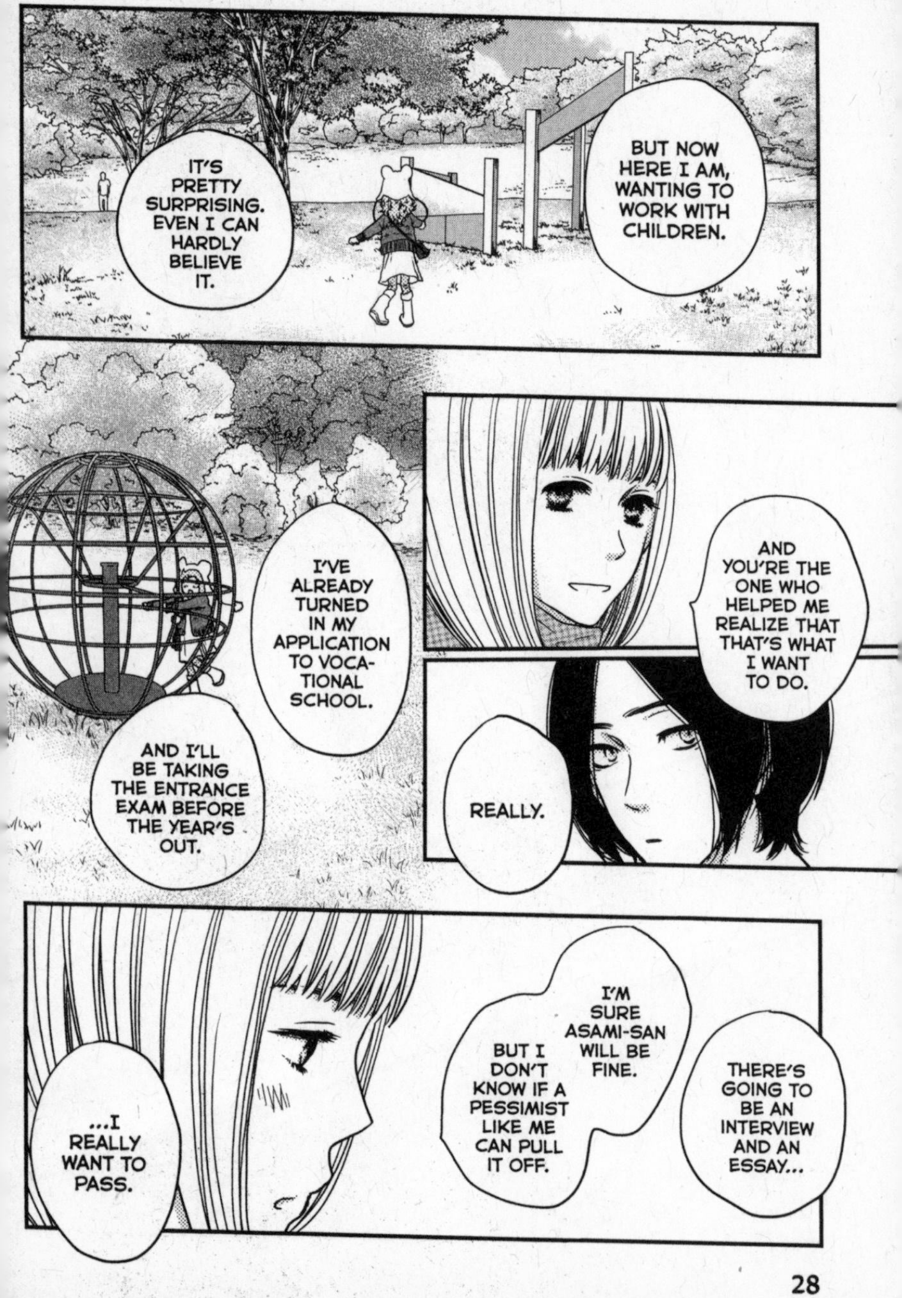
BUT NOW HERE I AM, WANTING TO WORK WITH CHILDREN.
IT'S PRETTY SURPRISING. EVEN I CAN HARDLY BELIEVE IT.
AND YOU'RE THE ONE WHO HELPED ME REALIZE THAT THAT'S WHAT I WANT TO DO.
REALLY.
I'VE ALREADY TURNED IN MY APPLICATION TO VOCA-TIONAL SCHOOL.
AND I'LL BE TAKING THE ENTRANCE EXAM BEFORE THE YEAR'S OUT.
THERE'S GOING TO BE AN INTERVIEW AND AN ESSAY...
I'M SURE ASAMI-SAN WILL BE FINE.
BUT I DON'T KNOW IF A PESSIMIST LIKE ME CAN PULL IT OFF.
...I REALLY WANT TO PASS.

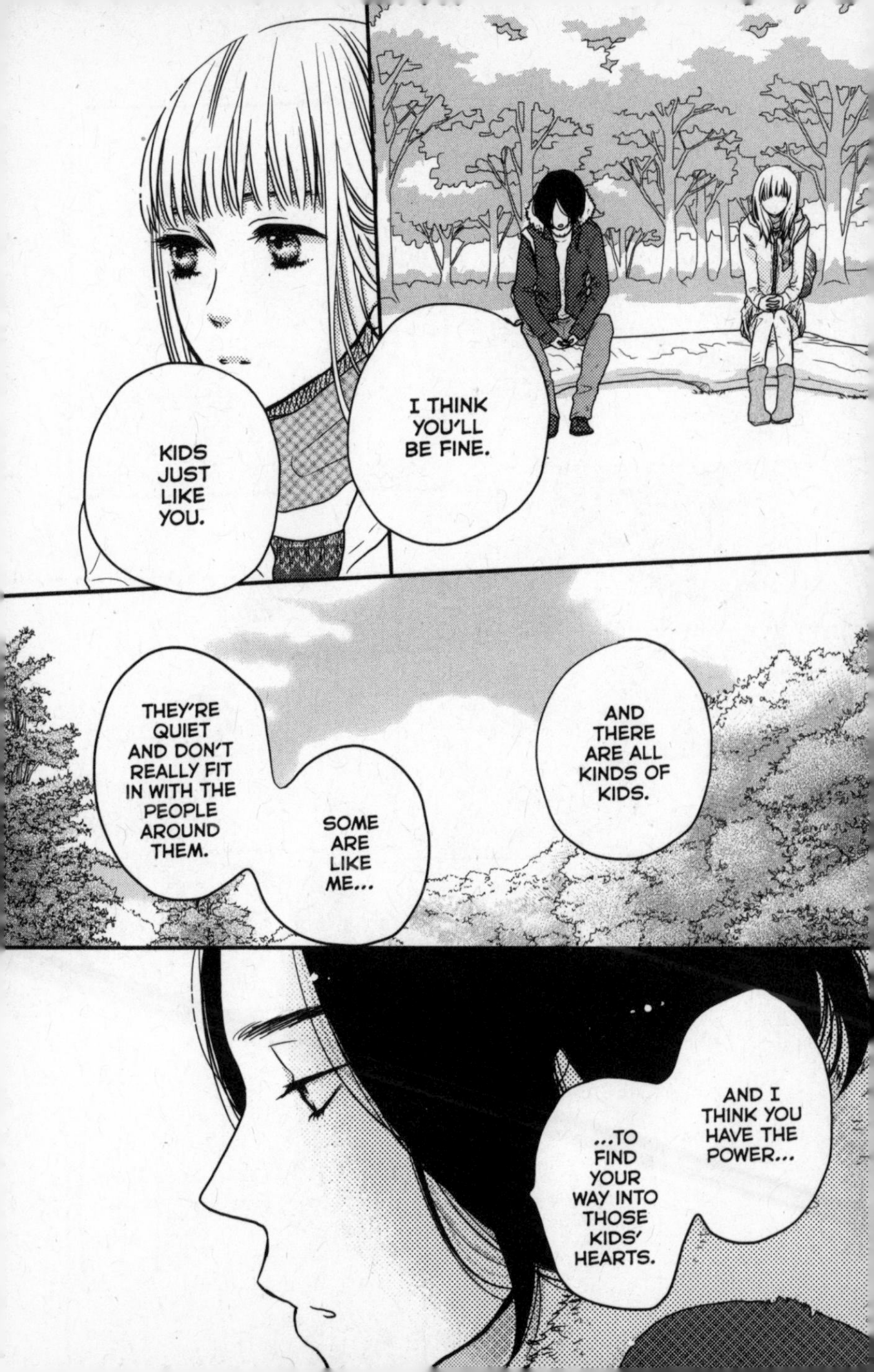
I THINK YOU'LL BE FINE.
KIDS JUST LIKE YOU.
AND THERE ARE ALL KINDS OF KIDS.
SOME ARE LIKE ME...
THEY'RE QUIET AND DON'T REALLY FIT IN WITH THE PEOPLE AROUND THEM.
AND I THINK YOU HAVE THE POWER...
...TO FIND YOUR WAY INTO THOSE KIDS' HEARTS.

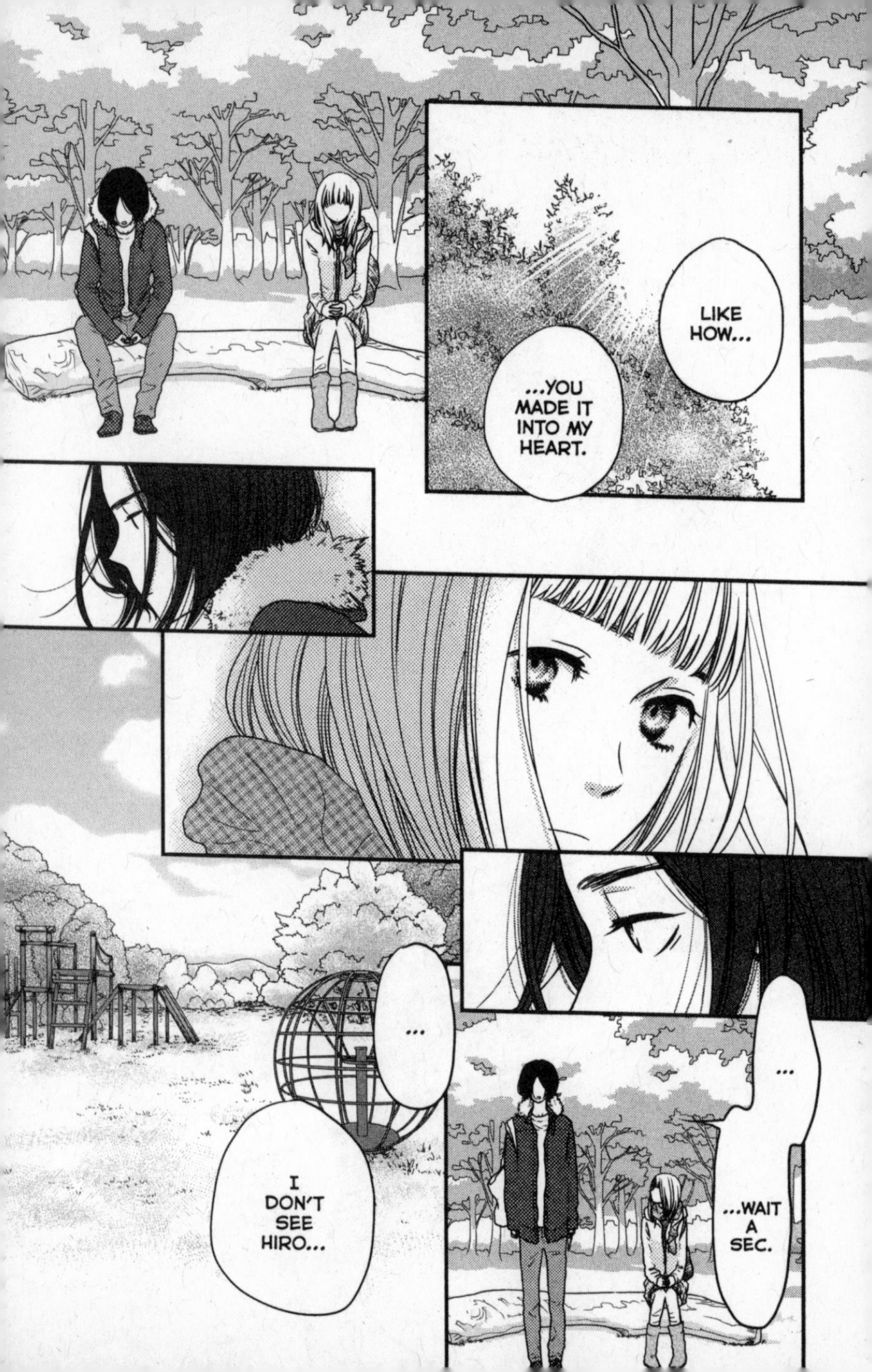
LIKE HOW...
...YOU MADE IT INTO MY HEART.
...
...WAIT A SEC.
...
I DON'T SEE HIRO...

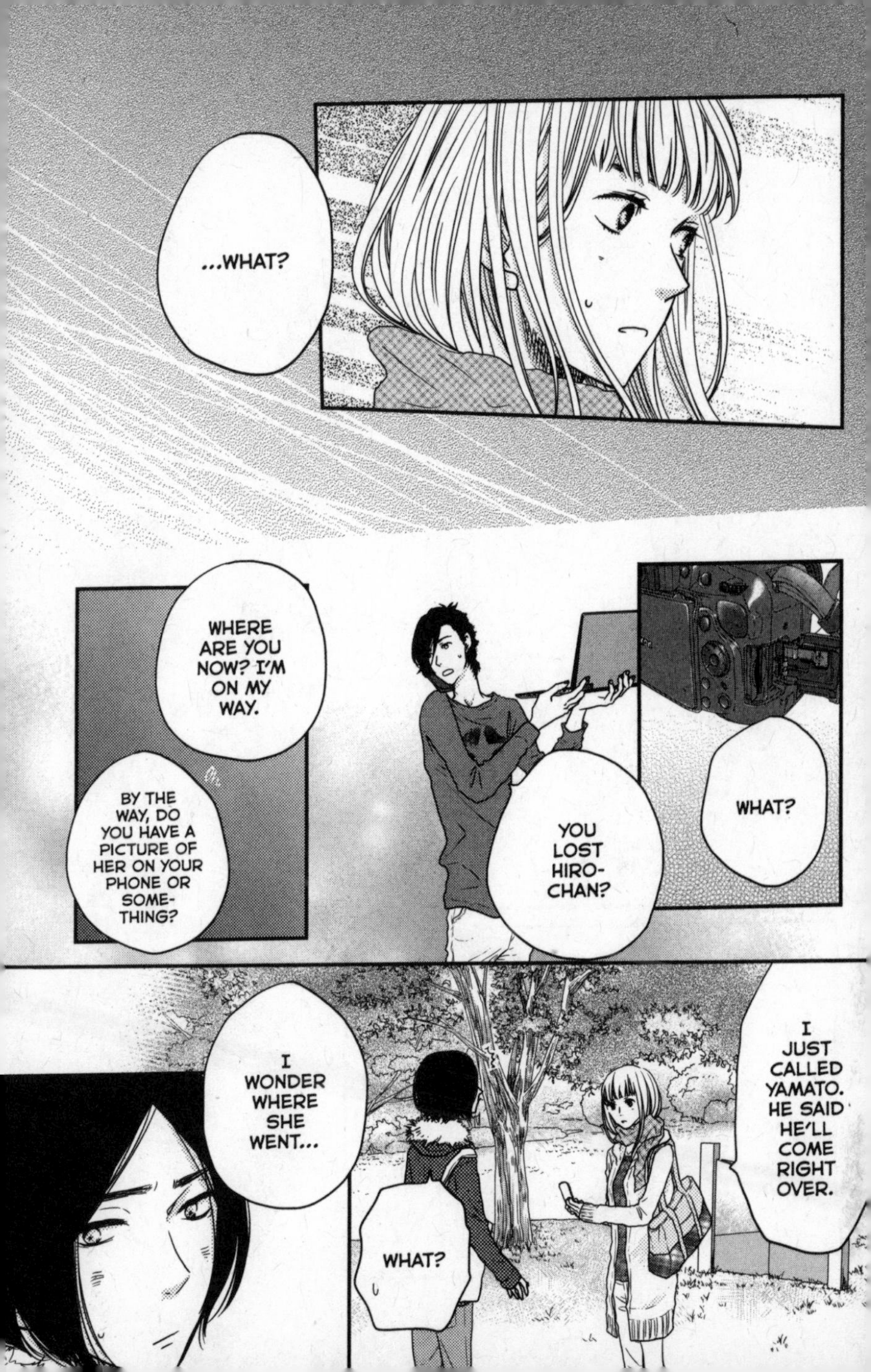
...WHAT?
WHAT?
YOU LOST HIRO-CHAN?
WHERE ARE YOU NOW? I'M ON MY WAY.
BY THE WAY, DO YOU HAVE A PICTURE OF HER ON YOUR PHONE OR SOME-THING?
I JUST CALLED YAMATO. HE SAID HE'LL COME RIGHT OVER.
WHAT?
I WONDER WHERE SHE WENT...

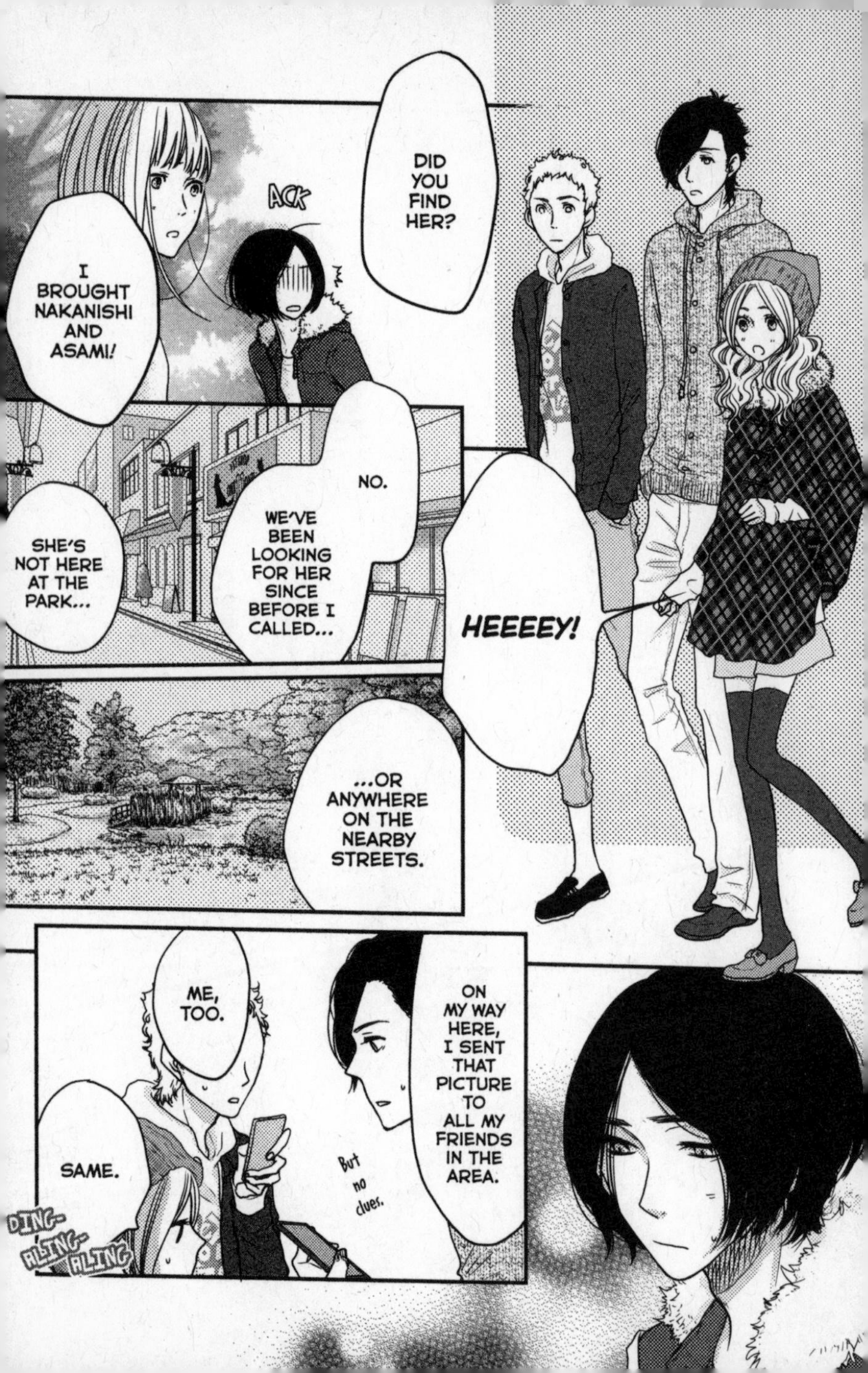
HEEEEY!
DID YOU FIND HER?
ACK
I BROUGHT NAKANISHI AND ASAMI!
NO.
WE'VE BEEN LOOKING FOR HER SINCE BEFORE I CALLED...
SHE'S NOT HERE AT THE PARK...
...OR ANYWHERE ON THE NEARBY STREETS.
ON MY WAY HERE, I SENT THAT PICTURE TO ALL MY FRIENDS IN THE AREA.
But no clues.
ME, TOO.
SAME.
DING-ALING-ALING

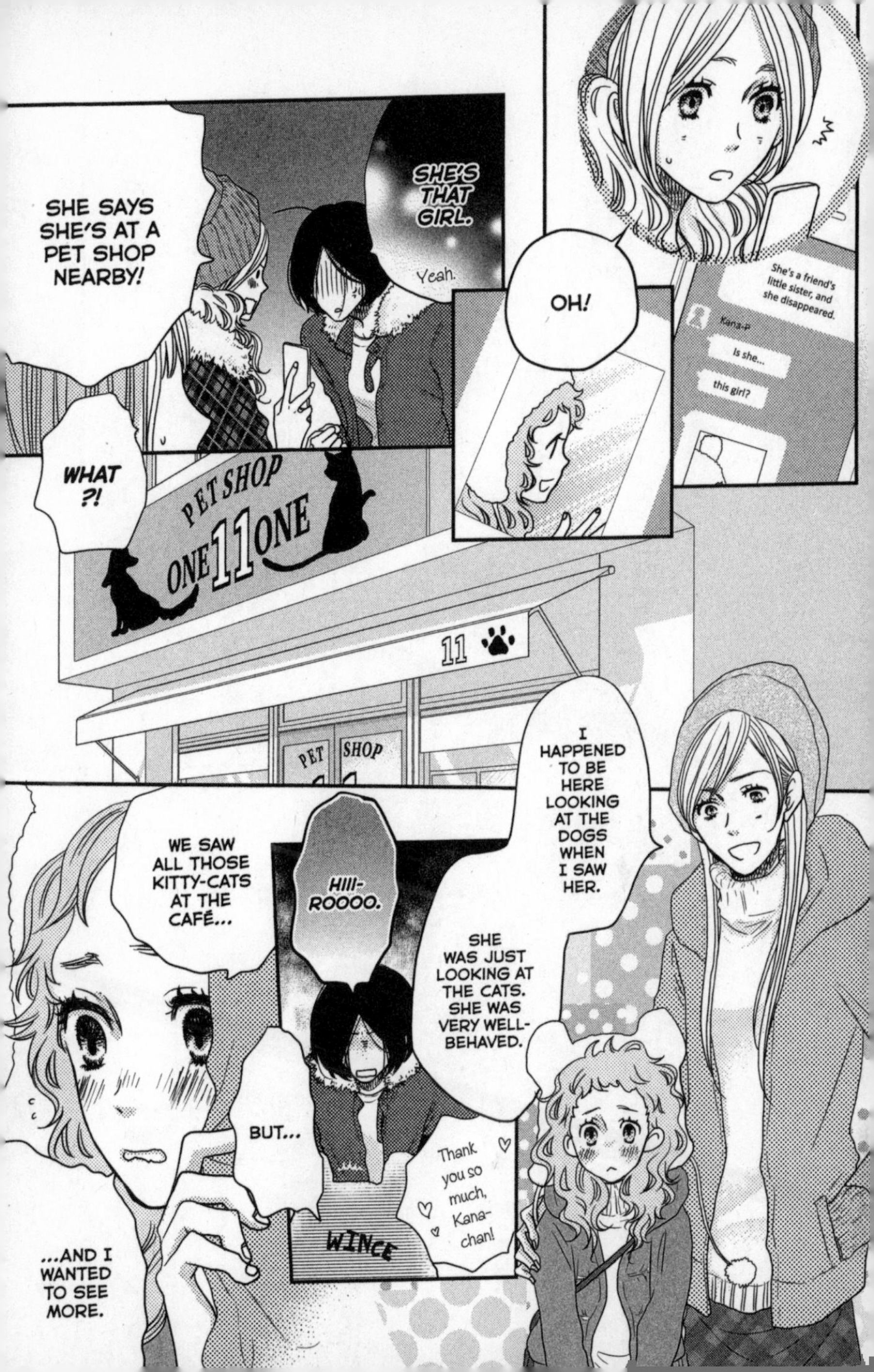
She's a friend's little sister, and she disappeared.
Kana-P
Is she...
this girl?
OH!
SHE'S THAT GIRL.
Yeah.
SHE SAYS SHE'S AT A PET SHOP NEARBY!
WHAT?!
PET SHOP
ONE 11 ONE
11
PET SHOP
I HAPPENED TO BE HERE LOOKING AT THE DOGS WHEN I SAW HER.
SHE WAS JUST LOOKING AT THE CATS. SHE WAS VERY WELL-BEHAVED.
Thank you so much, Kana-chan!
HIII-ROOOO.
WINCE
BUT...
WE SAW ALL THOSE KITTY-CATS AT THE CAFÉ...
...AND I WANTED TO SEE MORE.

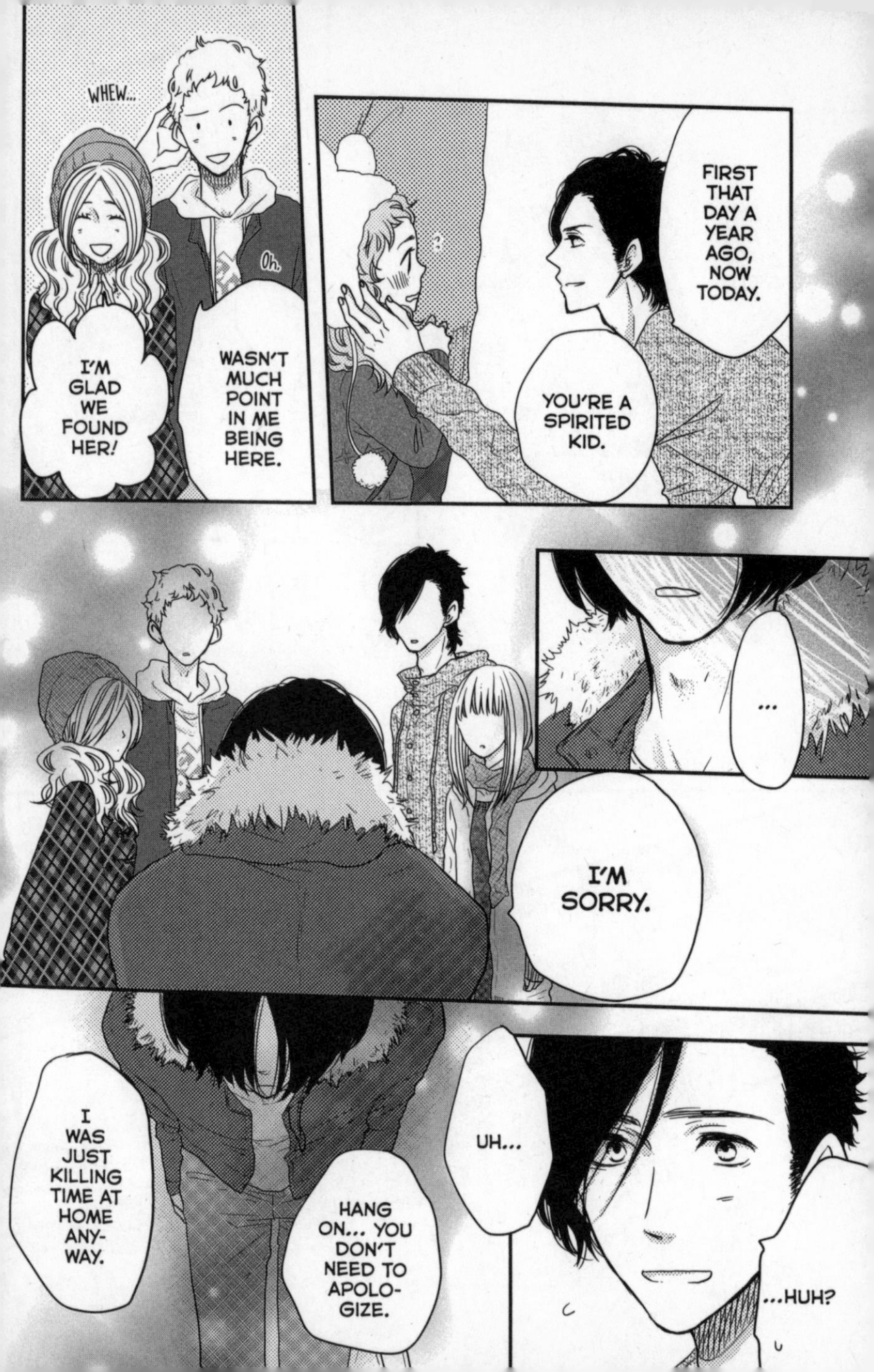

FIRST THAT DAY A YEAR AGO, NOW TODAY.
YOU'RE A SPIRITED KID.
WHEW...
Oh.
WASN'T MUCH POINT IN ME BEING HERE.
I'M GLAD WE FOUND HER!
...
I'M SORRY.
...HUH?
UH...
HANG ON... YOU DON'T NEED TO APOLOGIZE.
I WAS JUST KILLING TIME AT HOME ANYWAY.

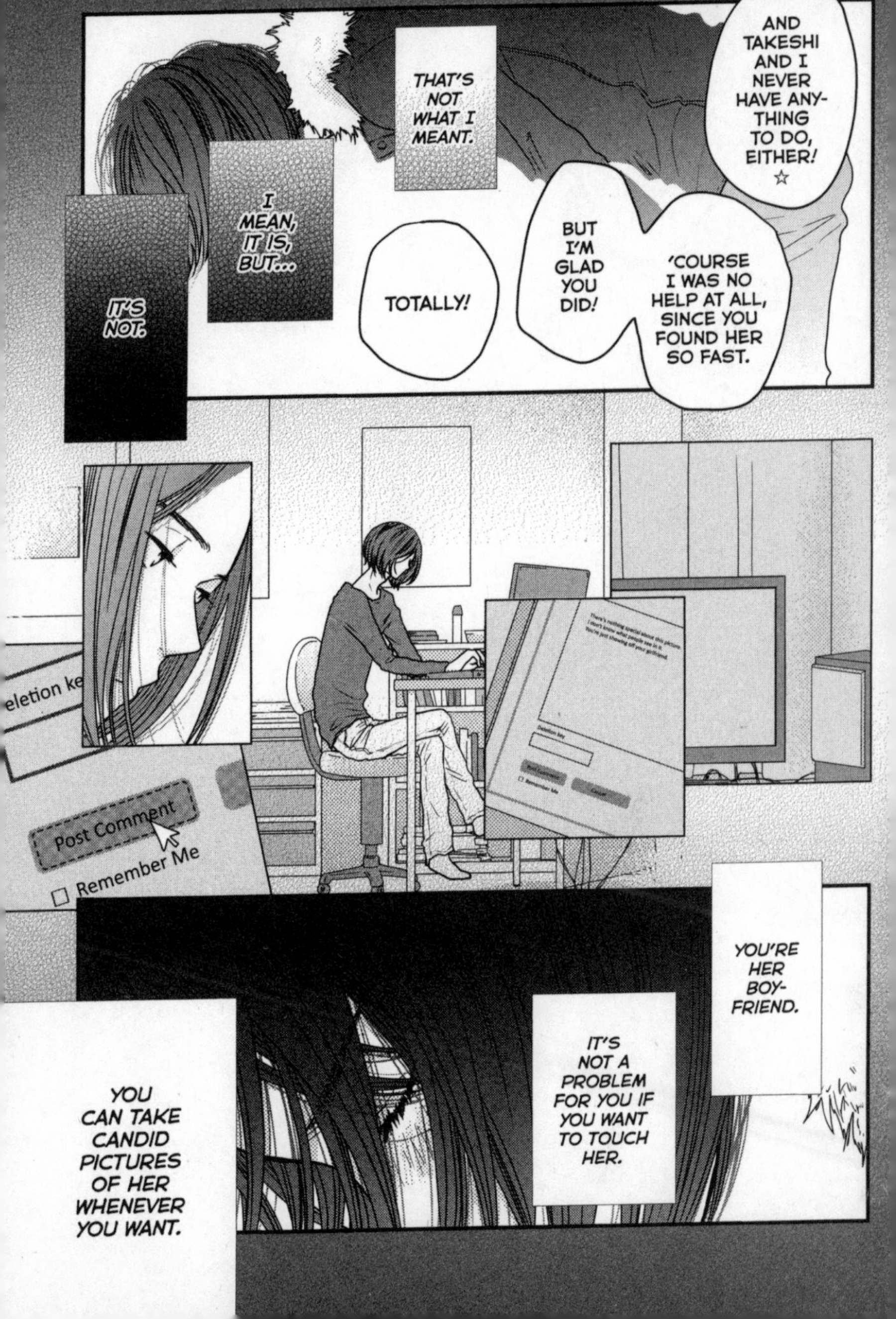
AND TAKESHI AND I NEVER HAVE ANY-THING TO DO, EITHER! ☆
'COURSE I WAS NO HELP AT ALL, SINCE YOU FOUND HER SO FAST.
BUT I'M GLAD YOU DID!
TOTALLY!
THAT'S NOT WHAT I MEANT.
I MEAN, IT IS, BUT...
IT'S NOT.
There's nothing special about this picture.
I don't know what people see in it.
You're just showing off your girlfriend.
Deletion key
Post Comment
Remember Me
Cancel
eletion ke
Post Comment
Remember Me
YOU'RE HER BOY-FRIEND.
IT'S NOT A PROBLEM FOR YOU IF YOU WANT TO TOUCH HER.
YOU CAN TAKE CANDID PICTURES OF HER WHENEVER YOU WANT.

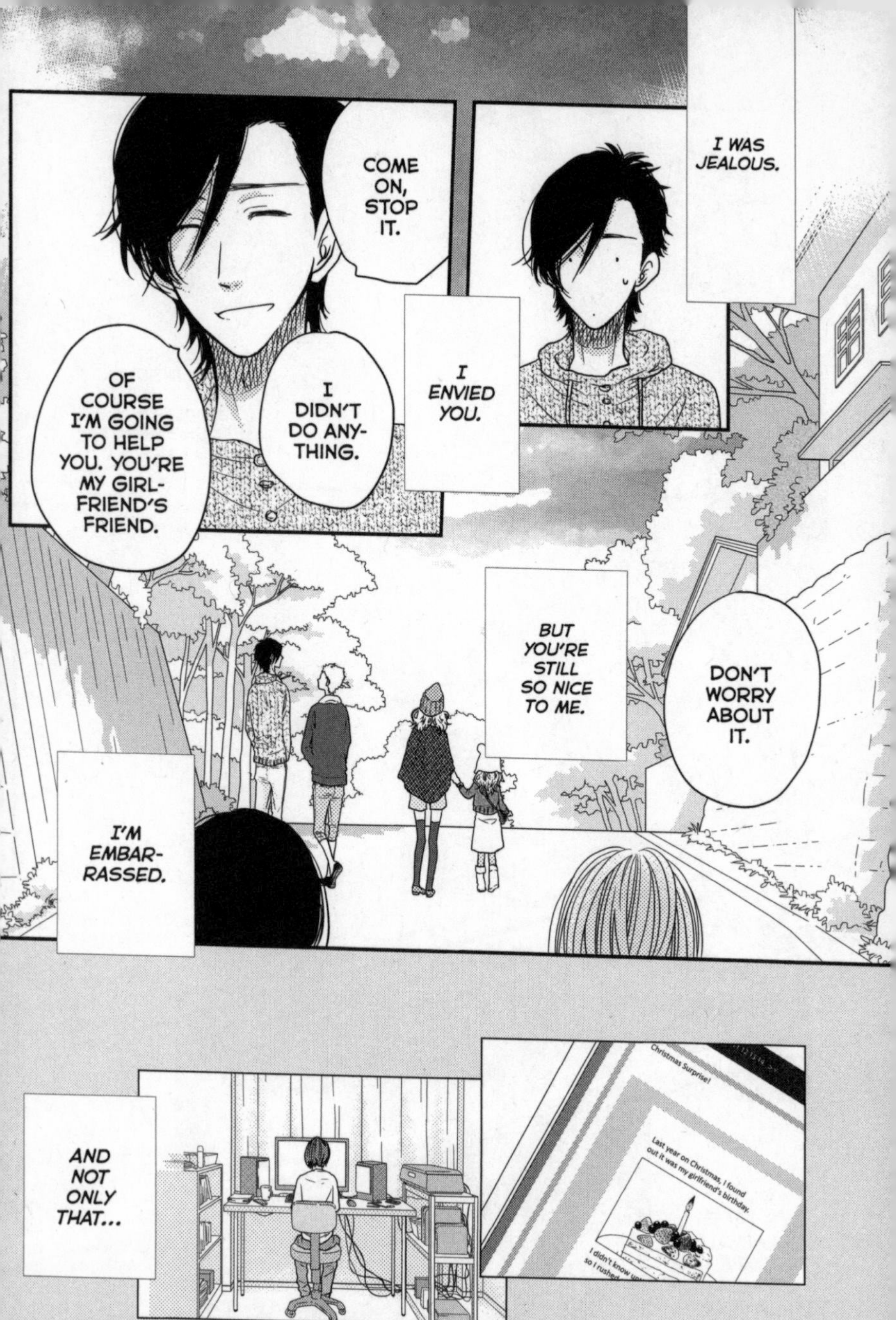
I WAS JEALOUS.
I ENVIED YOU.
COME ON, STOP IT.
I DIDN'T DO ANYTHING.
OF COURSE I'M GOING TO HELP YOU. YOU'RE MY GIRLFRIEND'S FRIEND.
DON'T WORRY ABOUT IT.
BUT YOU'RE STILL SO NICE TO ME.
I'M EMBARRASSED.
Christmas Surprise!
Last year on Christmas, I found out it was my girlfriend's birthday.
AND NOT ONLY THAT...

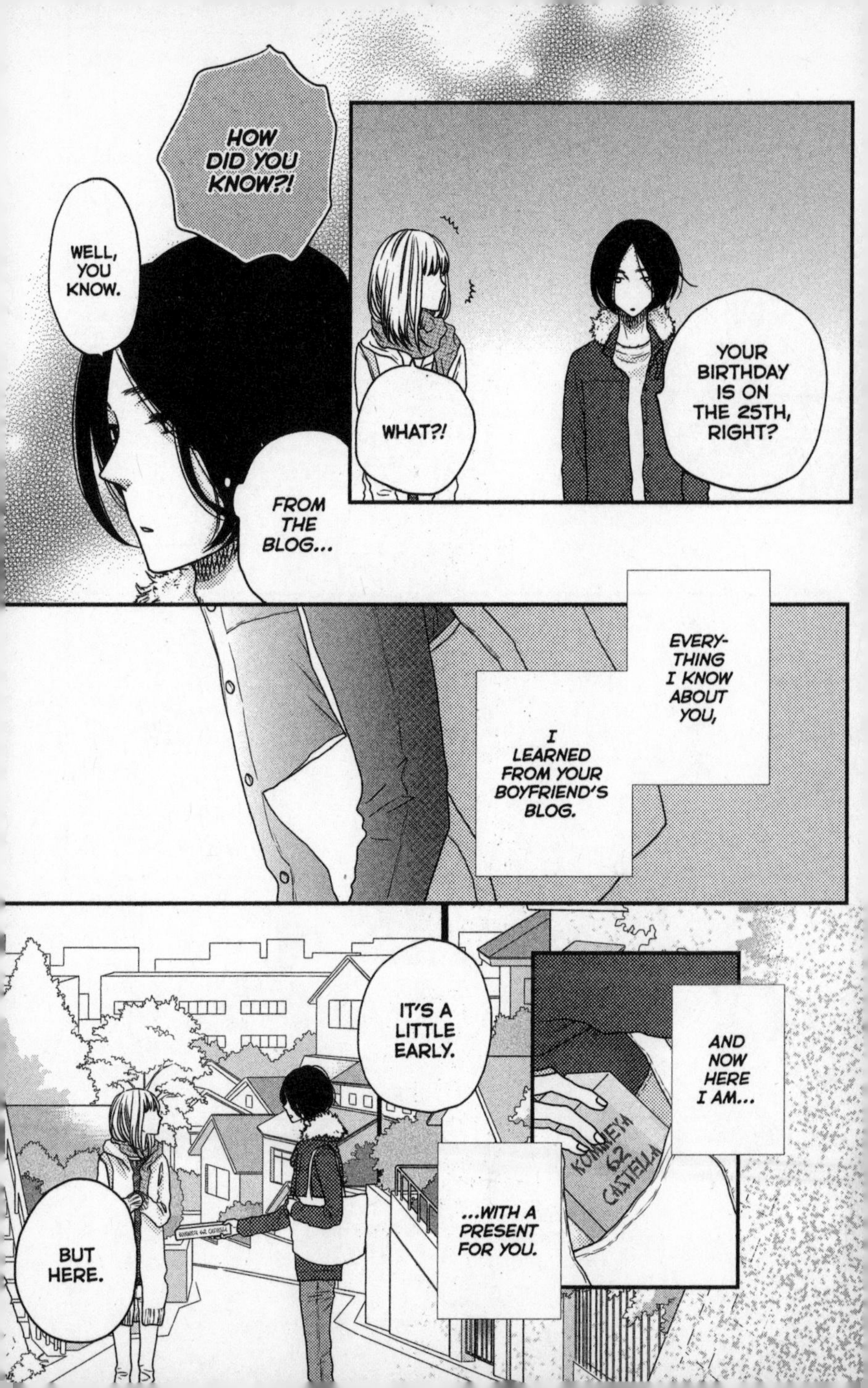
YOUR BIRTHDAY IS ON THE 25TH, RIGHT?
WHAT?!
HOW DID YOU KNOW?!
WELL, YOU KNOW.
FROM THE BLOG...
EVERY-THING I KNOW ABOUT YOU,
I LEARNED FROM YOUR BOYFRIEND'S BLOG.
AND NOW HERE I AM...
62
CASTELLA
...WITH A PRESENT FOR YOU.
IT'S A LITTLE EARLY.
BUT HERE.

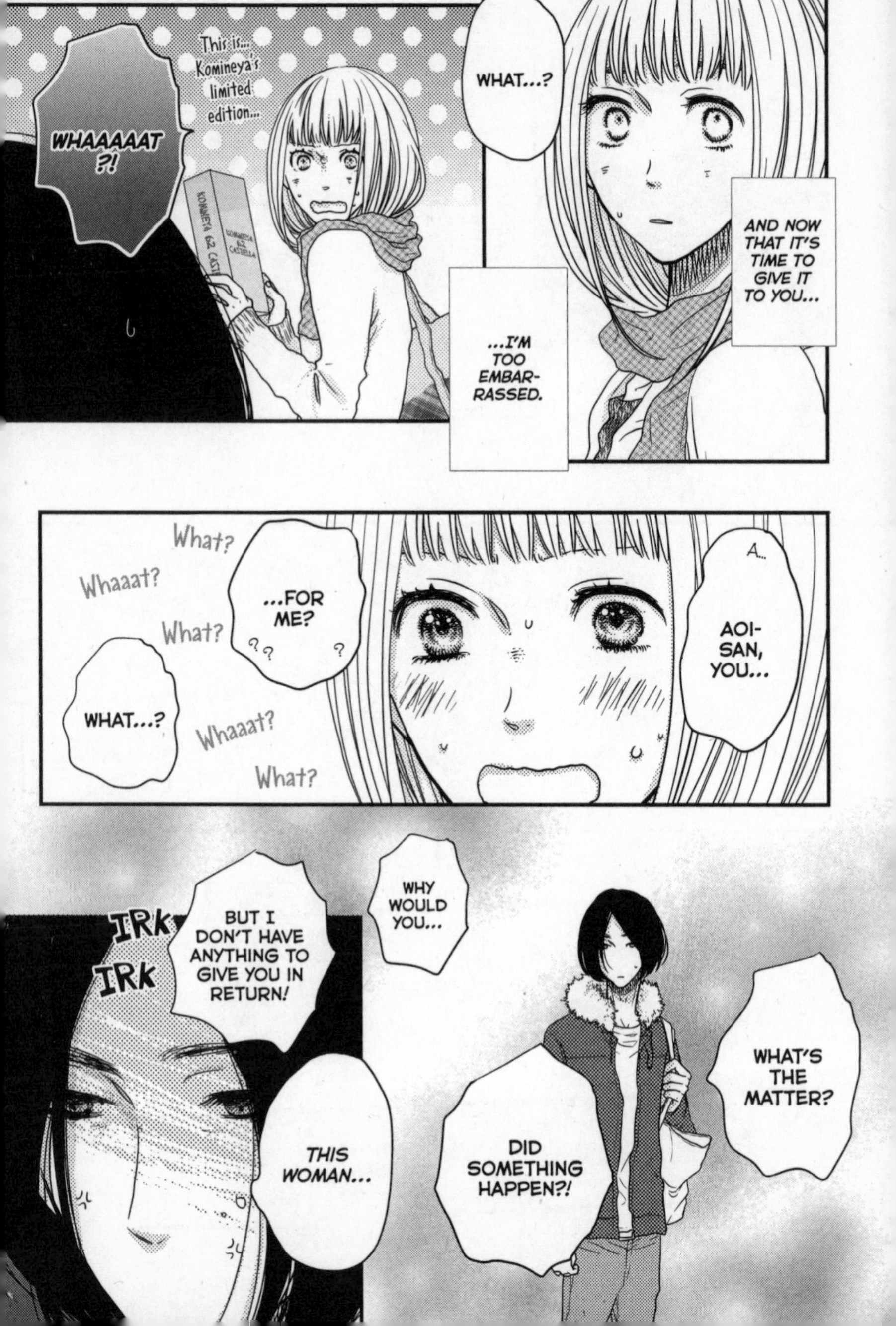
WHAT...?
AND NOW THAT IT'S TIME TO GIVE IT TO YOU...
...I'M TOO EMBARRASSED.
This is... Komineya's limited edition...
WHAAAAAT?!
KOMINEYA 62 CASTELLA
A... AOI-SAN, YOU...
...FOR ME?
What?
Whaaat?
What?
WHAT...?
Whaaat?
What?
WHAT'S THE MATTER?
DID SOMETHING HAPPEN?!
WHY WOULD YOU...
BUT I DON'T HAVE ANYTHING TO GIVE YOU IN RETURN!
IRK
IRK
THIS WOMAN...

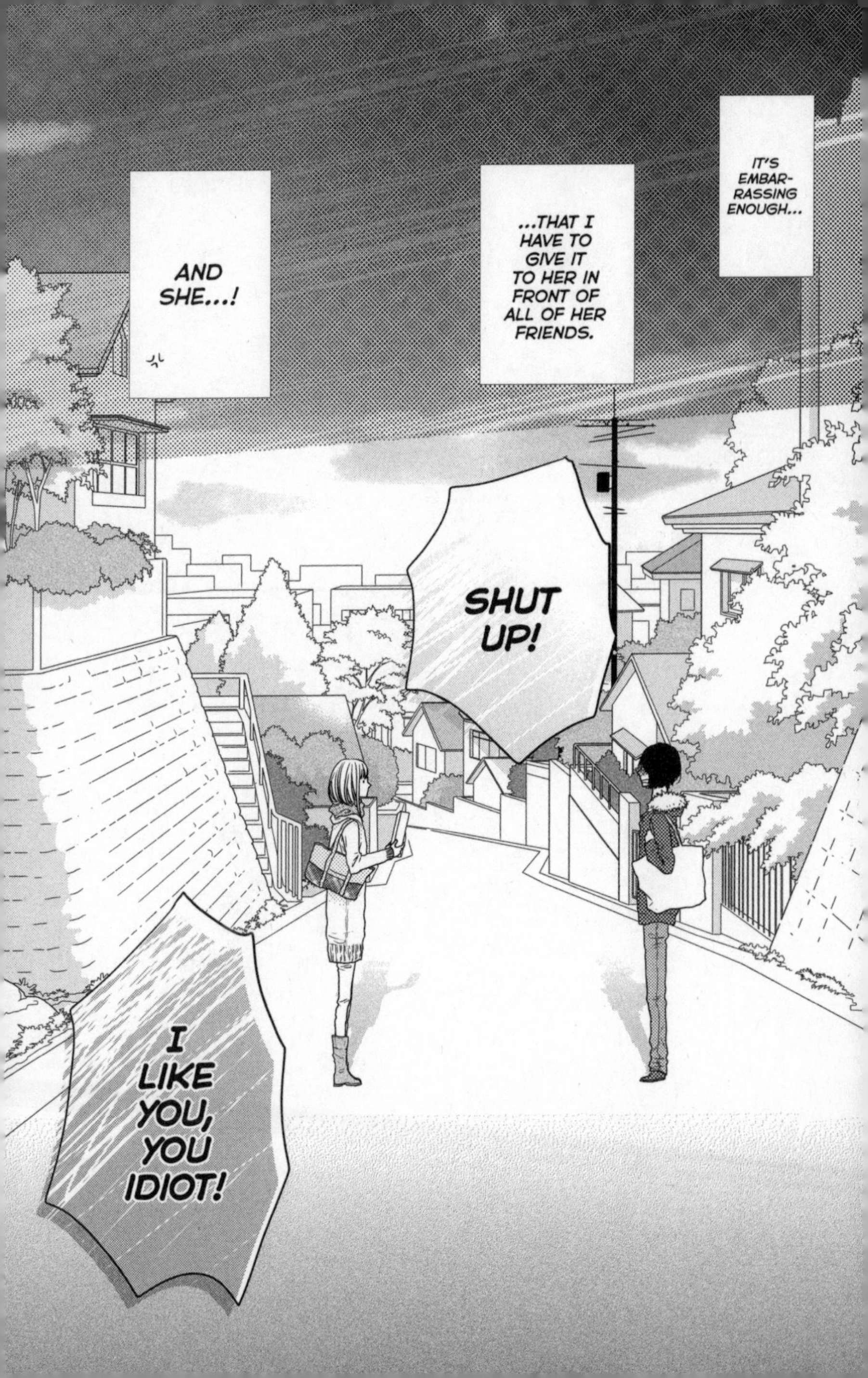
IT'S EMBAR-RASSING ENOUGH...
...THAT I HAVE TO GIVE IT TO HER IN FRONT OF ALL OF HER FRIENDS.
AND SHE...!
SHUT UP!
I LIKE YOU, YOU IDIOT!

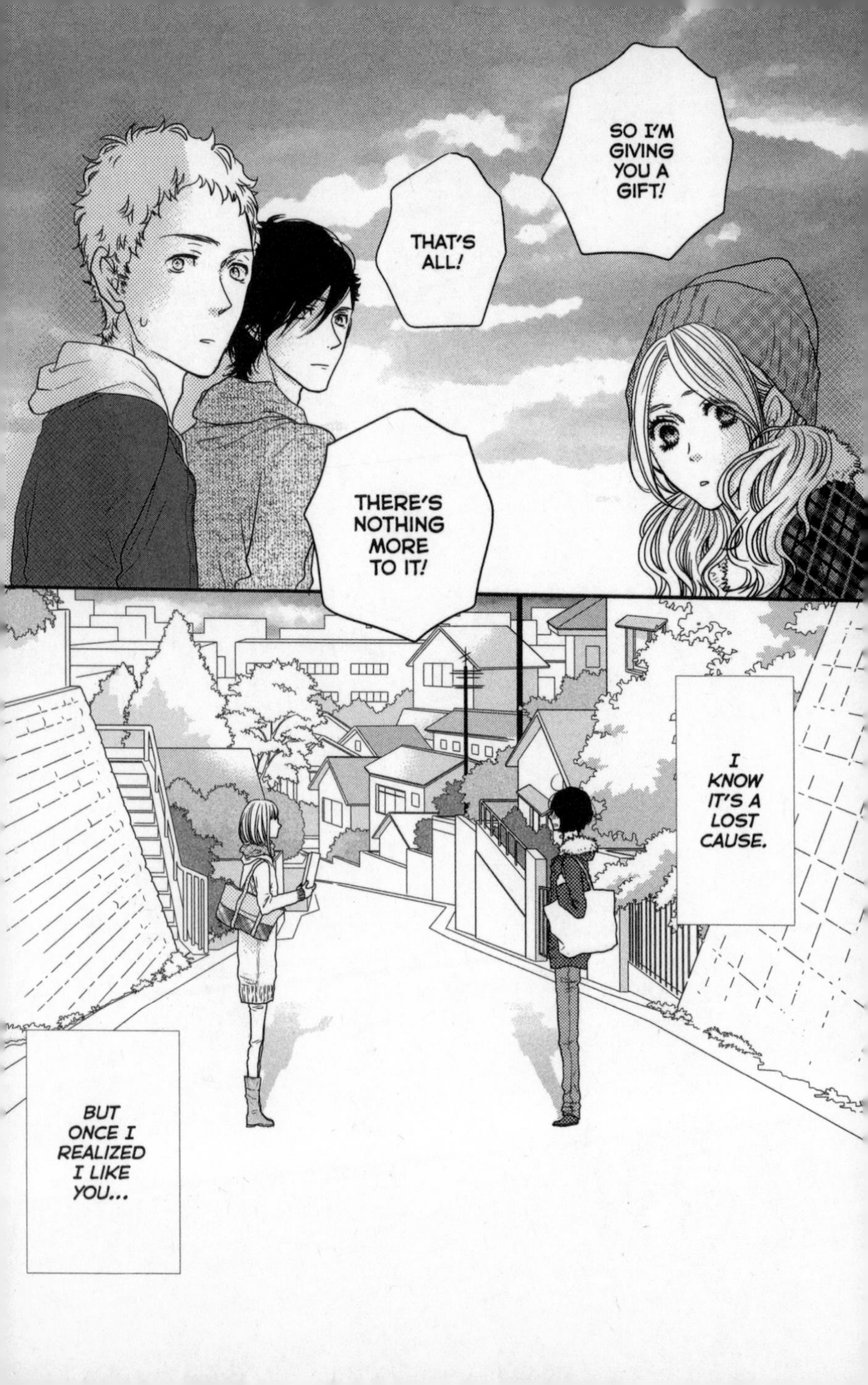
SO I'M GIVING YOU A GIFT!
THAT'S ALL!
THERE'S NOTHING MORE TO IT!
I KNOW IT'S A LOST CAUSE.
BUT ONCE I REALIZED I LIKE YOU...

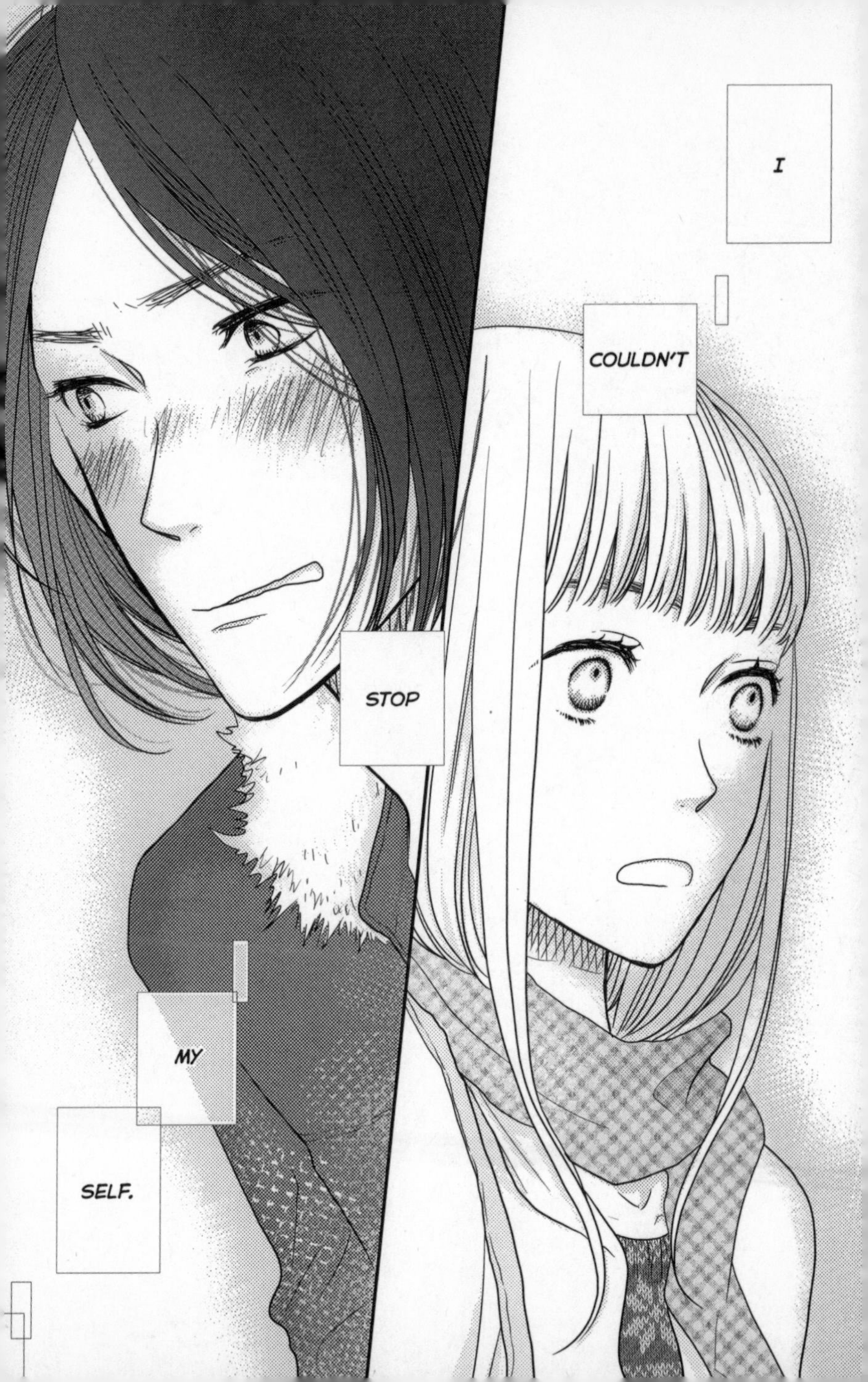
I
COULDN'T
STOP
MY
SELF.

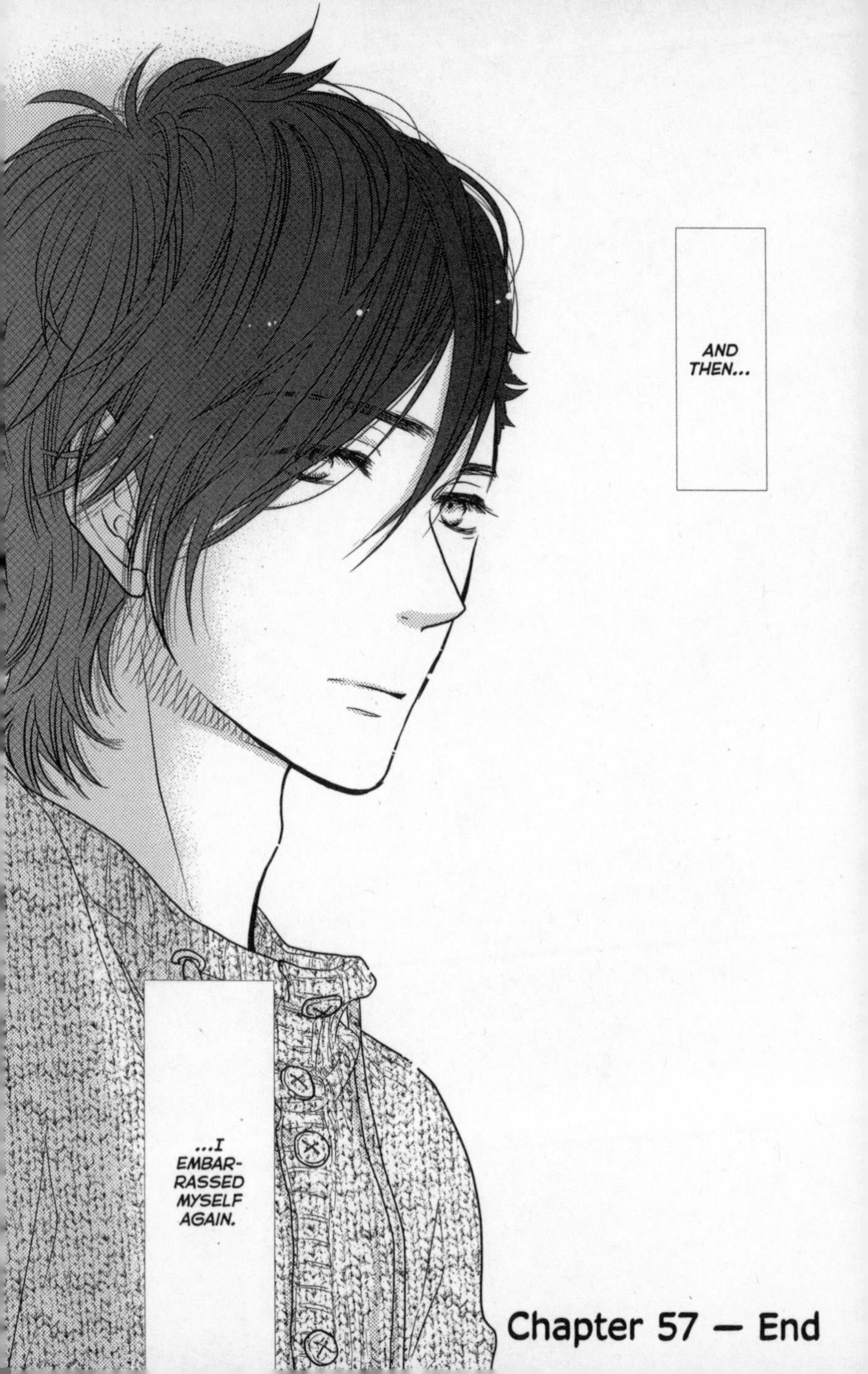
AND THEN...
...I EMBARRASSED MYSELF AGAIN.
Chapter 57 — End

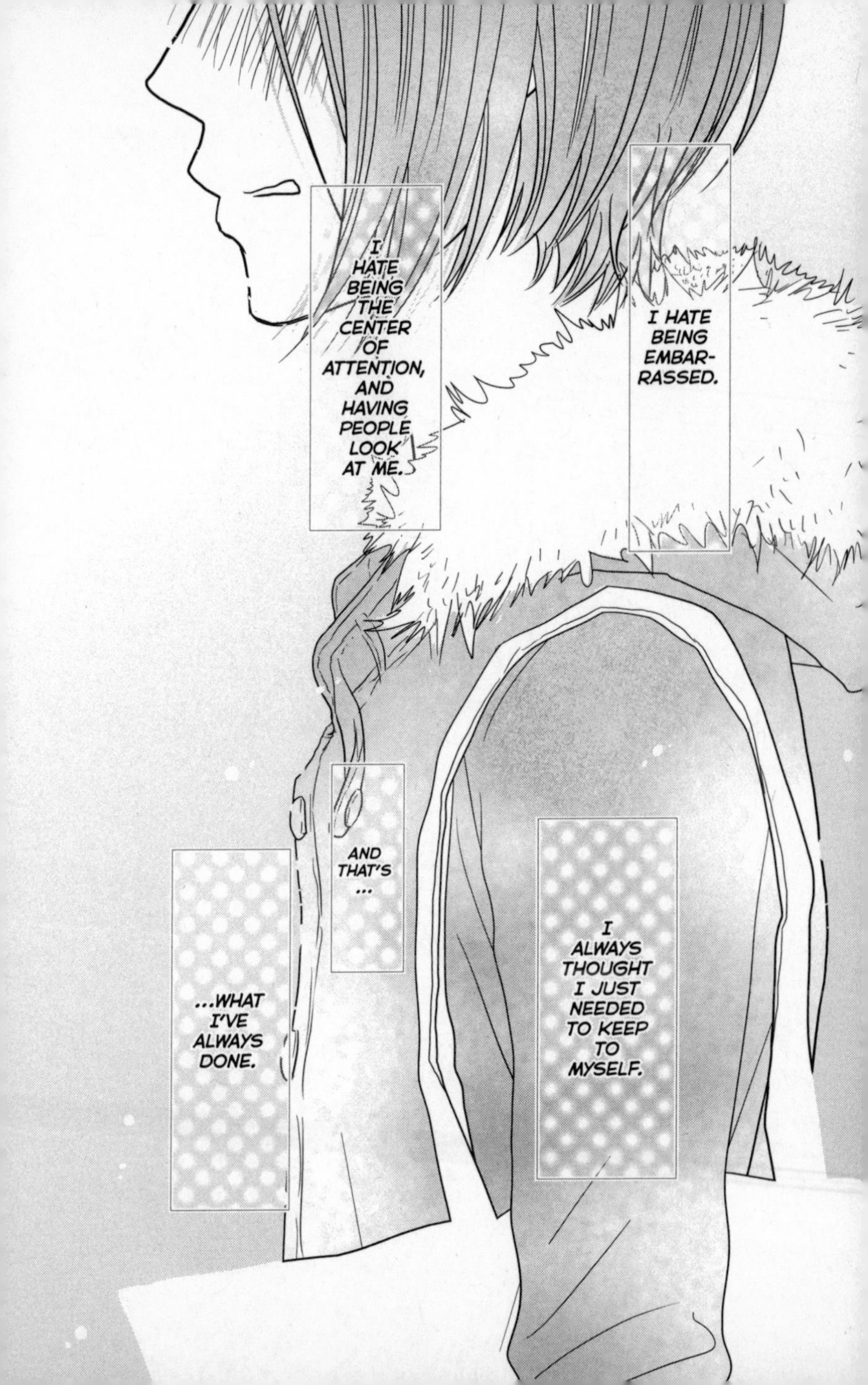
I HATE BEING EMBARRASSED.
I HATE BEING THE CENTER OF ATTENTION, AND HAVING PEOPLE LOOK AT ME.
I ALWAYS THOUGHT I JUST NEEDED TO KEEP TO MYSELF.
AND THAT'S...
...WHAT I'VE ALWAYS DONE.

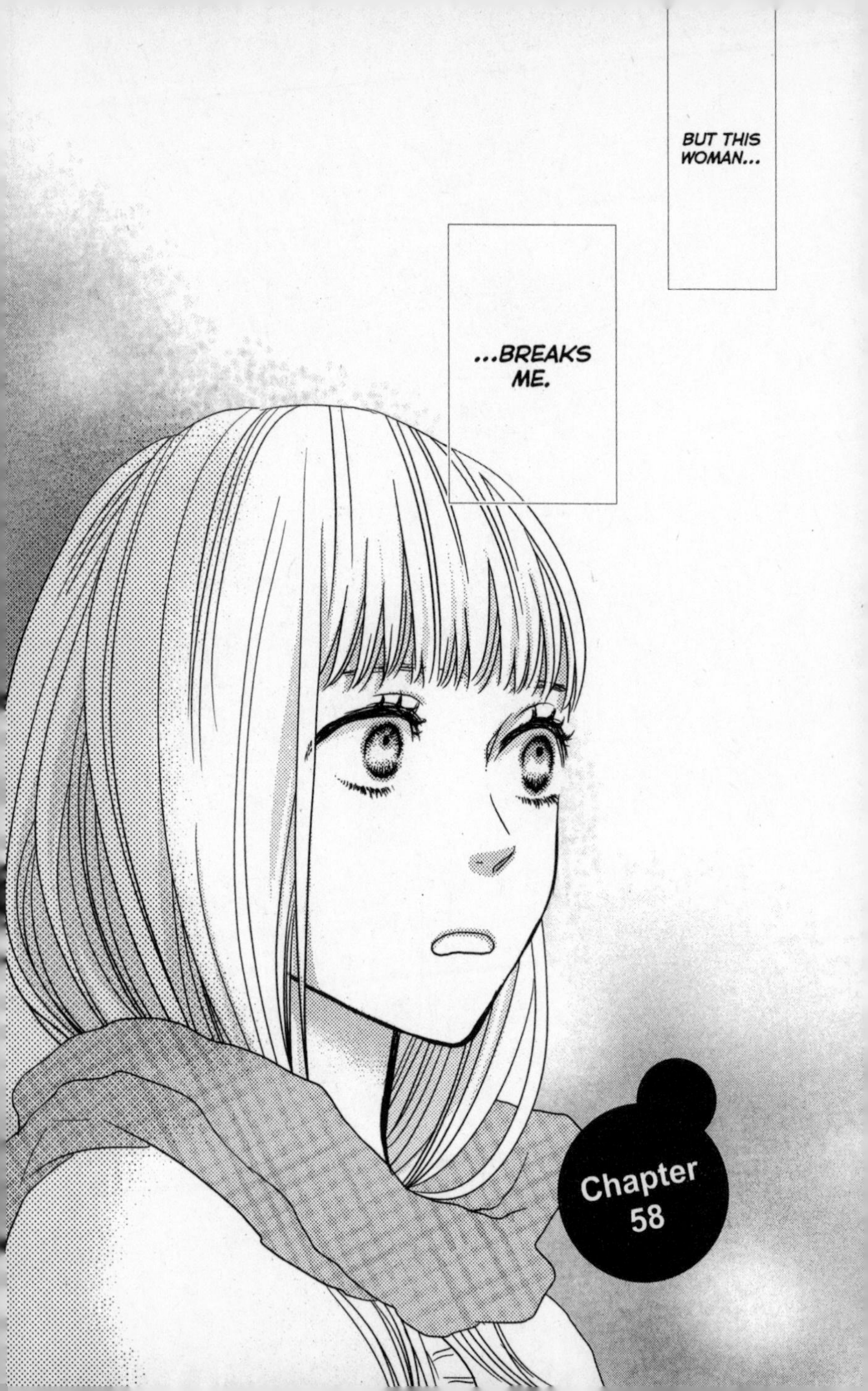
BUT THIS WOMAN...
...BREAKS ME.
Chapter 58

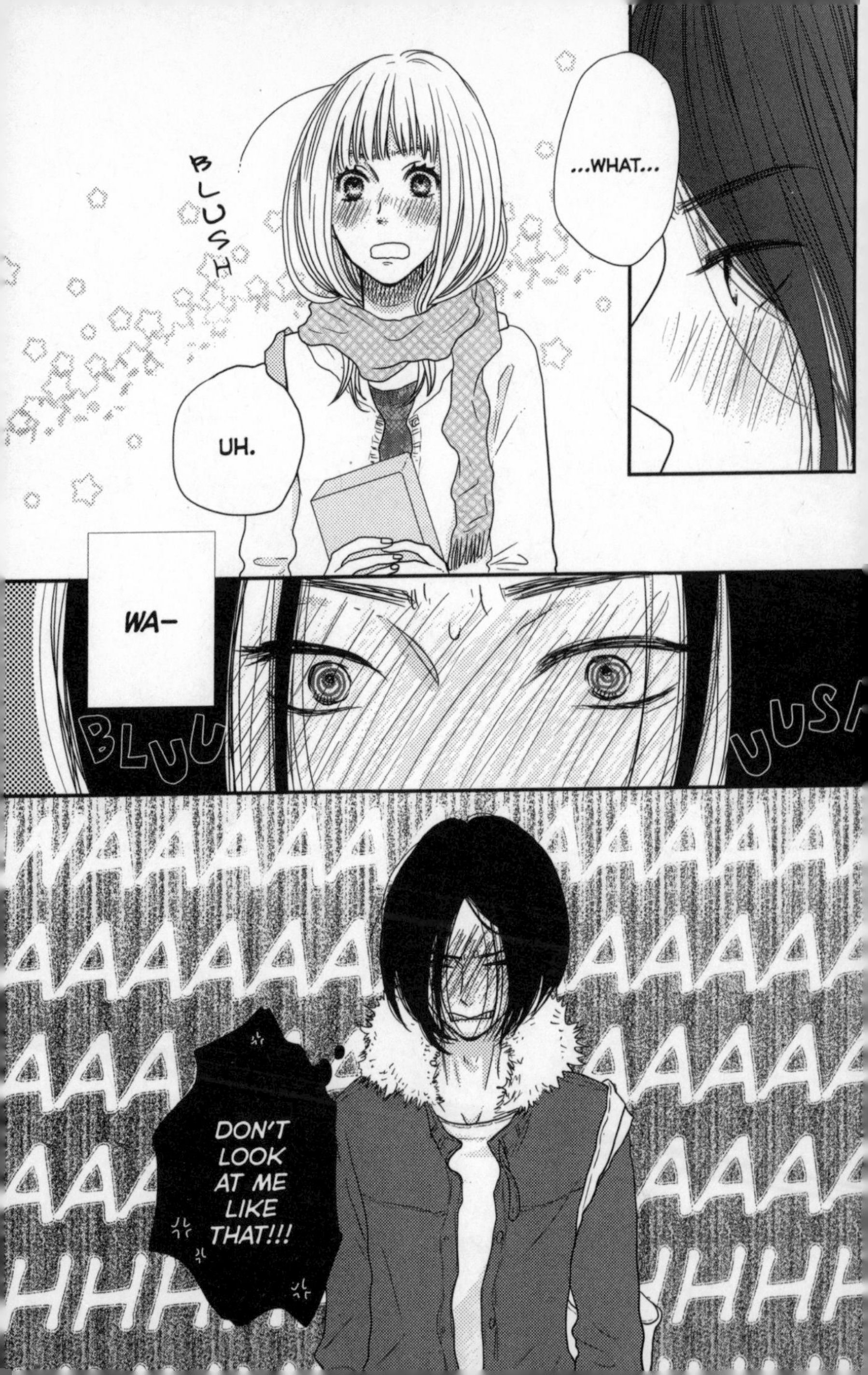
...WHAT...
BLUSH
UH.
WA-
BLUU
UUSH
DON'T LOOK AT ME LIKE THAT!!!

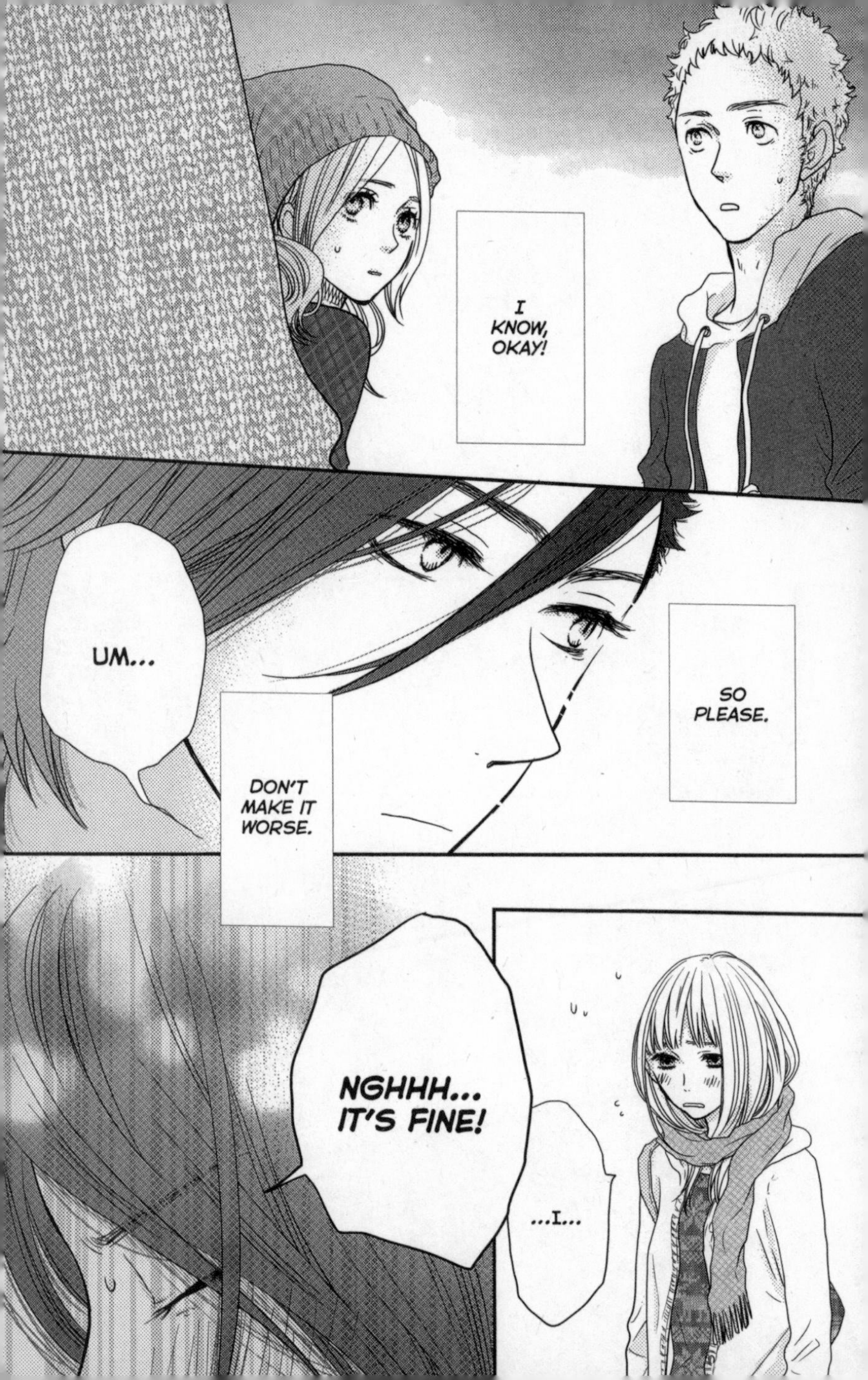
I KNOW, OKAY!
SO PLEASE.
DON'T MAKE IT WORSE.
UM...
...I...
NGHHH... IT'S FINE!

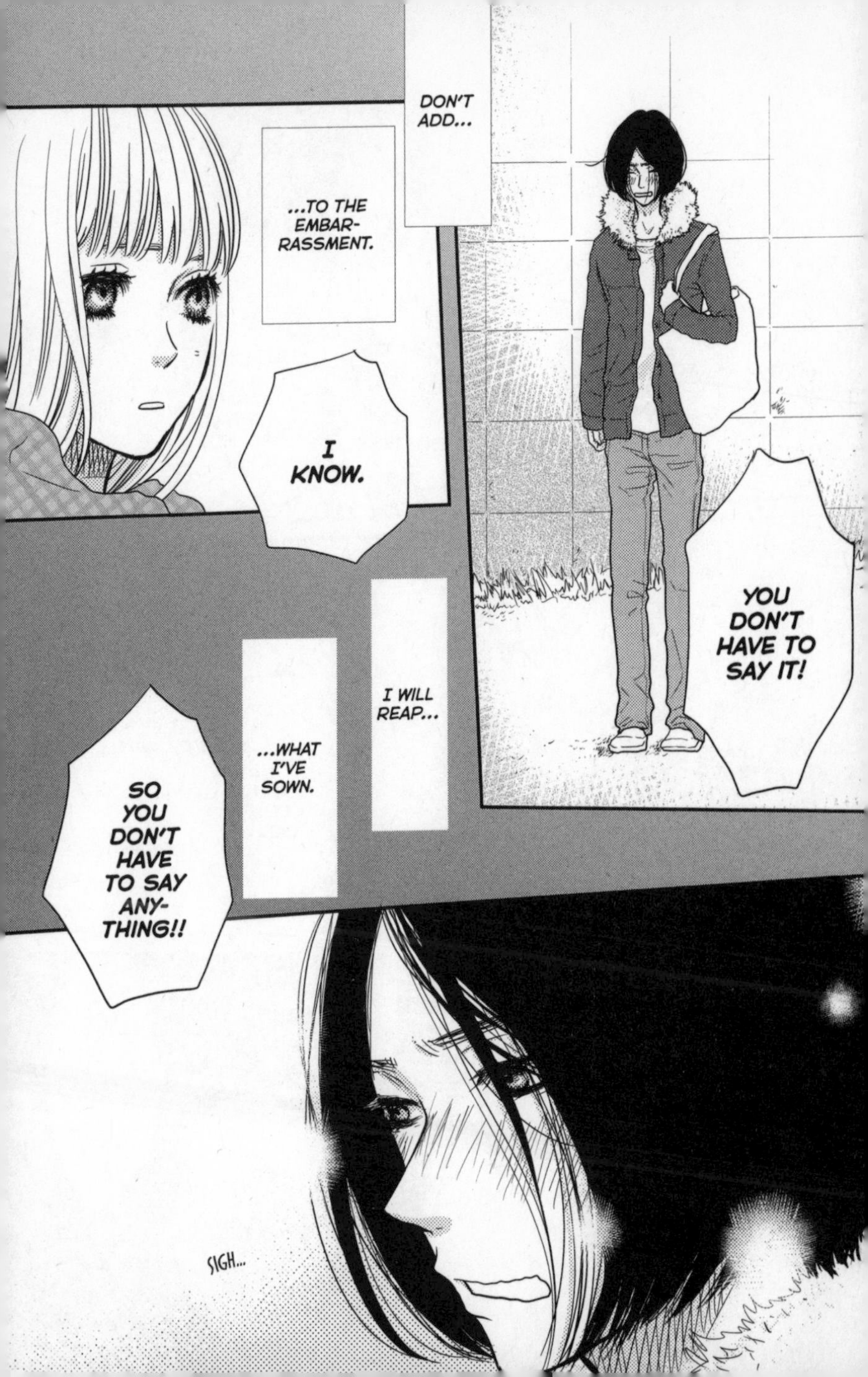
DON'T ADD...
YOU DON'T HAVE TO SAY IT!
...TO THE EMBARRASSMENT.
I KNOW.
I WILL REAP...
...WHAT I'VE SOWN.
SO YOU DON'T HAVE TO SAY ANYTHING!!
SIGH...

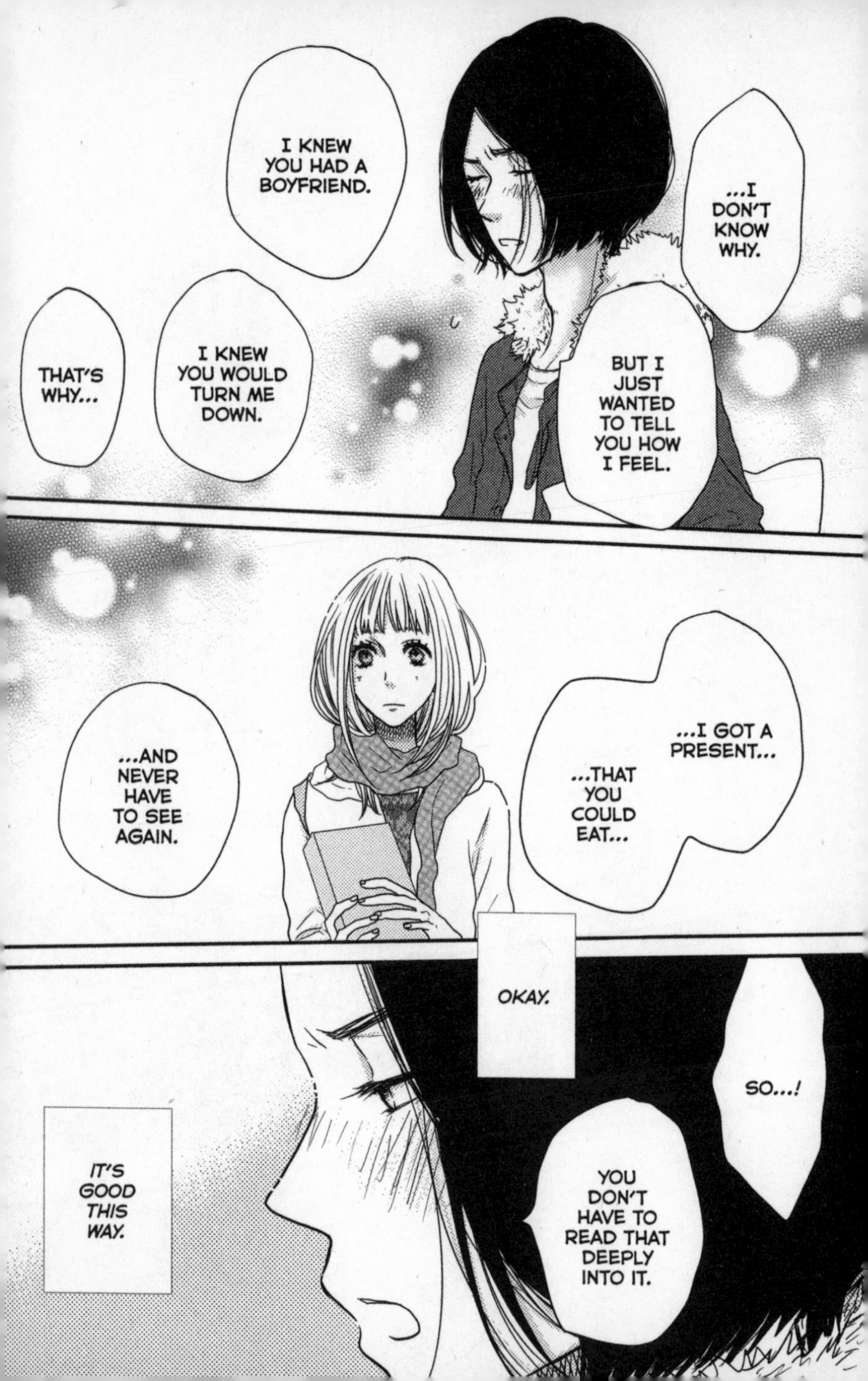
...I DON'T KNOW WHY.
BUT I JUST WANTED TO TELL YOU HOW I FEEL.
I KNEW YOU HAD A BOYFRIEND.
I KNEW YOU WOULD TURN ME DOWN.
THAT'S WHY...
...I GOT A PRESENT...
...THAT YOU COULD EAT...
...AND NEVER HAVE TO SEE AGAIN.
SO...!
YOU DON'T HAVE TO READ THAT DEEPLY INTO IT.
OKAY.
IT'S GOOD THIS WAY.

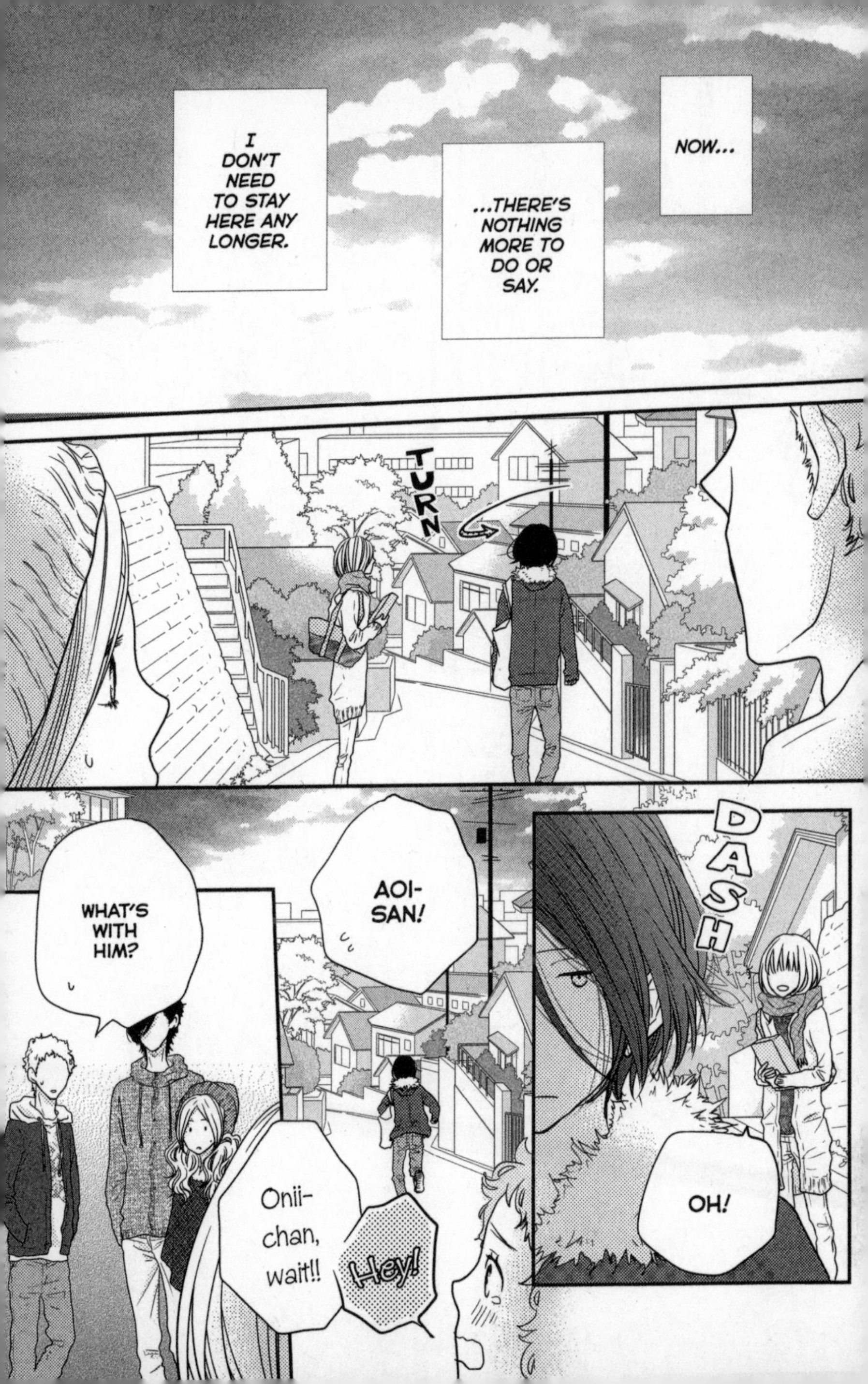
NOW...
...THERE'S NOTHING MORE TO DO OR SAY.
I DON'T NEED TO STAY HERE ANY LONGER.
TURN
DASH
OH!
AOI-SAN!
WHAT'S WITH HIM?
Hey!
Onii-chan, wait!!

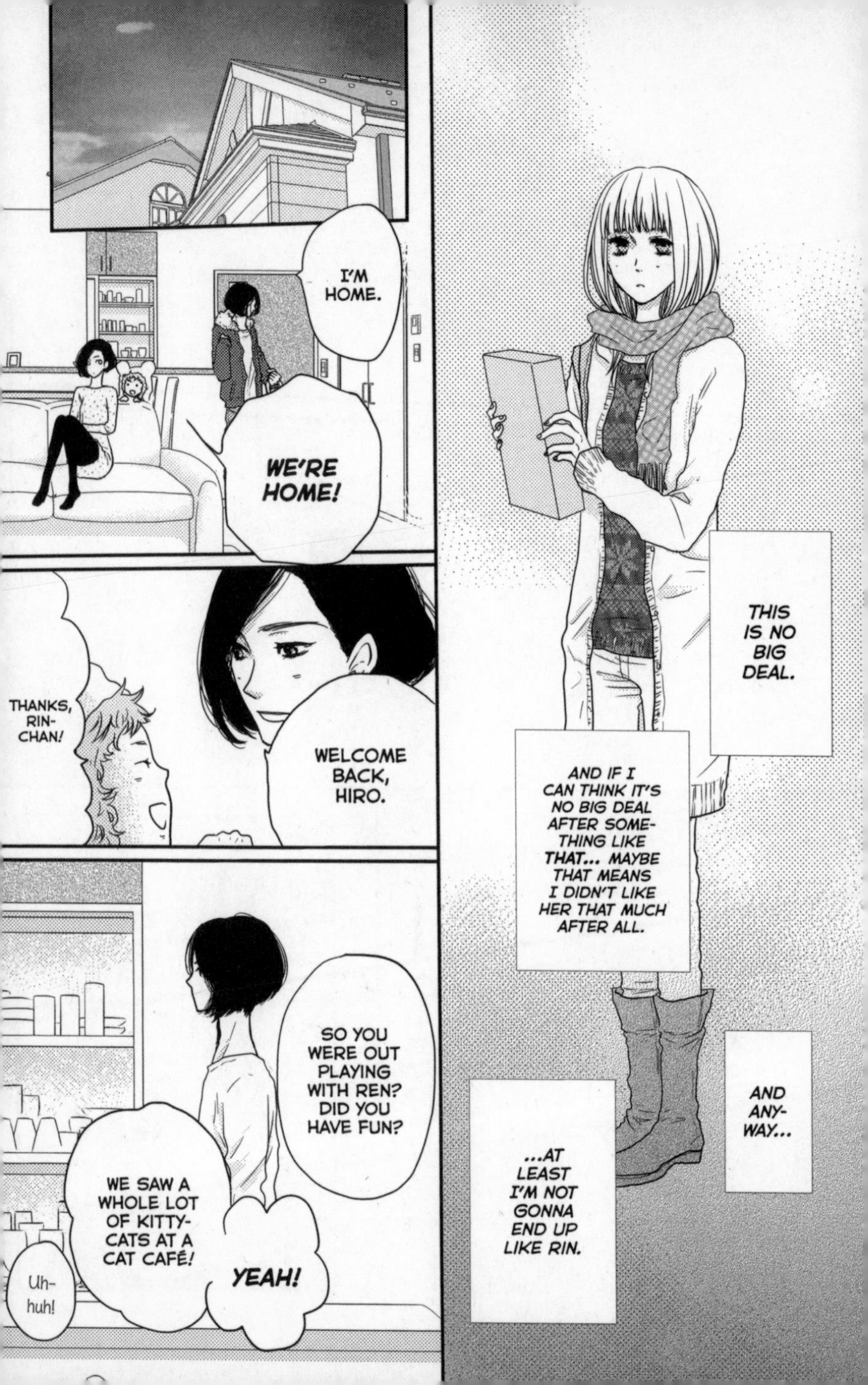
THIS IS NO BIG DEAL.
AND IF I CAN THINK IT'S NO BIG DEAL AFTER SOME-THING LIKE THAT... MAYBE THAT MEANS I DIDN'T LIKE HER THAT MUCH AFTER ALL.
AND ANY-WAY...
...AT LEAST I'M NOT GONNA END UP LIKE RIN.
I'M HOME.
WE'RE HOME!
WELCOME BACK, HIRO.
THANKS, RIN-CHAN!
SO YOU WERE OUT PLAYING WITH REN? DID YOU HAVE FUN?
YEAH!
WE SAW A WHOLE LOT OF KITTY-CATS AT A CAT CAFÉ!
Uh-huh!

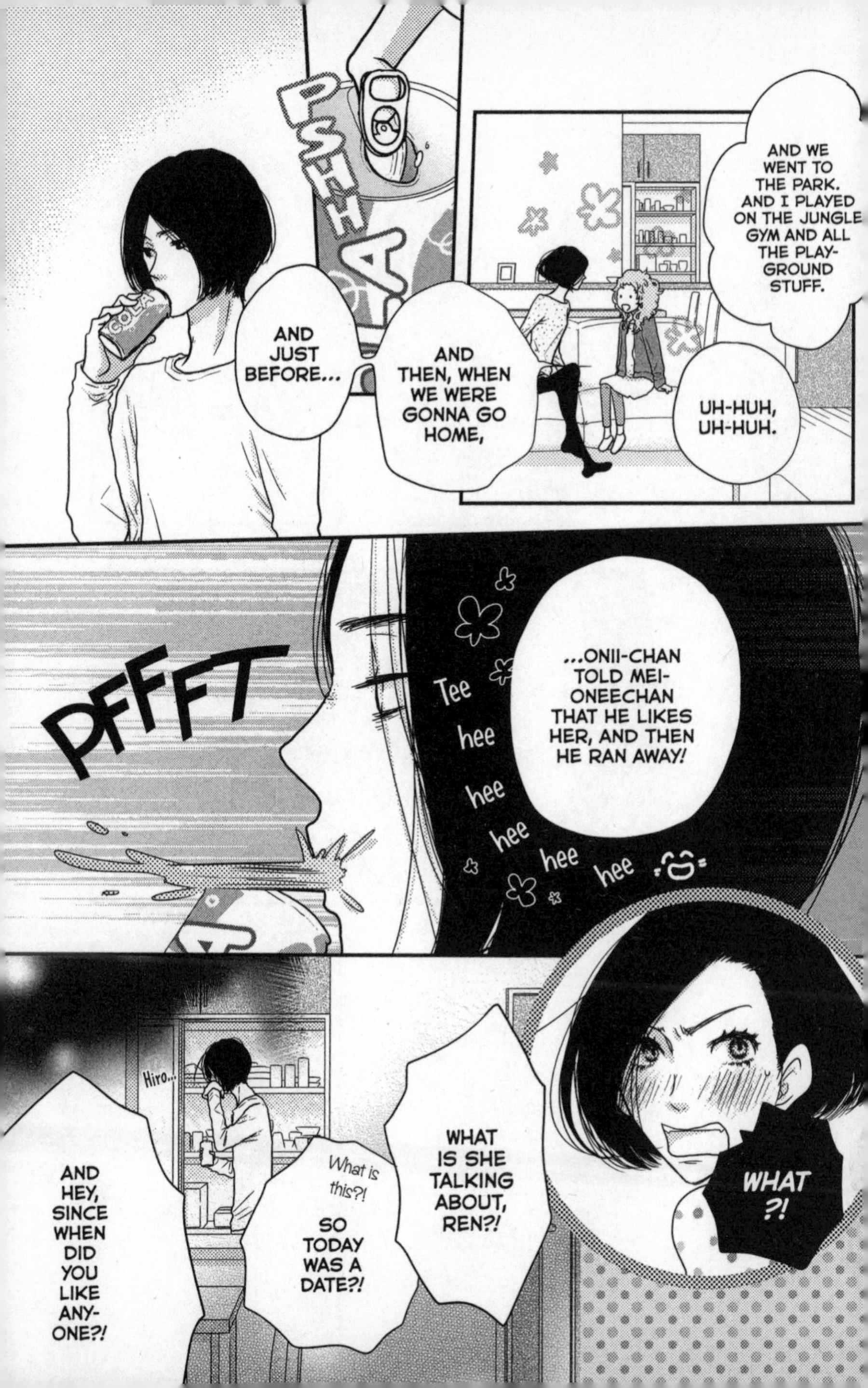
AND WE WENT TO THE PARK. AND I PLAYED ON THE JUNGLE GYM AND ALL THE PLAY-GROUND STUFF.
UH-HUH, UH-HUH.
AND THEN, WHEN WE WERE GONNA GO HOME,
PSHHA
AND JUST BEFORE...
...ONII-CHAN TOLD MEI-ONEECHAN THAT HE LIKES HER, AND THEN HE RAN AWAY!
Tee hee hee hee hee hee
PFFFT
WHAT ?!
WHAT IS SHE TALKING ABOUT, REN?!
What is this?!
SO TODAY WAS A DATE?!
Hiro...
AND HEY, SINCE WHEN DID YOU LIKE ANY-ONE?!

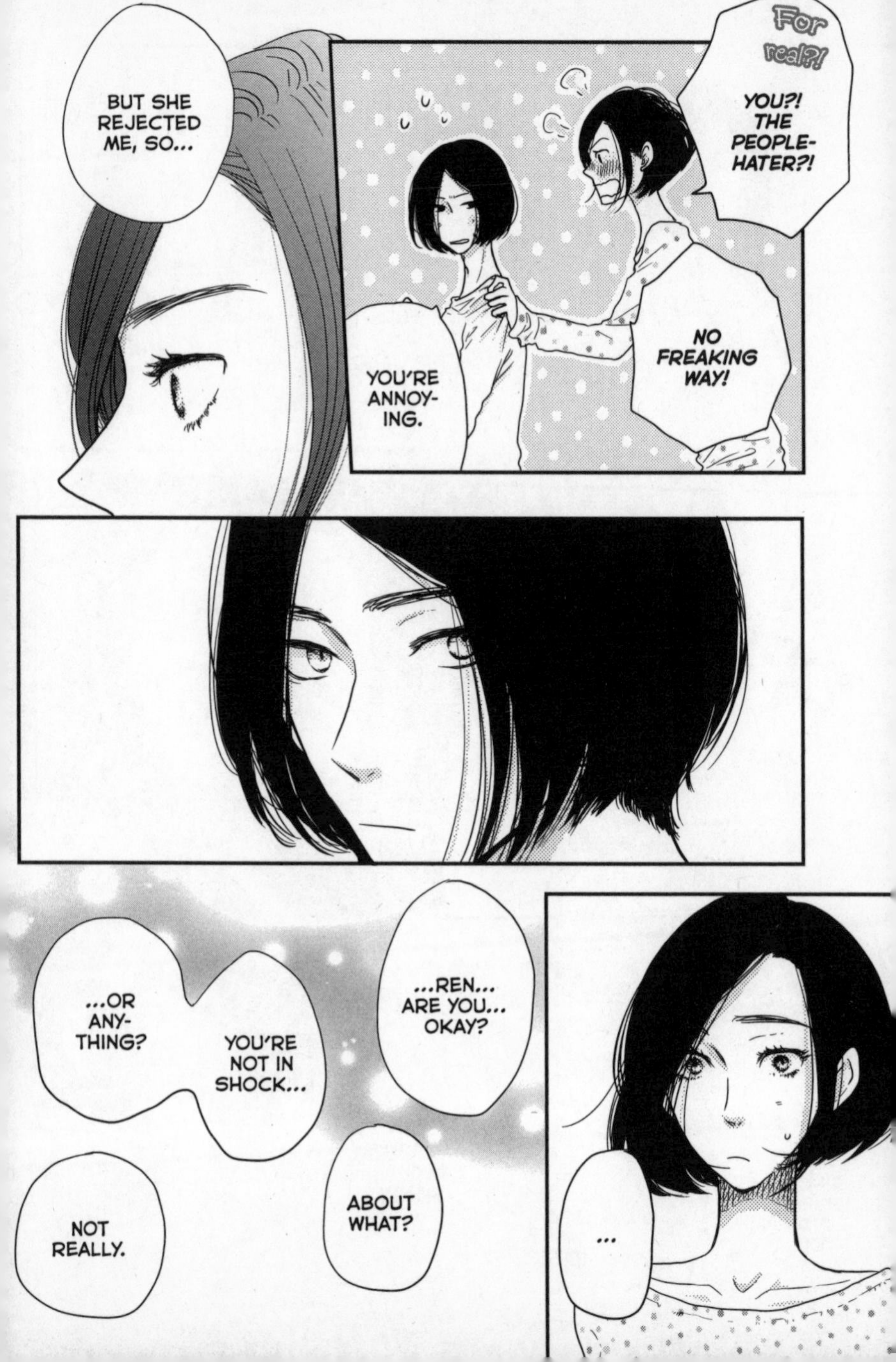
For real?!
YOU?! THE PEOPLE-HATER?!
NO FREAKING WAY!
YOU'RE ANNOY-ING.
BUT SHE REJECTED ME, SO...
...
...REN... ARE YOU... OKAY?
YOU'RE NOT IN SHOCK...
...OR ANY-THING?
ABOUT WHAT?
NOT REALLY.

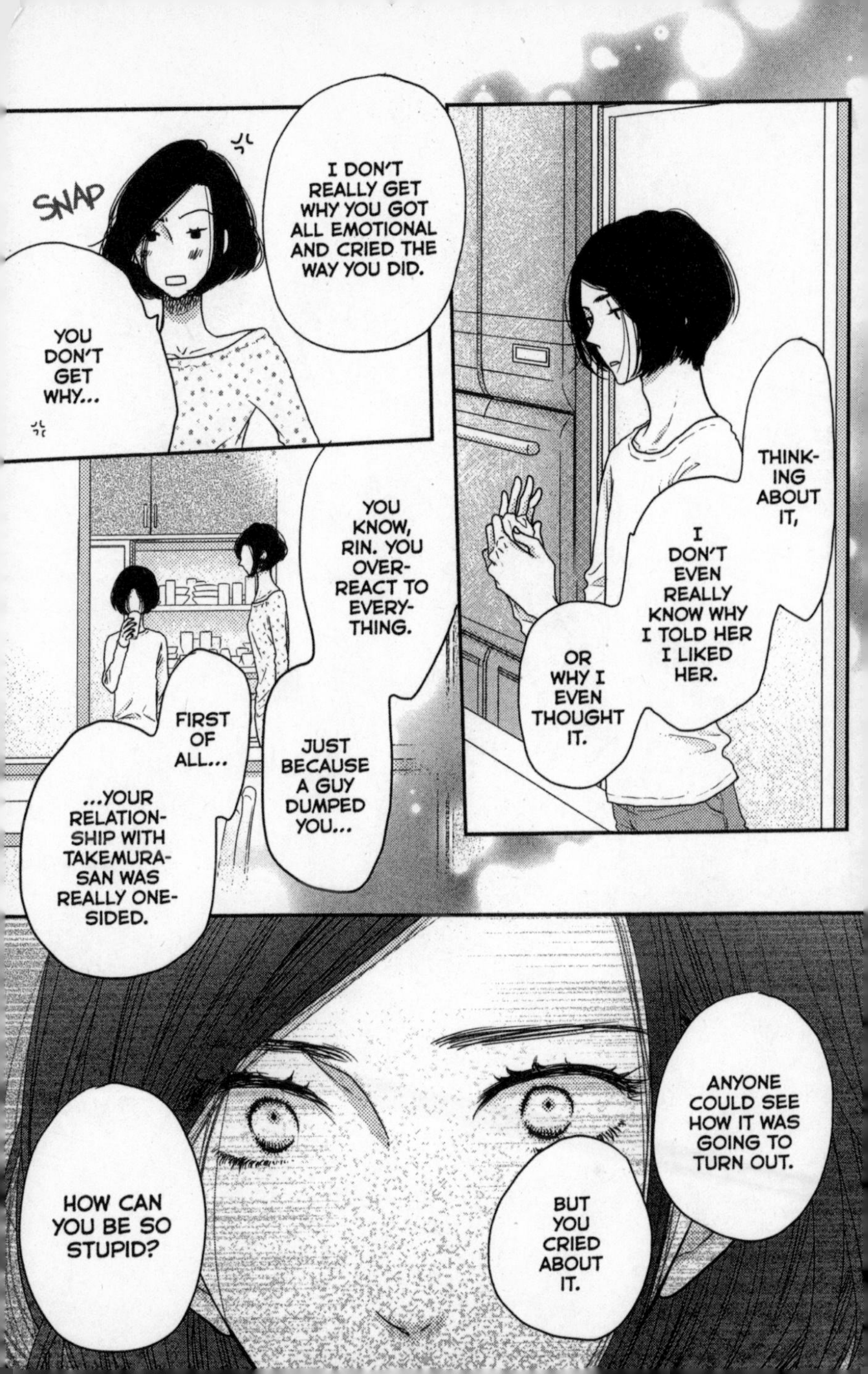
THINKING ABOUT IT,
I DON'T EVEN REALLY KNOW WHY I TOLD HER I LIKED HER.
OR WHY I EVEN THOUGHT IT.
I DON'T REALLY GET WHY YOU GOT ALL EMOTIONAL AND CRIED THE WAY YOU DID.
SNAP
YOU DON'T GET WHY...
YOU KNOW, RIN. YOU OVER-REACT TO EVERYTHING.
JUST BECAUSE A GUY DUMPED YOU...
FIRST OF ALL...
...YOUR RELATION-SHIP WITH TAKEMURA-SAN WAS REALLY ONE-SIDED.
ANYONE COULD SEE HOW IT WAS GOING TO TURN OUT.
BUT YOU CRIED ABOUT IT.
HOW CAN YOU BE SO STUPID?

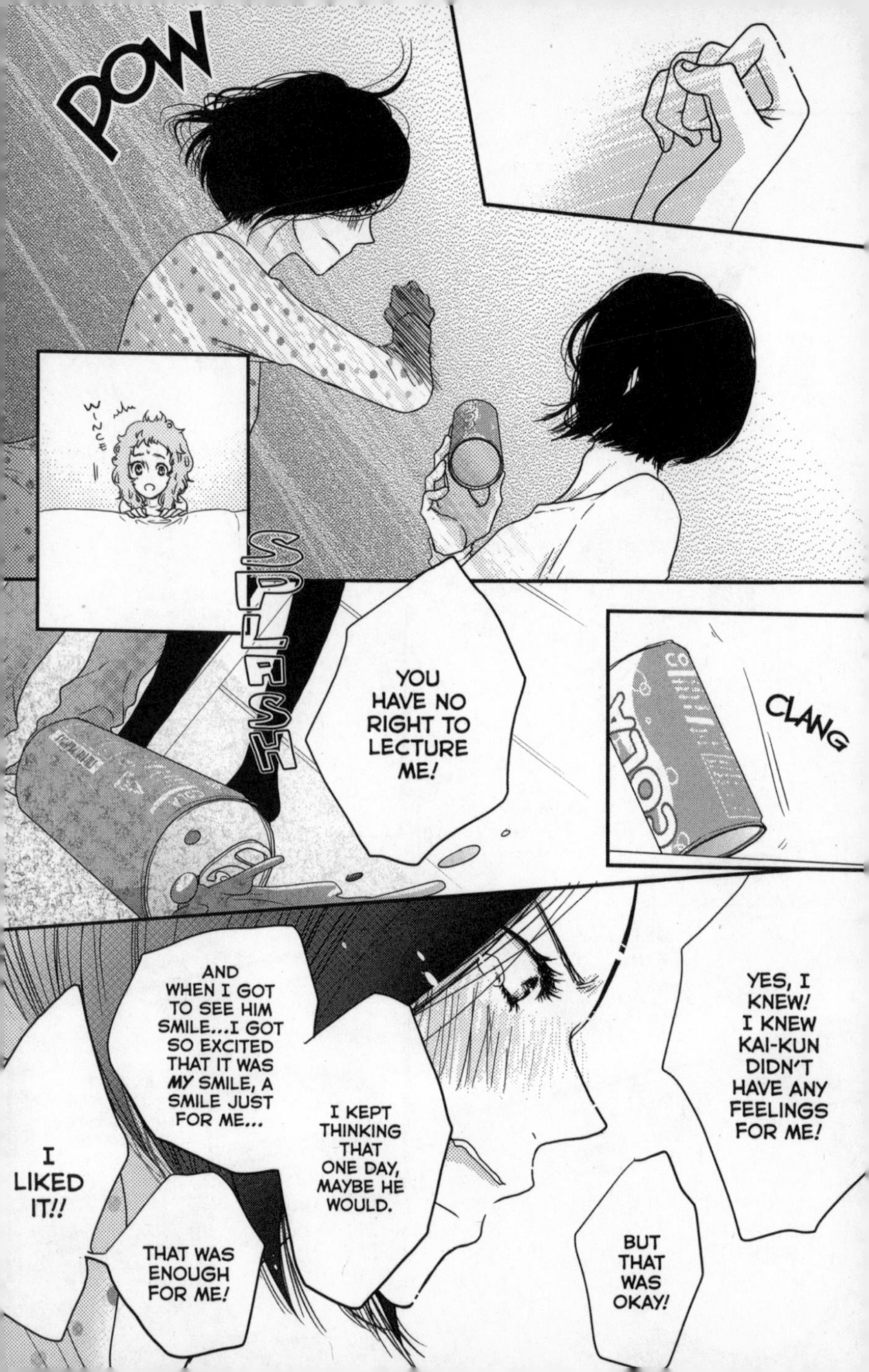
POW
W-INCE
CLANG
YOU HAVE NO RIGHT TO LECTURE ME!
SPLASH
YES, I KNEW! I KNEW KAI-KUN DIDN'T HAVE ANY FEELINGS FOR ME!
BUT THAT WAS OKAY!
I KEPT THINKING THAT ONE DAY, MAYBE HE WOULD.
AND WHEN I GOT TO SEE HIM SMILE...I GOT SO EXCITED THAT IT WAS *MY* SMILE, A SMILE JUST FOR ME...
THAT WAS ENOUGH FOR ME!
I LIKED IT!!

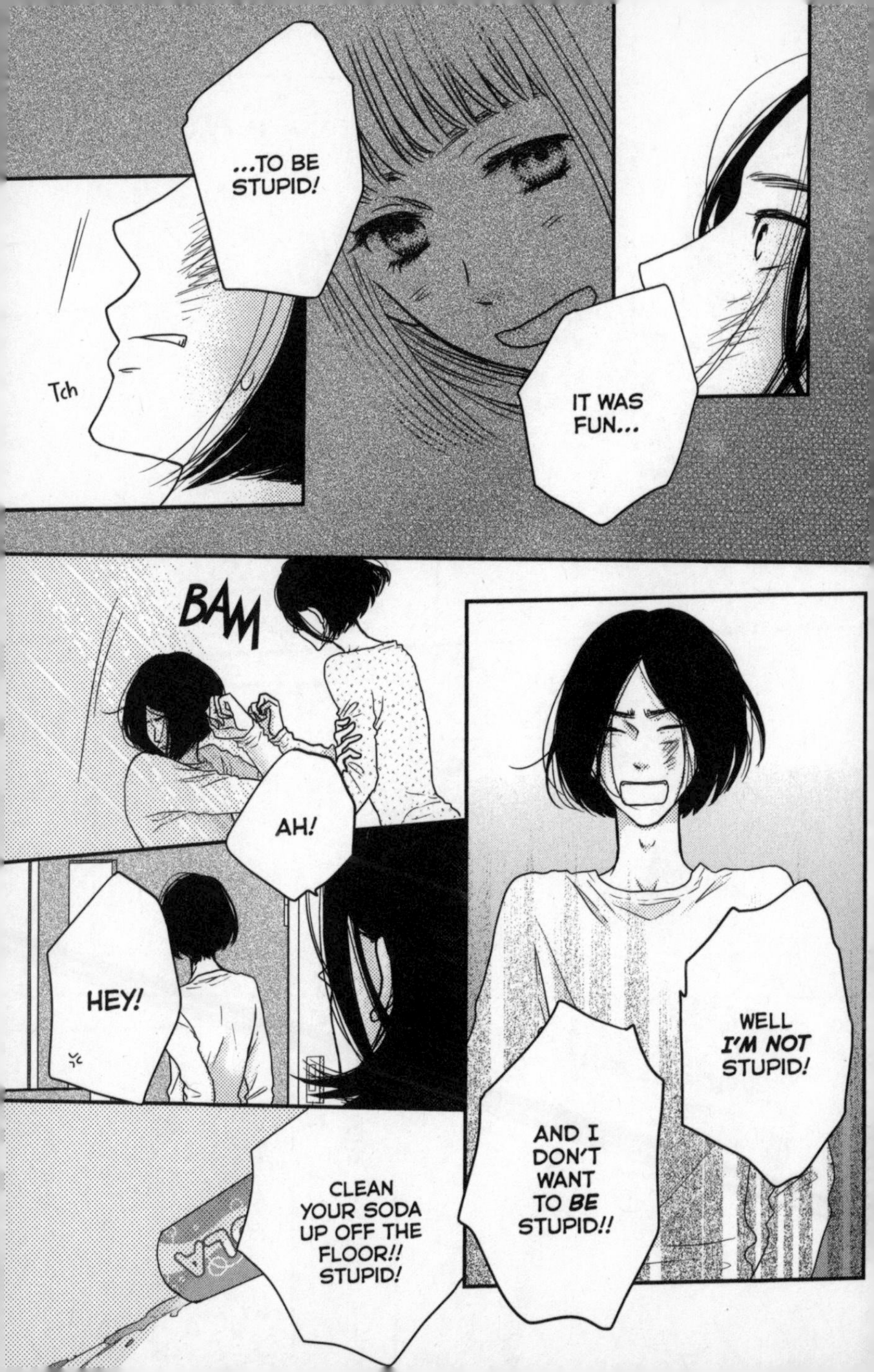
IT WAS FUN...
...TO BE STUPID!
Tch
WELL I'M NOT STUPID!
AND I DON'T WANT TO BE STUPID!!
BAM
AH!
HEY!
CLEAN YOUR SODA UP OFF THE FLOOR!! STUPID!

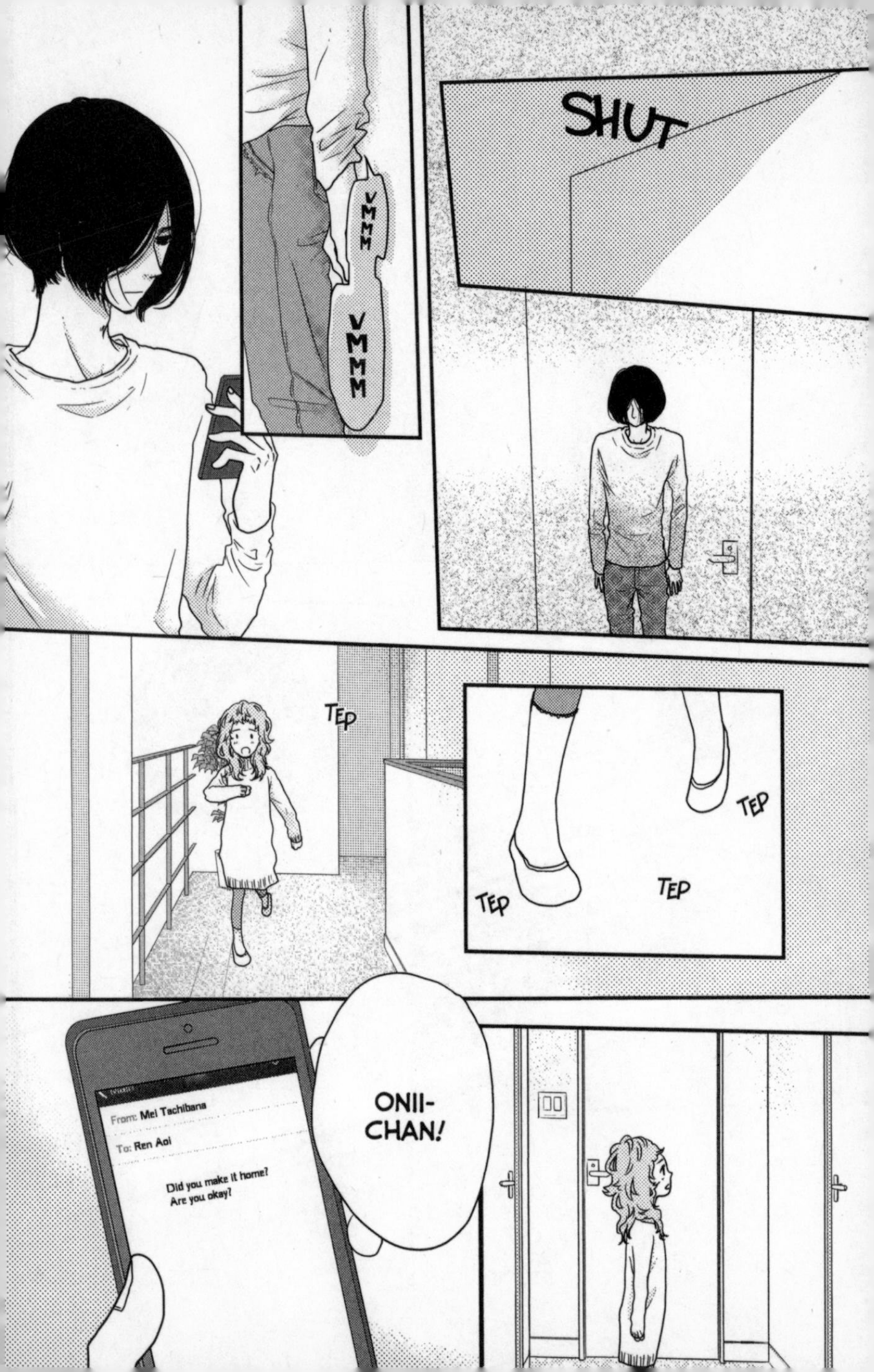
SHUT
VMMM
VMMM
TEP
TEP
TEP
TEP
ONII-CHAN!
From: Mei Tachibana
To: Ren Aoi
Did you make it home?
Are you okay?

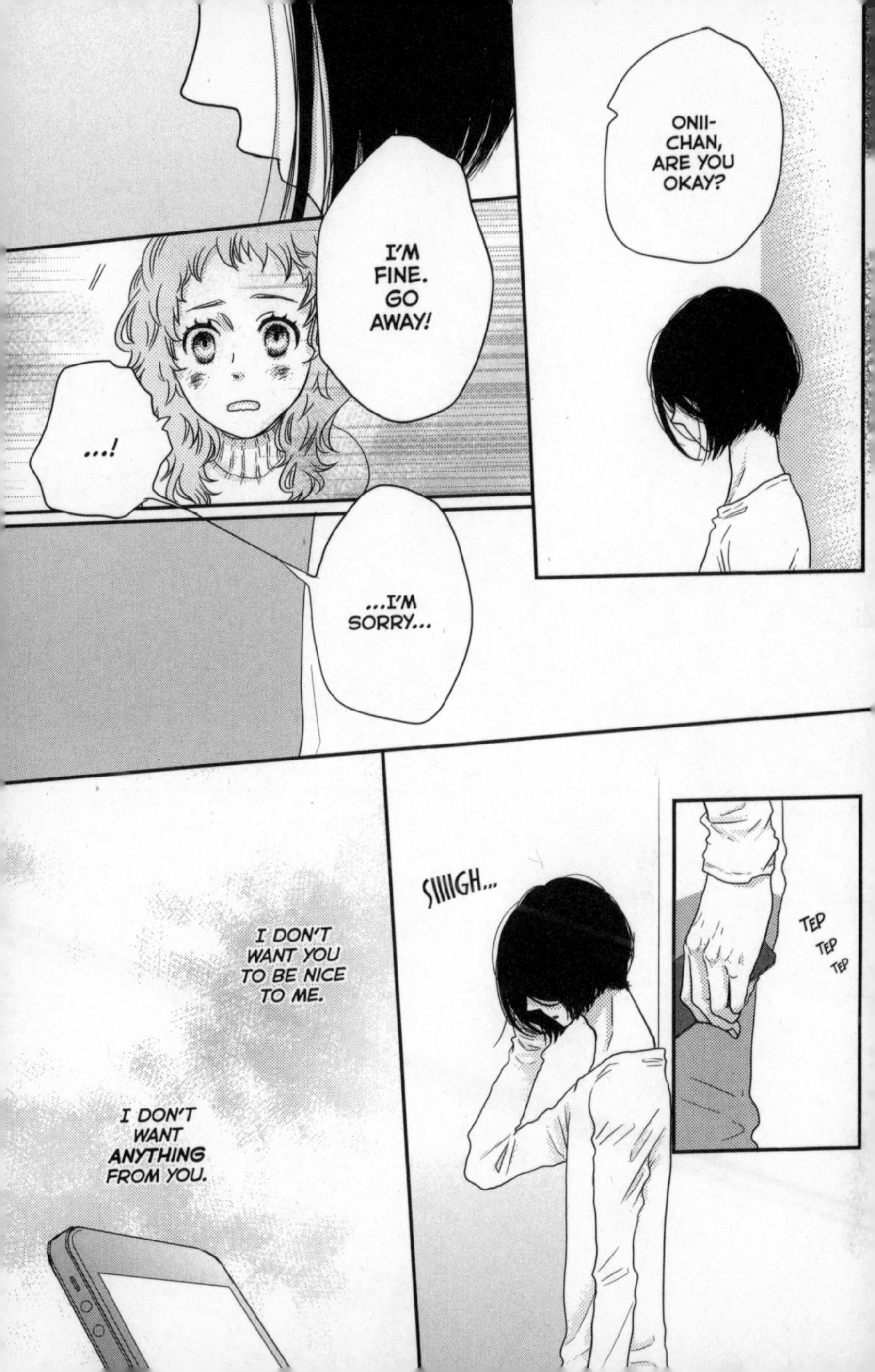
ONII-CHAN, ARE YOU OKAY?
I'M FINE. GO AWAY!
...!
...I'M SORRY...
TEP TEP TEP
SIIIIGH...
I DON'T WANT YOU TO BE NICE TO ME.
I DON'T WANT ANYTHING FROM YOU.

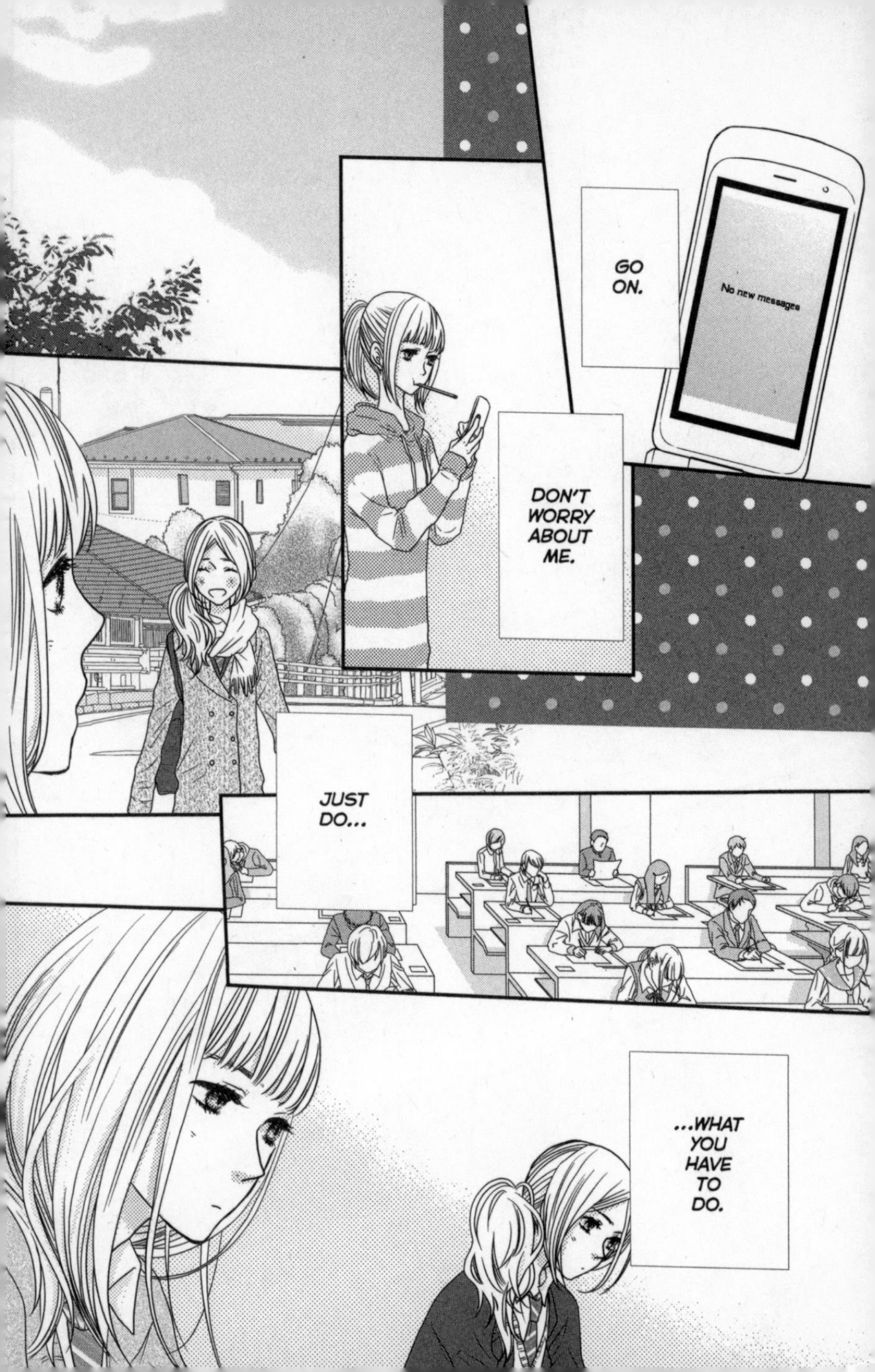
No new messages
GO ON.
DON'T WORRY ABOUT ME.
JUST DO...
...WHAT YOU HAVE TO DO.

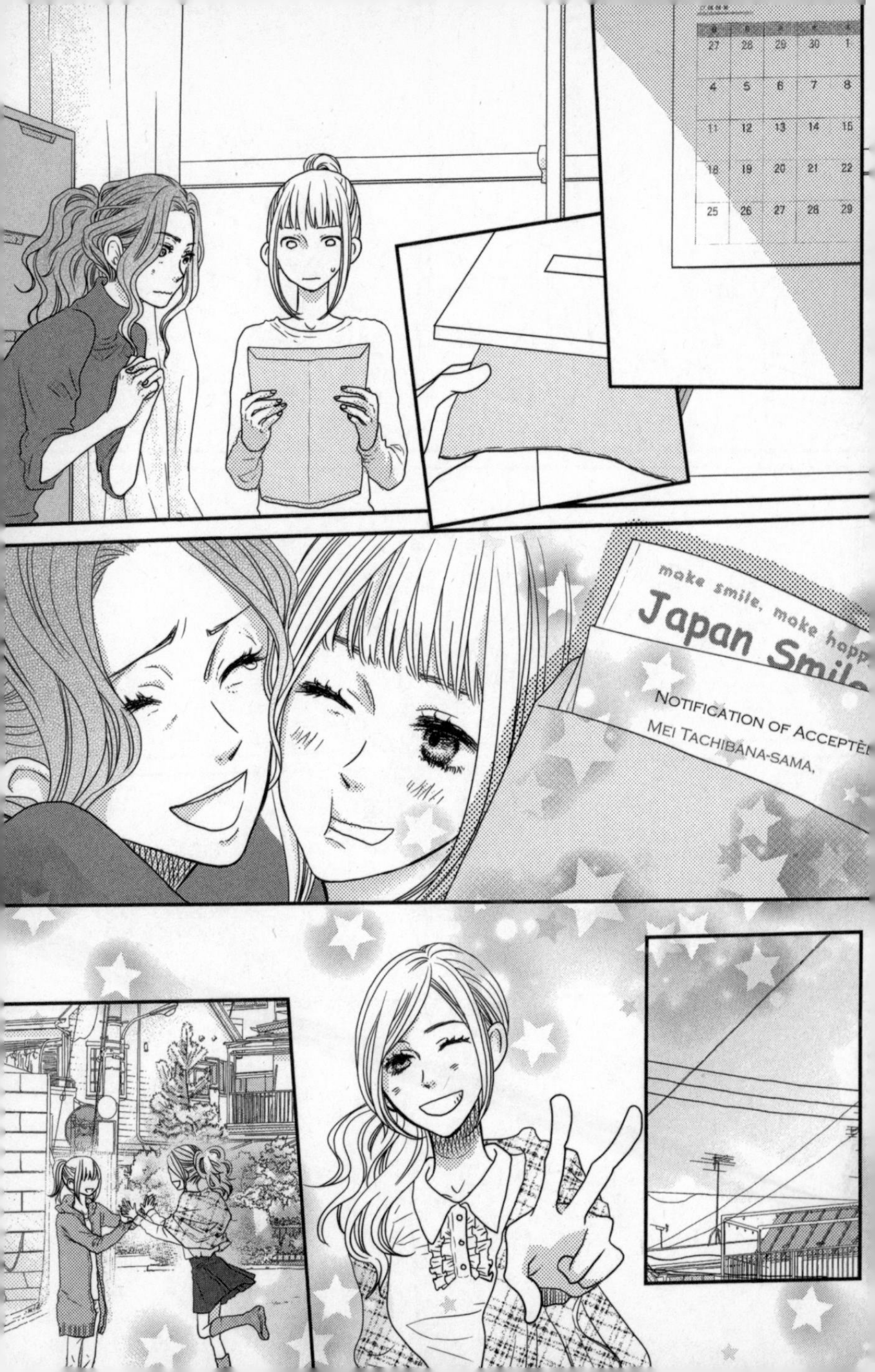
make smile, make happ
Japan Smil
NOTIFICATION OF ACCEPTE
MEI TACHIBANA-SAMA,

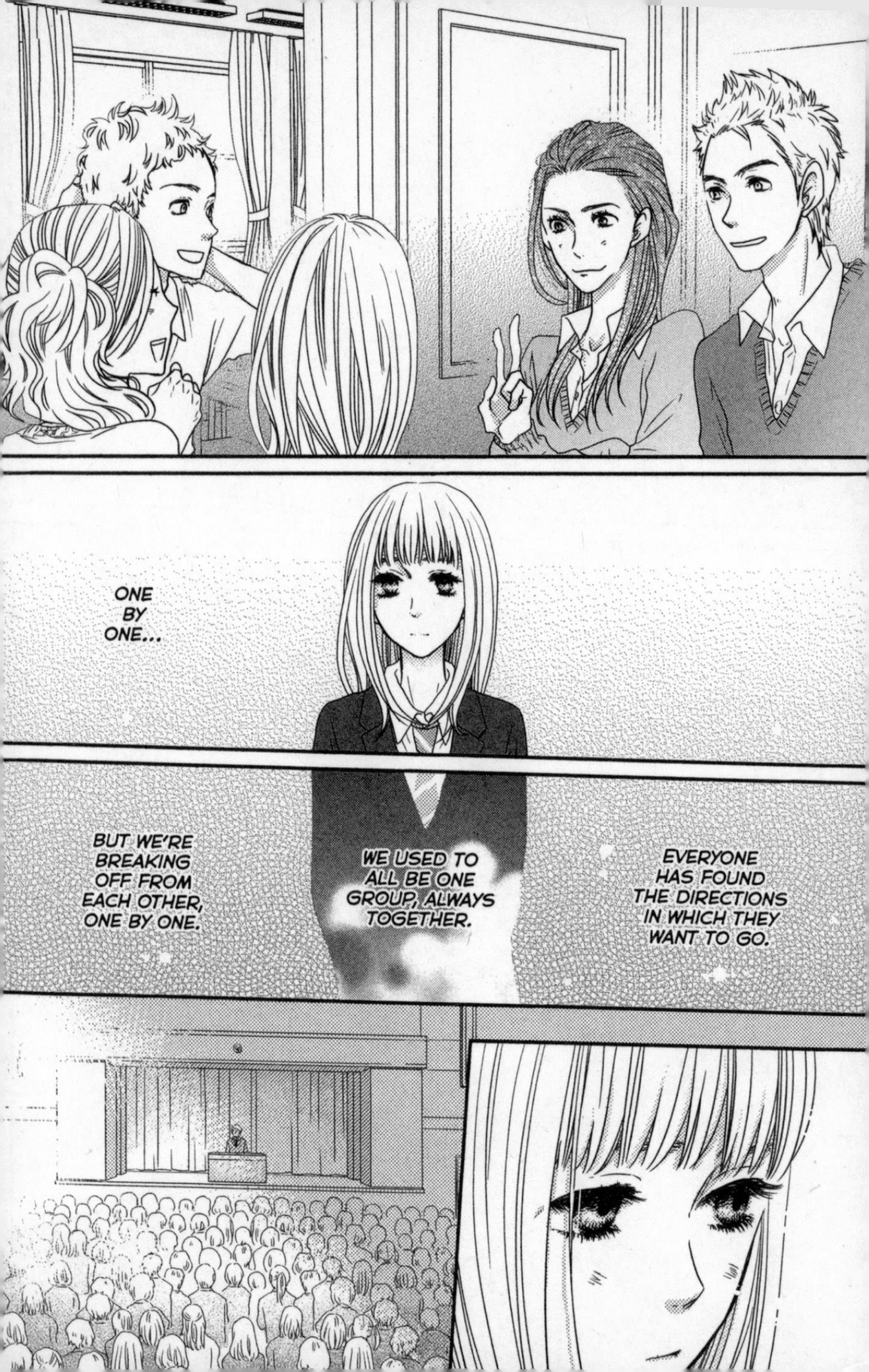
ONE BY ONE...
EVERYONE HAS FOUND THE DIRECTIONS IN WHICH THEY WANT TO GO.
WE USED TO ALL BE ONE GROUP, ALWAYS TOGETHER.
BUT WE'RE BREAKING OFF FROM EACH OTHER, ONE BY ONE.

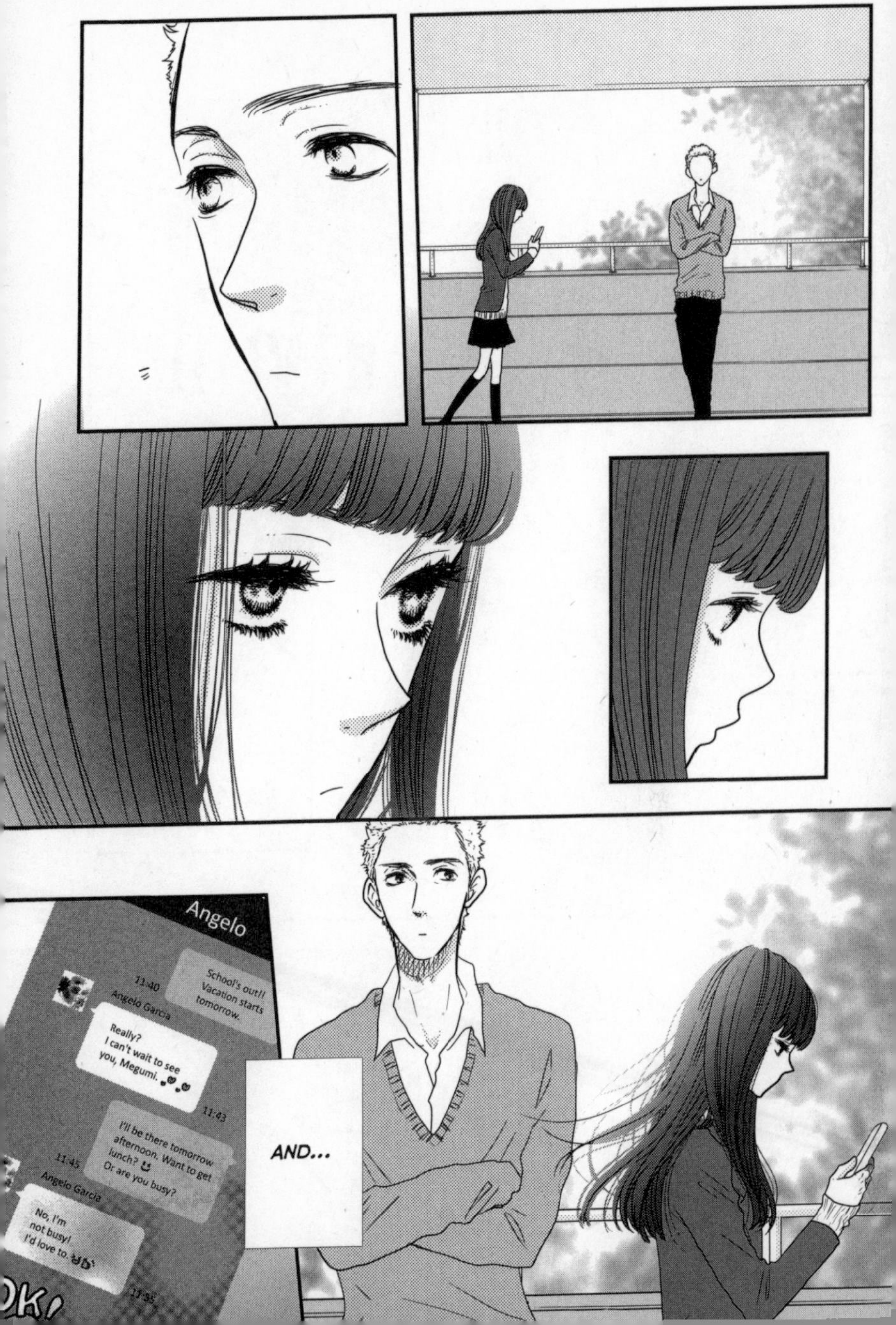
AND...
Angelo
School's out!! Vacation starts tomorrow.
11:40
Angelo Garcia
Really? I can't wait to see you, Megumi.
11:43
I'll be there tomorrow afternoon. Want to get lunch? Or are you busy?
11:45
Angelo Garcia
No, I'm not busy! I'd love to.

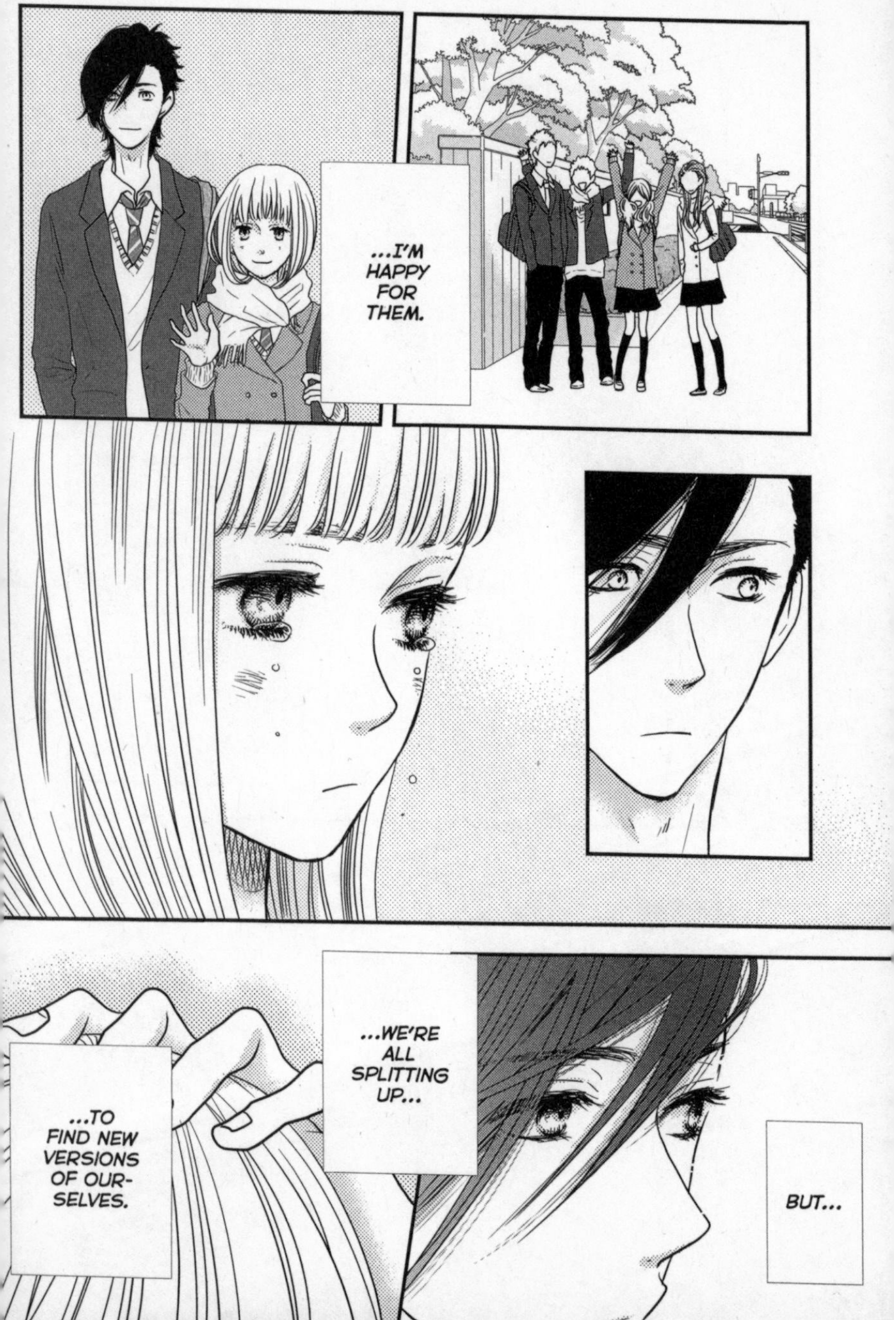
...I'M HAPPY FOR THEM.
BUT...
...WE'RE ALL SPLITTING UP...
...TO FIND NEW VERSIONS OF OUR-SELVES.

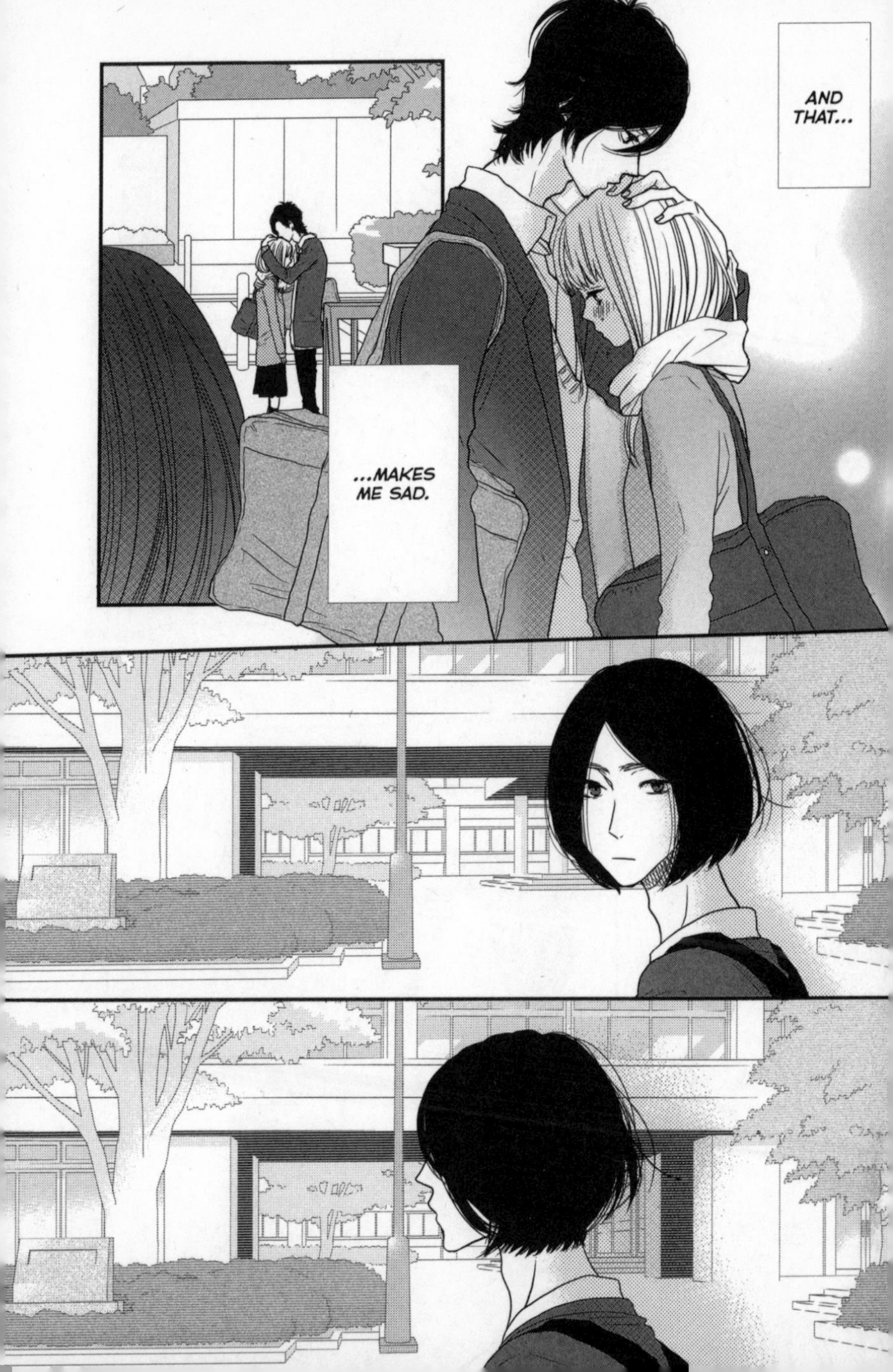
AND THAT...
...MAKES ME SAD.

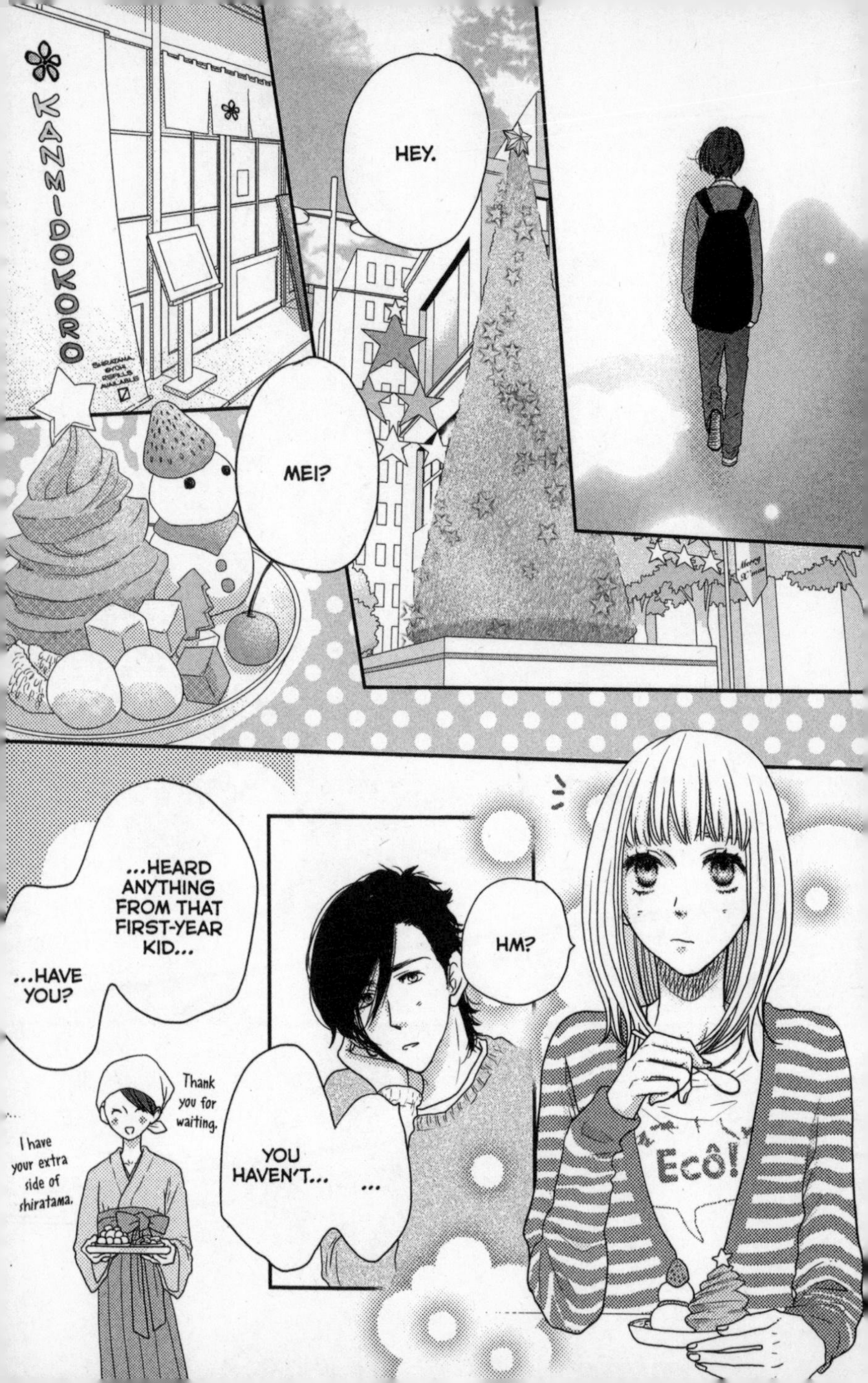
HEY.
MEI?
KANMIDOKORO
...HEARD ANYTHING FROM THAT FIRST-YEAR KID...
...HAVE YOU?
HM?
YOU HAVEN'T...
...
Thank you for waiting.
I have your extra side of shiratama.
Ecô!

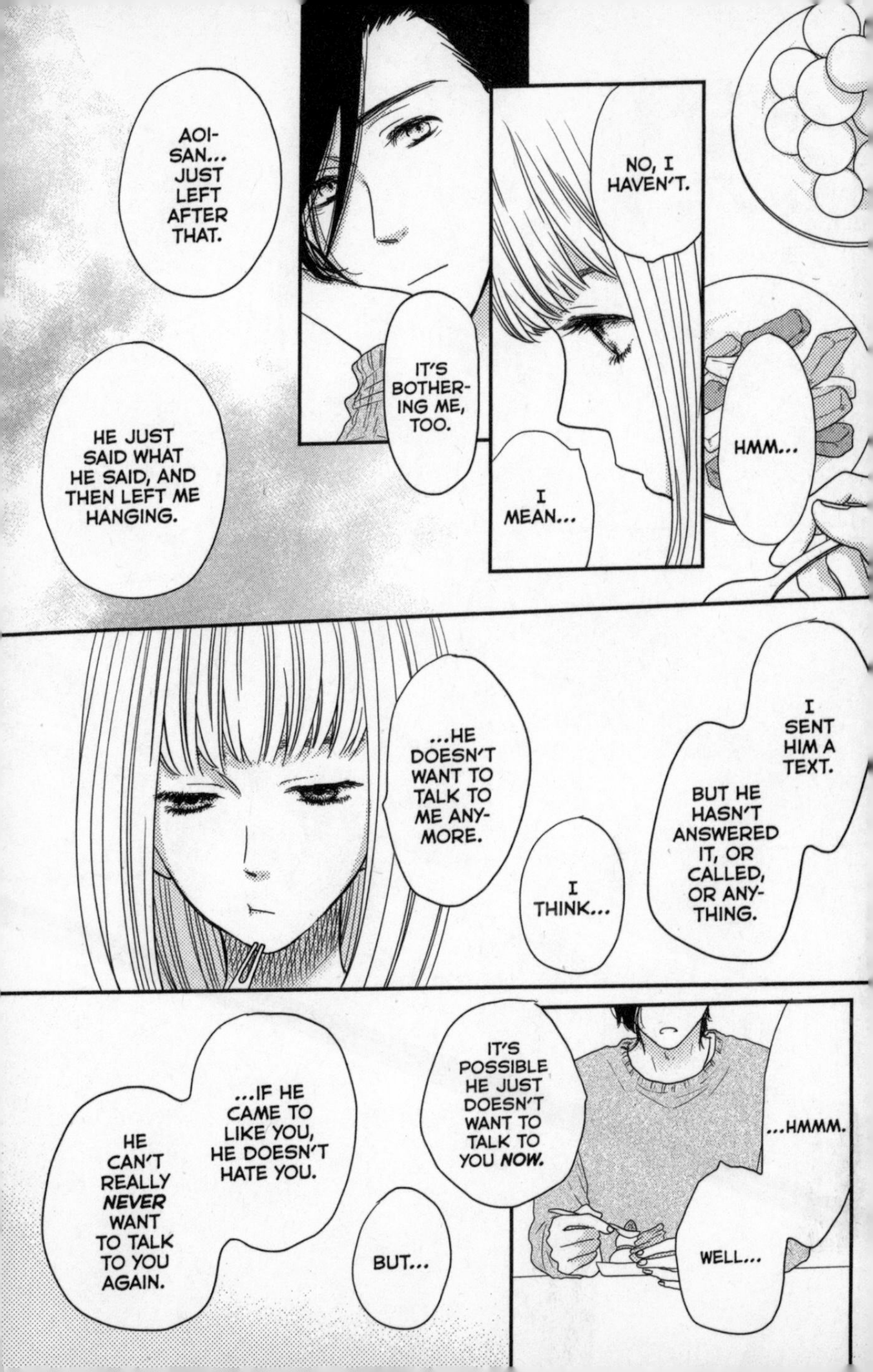
NO, I HAVEN'T.
HMM...
I MEAN...
IT'S BOTHERING ME, TOO.
AOI-SAN... JUST LEFT AFTER THAT.
HE JUST SAID WHAT HE SAID, AND THEN LEFT ME HANGING.
I SENT HIM A TEXT.
BUT HE HASN'T ANSWERED IT, OR CALLED, OR ANYTHING.
I THINK...
...HE DOESN'T WANT TO TALK TO ME ANYMORE.
...HMMM.
IT'S POSSIBLE HE JUST DOESN'T WANT TO TALK TO YOU *NOW.*
WELL...
BUT...
...IF HE CAME TO LIKE YOU, HE DOESN'T HATE YOU.
HE CAN'T REALLY *NEVER* WANT TO TALK TO YOU AGAIN.

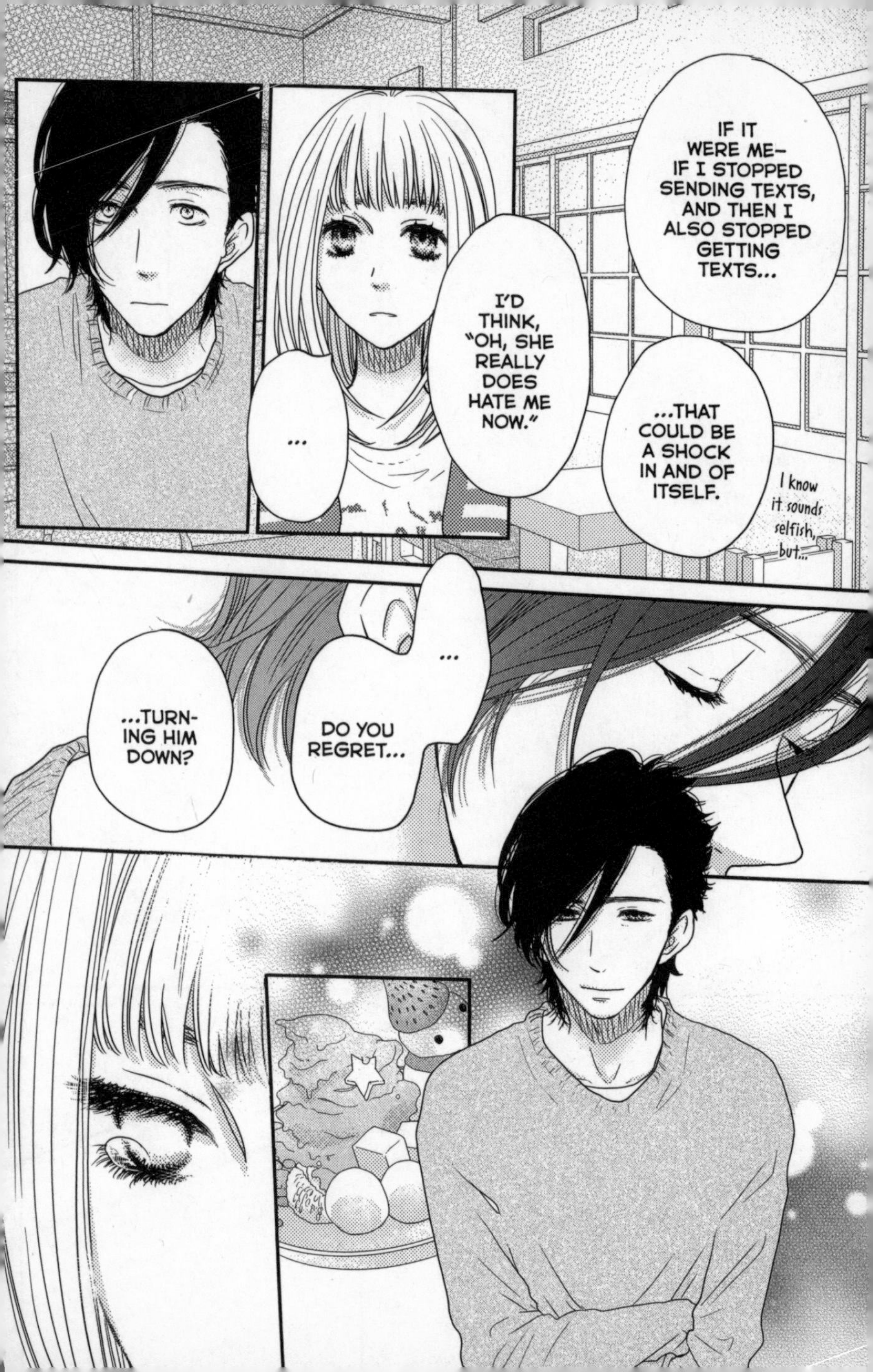
IF IT WERE ME— IF I STOPPED SENDING TEXTS, AND THEN I ALSO STOPPED GETTING TEXTS...
...THAT COULD BE A SHOCK IN AND OF ITSELF.
I know it sounds selfish, but...
I'D THINK, "OH, SHE REALLY DOES HATE ME NOW."
...
...
DO YOU REGRET...
...TURNING HIM DOWN?

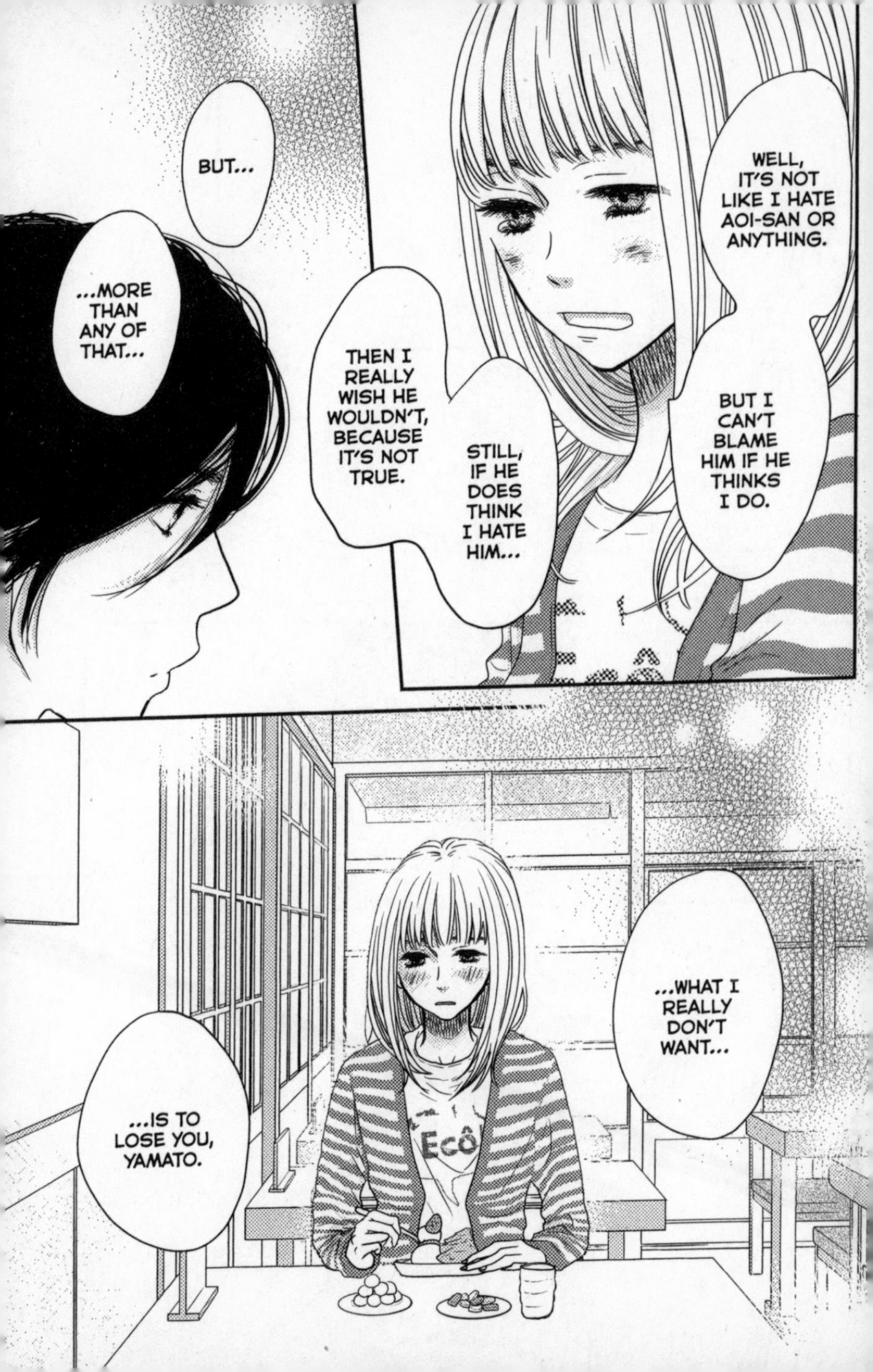
WELL, IT'S NOT LIKE I HATE AOI-SAN OR ANYTHING.
BUT I CAN'T BLAME HIM IF HE THINKS I DO.
STILL, IF HE DOES THINK I HATE HIM...
THEN I REALLY WISH HE WOULDN'T, BECAUSE IT'S NOT TRUE.
BUT...
...MORE THAN ANY OF THAT...
...WHAT I REALLY DON'T WANT...
...IS TO LOSE YOU, YAMATO.

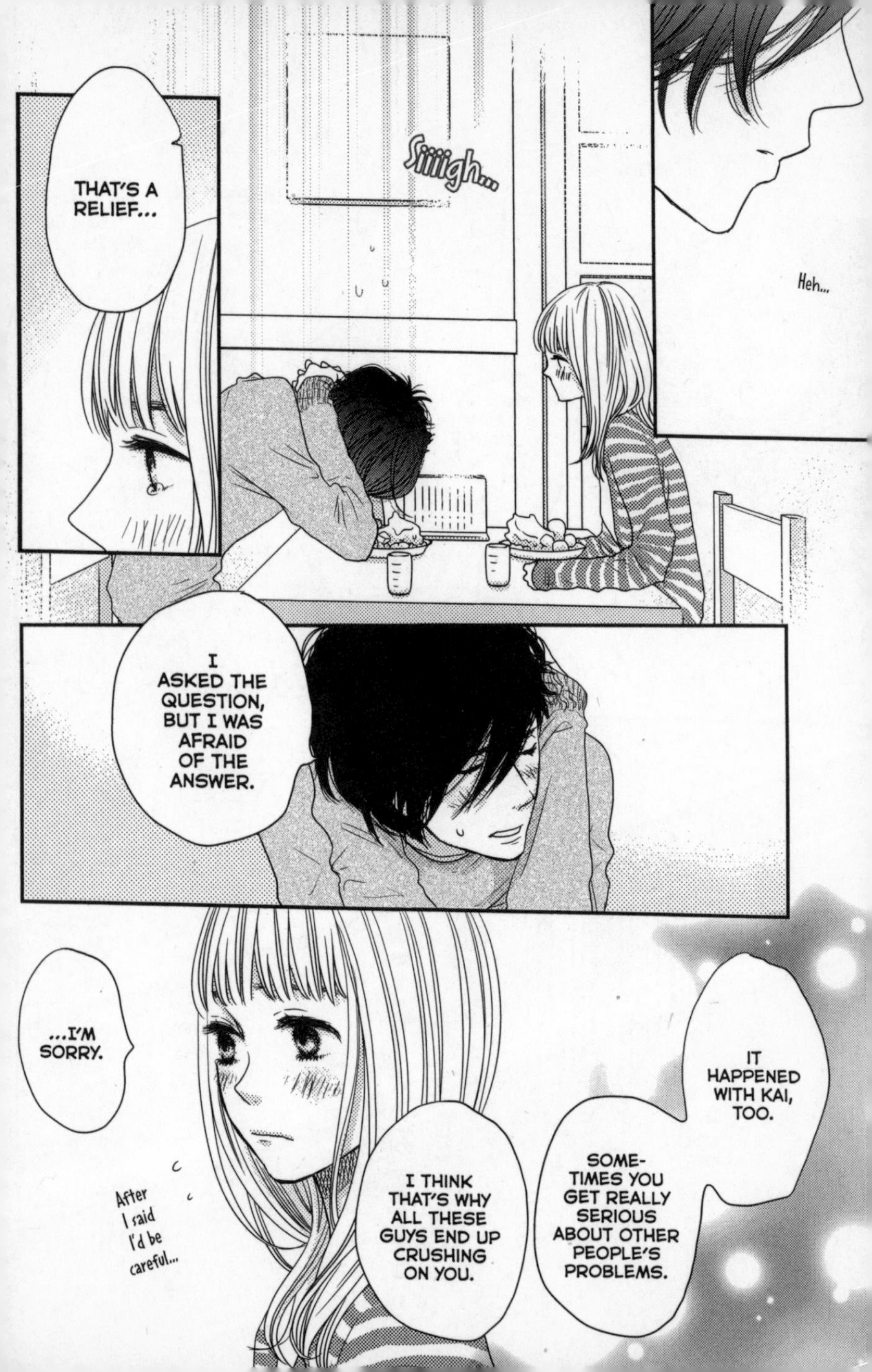
Heh...
Siiiigh...
THAT'S A RELIEF...
I ASKED THE QUESTION, BUT I WAS AFRAID OF THE ANSWER.
IT HAPPENED WITH KAI, TOO.
SOME-TIMES YOU GET REALLY SERIOUS ABOUT OTHER PEOPLE'S PROBLEMS.
I THINK THAT'S WHY ALL THESE GUYS END UP CRUSHING ON YOU.
...I'M SORRY.
After I said I'd be careful...

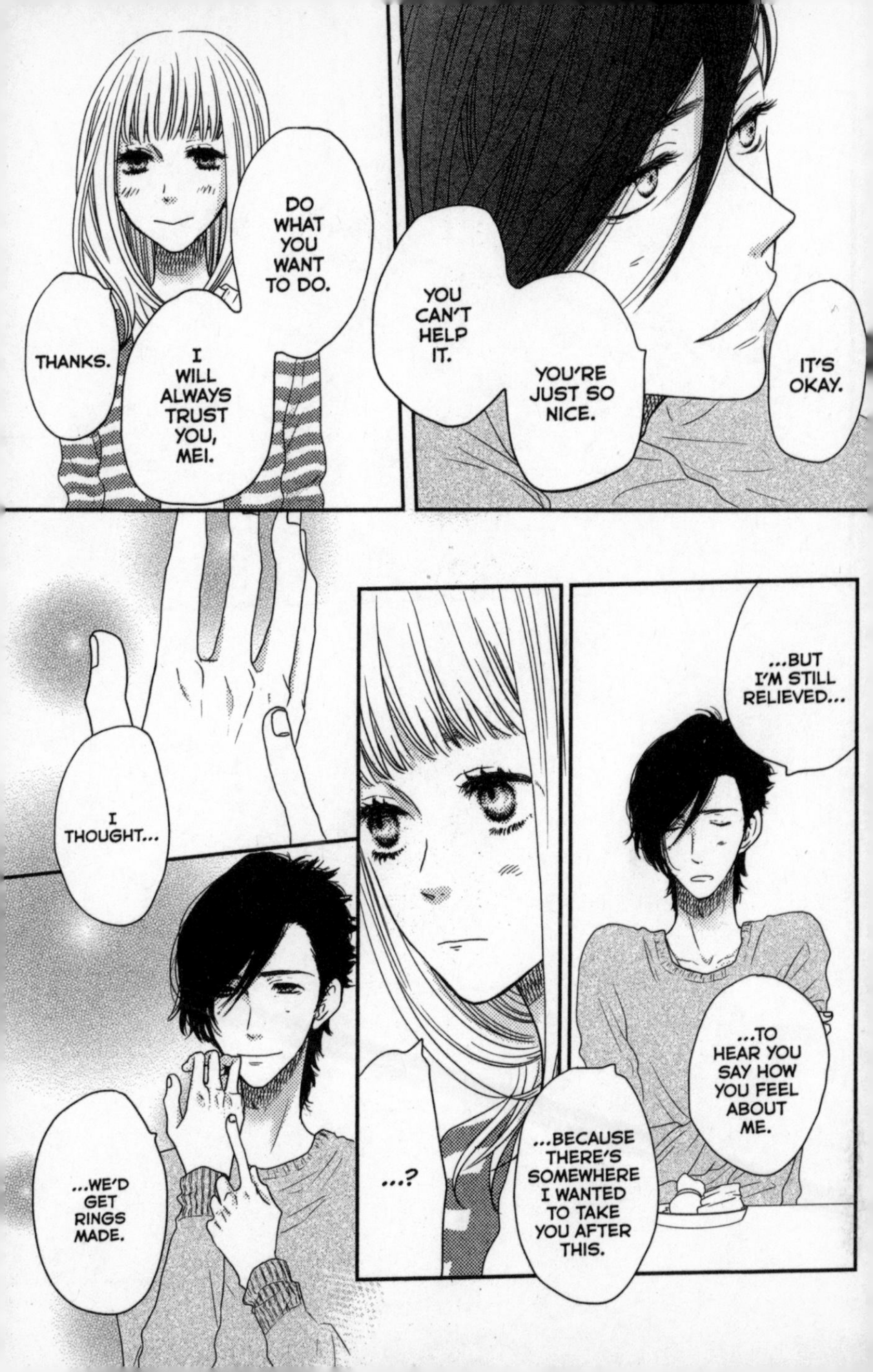
IT'S OKAY.
YOU'RE JUST SO NICE.
YOU CAN'T HELP IT.
DO WHAT YOU WANT TO DO.
I WILL ALWAYS TRUST YOU, MEI.
THANKS.
...BUT I'M STILL RELIEVED...
...TO HEAR YOU SAY HOW YOU FEEL ABOUT ME.
...BECAUSE THERE'S SOMEWHERE I WANTED TO TAKE YOU AFTER THIS.
...?
I THOUGHT...
...WE'D GET RINGS MADE.

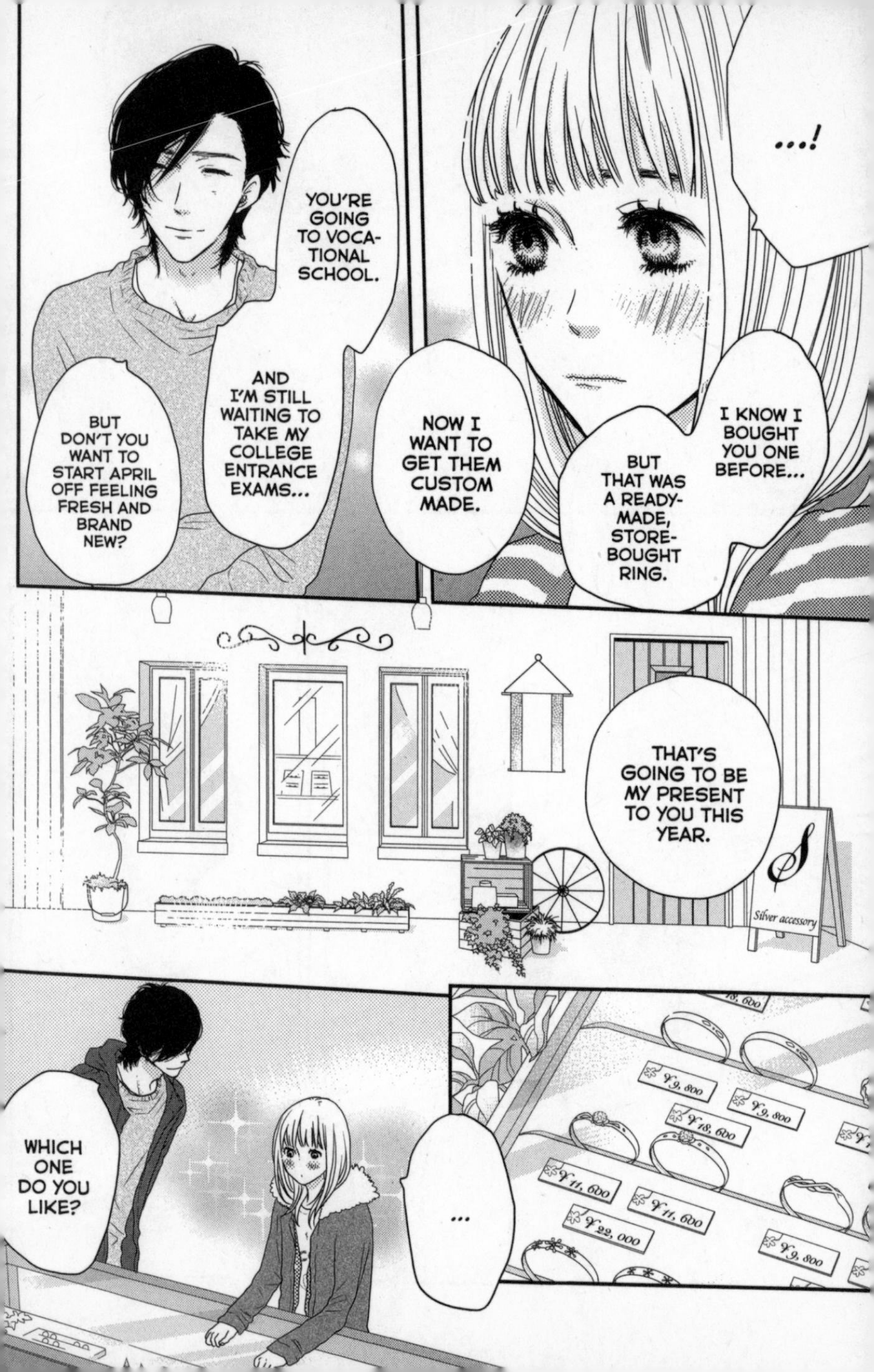
...!
I KNOW I BOUGHT YOU ONE BEFORE...
BUT THAT WAS A READY-MADE, STORE-BOUGHT RING.
NOW I WANT TO GET THEM CUSTOM MADE.
YOU'RE GOING TO VOCATIONAL SCHOOL.
AND I'M STILL WAITING TO TAKE MY COLLEGE ENTRANCE EXAMS...
BUT DON'T YOU WANT TO START APRIL OFF FEELING FRESH AND BRAND NEW?
THAT'S GOING TO BE MY PRESENT TO YOU THIS YEAR.
Silver accessory
...
WHICH ONE DO YOU LIKE?

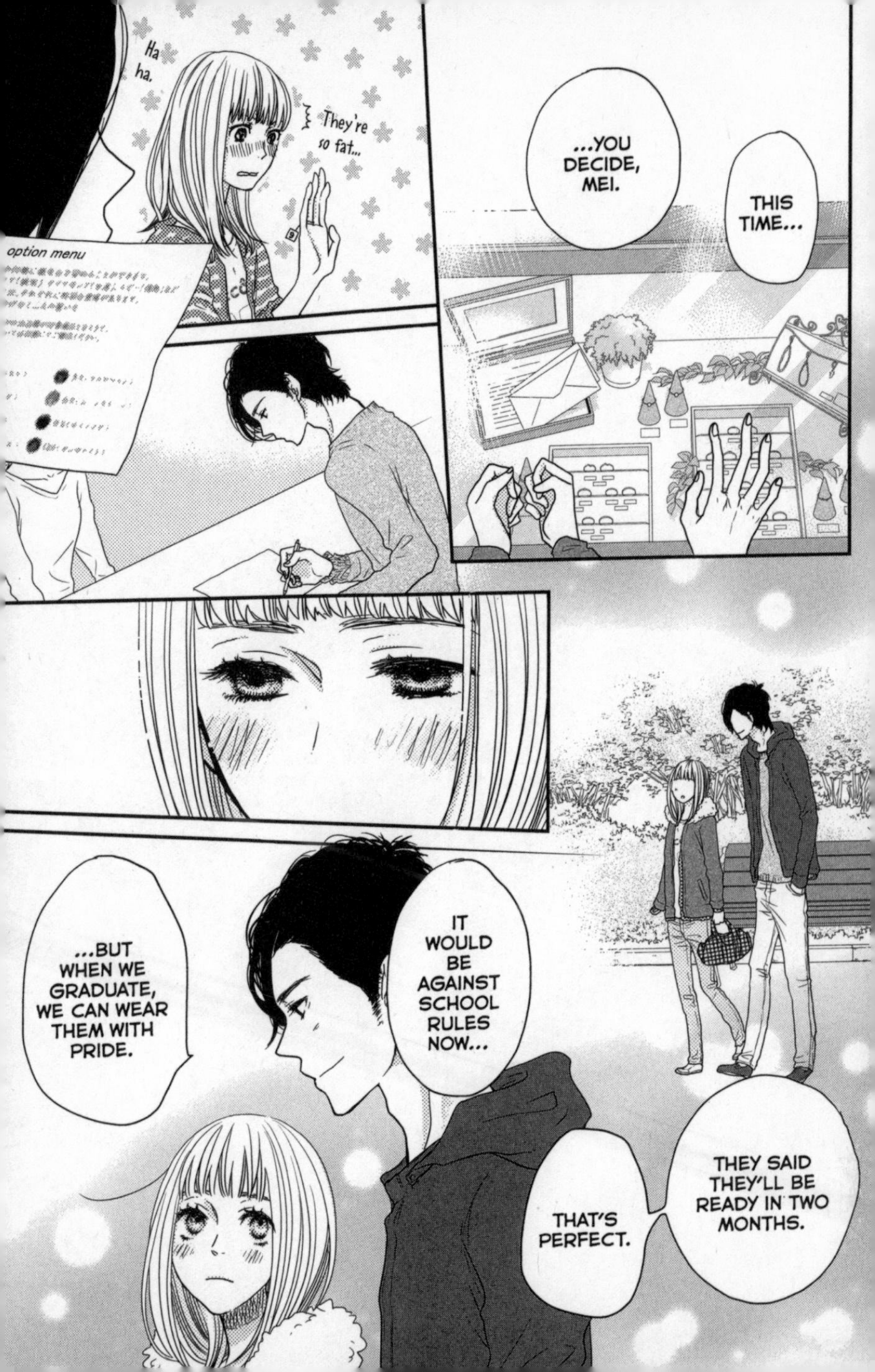
THIS TIME...
...YOU DECIDE, MEI.
They're so fat...
Ha ha.
option menu
THEY SAID THEY'LL BE READY IN TWO MONTHS.
THAT'S PERFECT.
IT WOULD BE AGAINST SCHOOL RULES NOW...
...BUT WHEN WE GRADUATE, WE CAN WEAR THEM WITH PRIDE.

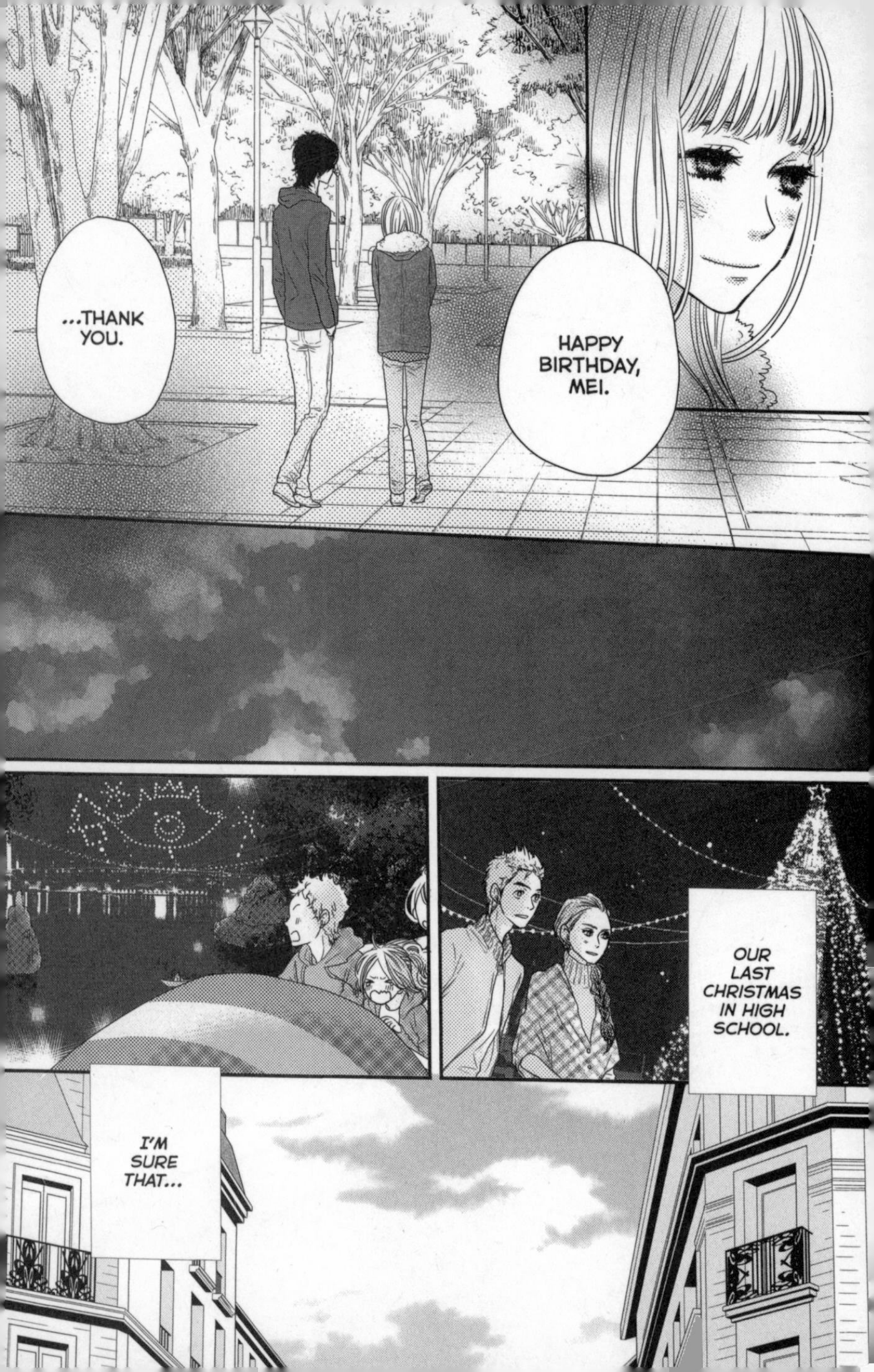
HAPPY BIRTHDAY, MEI.
...THANK YOU.
OUR LAST CHRISTMAS IN HIGH SCHOOL.
I'M SURE THAT...

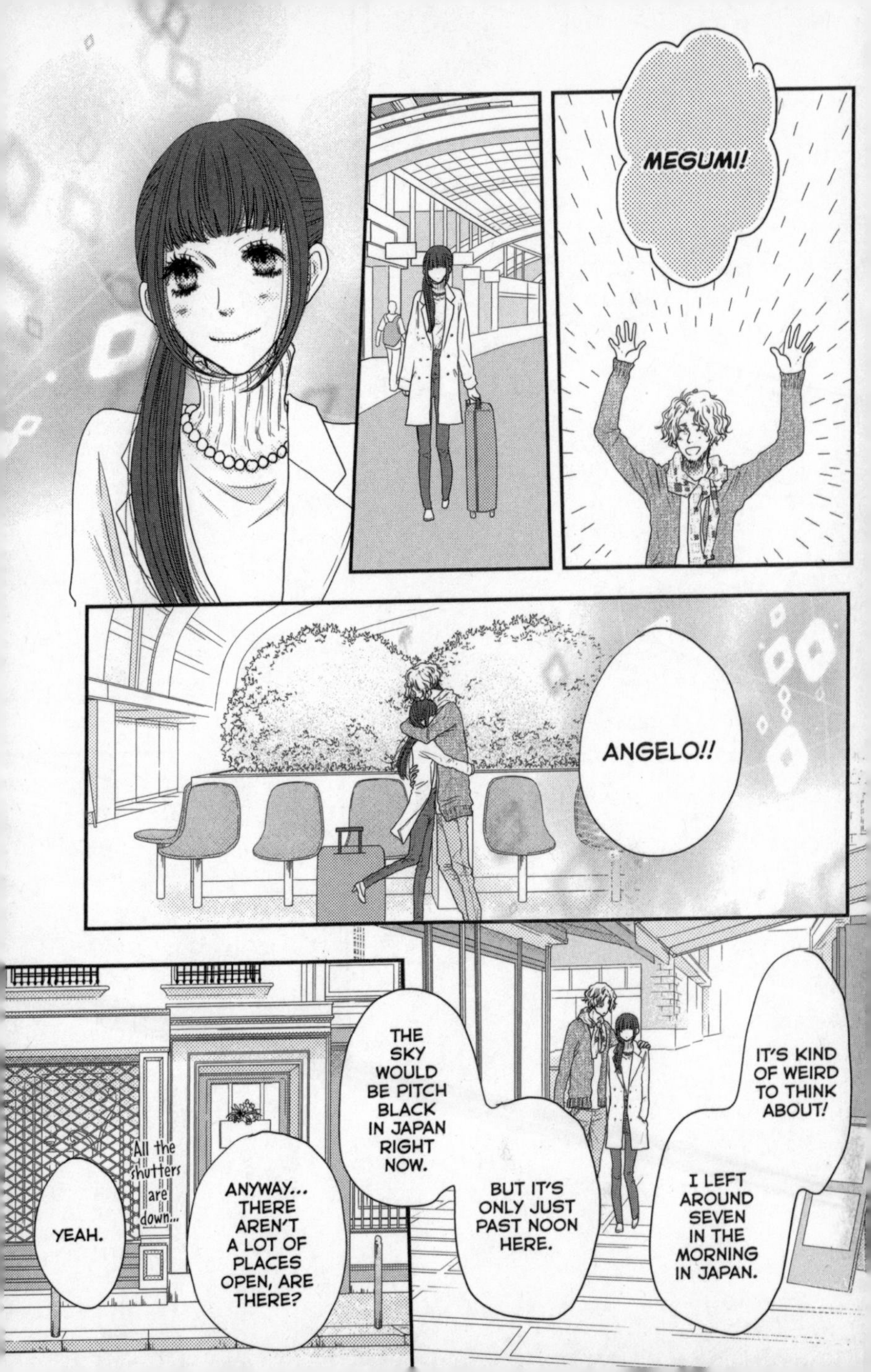
MEGUMI!
ANGELO!!
IT'S KIND OF WEIRD TO THINK ABOUT!
I LEFT AROUND SEVEN IN THE MORNING IN JAPAN.
THE SKY WOULD BE PITCH BLACK IN JAPAN RIGHT NOW.
BUT IT'S ONLY JUST PAST NOON HERE.
ANYWAY... THERE AREN'T A LOT OF PLACES OPEN, ARE THERE?
All the shutters are down...
YEAH.

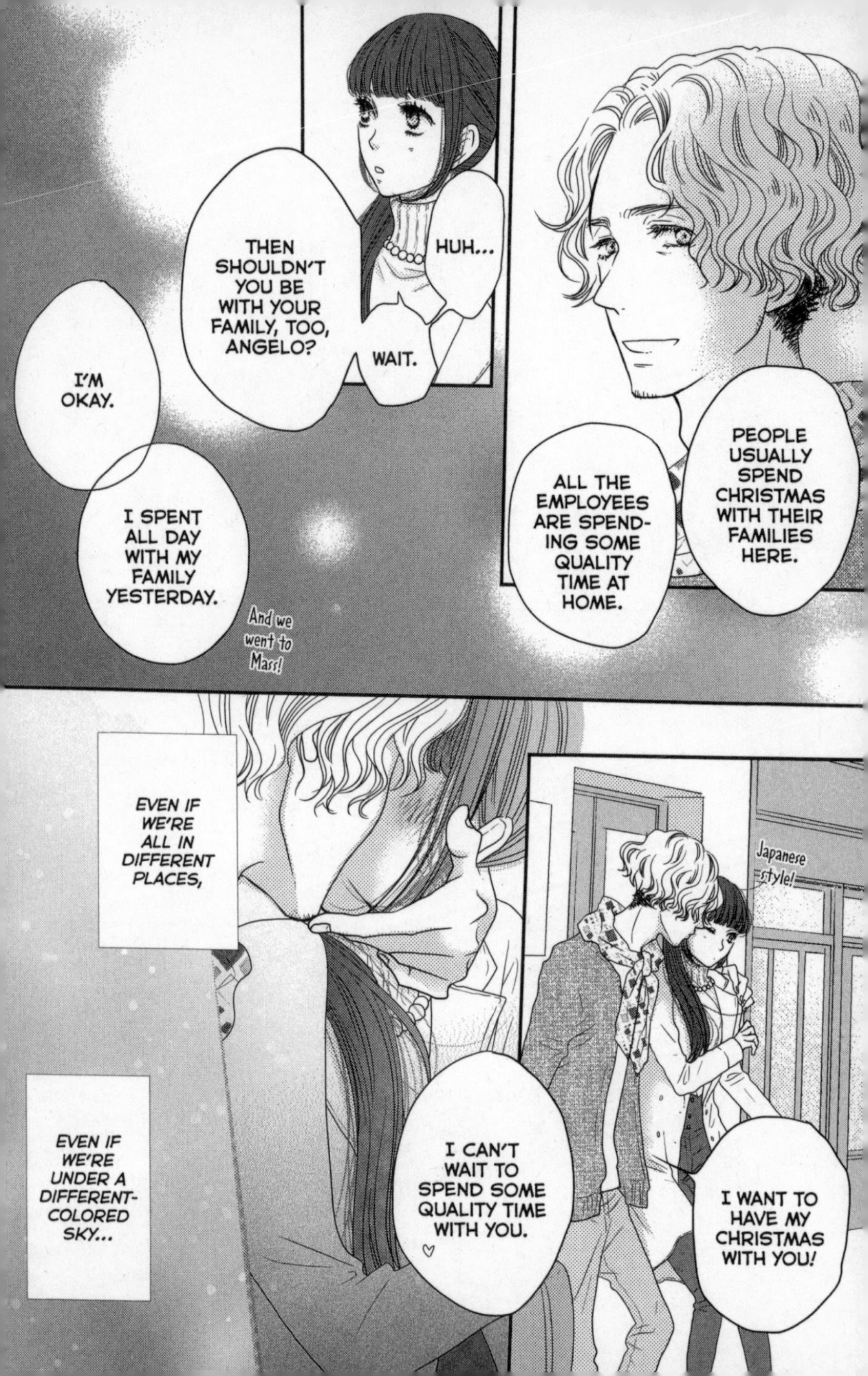
PEOPLE USUALLY SPEND CHRISTMAS WITH THEIR FAMILIES HERE.
ALL THE EMPLOYEES ARE SPENDING SOME QUALITY TIME AT HOME.
HUH...
WAIT.
THEN SHOULDN'T YOU BE WITH YOUR FAMILY, TOO, ANGELO?
I'M OKAY.
I SPENT ALL DAY WITH MY FAMILY YESTERDAY.
And we went to Mass!
I WANT TO HAVE MY CHRISTMAS WITH YOU!
Japanese style!
I CAN'T WAIT TO SPEND SOME QUALITY TIME WITH YOU. ♡
EVEN IF WE'RE ALL IN DIFFERENT PLACES,
EVEN IF WE'RE UNDER A DIFFERENT-COLORED SKY...

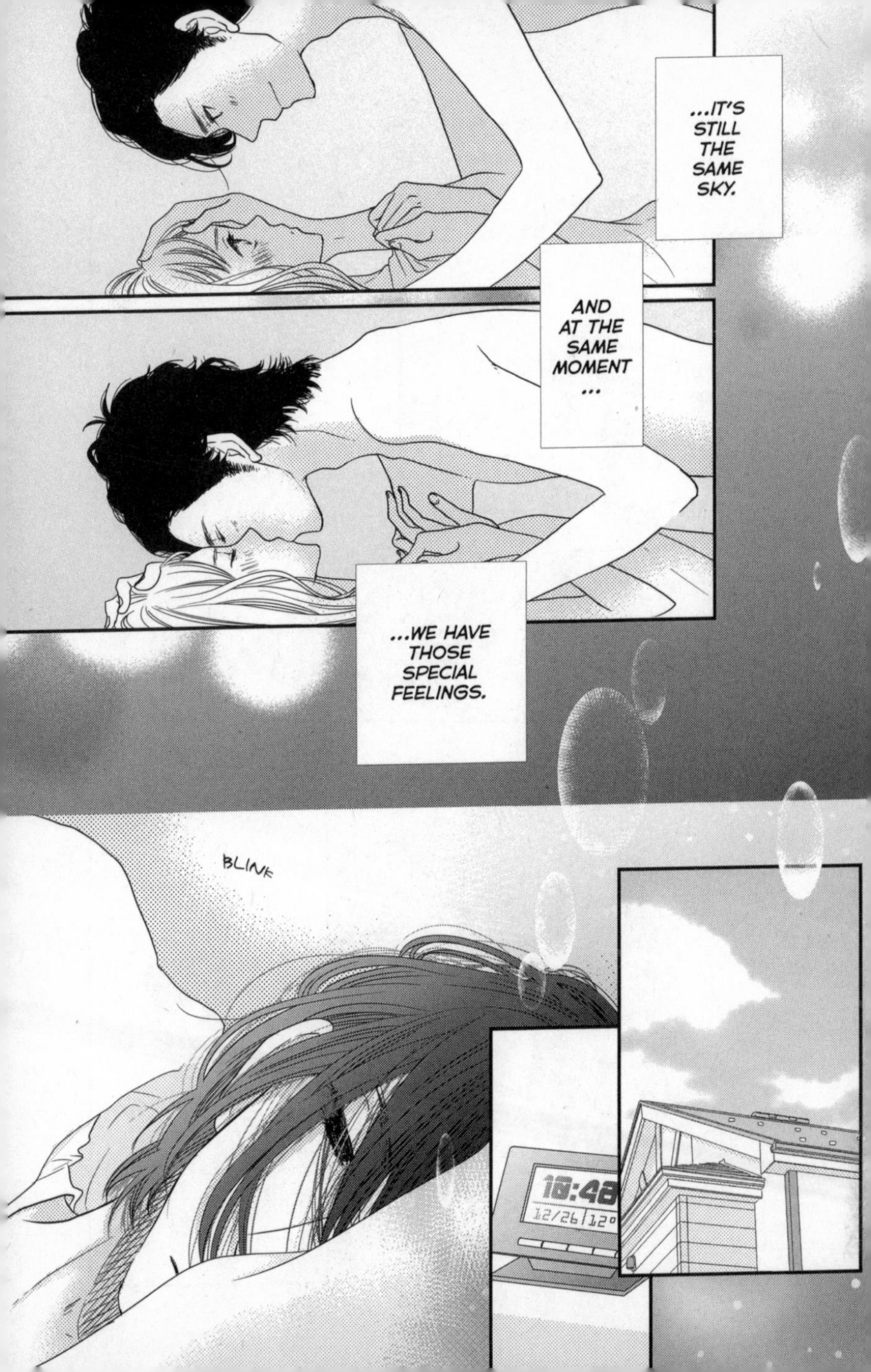
...IT'S STILL THE SAME SKY.
AND AT THE SAME MOMENT ...
...WE HAVE THOSE SPECIAL FEELINGS.
BLINK
10:48
12/26 12°

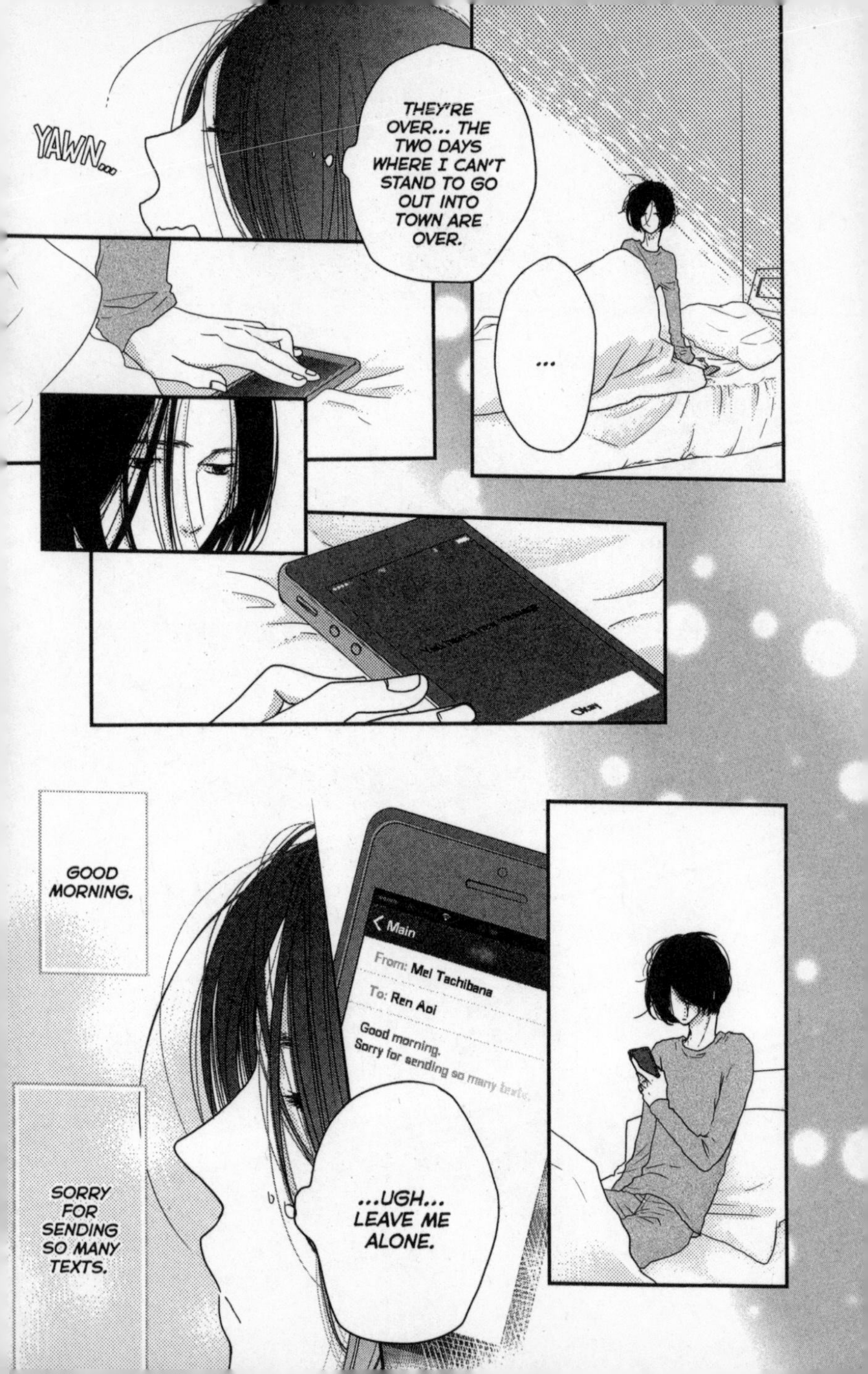
...
YAWN...
THEY'RE OVER... THE TWO DAYS WHERE I CAN'T STAND TO GO OUT INTO TOWN ARE OVER.
Okay
Main
From: Mei Tachibana
To: Ren Aoi
Good morning.
Sorry for sending so many texts.
GOOD MORNING.
SORRY FOR SENDING SO MANY TEXTS.
...UGH... LEAVE ME ALONE.

...WITH THE THINGS YOU'VE SAID SINCE WE BECAME FRIENDS.

YOU'VE GIVEN ME A LOT OF COURAGE...

...YOUR FEELINGS FOR ME.

AND I APPRECI-ATE...

THANK YOU FOR THE PRESENT.

I FEEL LIKE THE VAGUE IDEA OF WHAT I WANTED TO DO IS FINALLY TAKING SHAPE.

I HAVE A HARD TIME INTER-ACTING WITH PEOPLE, AND I WAS REALLY WORRIED THAT I'D CHOSEN THE WRONG CAREER.

...AND I LEARNED WHAT FUN AND JOY THERE IS IN WORKING WITH CHILDREN AND BEING SOMEONE THEY RELY ON.

BUT YOU TOOK ME TO VOLUNTEER WITH YOU...

AND I REALLY COULDN'T HAVE DONE IT WITHOUT YOU, AOI-SAN!

THE COURAGE THAT YOU GAVE ME HELPED ME TAKE THE ENTRANCE EXAM FOR A VOCATIONAL SCHOOL.

WHEW...

AND I ACTUALLY GOT ACCEPTED.

SHE PASSED?

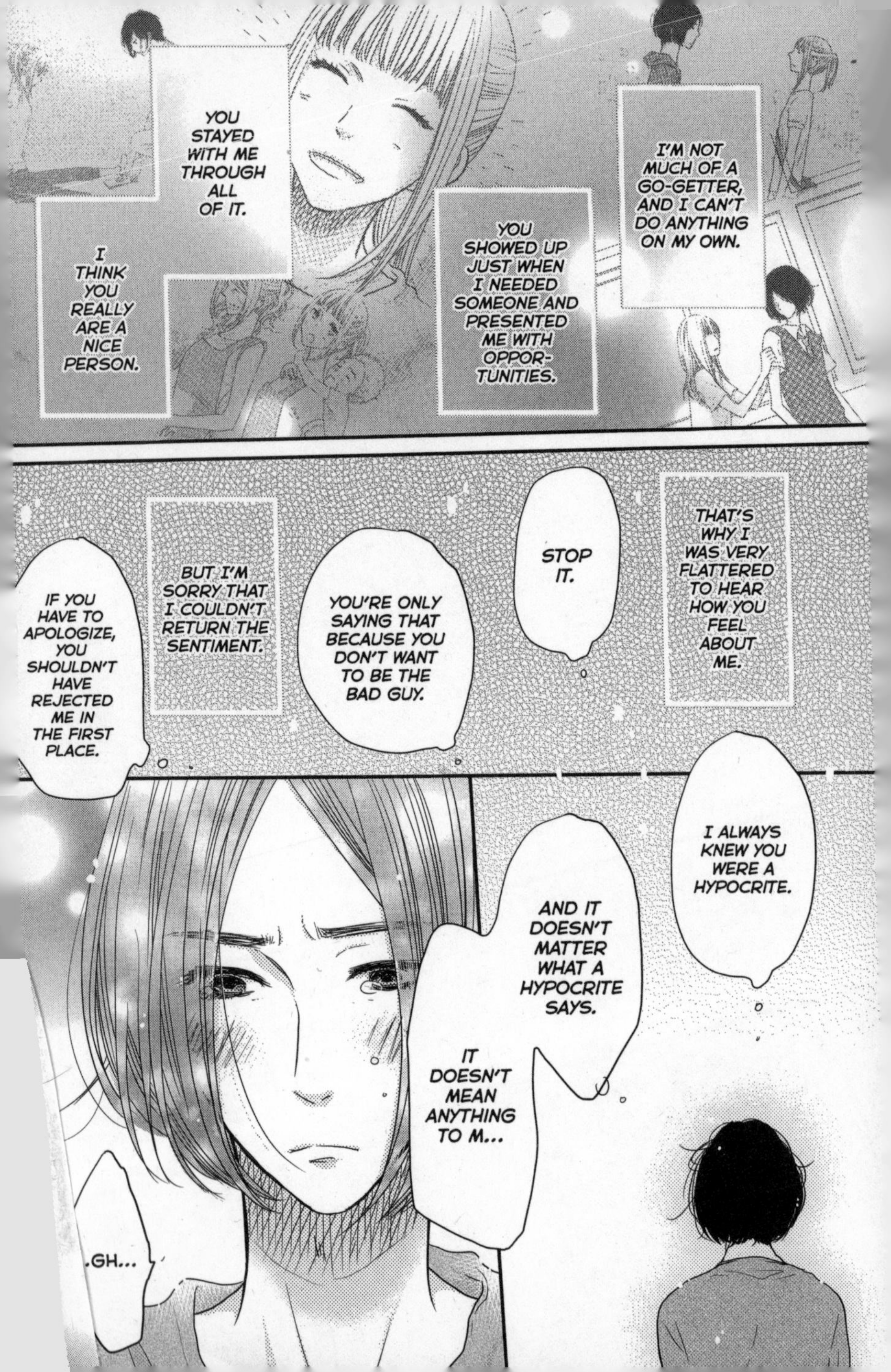
I'M NOT MUCH OF A GO-GETTER, AND I CAN'T DO ANYTHING ON MY OWN.
YOU SHOWED UP JUST WHEN I NEEDED SOMEONE AND PRESENTED ME WITH OPPOR-TUNITIES.
YOU STAYED WITH ME THROUGH ALL OF IT.
I THINK YOU REALLY ARE A NICE PERSON.
THAT'S WHY I WAS VERY FLATTERED TO HEAR HOW YOU FEEL ABOUT ME.
STOP IT.
YOU'RE ONLY SAYING THAT BECAUSE YOU DON'T WANT TO BE THE BAD GUY.
BUT I'M SORRY THAT I COULDN'T RETURN THE SENTIMENT.
IF YOU HAVE TO APOLOGIZE, YOU SHOULDN'T HAVE REJECTED ME IN THE FIRST PLACE.
I ALWAYS KNEW YOU WERE A HYPOCRITE.
AND IT DOESN'T MATTER WHAT A HYPOCRITE SAYS.
IT DOESN'T MEAN ANYTHING TO M...
.GH...

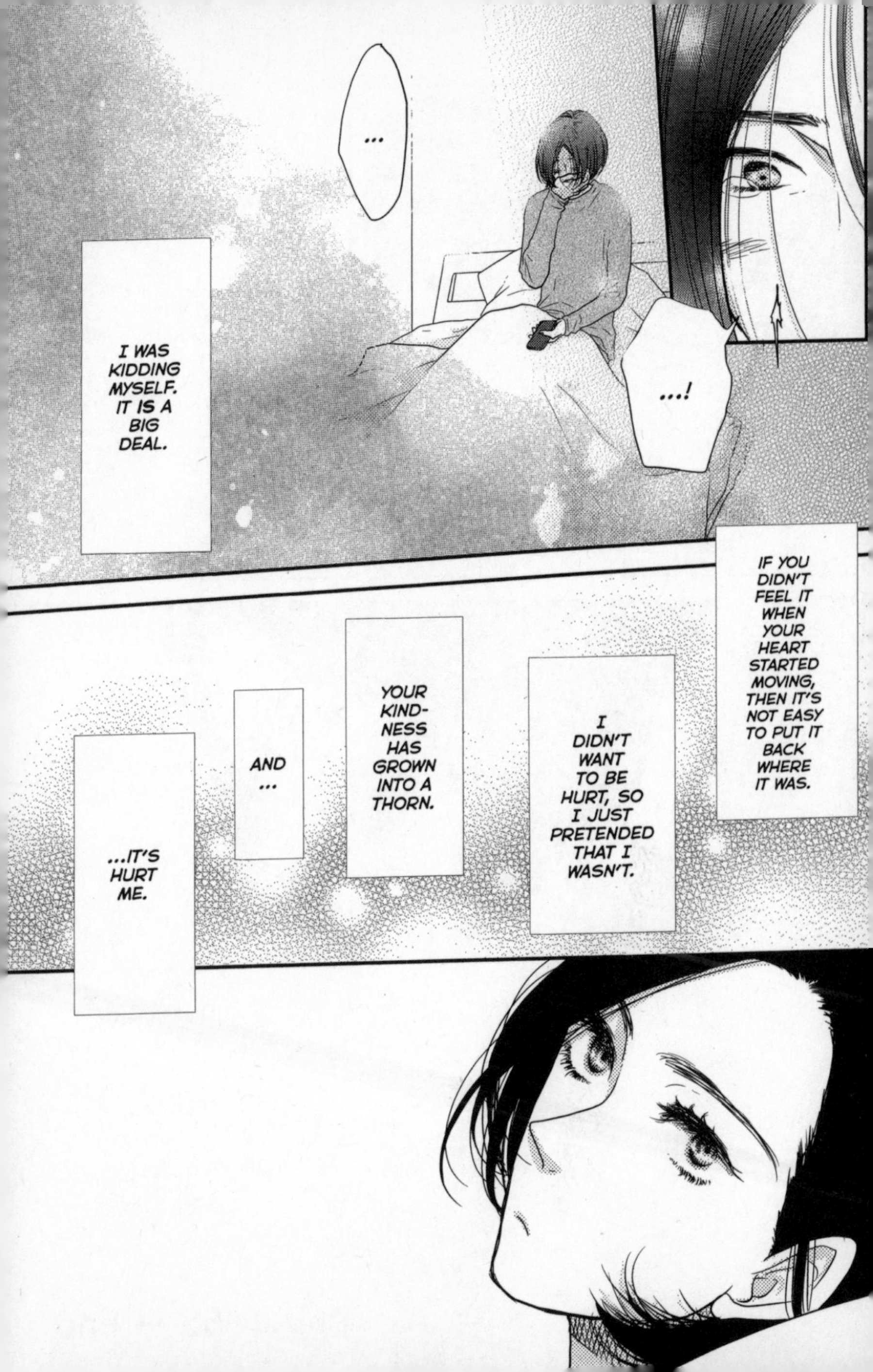
...!
...
I WAS KIDDING MYSELF. IT IS A BIG DEAL.
IF YOU DIDN'T FEEL IT WHEN YOUR HEART STARTED MOVING, THEN IT'S NOT EASY TO PUT IT BACK WHERE IT WAS.
I DIDN'T WANT TO BE HURT, SO I JUST PRETENDED THAT I WASN'T.
YOUR KIND-NESS HAS GROWN INTO A THORN.
AND ...
...IT'S HURT ME.

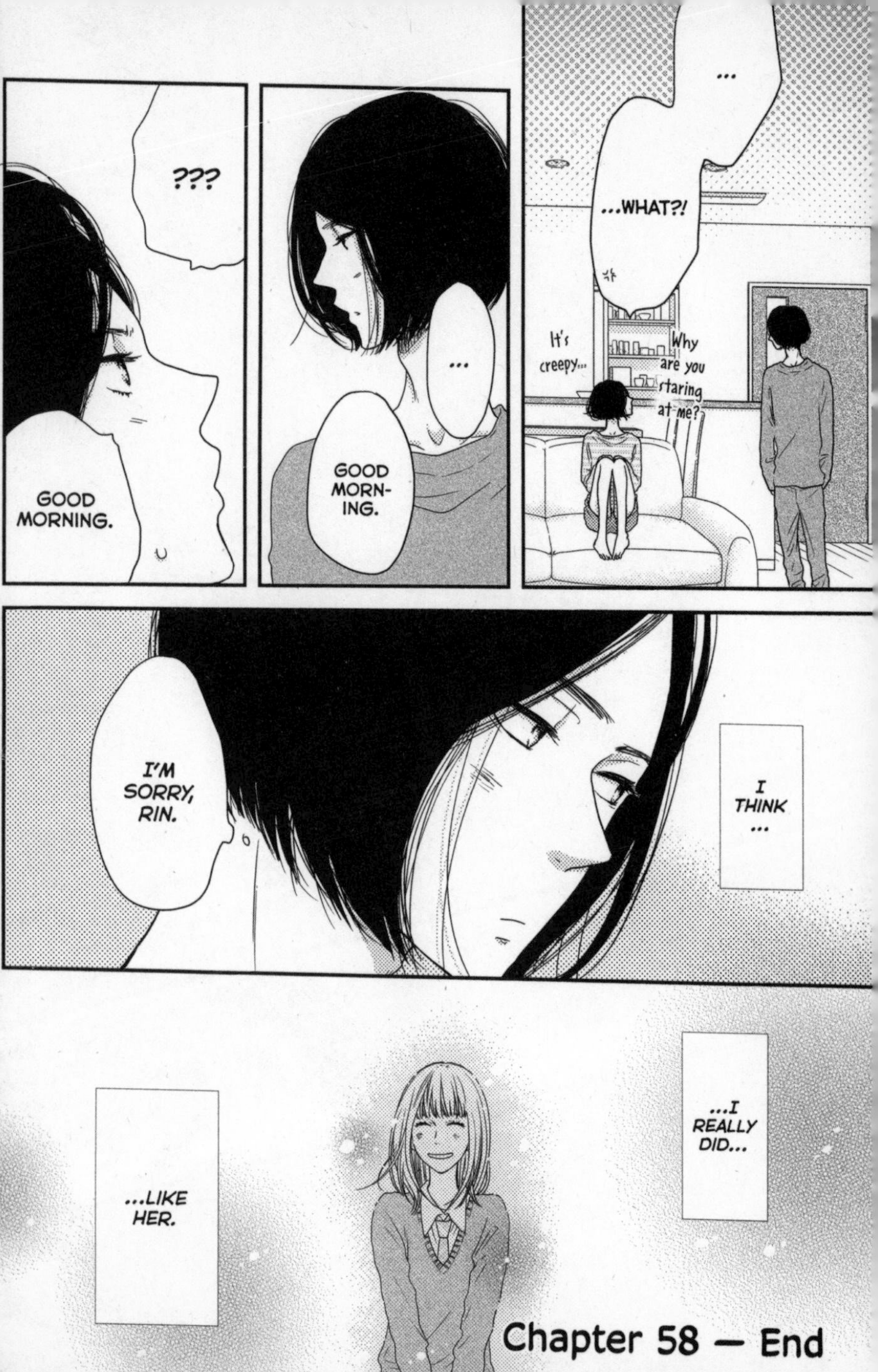
...
...WHAT?!
Why are you staring at me?
It's creepy...
...
GOOD MORNING.
???
GOOD MORNING.
I THINK ...
I'M SORRY, RIN.
...I REALLY DID...
...LIKE HER.
Chapter 58 — End

Say "I love you".

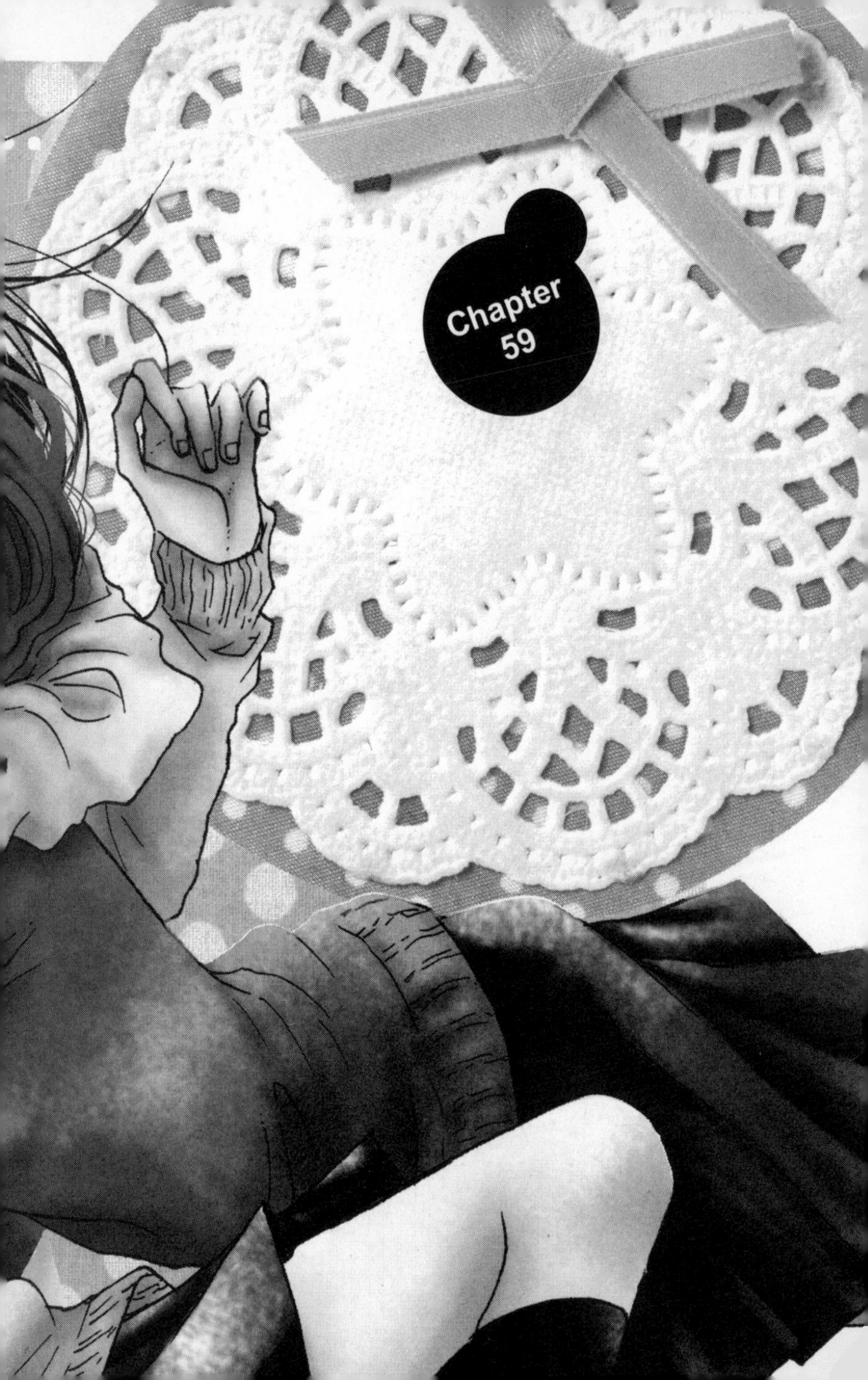
Chapter
59

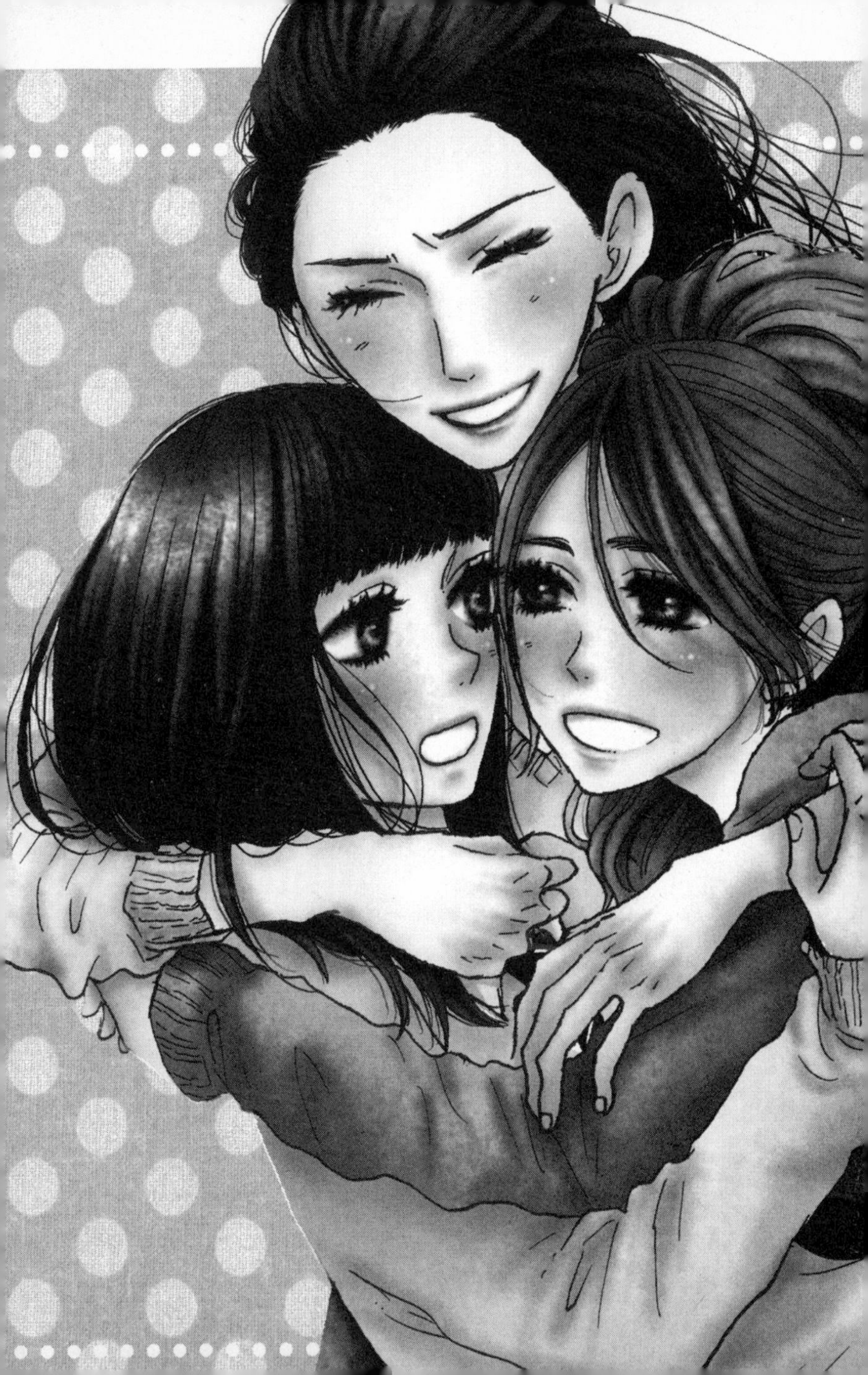

Say "I love you".

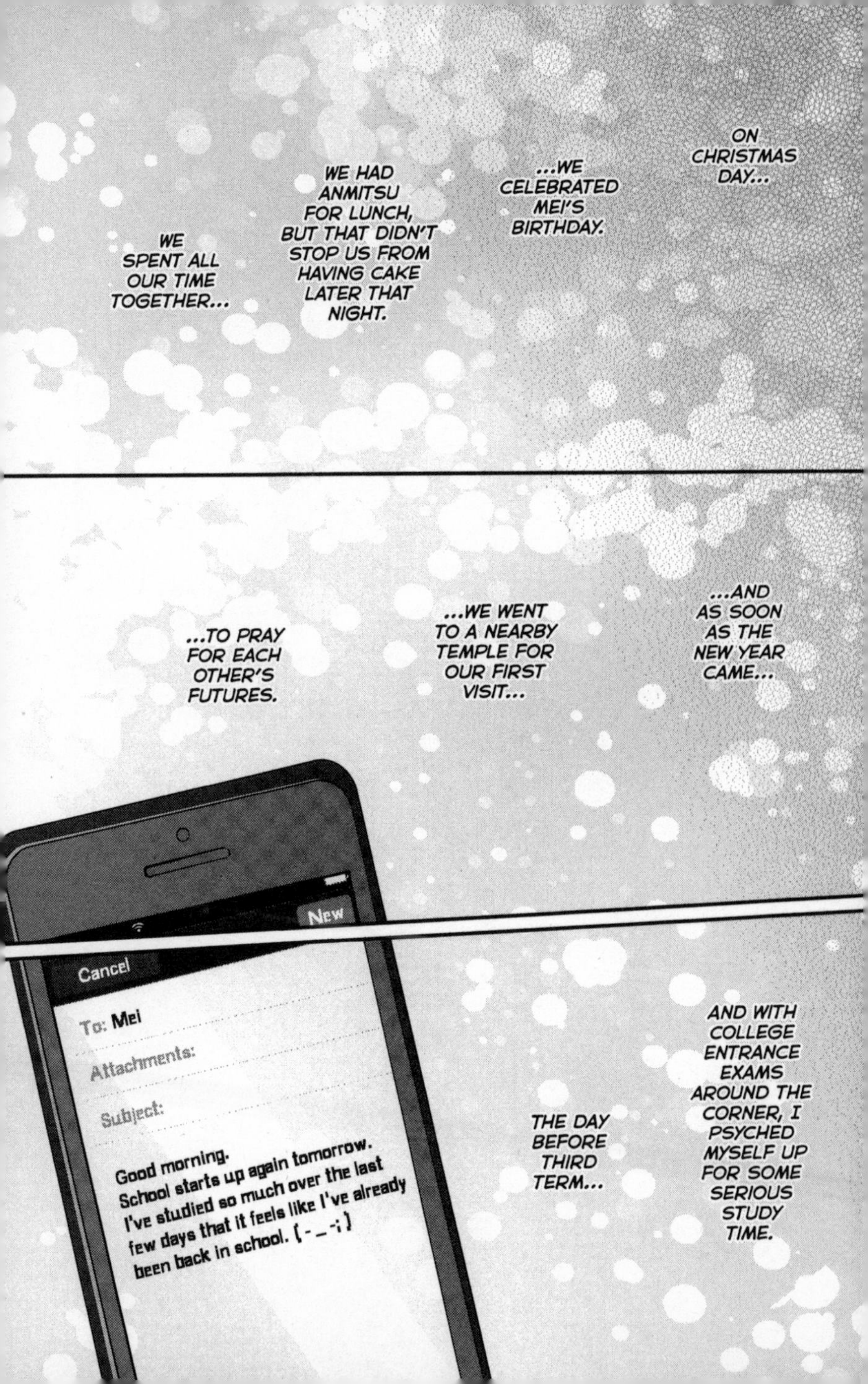
ON CHRISTMAS DAY...
...WE CELEBRATED MEI'S BIRTHDAY.
WE HAD ANMITSU FOR LUNCH, BUT THAT DIDN'T STOP US FROM HAVING CAKE LATER THAT NIGHT.
WE SPENT ALL OUR TIME TOGETHER...
...AND AS SOON AS THE NEW YEAR CAME...
...WE WENT TO A NEARBY TEMPLE FOR OUR FIRST VISIT...
...TO PRAY FOR EACH OTHER'S FUTURES.
AND WITH COLLEGE ENTRANCE EXAMS AROUND THE CORNER, I PSYCHED MYSELF UP FOR SOME SERIOUS STUDY TIME.
THE DAY BEFORE THIRD TERM...
New
Cancel
To: Mei
Attachments:
Subject:
Good morning.
School starts up again tomorrow.
I've studied so much over the last few days that it feels like I've already been back in school. (-_-;)

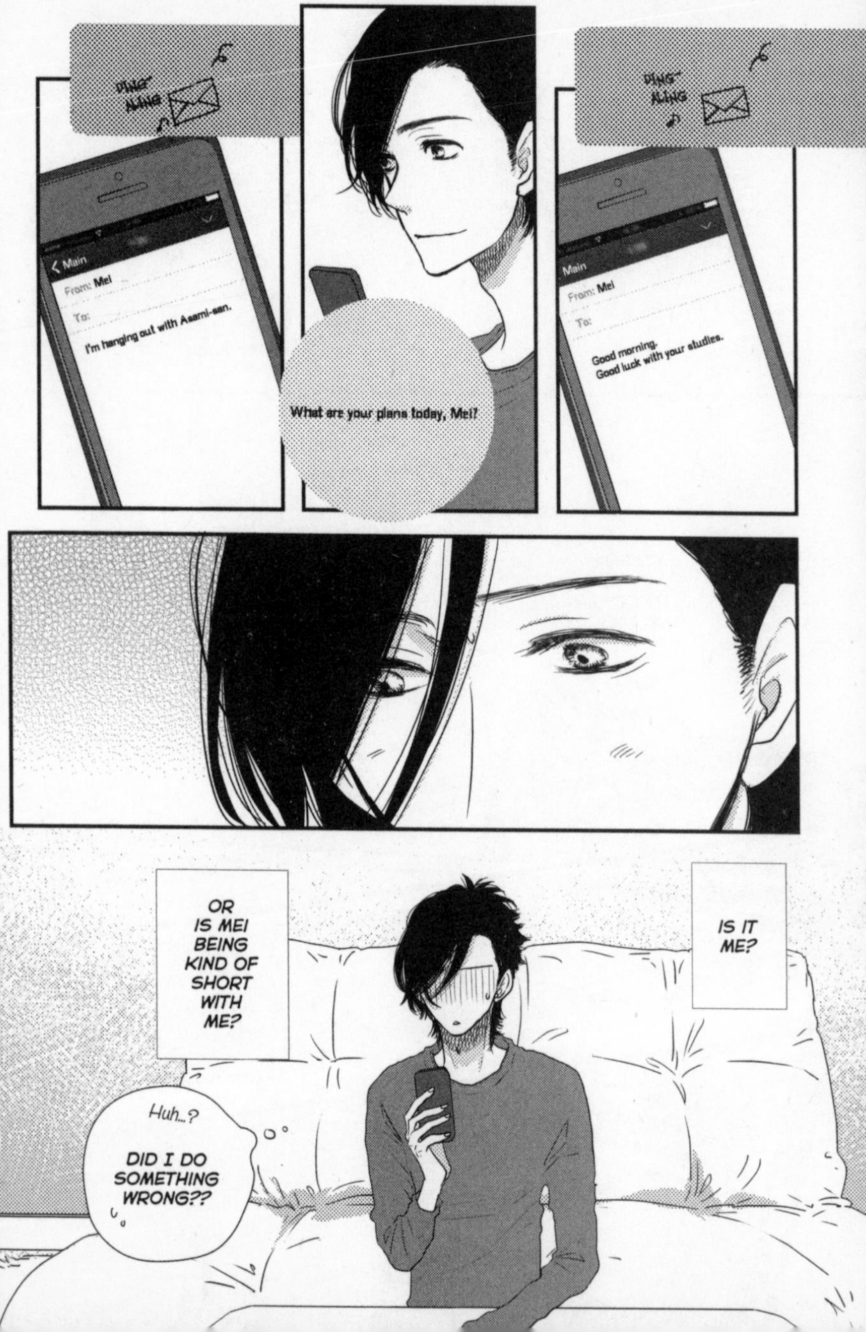
DING ALING
Main
From: Mei
To:
Good morning.
Good luck with your studies.
What are your plans today, Mei?
DING ALING
Main
From: Mei
To:
I'm hanging out with Asami-san.
IS IT ME?
OR IS MEI BEING KIND OF SHORT WITH ME?
Huh...?
DID I DO SOMETHING WRONG??

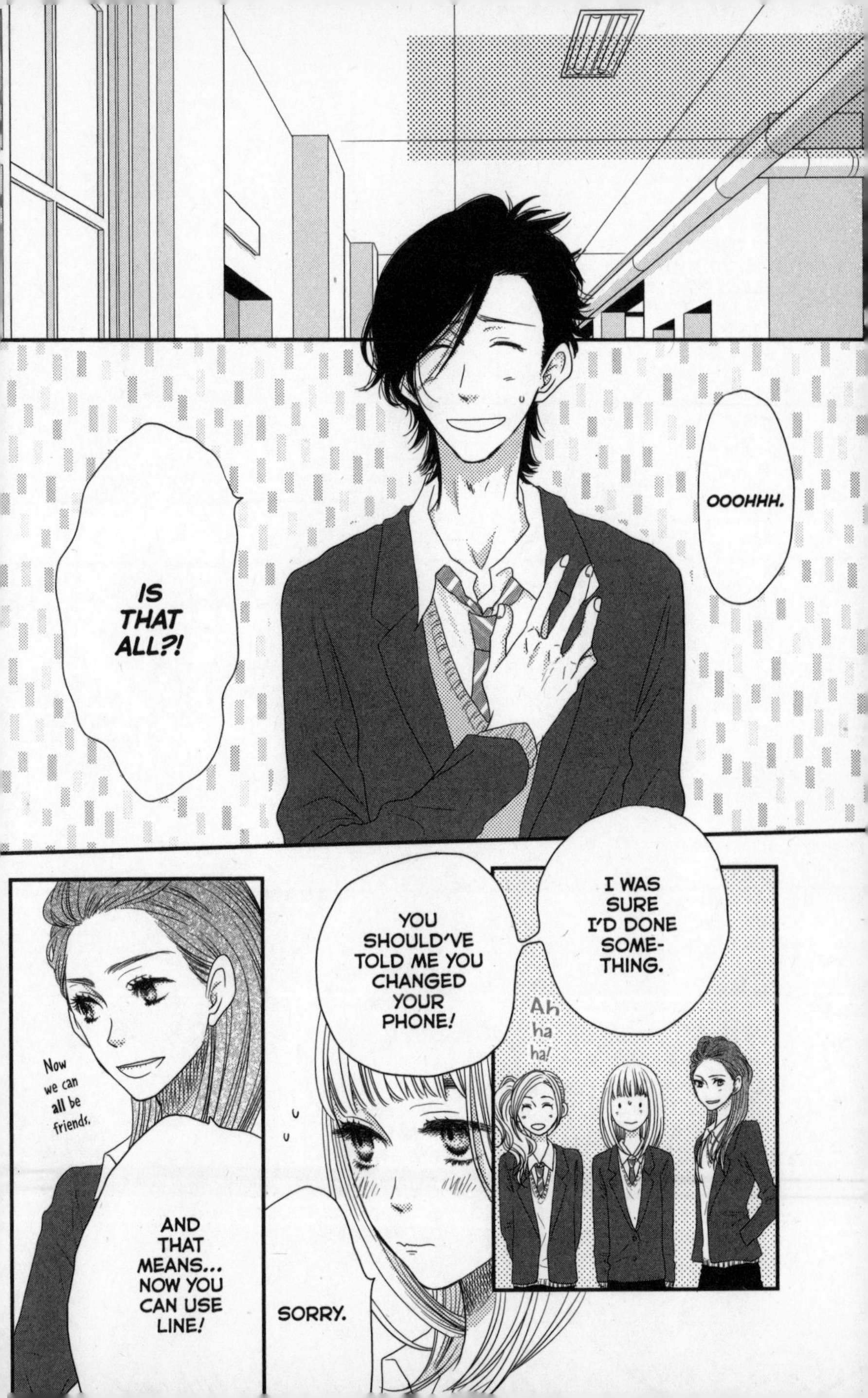
OOOHHH.
IS THAT ALL?!
I WAS SURE I'D DONE SOMETHING.
Ah ha ha!
YOU SHOULD'VE TOLD ME YOU CHANGED YOUR PHONE!
SORRY.
Now we can all be friends.
AND THAT MEANS... NOW YOU CAN USE LINE!

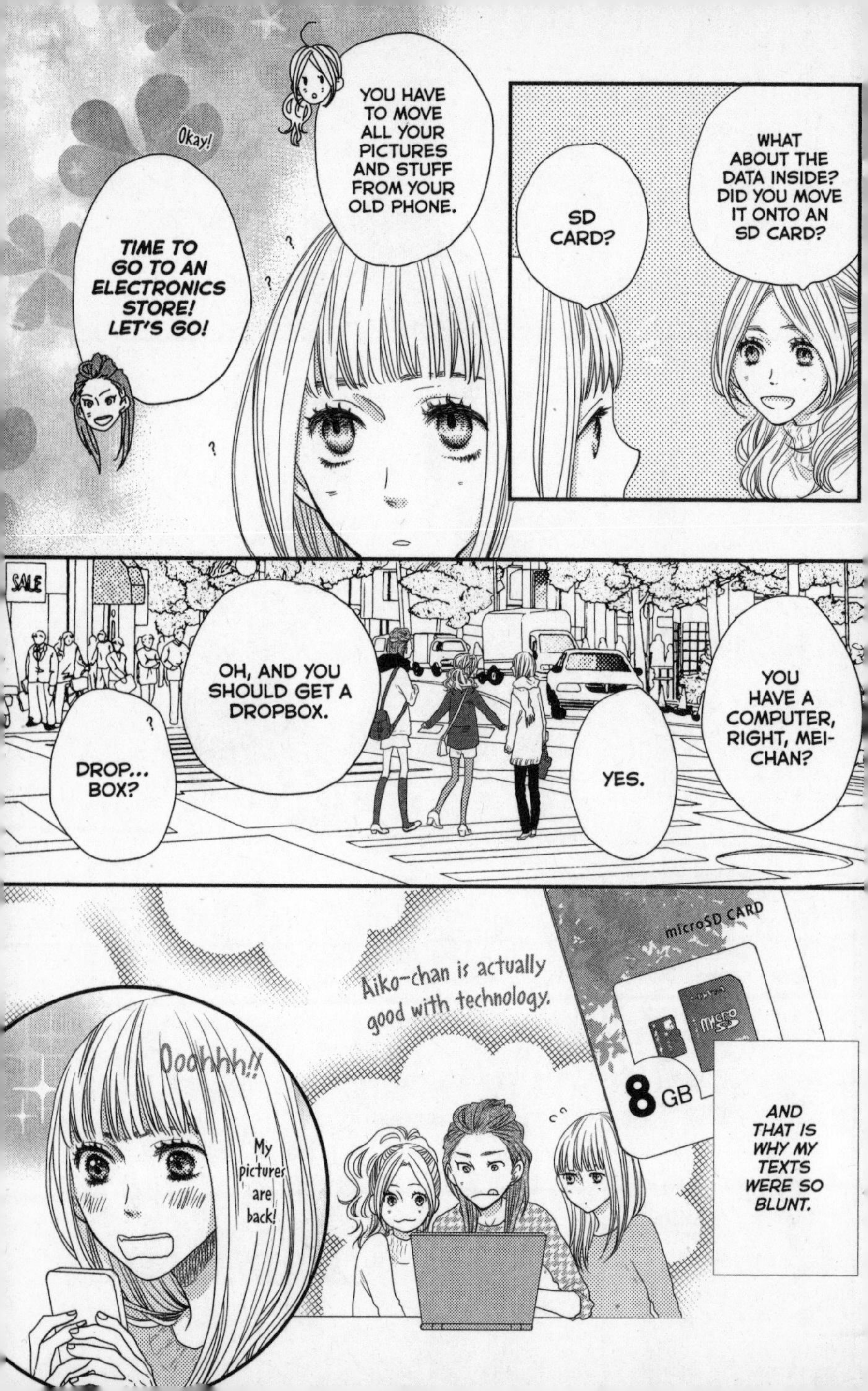
WHAT ABOUT THE DATA INSIDE? DID YOU MOVE IT ONTO AN SD CARD?
SD CARD?
YOU HAVE TO MOVE ALL YOUR PICTURES AND STUFF FROM YOUR OLD PHONE.
Okay!
TIME TO GO TO AN ELECTRONICS STORE! LET'S GO!
YOU HAVE A COMPUTER, RIGHT, MEI-CHAN?
YES.
OH, AND YOU SHOULD GET A DROPBOX.
DROP... BOX?
SALE
microSD CARD
8 GB
AND THAT IS WHY MY TEXTS WERE SO BLUNT.
Aiko-chan is actually good with technology.
Ooohhh!!
My pictures are back!

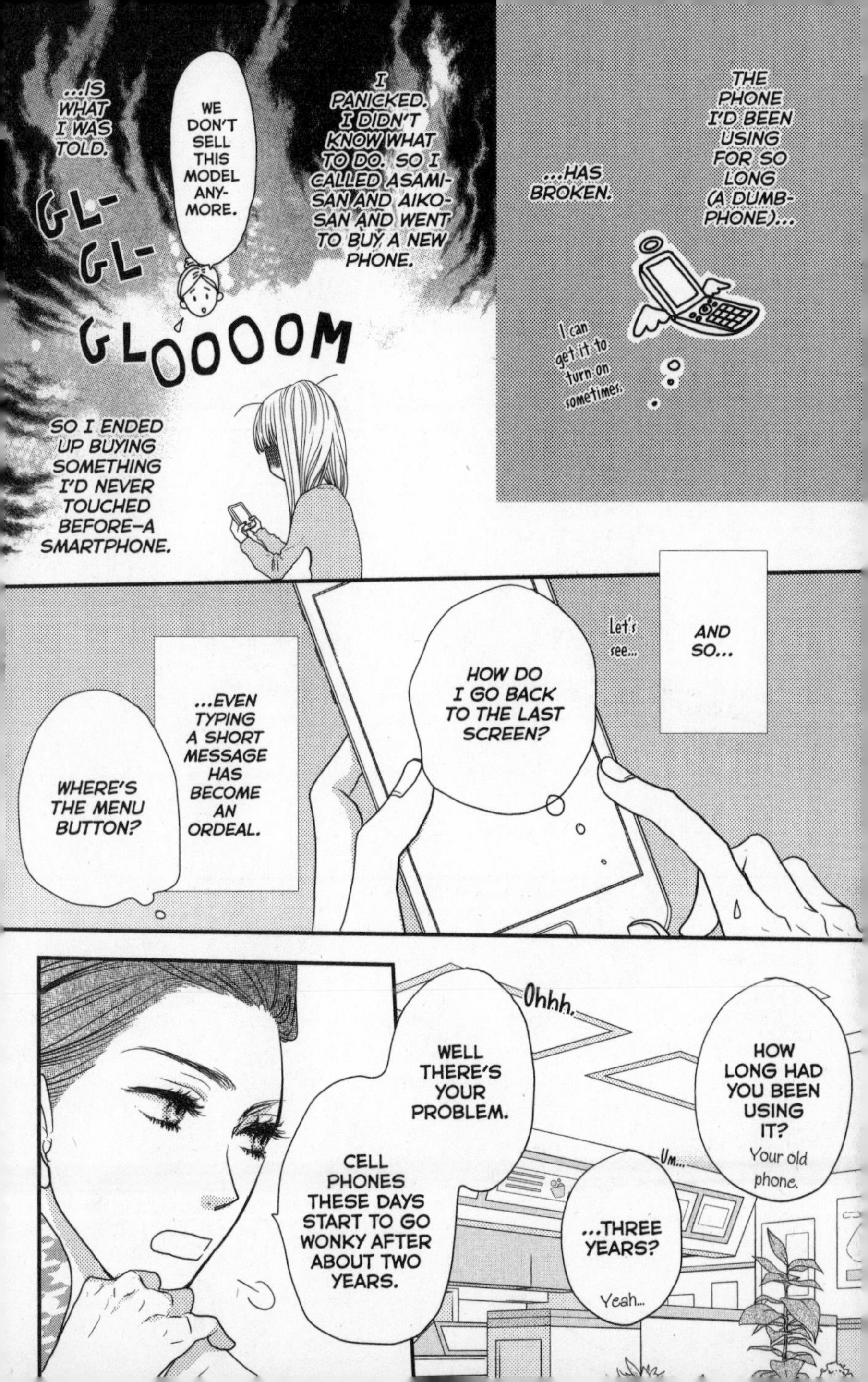
THE PHONE I'D BEEN USING FOR SO LONG (A DUMB-PHONE)...
...HAS BROKEN.
I can get it to turn on sometimes.
I PANICKED. I DIDN'T KNOW WHAT TO DO. SO I CALLED ASAMI-SAN AND AIKO-SAN AND WENT TO BUY A NEW PHONE.
WE DON'T SELL THIS MODEL ANYMORE.
...IS WHAT I WAS TOLD.
GL-GL-GLOOOOM
SO I ENDED UP BUYING SOMETHING I'D NEVER TOUCHED BEFORE—A SMARTPHONE.
AND SO...
Let's see...
HOW DO I GO BACK TO THE LAST SCREEN?
...EVEN TYPING A SHORT MESSAGE HAS BECOME AN ORDEAL.
WHERE'S THE MENU BUTTON?
HOW LONG HAD YOU BEEN USING IT? Your old phone.
Um...
...THREE YEARS?
Yeah...
Ohhh.
WELL THERE'S YOUR PROBLEM.
CELL PHONES THESE DAYS START TO GO WONKY AFTER ABOUT TWO YEARS.

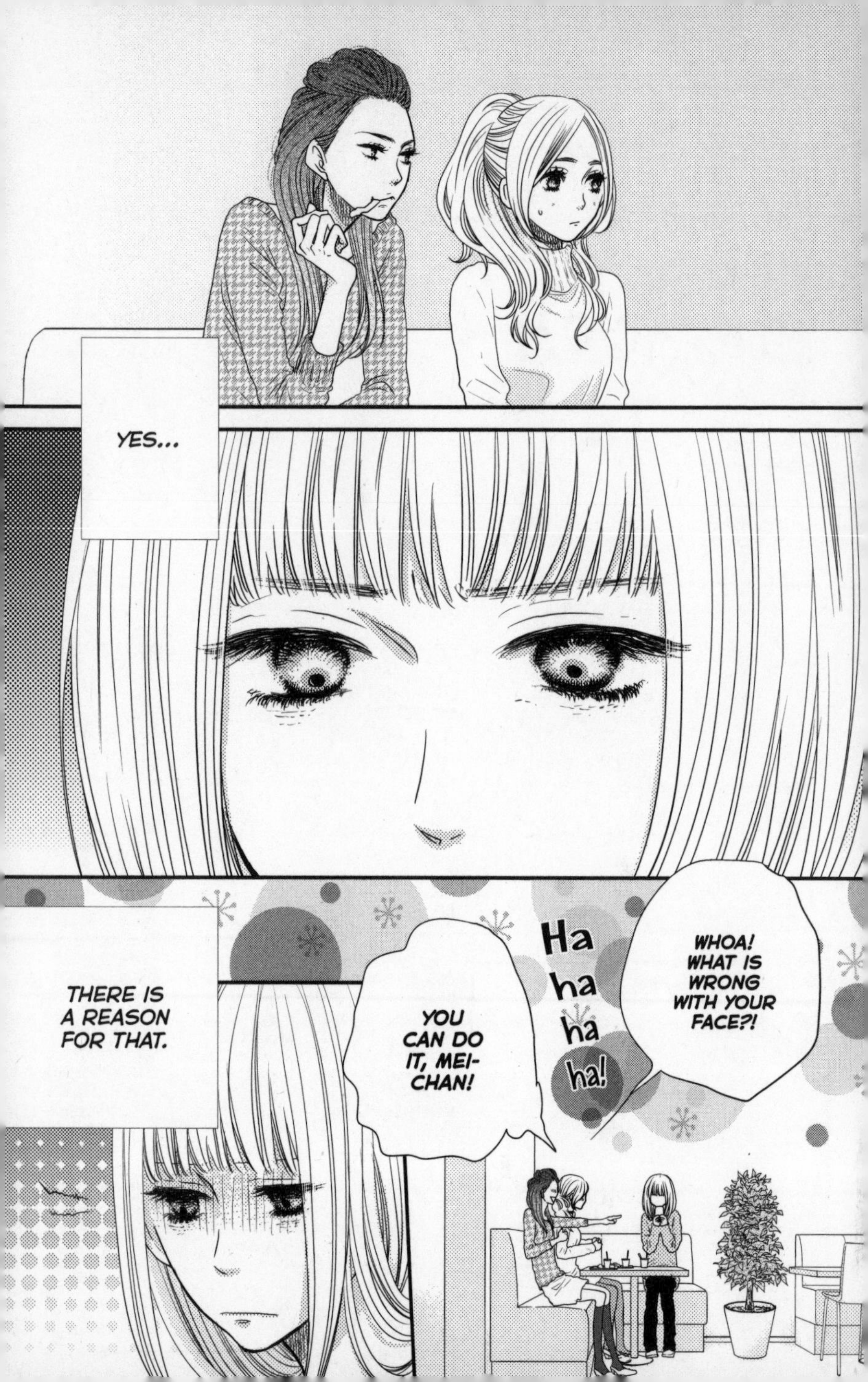
YES...
WHOA! WHAT IS WRONG WITH YOUR FACE?!
Ha ha ha ha!
YOU CAN DO IT, MEI-CHAN!
THERE IS A REASON FOR THAT.

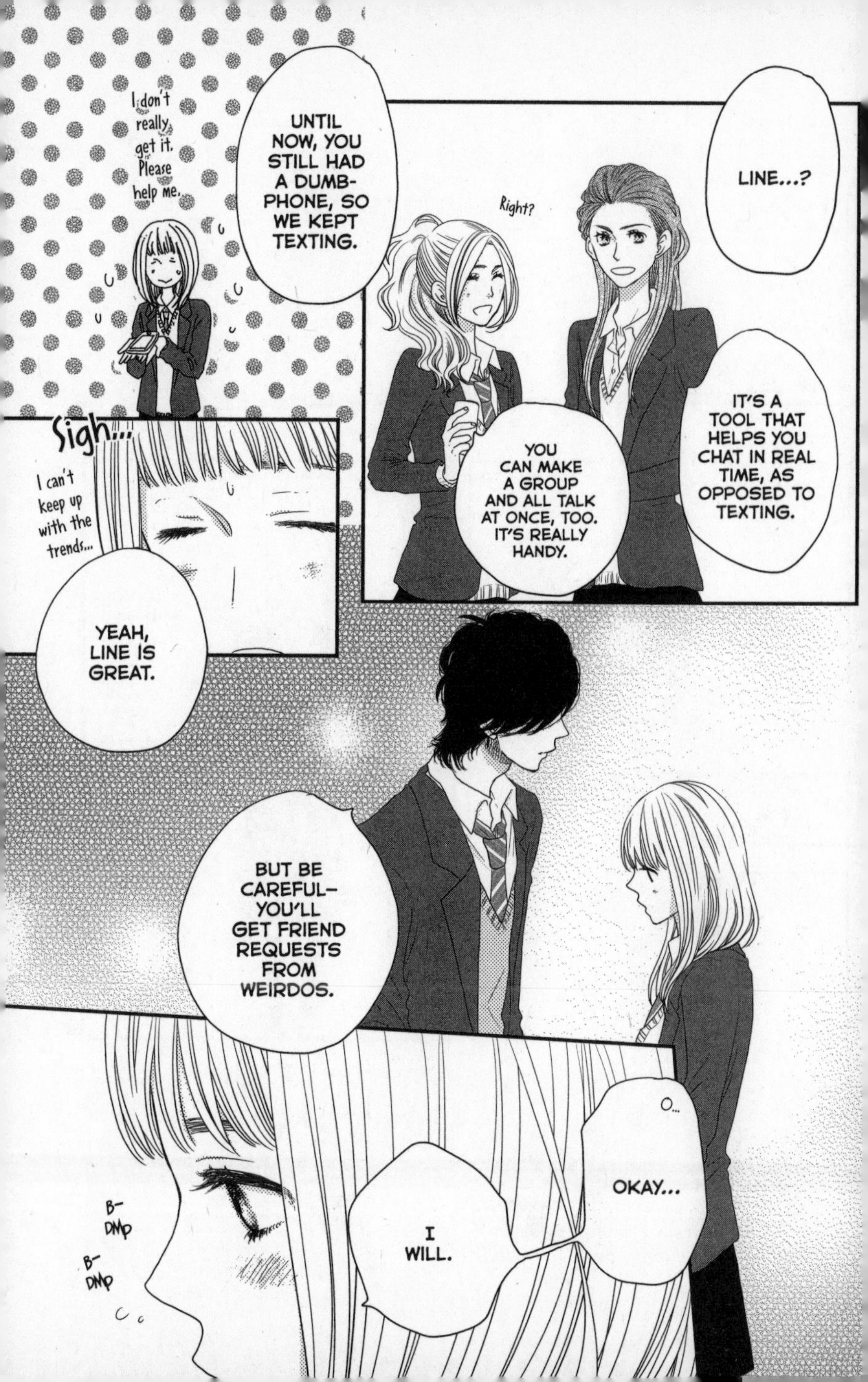

LINE...?
Right?
IT'S A TOOL THAT HELPS YOU CHAT IN REAL TIME, AS OPPOSED TO TEXTING.
YOU CAN MAKE A GROUP AND ALL TALK AT ONCE, TOO. IT'S REALLY HANDY.
UNTIL NOW, YOU STILL HAD A DUMB-PHONE, SO WE KEPT TEXTING.
I don't really get it. Please help me.
Sigh...
I can't keep up with the trends...
YEAH, LINE IS GREAT.
BUT BE CAREFUL-YOU'LL GET FRIEND REQUESTS FROM WEIRDOS.
O...
OKAY...
I WILL.
B-DMP
B-DMP

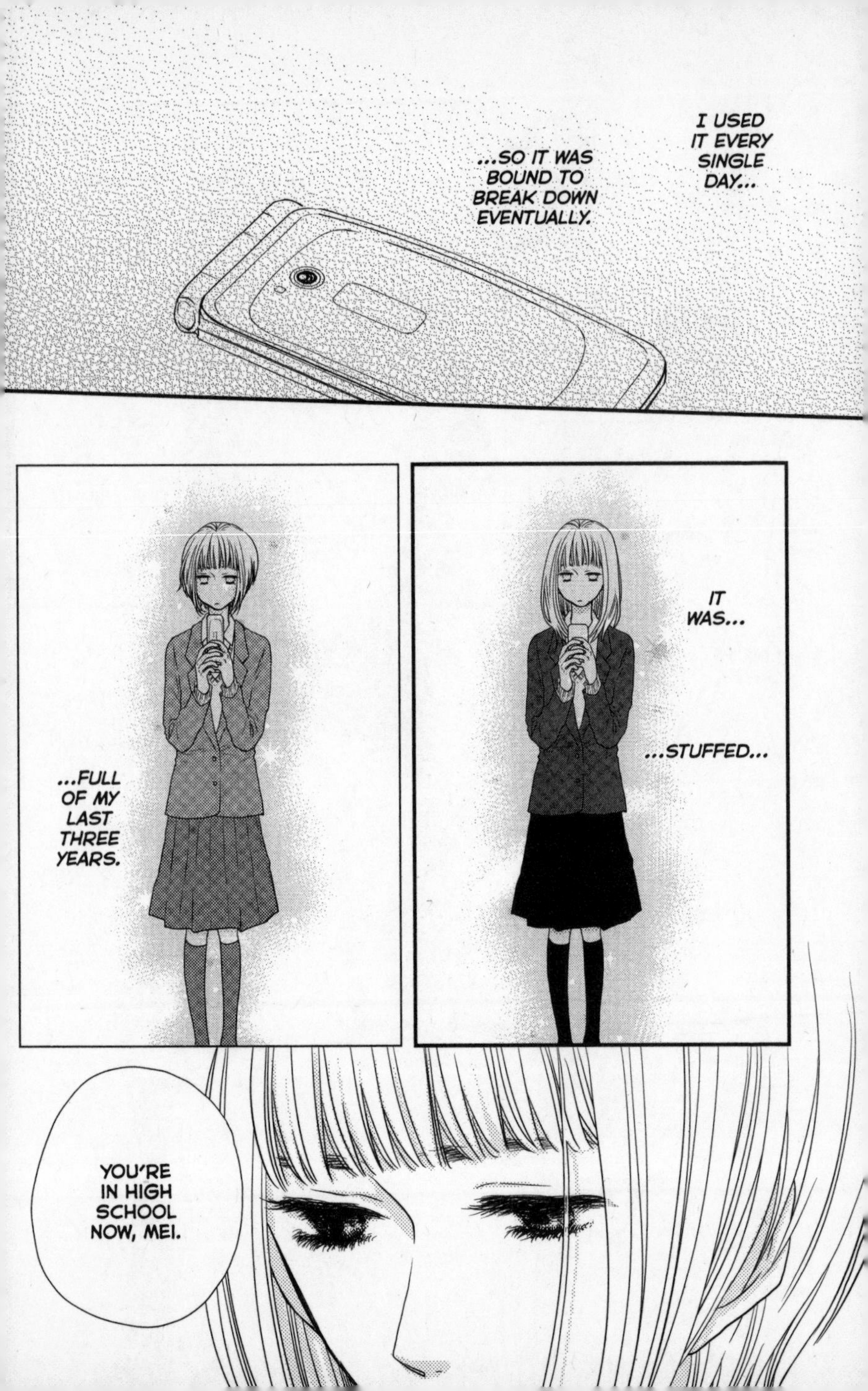
I USED IT EVERY SINGLE DAY...
...SO IT WAS BOUND TO BREAK DOWN EVENTUALLY.
IT WAS...
...STUFFED...
...FULL OF MY LAST THREE YEARS.
YOU'RE IN HIGH SCHOOL NOW, MEI.

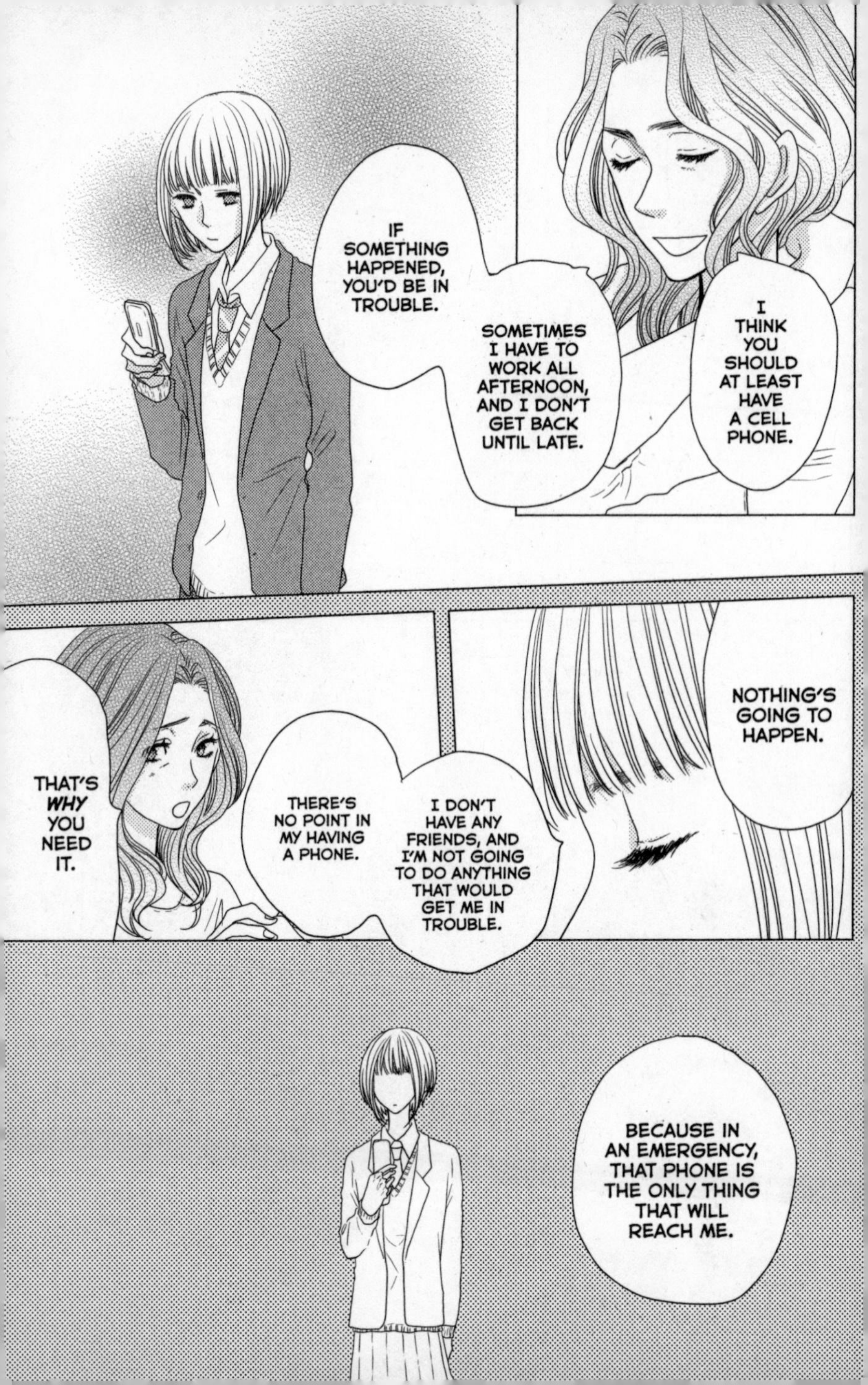
I THINK YOU SHOULD AT LEAST HAVE A CELL PHONE.
SOMETIMES I HAVE TO WORK ALL AFTERNOON, AND I DON'T GET BACK UNTIL LATE.
IF SOMETHING HAPPENED, YOU'D BE IN TROUBLE.
NOTHING'S GOING TO HAPPEN.
I DON'T HAVE ANY FRIENDS, AND I'M NOT GOING TO DO ANYTHING THAT WOULD GET ME IN TROUBLE.
THERE'S NO POINT IN MY HAVING A PHONE.
THAT'S *WHY* YOU NEED IT.
BECAUSE IN AN EMERGENCY, THAT PHONE IS THE ONLY THING THAT WILL REACH ME.

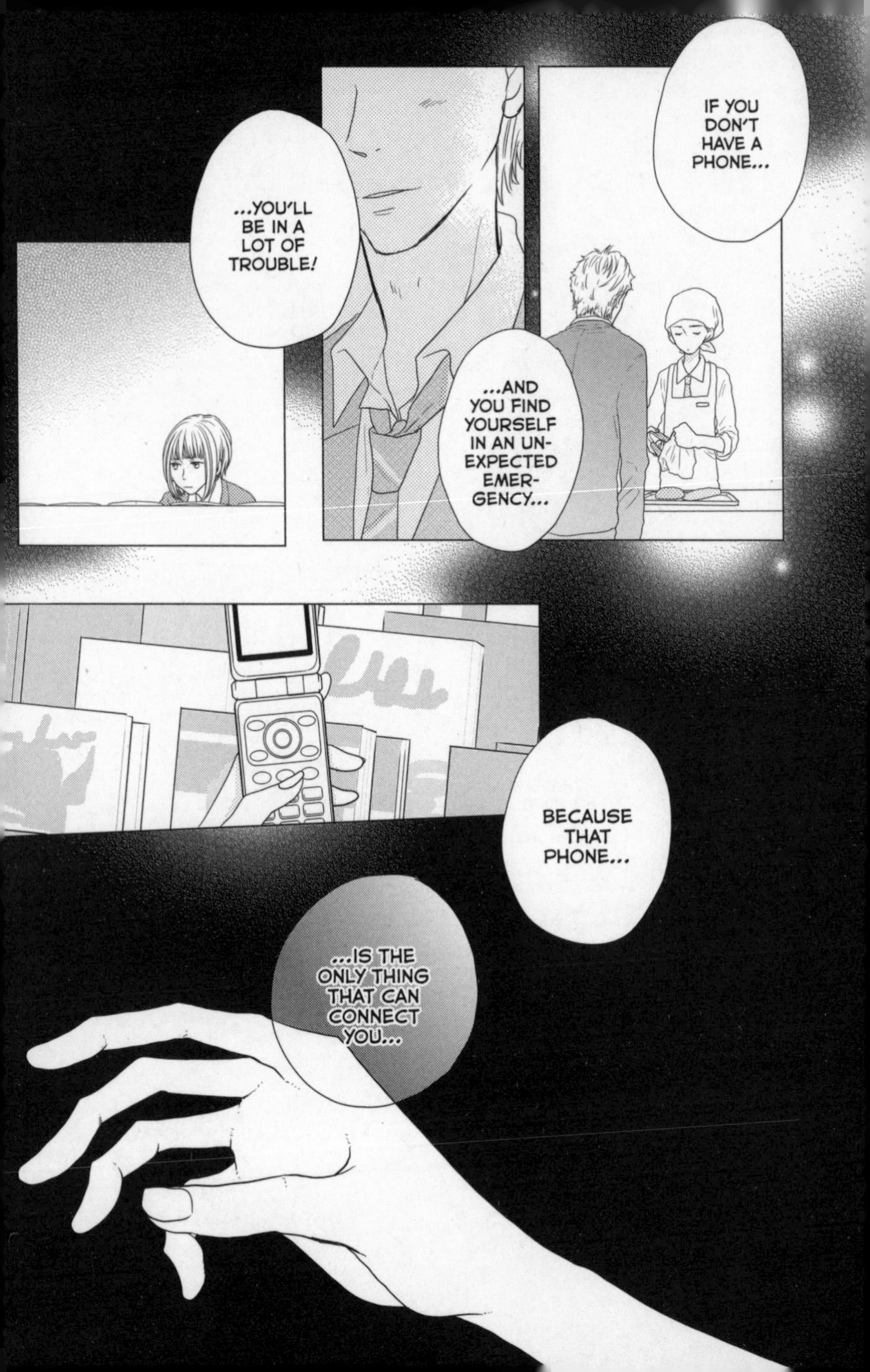
IF YOU DON'T HAVE A PHONE...
...AND YOU FIND YOURSELF IN AN UN-EXPECTED EMER-GENCY...
...YOU'LL BE IN A LOT OF TROUBLE!
BECAUSE THAT PHONE...
...IS THE ONLY THING THAT CAN CONNECT YOU...

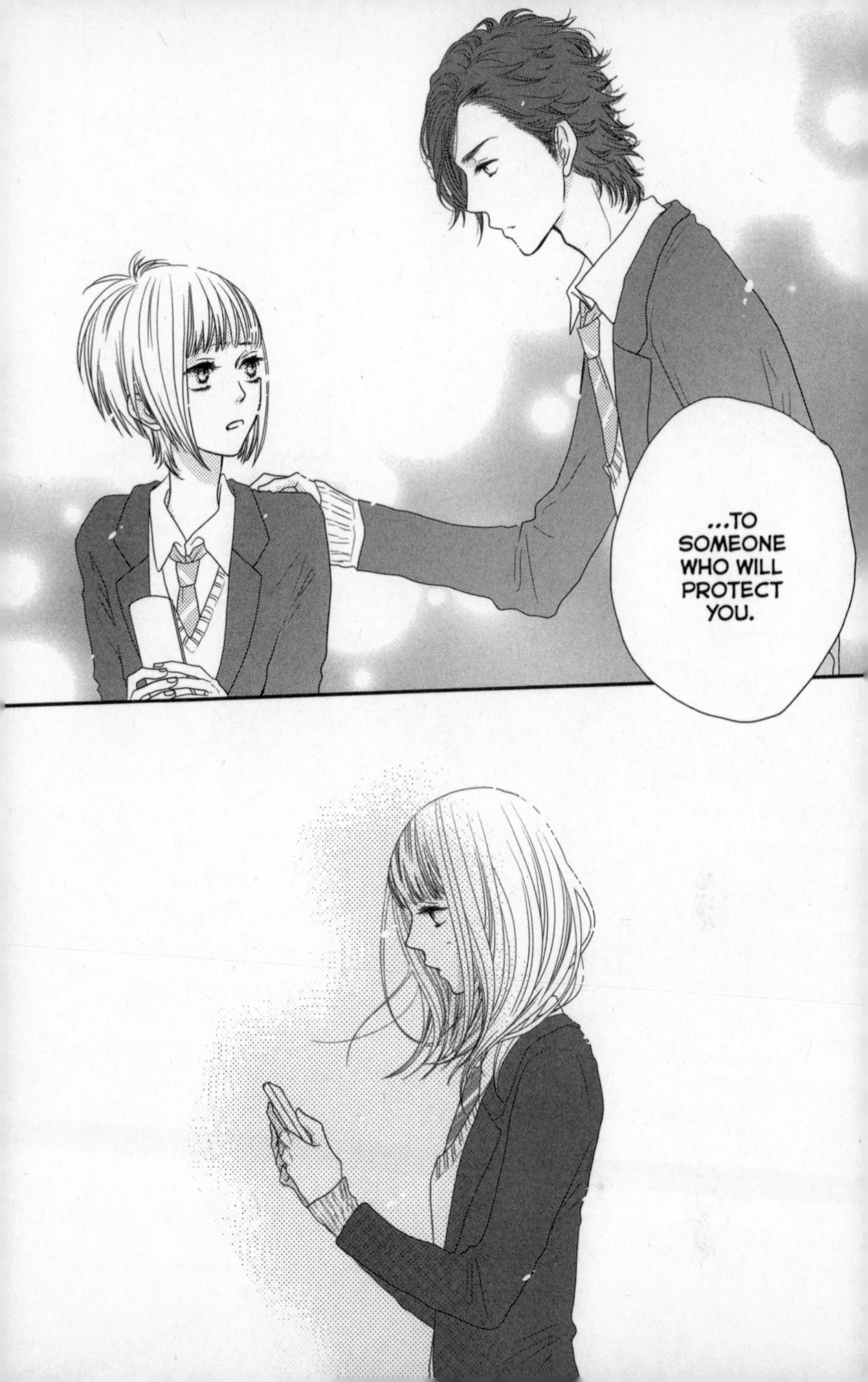
...TO SOMEONE WHO WILL PROTECT YOU.

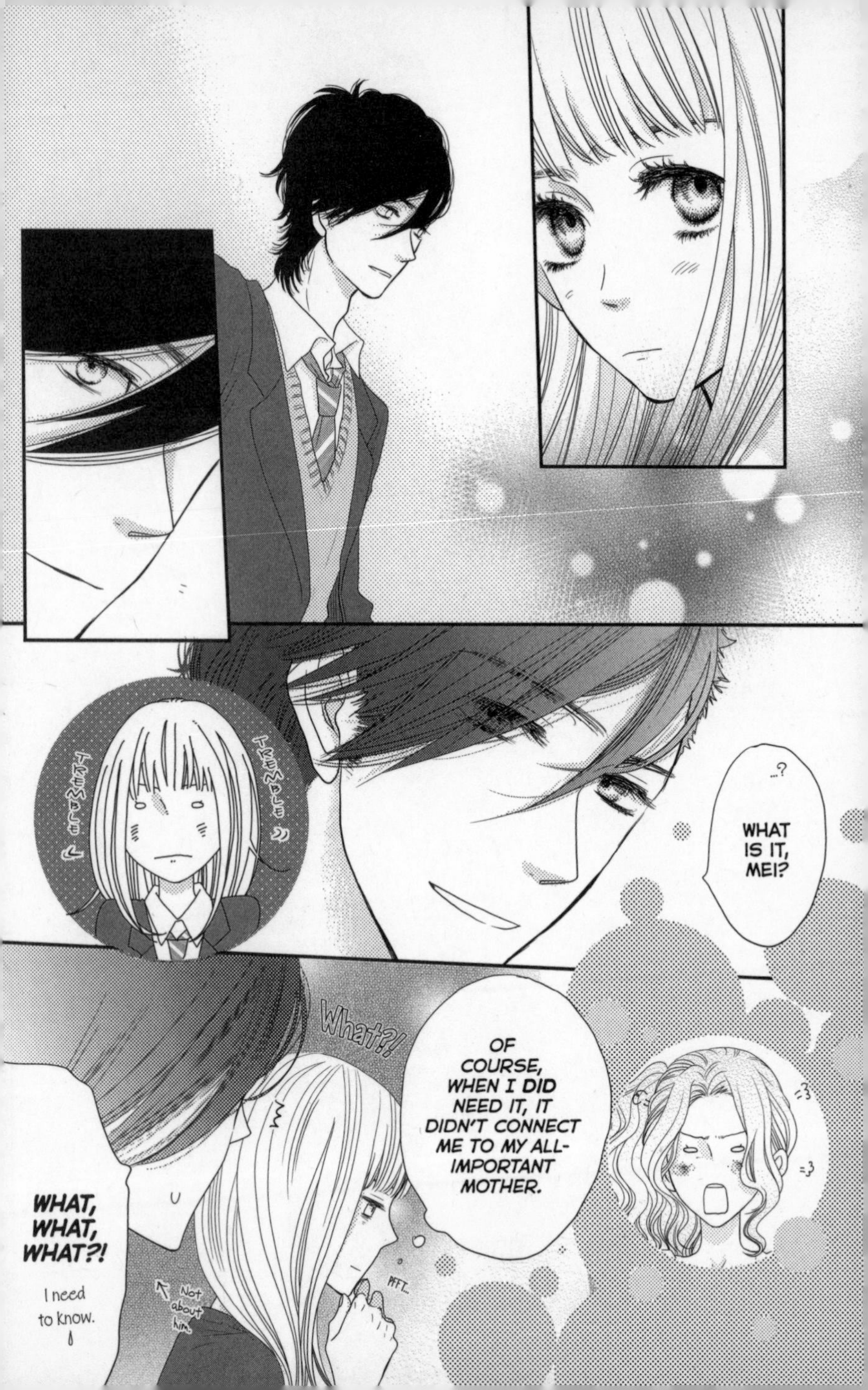
...?
WHAT IS IT, MEI?
TREMBLE
TREMBLE
OF COURSE, WHEN I **DID** NEED IT, IT DIDN'T CONNECT ME TO MY ALL-IMPORTANT MOTHER.
What?!
PFFT...
Not about him
WHAT, WHAT, WHAT?!
I need to know.

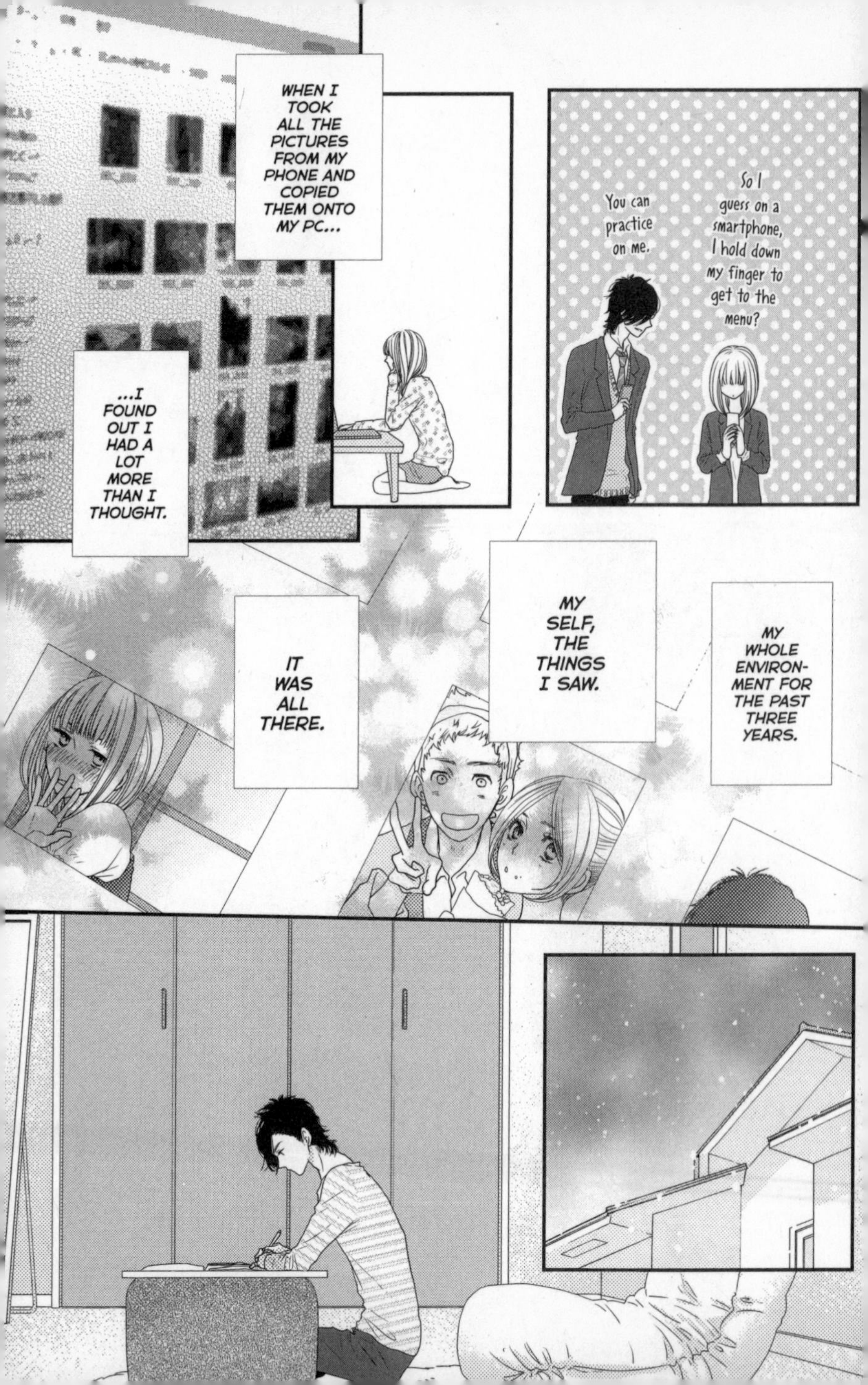
So I guess on a smartphone, I hold down my finger to get to the menu?
You can practice on me.
WHEN I TOOK ALL THE PICTURES FROM MY PHONE AND COPIED THEM ONTO MY PC...
...I FOUND OUT I HAD A LOT MORE THAN I THOUGHT.
MY WHOLE ENVIRONMENT FOR THE PAST THREE YEARS.
MY SELF, THE THINGS I SAW.
IT WAS ALL THERE.

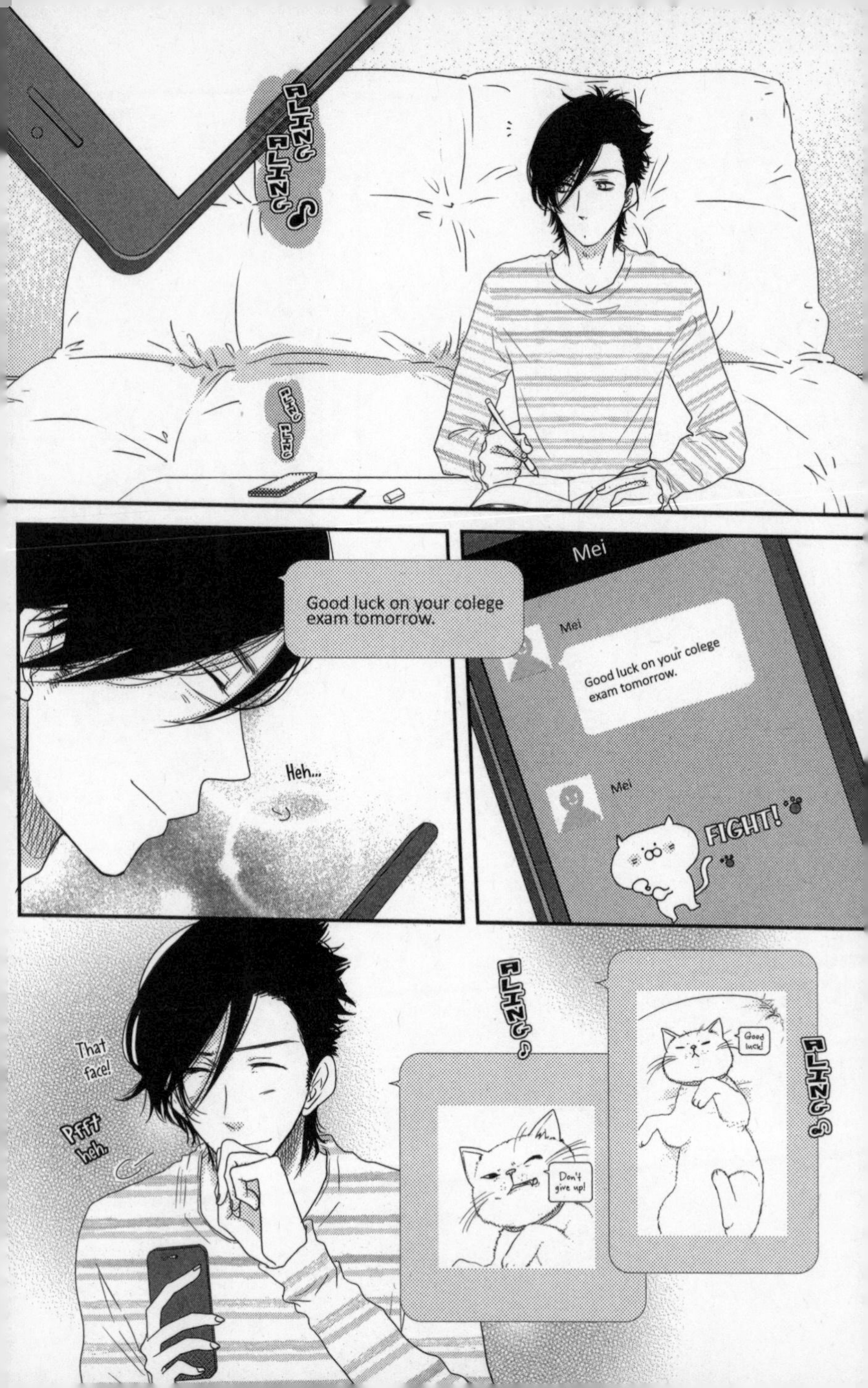
ALING ALING
ALING ALING
Mei
Mei
Good luck on your colege exam tomorrow.
Mei
FIGHT!
Good luck on your colege exam tomorrow.
Heh...
ALING
Good luck!
ALING
Don't give up!
That face!
Pfft heh.

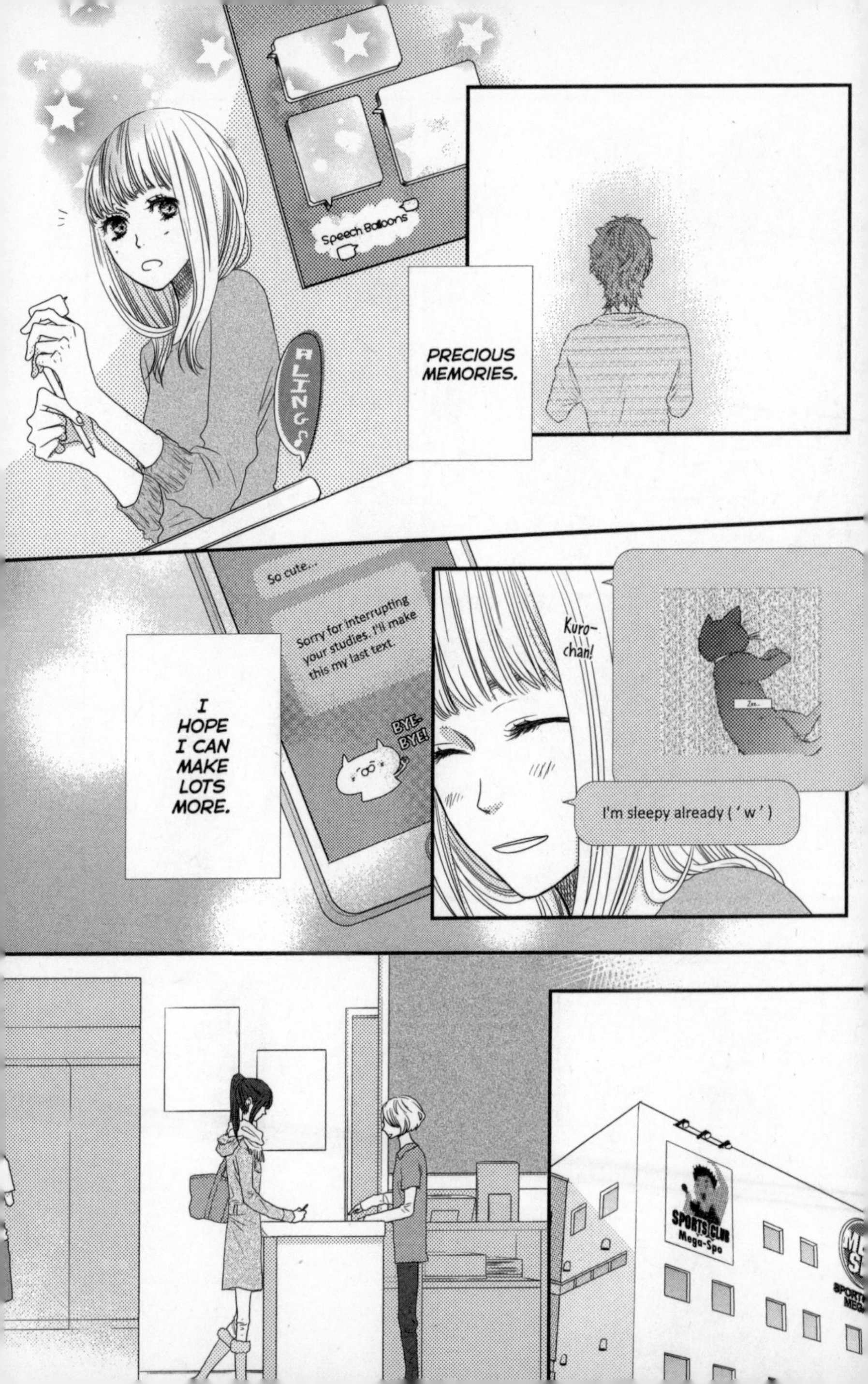
PRECIOUS MEMORIES.
Speech Balloons
ALING
Kuro-chan!
I'm sleepy already (' w ')
So cute...
Sorry for interrupting your studies. I'll make this my last text.
BYE-BYE!
I HOPE I CAN MAKE LOTS MORE.
SPORTS CLUB Mega-Spo

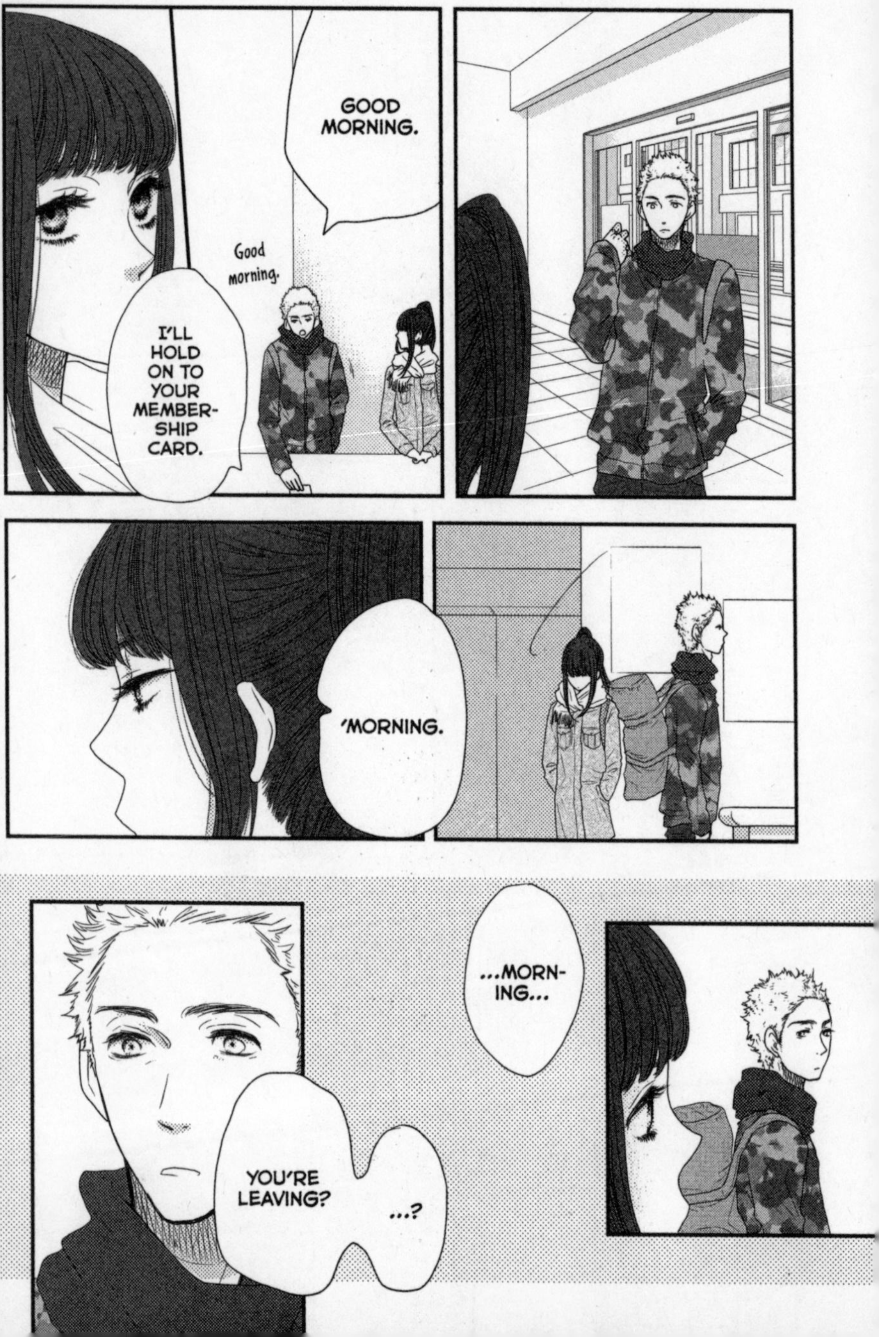
GOOD MORNING.
Good morning.
I'LL HOLD ON TO YOUR MEMBER-SHIP CARD.
'MORNING.
...MORN-ING...
YOU'RE LEAVING?
...?

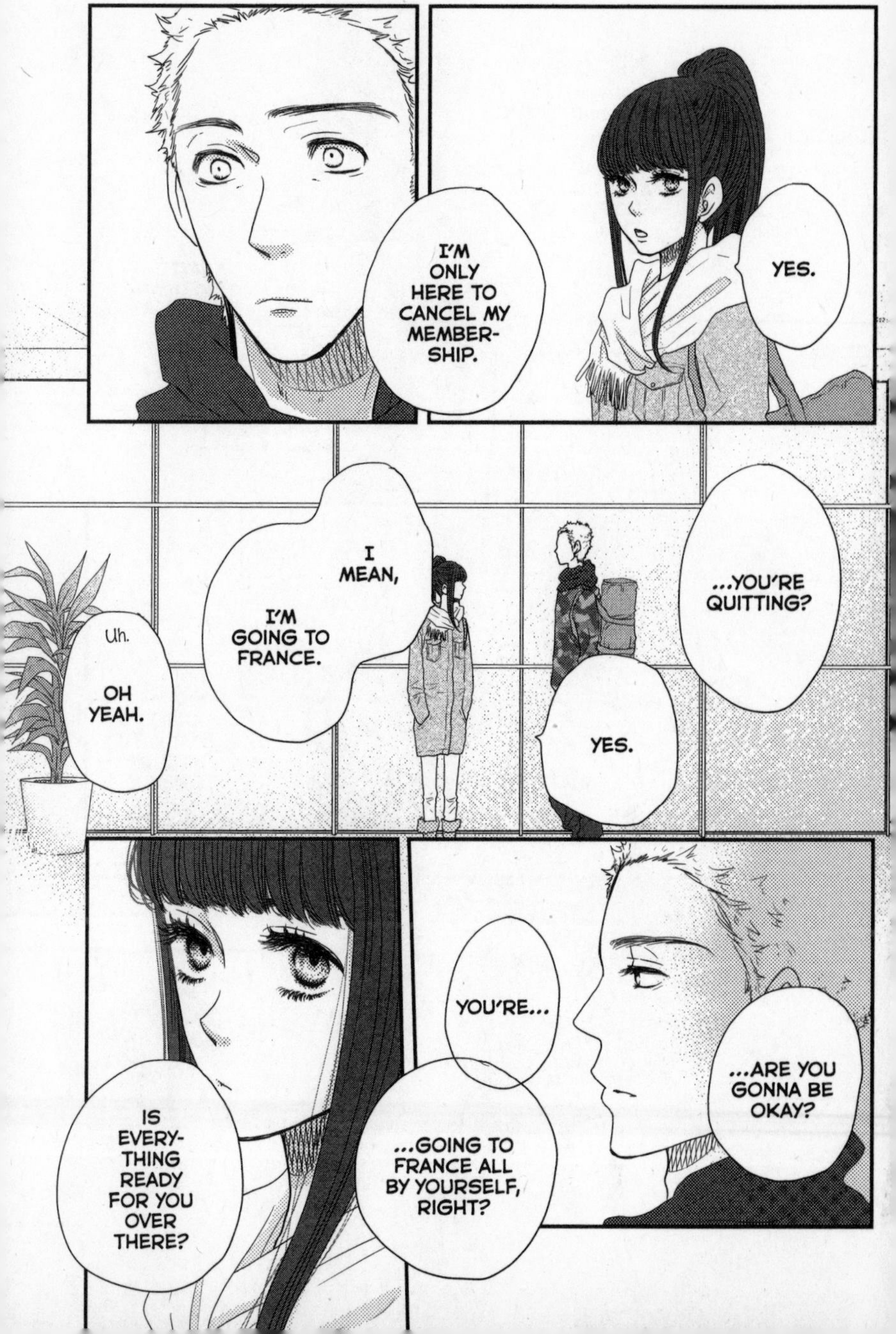
YES.
I'M ONLY HERE TO CANCEL MY MEMBER-SHIP.
...YOU'RE QUITTING?
YES.
I MEAN, I'M GOING TO FRANCE.
Uh. OH YEAH.
YOU'RE...
...GOING TO FRANCE ALL BY YOURSELF, RIGHT?
...ARE YOU GONNA BE OKAY?
IS EVERY-THING READY FOR YOU OVER THERE?

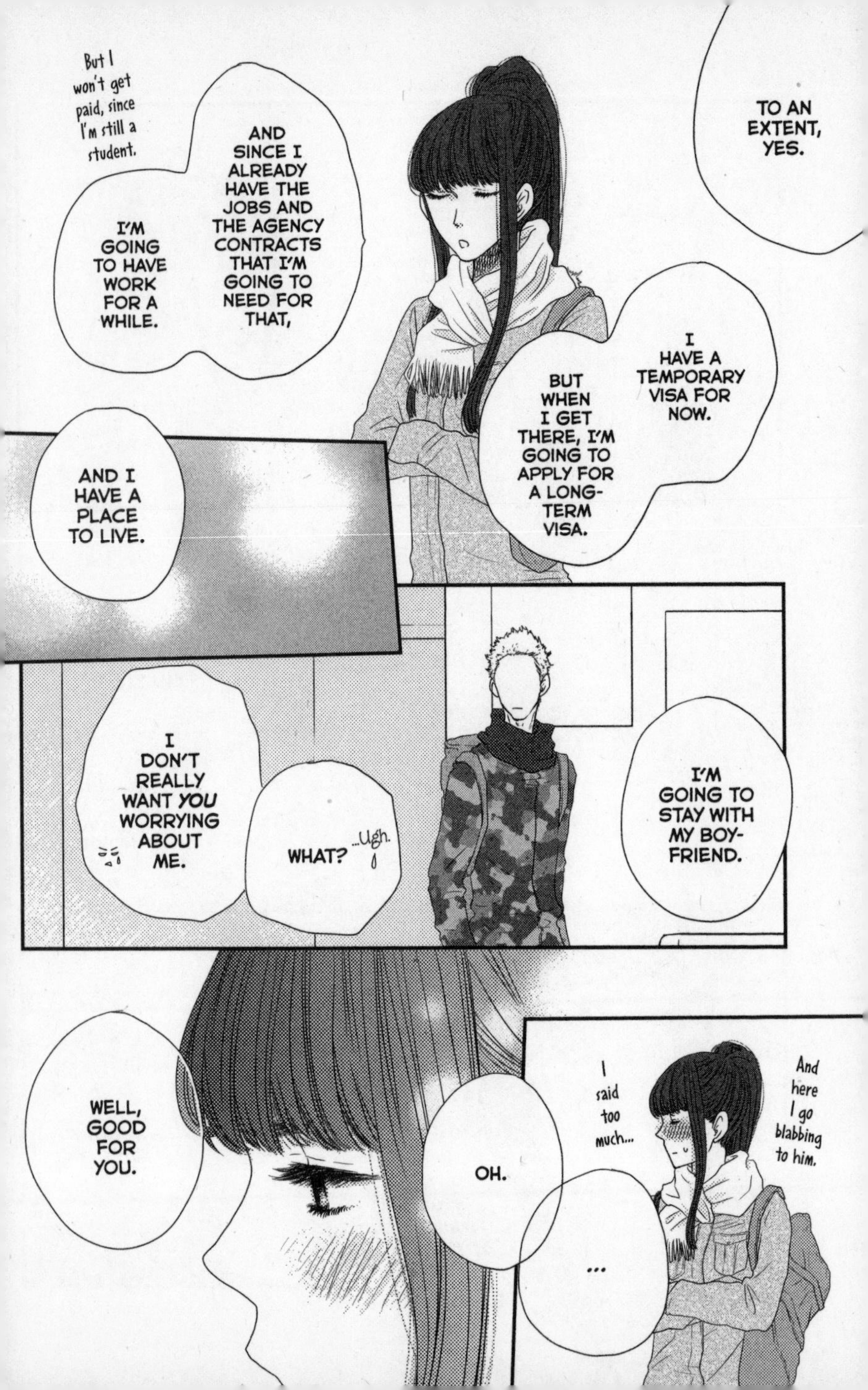

TO AN EXTENT, YES.
I HAVE A TEMPORARY VISA FOR NOW.
BUT WHEN I GET THERE, I'M GOING TO APPLY FOR A LONG-TERM VISA.
AND SINCE I ALREADY HAVE THE JOBS AND THE AGENCY CONTRACTS THAT I'M GOING TO NEED FOR THAT,
I'M GOING TO HAVE WORK FOR A WHILE.
But I won't get paid, since I'm still a student.
AND I HAVE A PLACE TO LIVE.
I'M GOING TO STAY WITH MY BOY-FRIEND.
...Ugh.
WHAT?
I DON'T REALLY WANT *YOU* WORRYING ABOUT ME.
And here I go blabbing to him.
I said too much...
OH.
...
WELL, GOOD FOR YOU.

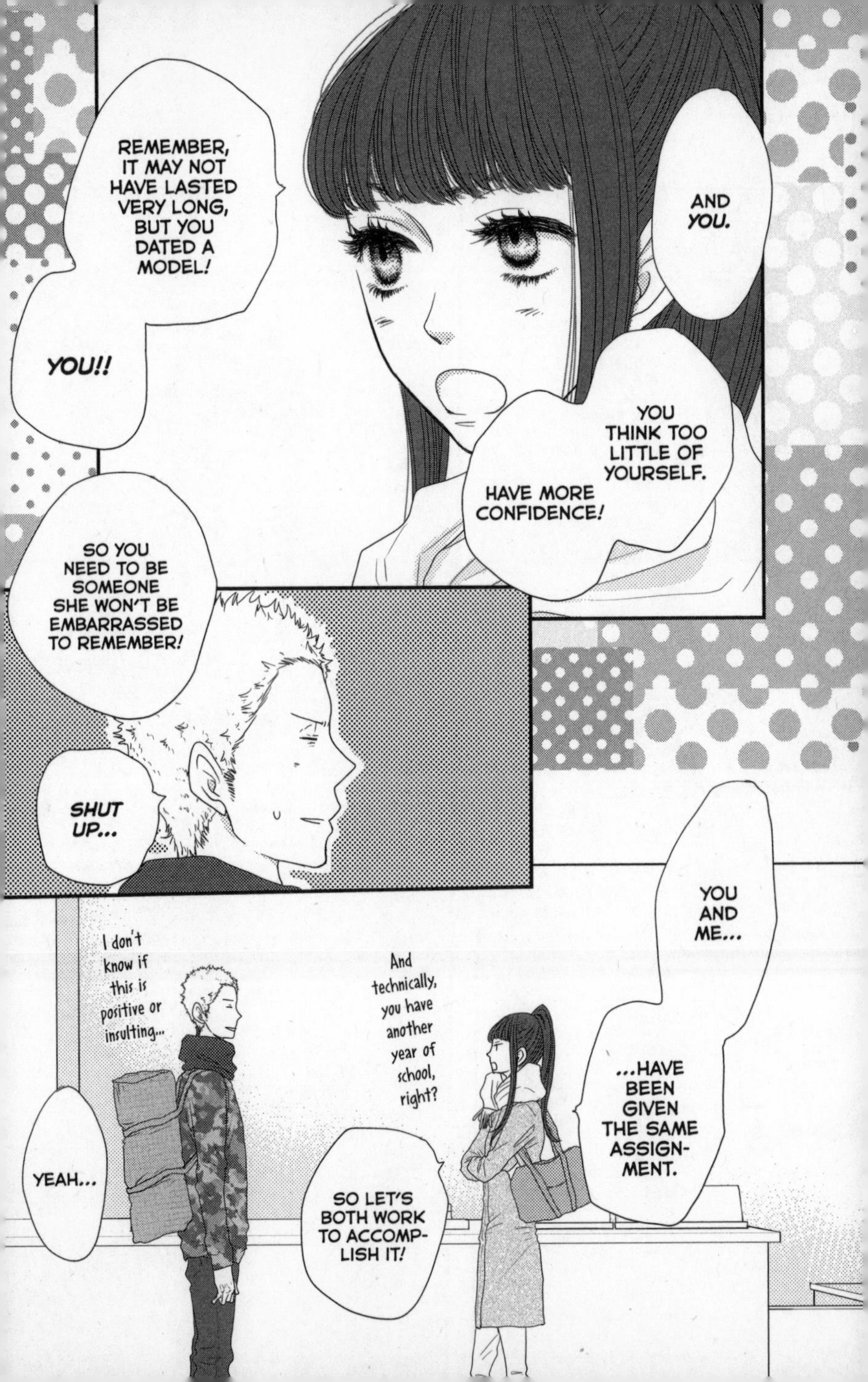
AND YOU.
YOU THINK TOO LITTLE OF YOURSELF. HAVE MORE CONFIDENCE!
REMEMBER, IT MAY NOT HAVE LASTED VERY LONG, BUT YOU DATED A MODEL! YOU!!
SO YOU NEED TO BE SOMEONE SHE WON'T BE EMBARRASSED TO REMEMBER!
SHUT UP...
YOU AND ME...
...HAVE BEEN GIVEN THE SAME ASSIGN-MENT.
And technically, you have another year of school, right?
SO LET'S BOTH WORK TO ACCOMP-LISH IT!
I don't know if this is positive or insulting...
YEAH...

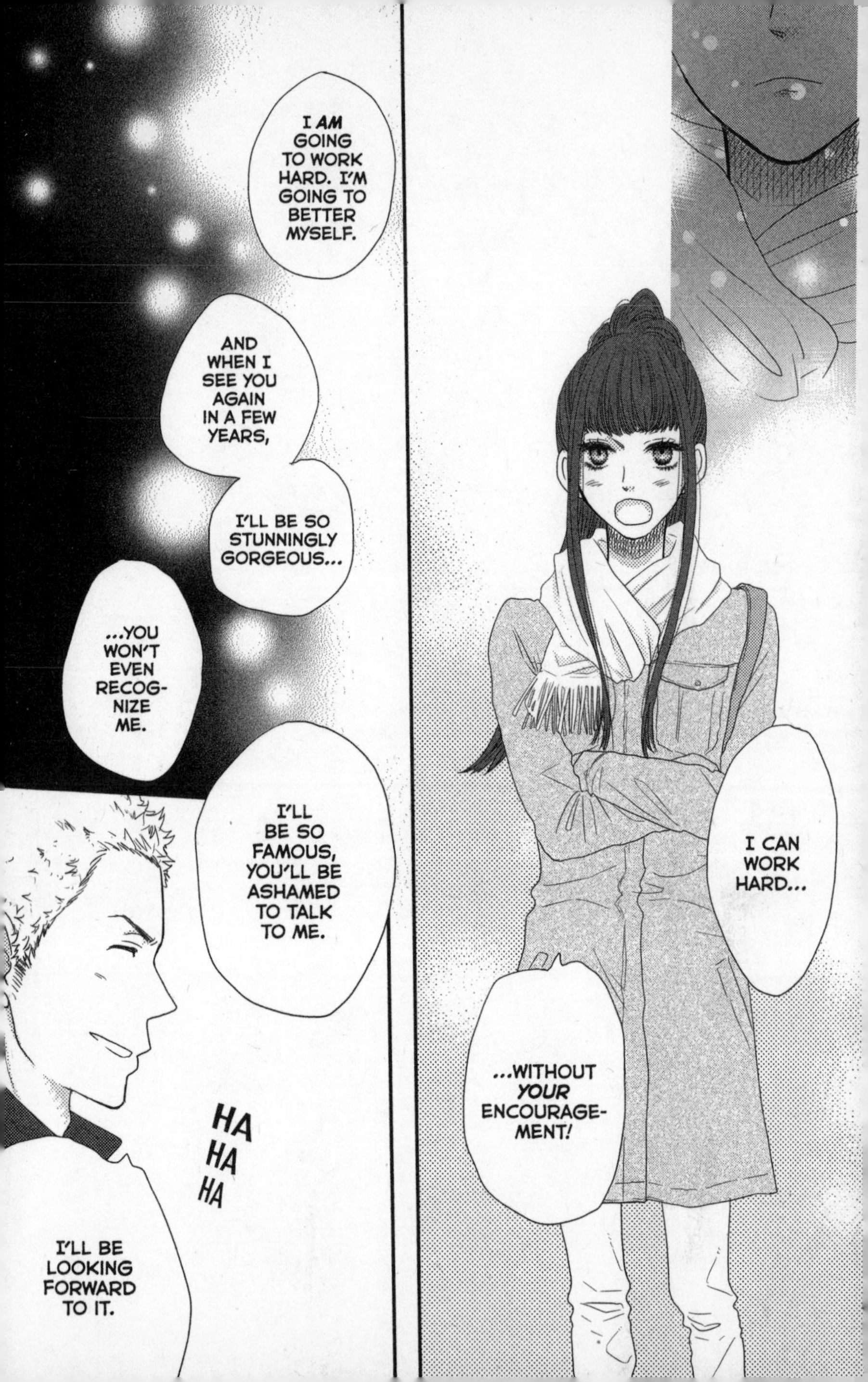
I CAN WORK HARD...
...WITHOUT YOUR ENCOURAGEMENT!
I AM GOING TO WORK HARD. I'M GOING TO BETTER MYSELF.
AND WHEN I SEE YOU AGAIN IN A FEW YEARS,
I'LL BE SO STUNNINGLY GORGEOUS...
...YOU WON'T EVEN RECOGNIZE ME.
I'LL BE SO FAMOUS, YOU'LL BE ASHAMED TO TALK TO ME.
HA HA HA
I'LL BE LOOKING FORWARD TO IT.

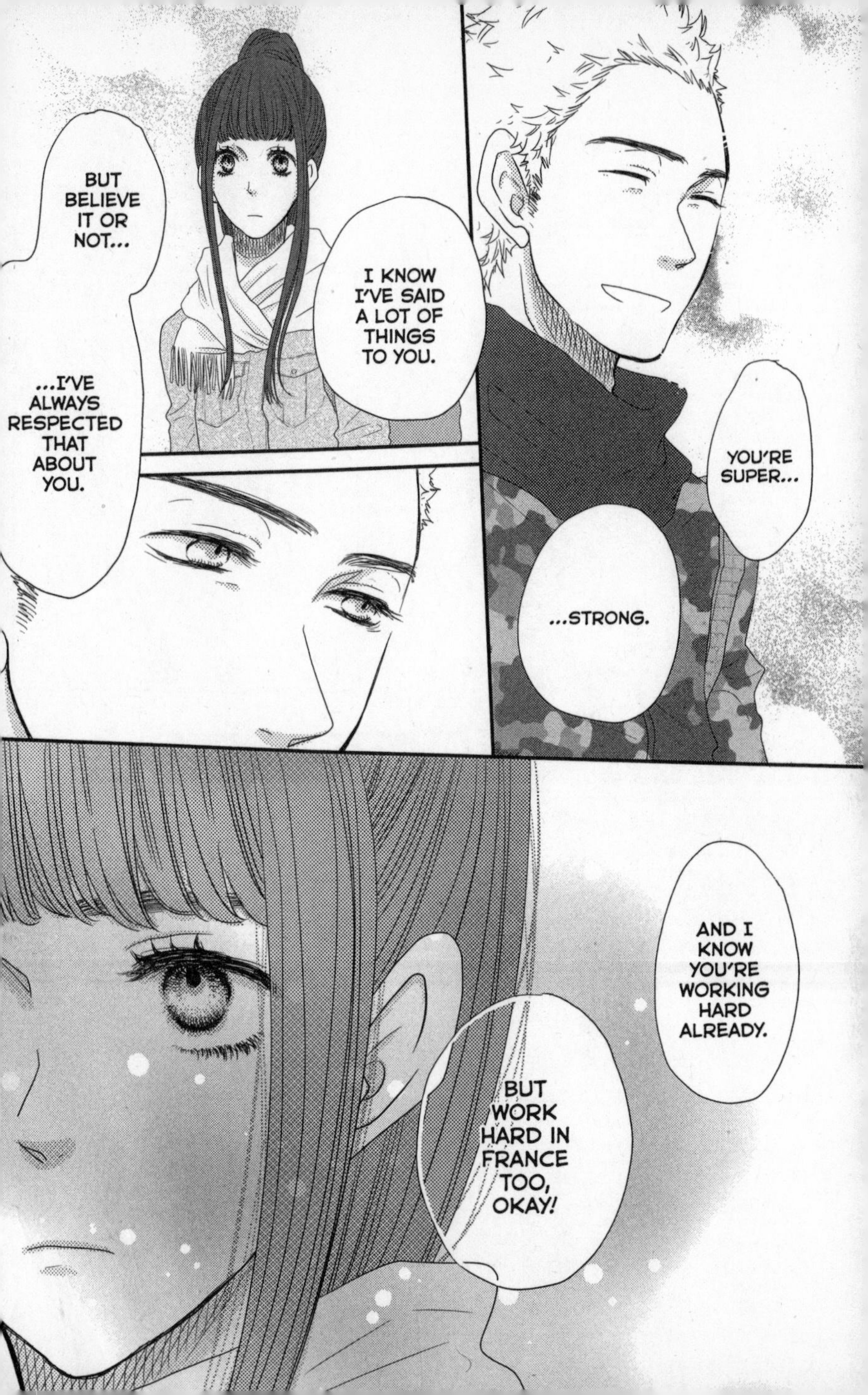
YOU'RE SUPER...
...STRONG.
I KNOW I'VE SAID A LOT OF THINGS TO YOU.
BUT BELIEVE IT OR NOT...
...I'VE ALWAYS RESPECTED THAT ABOUT YOU.
AND I KNOW YOU'RE WORKING HARD ALREADY.
BUT WORK HARD IN FRANCE TOO, OKAY!

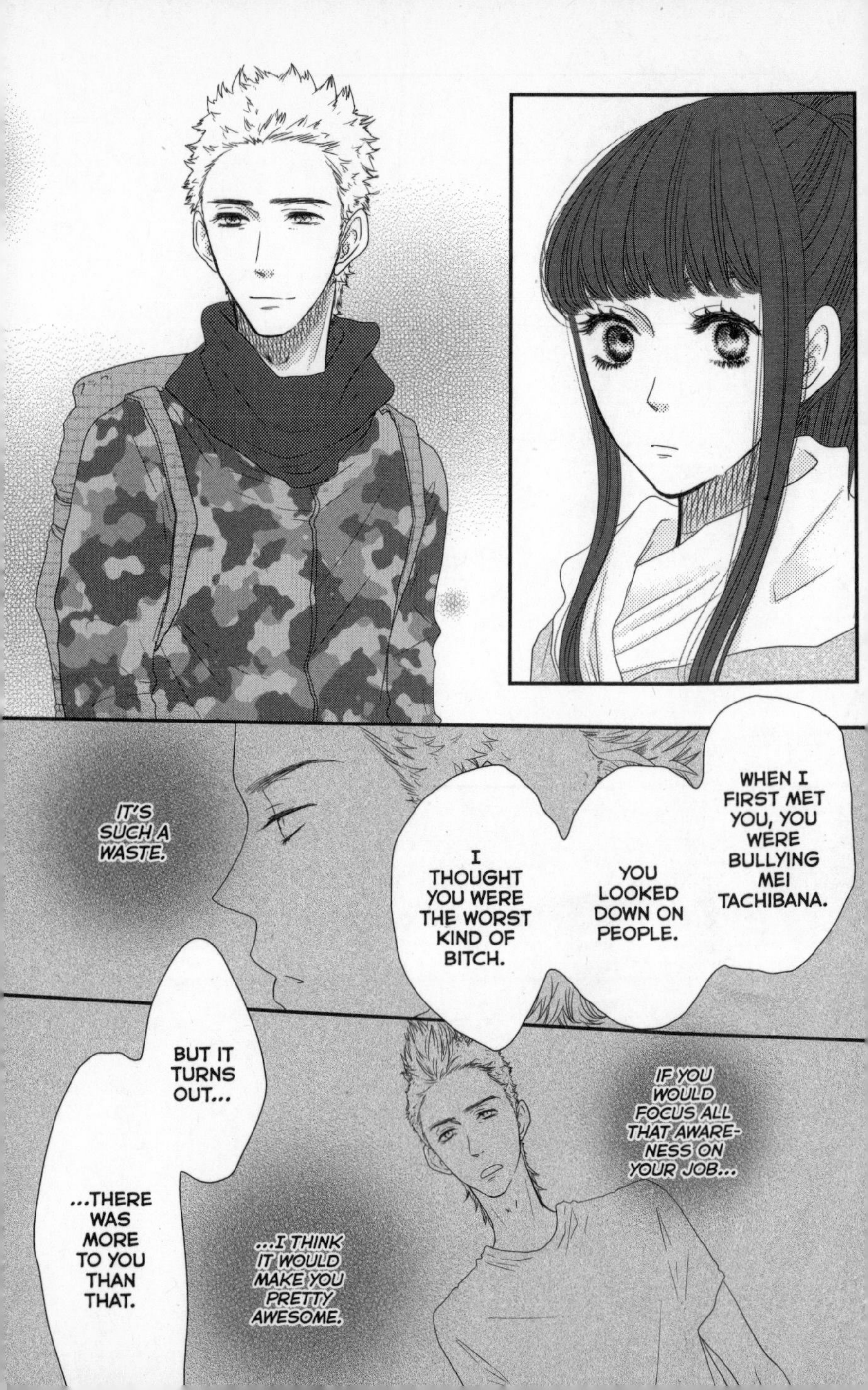
WHEN I FIRST MET YOU, YOU WERE BULLYING MEI TACHIBANA.
YOU LOOKED DOWN ON PEOPLE.
I THOUGHT YOU WERE THE WORST KIND OF BITCH.
BUT IT TURNS OUT...
...THERE WAS MORE TO YOU THAN THAT.
IT'S SUCH A WASTE.
IF YOU WOULD FOCUS ALL THAT AWARE-NESS ON YOUR JOB...
...I THINK IT WOULD MAKE YOU PRETTY AWESOME.

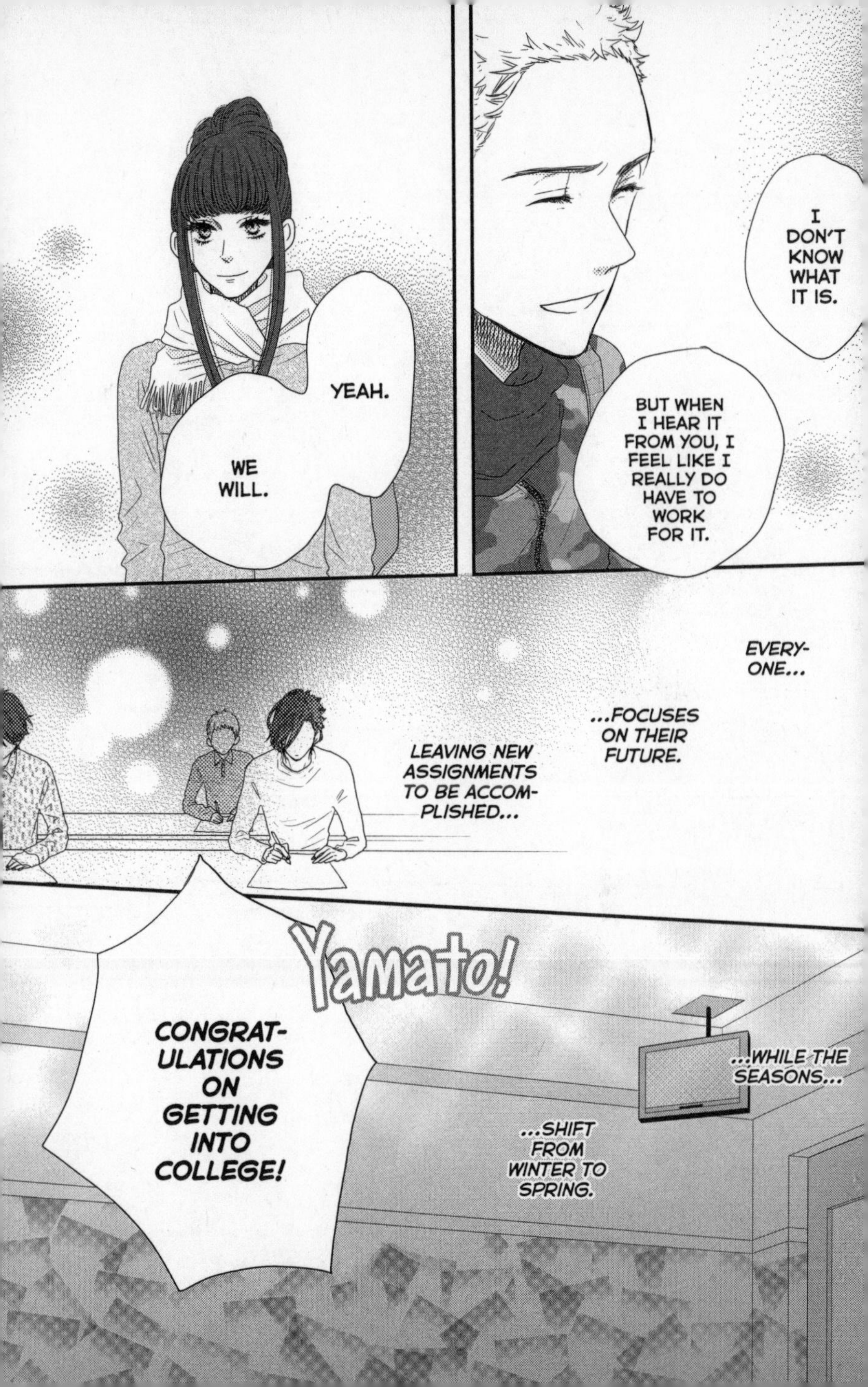

I DON'T KNOW WHAT IT IS.
BUT WHEN I HEAR IT FROM YOU, I FEEL LIKE I REALLY DO HAVE TO WORK FOR IT.
YEAH.
WE WILL.
EVERY-ONE...
...FOCUSES ON THEIR FUTURE.
LEAVING NEW ASSIGNMENTS TO BE ACCOM-PLISHED...
...WHILE THE SEASONS...
...SHIFT FROM WINTER TO SPRING.
Yamato!
CONGRAT-ULATIONS ON GETTING INTO COLLEGE!

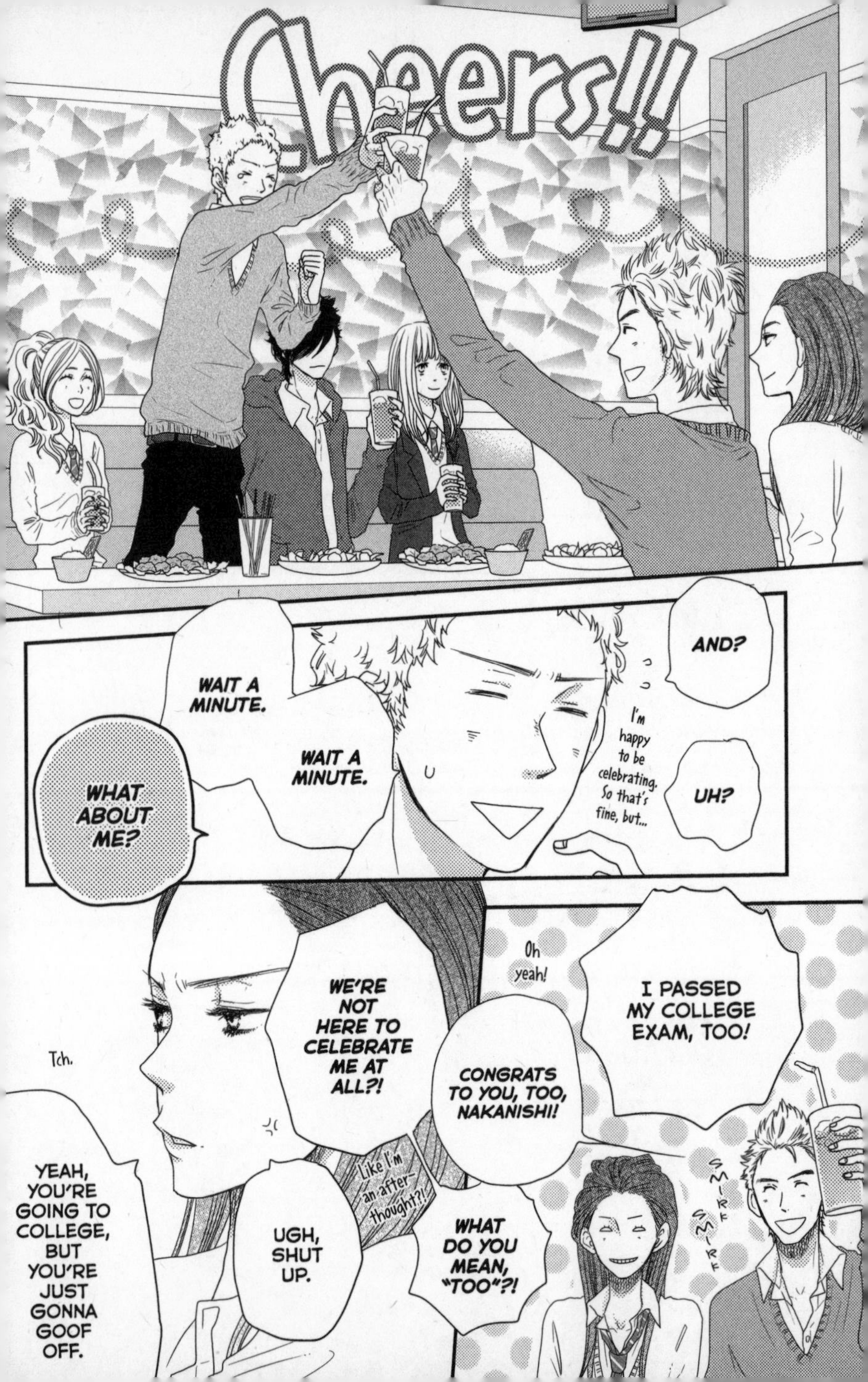
Cheers!!
AND?
UH?
I'm happy to be celebrating. So that's fine, but...
WAIT A MINUTE.
WAIT A MINUTE.
WHAT ABOUT ME?
I PASSED MY COLLEGE EXAM, TOO!
Oh yeah!
CONGRATS TO YOU, TOO, NAKANISHI!
SMIRK SMIRK
WHAT DO YOU MEAN, "TOO"?!
WE'RE NOT HERE TO CELEBRATE ME AT ALL?!
Tch.
Like I'm an after-thought?!
UGH, SHUT UP.
YEAH, YOU'RE GOING TO COLLEGE, BUT YOU'RE JUST GONNA GOOF OFF.

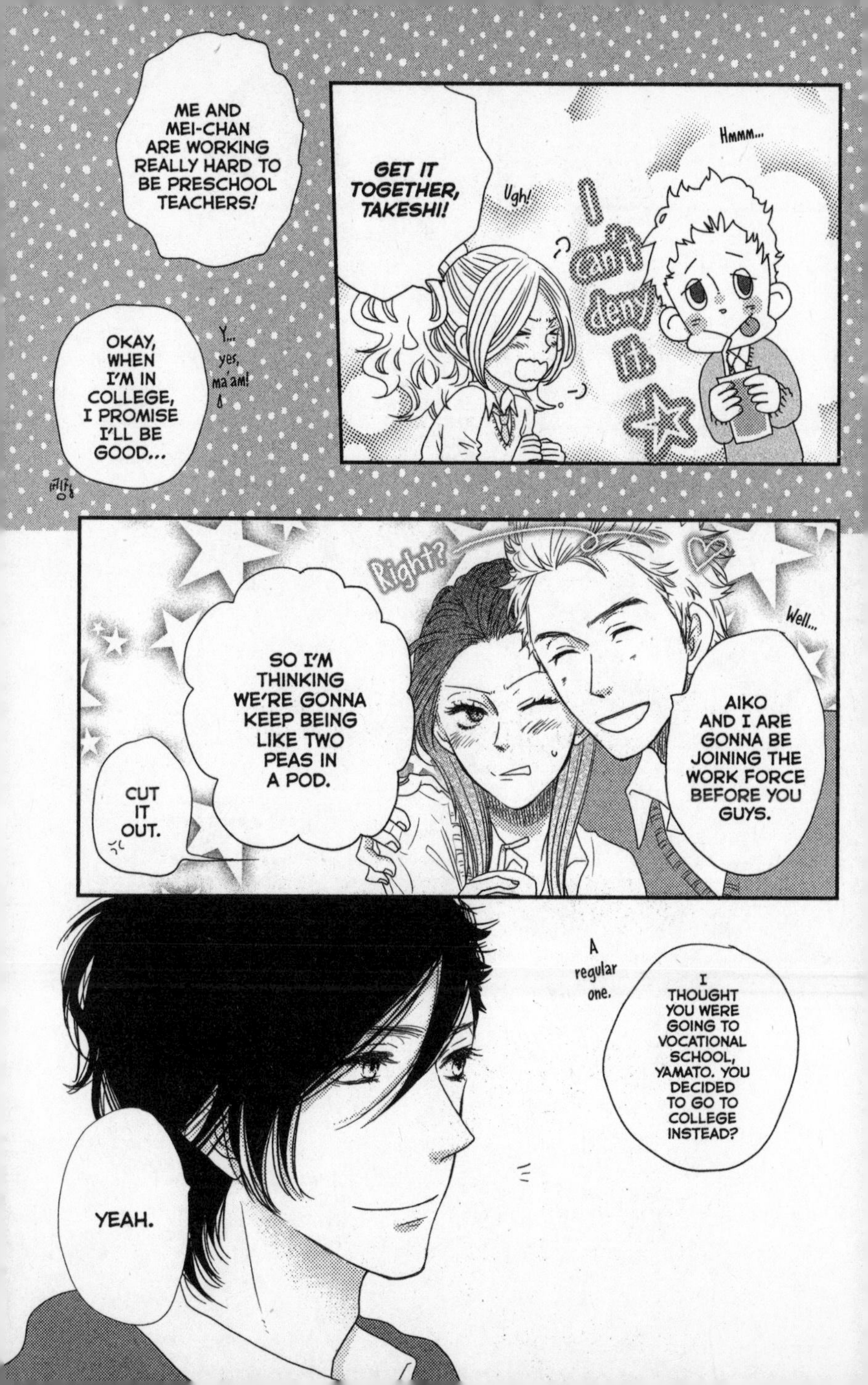
ME AND MEI-CHAN ARE WORKING REALLY HARD TO BE PRESCHOOL TEACHERS!
Hmmm...
GET IT TOGETHER, TAKESHI!
Ugh!
I can't deny it.
Y... yes, ma'am!
OKAY, WHEN I'M IN COLLEGE, I PROMISE I'LL BE GOOD...
Well...
AIKO AND I ARE GONNA BE JOINING THE WORK FORCE BEFORE YOU GUYS.
Right?
SO I'M THINKING WE'RE GONNA KEEP BEING LIKE TWO PEAS IN A POD.
CUT IT OUT.
I THOUGHT YOU WERE GOING TO VOCATIONAL SCHOOL, YAMATO. YOU DECIDED TO GO TO COLLEGE INSTEAD?
A regular one.
YEAH.

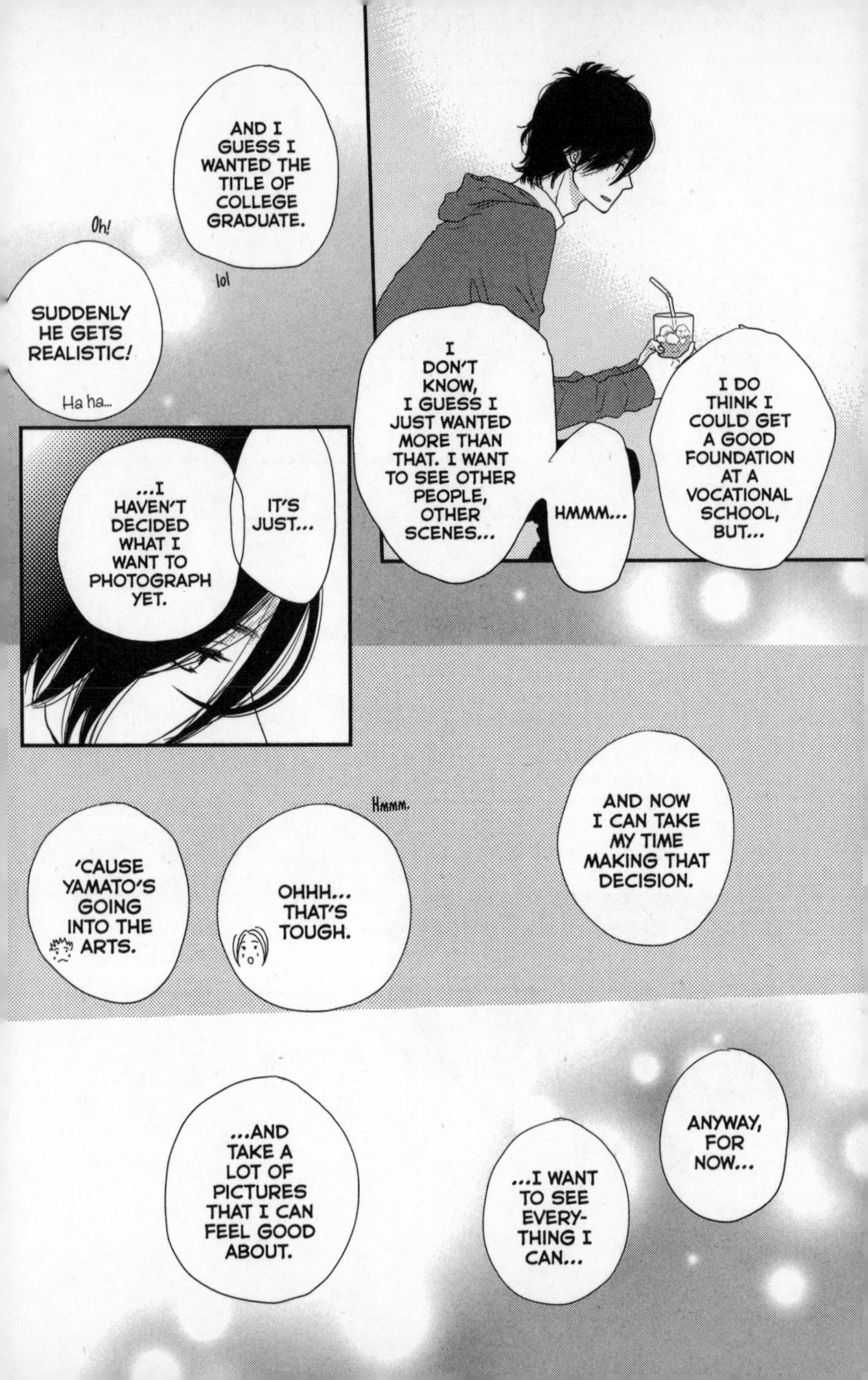
I DO THINK I COULD GET A GOOD FOUNDATION AT A VOCATIONAL SCHOOL, BUT...
HMMM...
I DON'T KNOW, I GUESS I JUST WANTED MORE THAN THAT. I WANT TO SEE OTHER PEOPLE, OTHER SCENES...
AND I GUESS I WANTED THE TITLE OF COLLEGE GRADUATE.
lol
Oh!
SUDDENLY HE GETS REALISTIC!
Ha ha...
IT'S JUST...
...I HAVEN'T DECIDED WHAT I WANT TO PHOTOGRAPH YET.
AND NOW I CAN TAKE MY TIME MAKING THAT DECISION.
Hmmm.
OHHH... THAT'S TOUGH.
'CAUSE YAMATO'S GOING INTO THE ARTS.
ANYWAY, FOR NOW...
...I WANT TO SEE EVERY-THING I CAN...
...AND TAKE A LOT OF PICTURES THAT I CAN FEEL GOOD ABOUT.

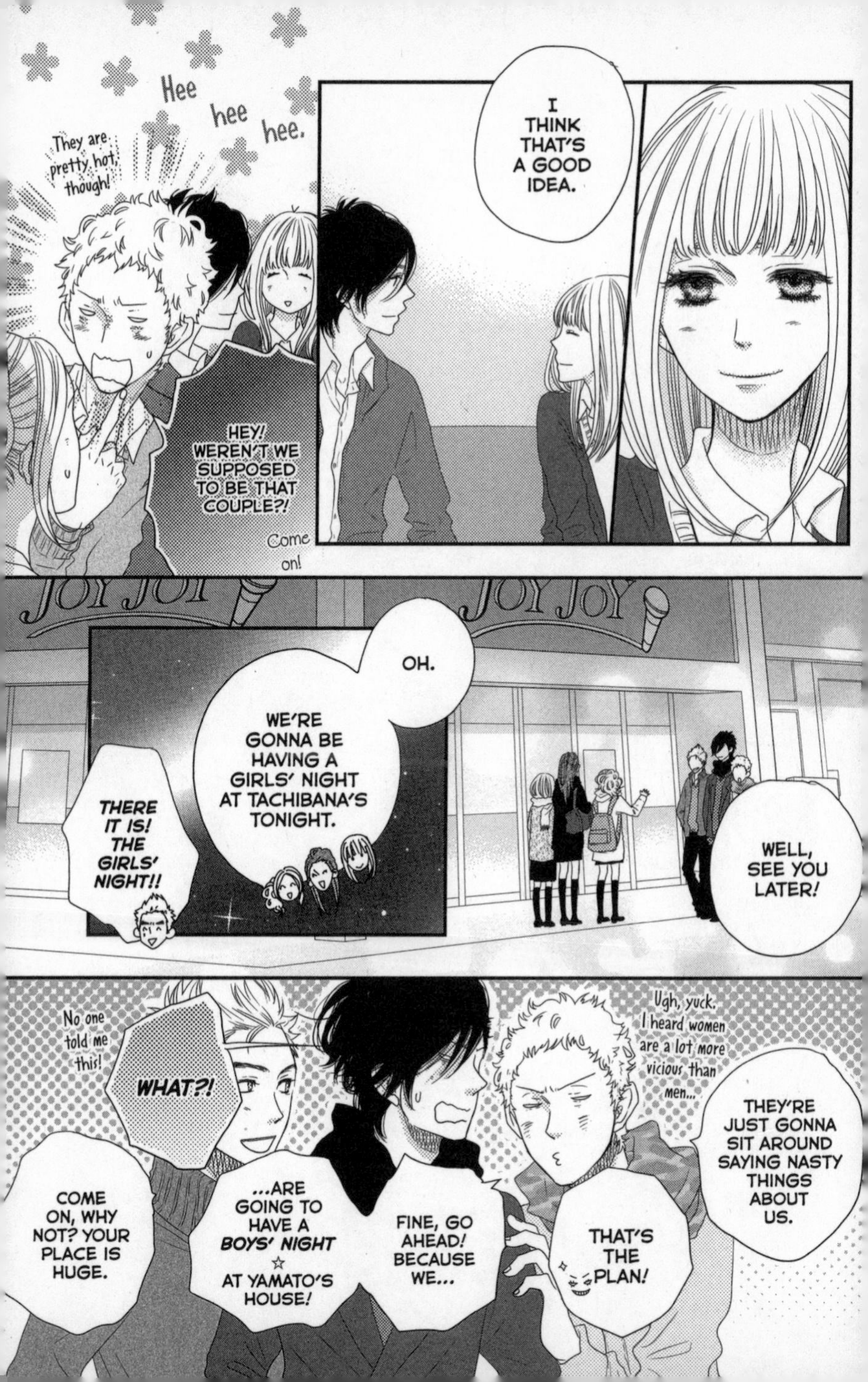
I THINK THAT'S A GOOD IDEA.
Hee hee hee.
They are pretty hot, though!
HEY! WEREN'T WE SUPPOSED TO BE THAT COUPLE?!
Come on!
JOY JOY
JOY JOY
WELL, SEE YOU LATER!
OH.
WE'RE GONNA BE HAVING A GIRLS' NIGHT AT TACHIBANA'S TONIGHT.
THERE IT IS! THE GIRLS' NIGHT!!
THEY'RE JUST GONNA SIT AROUND SAYING NASTY THINGS ABOUT US.
Ugh, yuck. I heard women are a lot more vicious than men...
THAT'S THE PLAN!
FINE, GO AHEAD! BECAUSE WE...
...ARE GOING TO HAVE A BOYS' NIGHT ☆ AT YAMATO'S HOUSE!
WHAT?!
No one told me this!
COME ON, WHY NOT? YOUR PLACE IS HUGE.

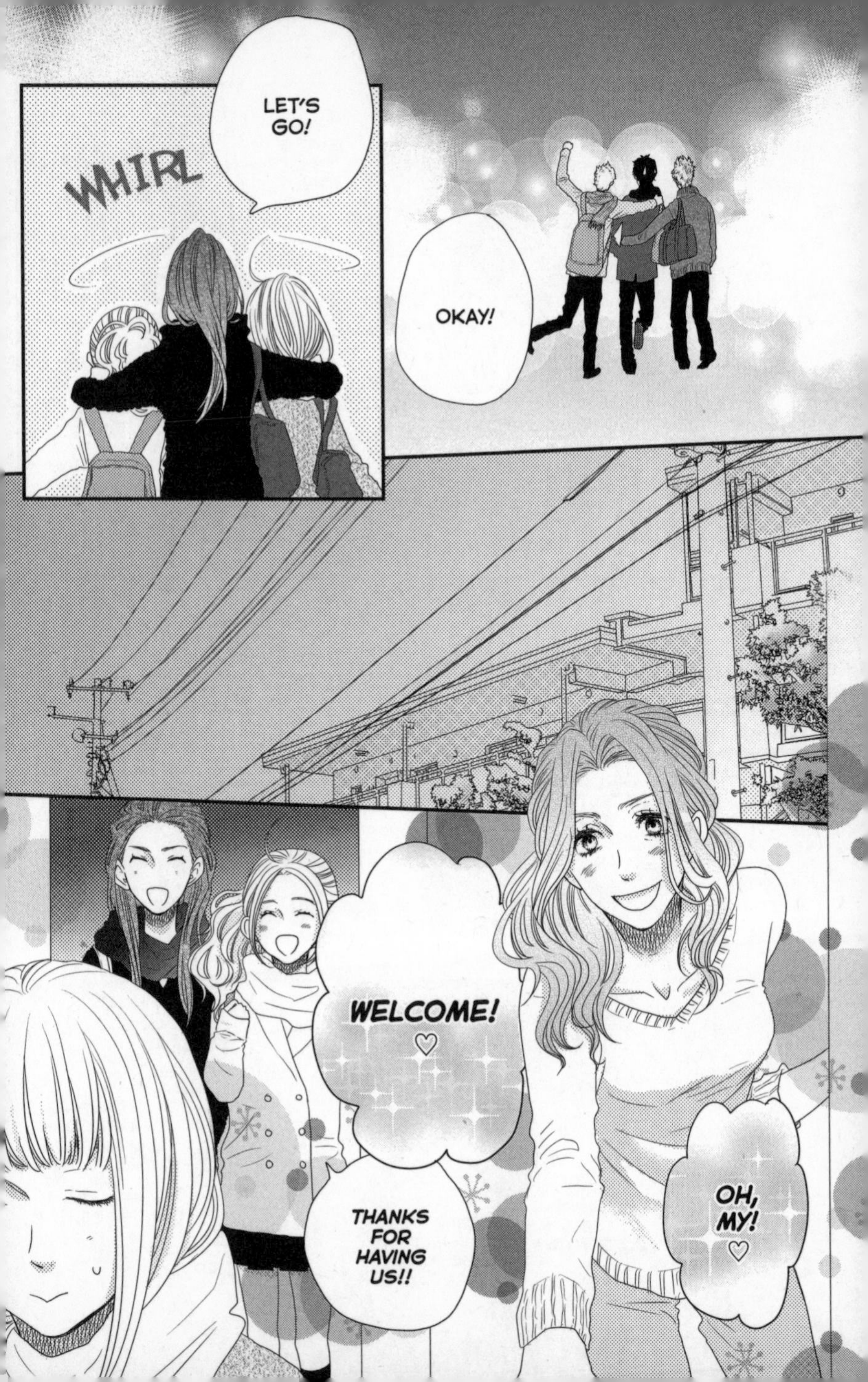
LET'S GO!
OKAY!
WHIRL
WELCOME! ♡
OH, MY! ♡
THANKS FOR HAVING US!!

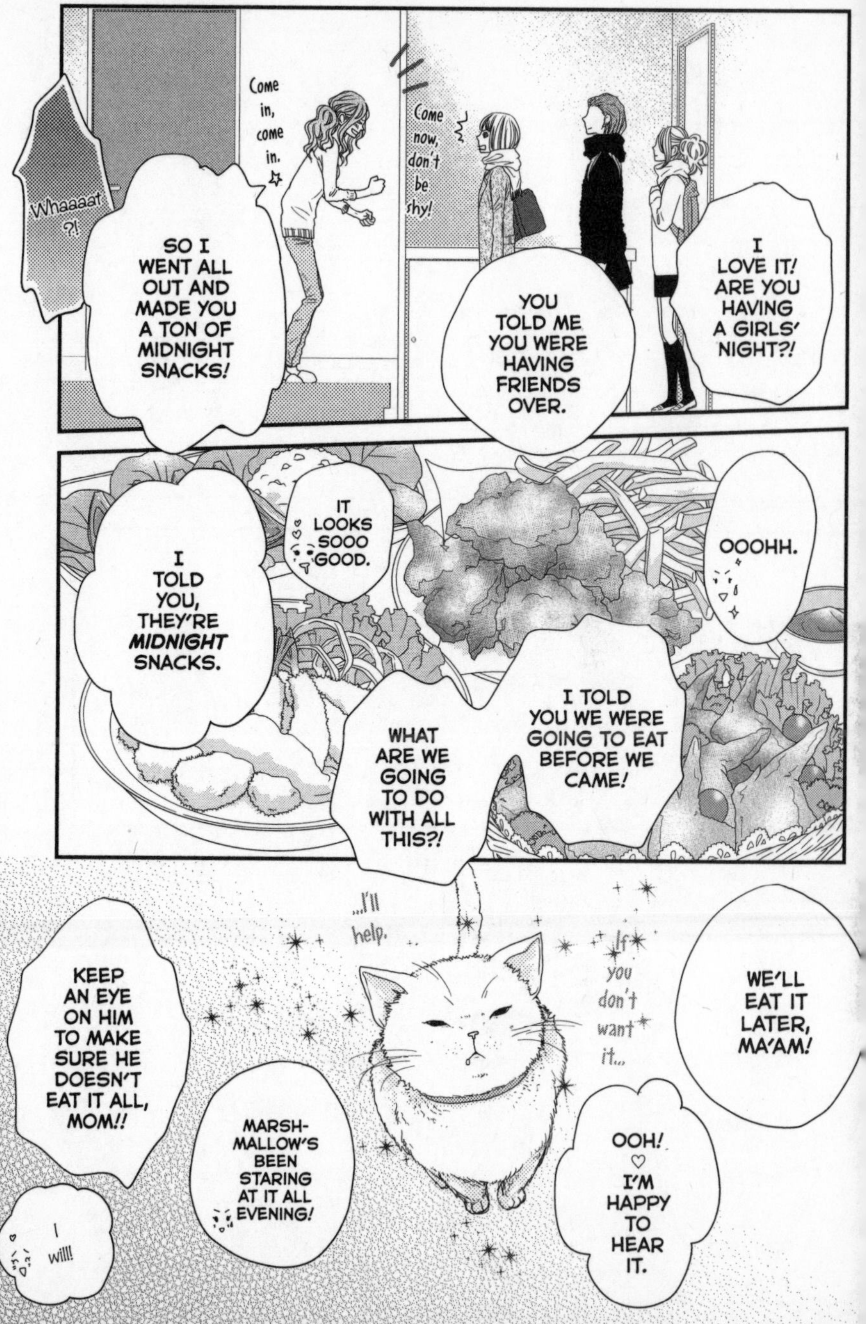
I LOVE IT! ARE YOU HAVING A GIRLS' NIGHT?!
YOU TOLD ME YOU WERE HAVING FRIENDS OVER.
Come now, don't be shy!
Come in, come in.
SO I WENT ALL OUT AND MADE YOU A TON OF MIDNIGHT SNACKS!
Whaaaat?!
OOOHH.
I TOLD YOU WE WERE GOING TO EAT BEFORE WE CAME!
WHAT ARE WE GOING TO DO WITH ALL THIS?!
IT LOOKS SOOO GOOD.
I TOLD YOU, THEY'RE *MIDNIGHT* SNACKS.
WE'LL EAT IT LATER, MA'AM!
If you don't want it...
...I'll help.
OOH! ♡ I'M HAPPY TO HEAR IT.
KEEP AN EYE ON HIM TO MAKE SURE HE DOESN'T EAT IT ALL, MOM!!
MARSH-MALLOW'S BEEN STARING AT IT ALL EVENING!
I will!

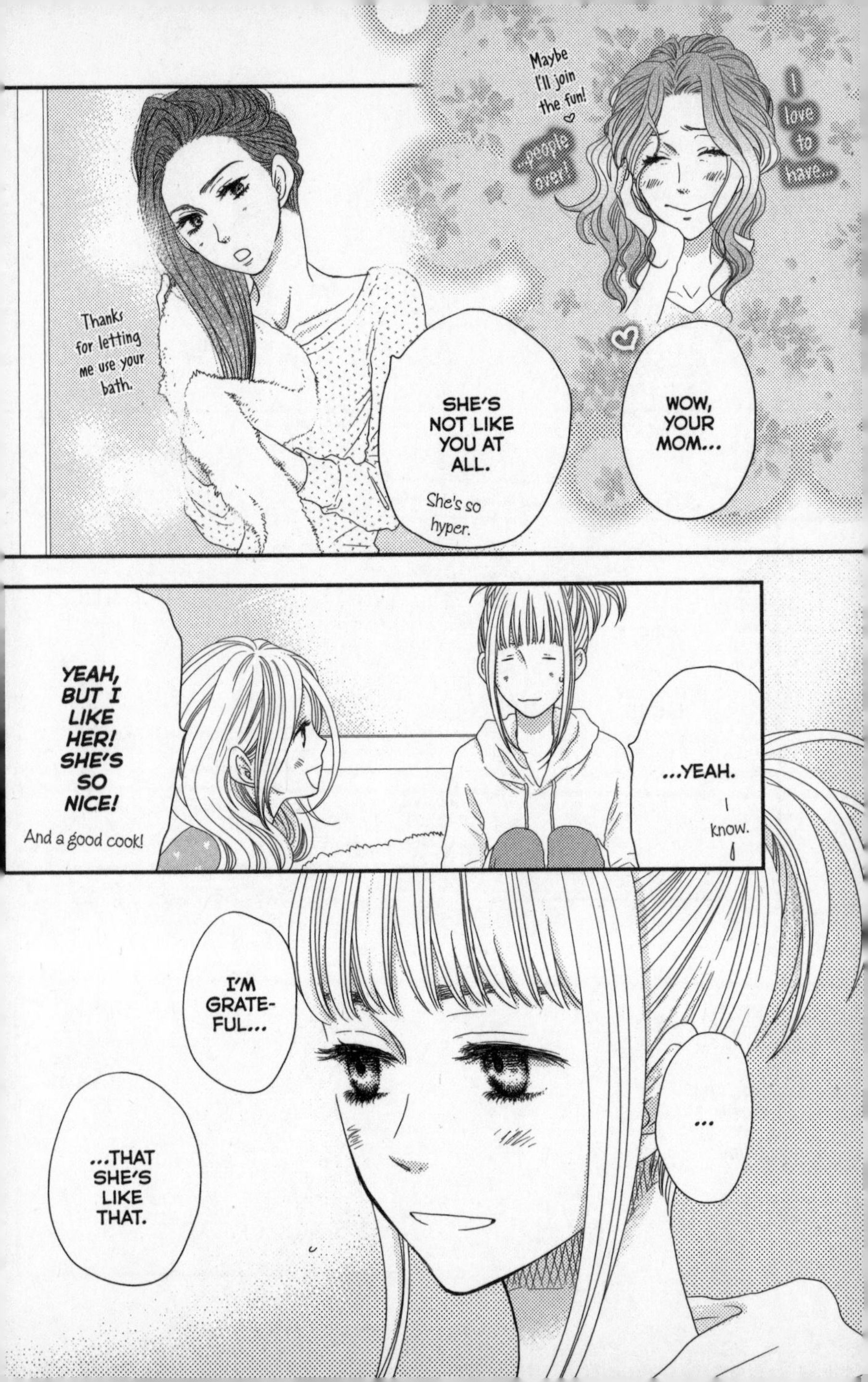
I love to have...
...people over!
Maybe I'll join the fun!
WOW, YOUR MOM...
SHE'S NOT LIKE YOU AT ALL.
She's so hyper.
Thanks for letting me use your bath.
...YEAH.
I know.
YEAH, BUT I LIKE HER! SHE'S SO NICE!
And a good cook!
...
I'M GRATE-FUL...
...THAT SHE'S LIKE THAT.

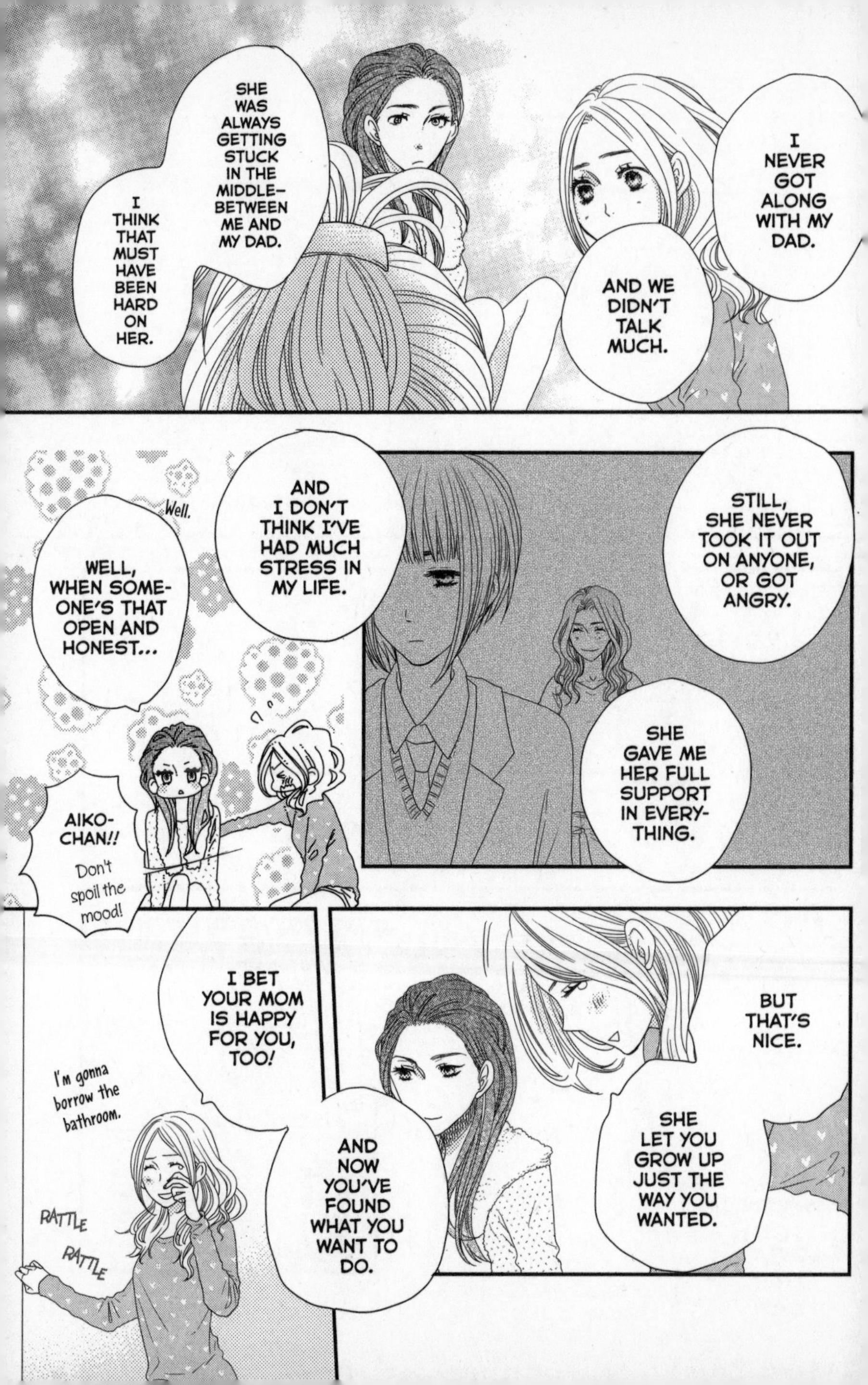
I NEVER GOT ALONG WITH MY DAD.
AND WE DIDN'T TALK MUCH.
SHE WAS ALWAYS GETTING STUCK IN THE MIDDLE—BETWEEN ME AND MY DAD.
I THINK THAT MUST HAVE BEEN HARD ON HER.
STILL, SHE NEVER TOOK IT OUT ON ANYONE, OR GOT ANGRY.
SHE GAVE ME HER FULL SUPPORT IN EVERYTHING.
AND I DON'T THINK I'VE HAD MUCH STRESS IN MY LIFE.
Well.
WELL, WHEN SOMEONE'S THAT OPEN AND HONEST...
AIKO-CHAN!!
Don't spoil the mood!
BUT THAT'S NICE.
SHE LET YOU GROW UP JUST THE WAY YOU WANTED.
AND NOW YOU'VE FOUND WHAT YOU WANT TO DO.
I BET YOUR MOM IS HAPPY FOR YOU, TOO!
I'm gonna borrow the bathroom.
RATTLE
RATTLE

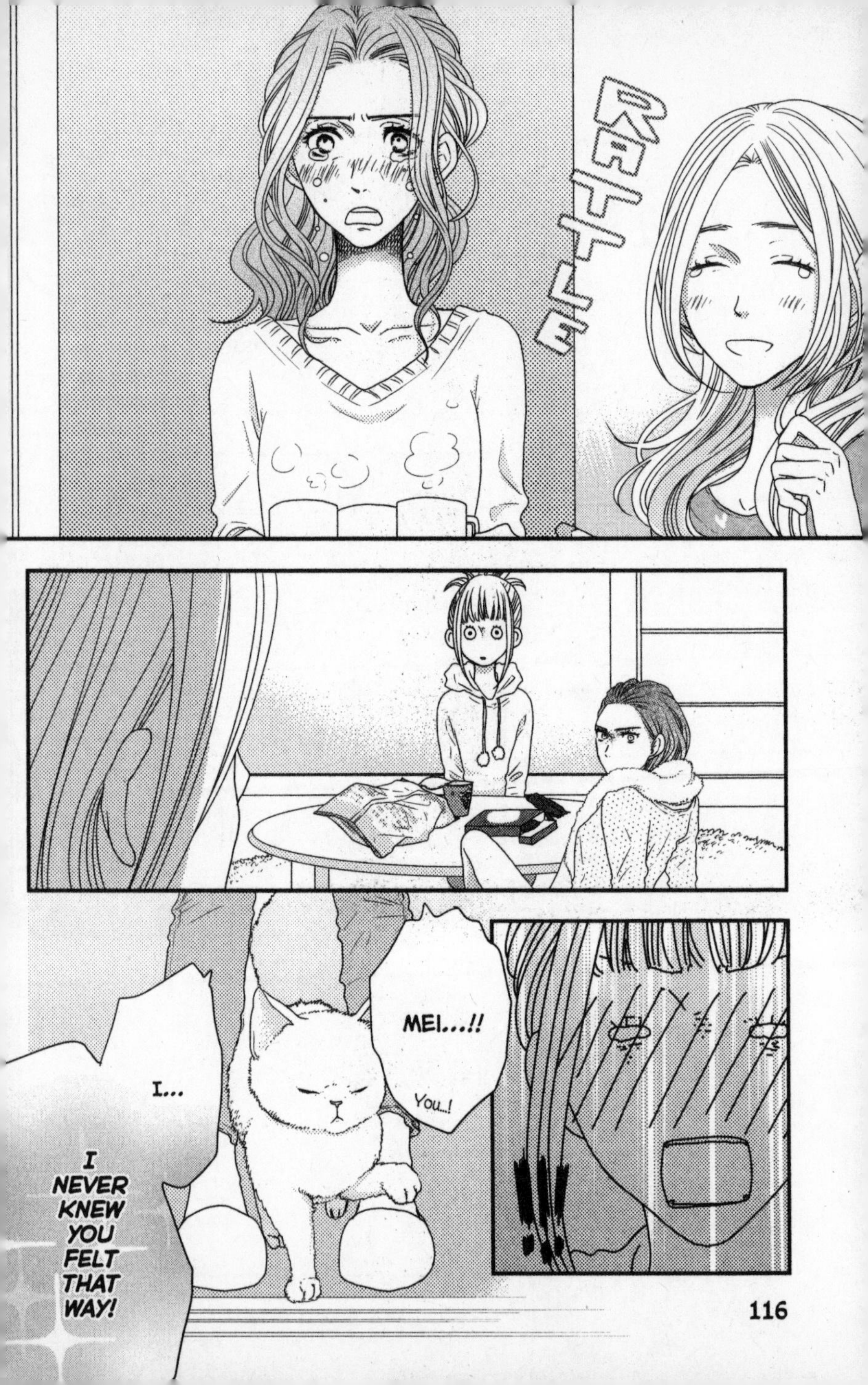
RATTLE
MEI...!!
You..!
I...
I NEVER KNEW YOU FELT THAT WAY!

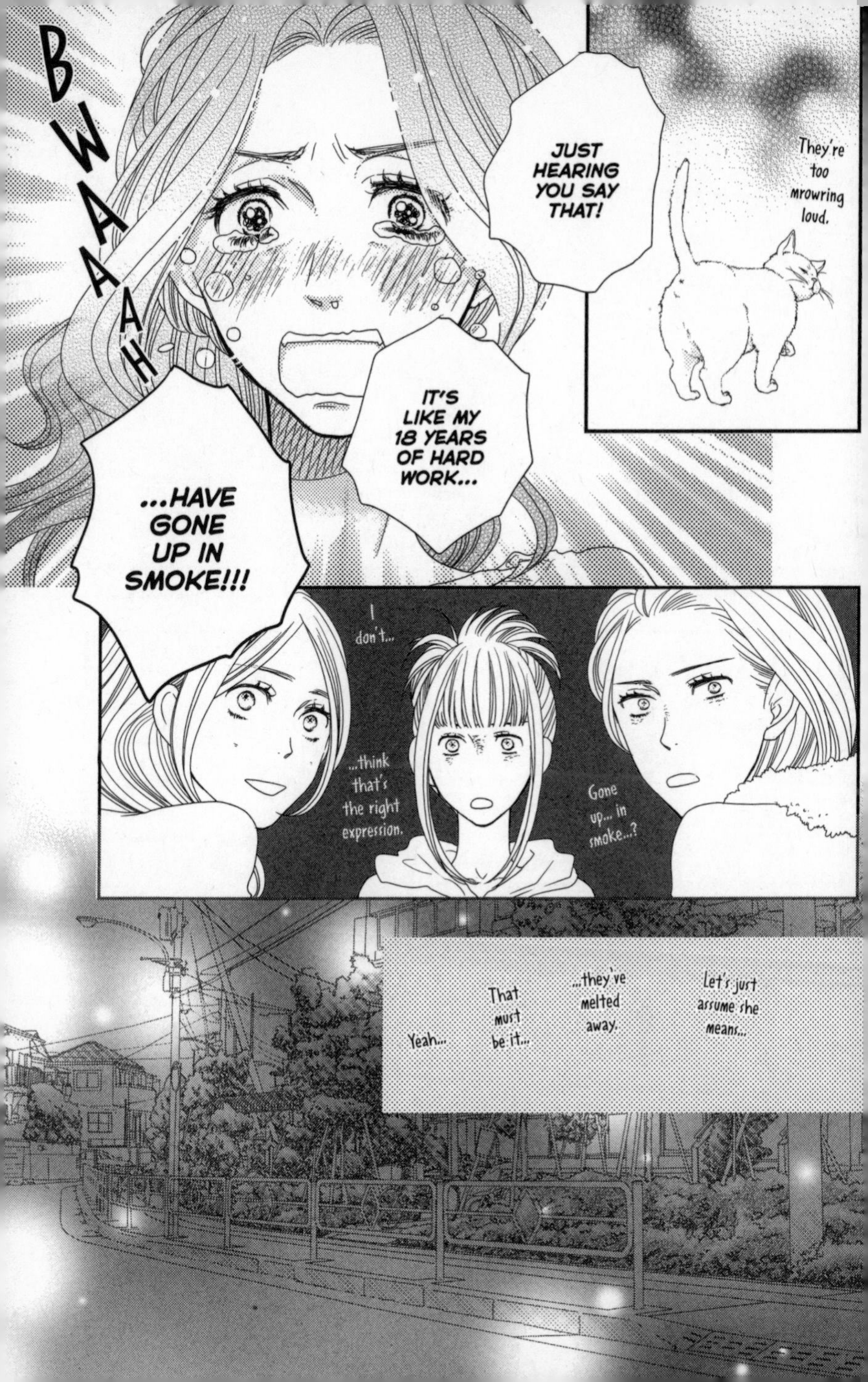
They're too mrowring loud.
JUST HEARING YOU SAY THAT!
BWAAAAH
IT'S LIKE MY 18 YEARS OF HARD WORK...
...HAVE GONE UP IN SMOKE!!!
Gone up... in smoke...?
I don't...
...think that's the right expression.
Let's just assume she means...
...they've melted away.
That must be it...
Yeah...

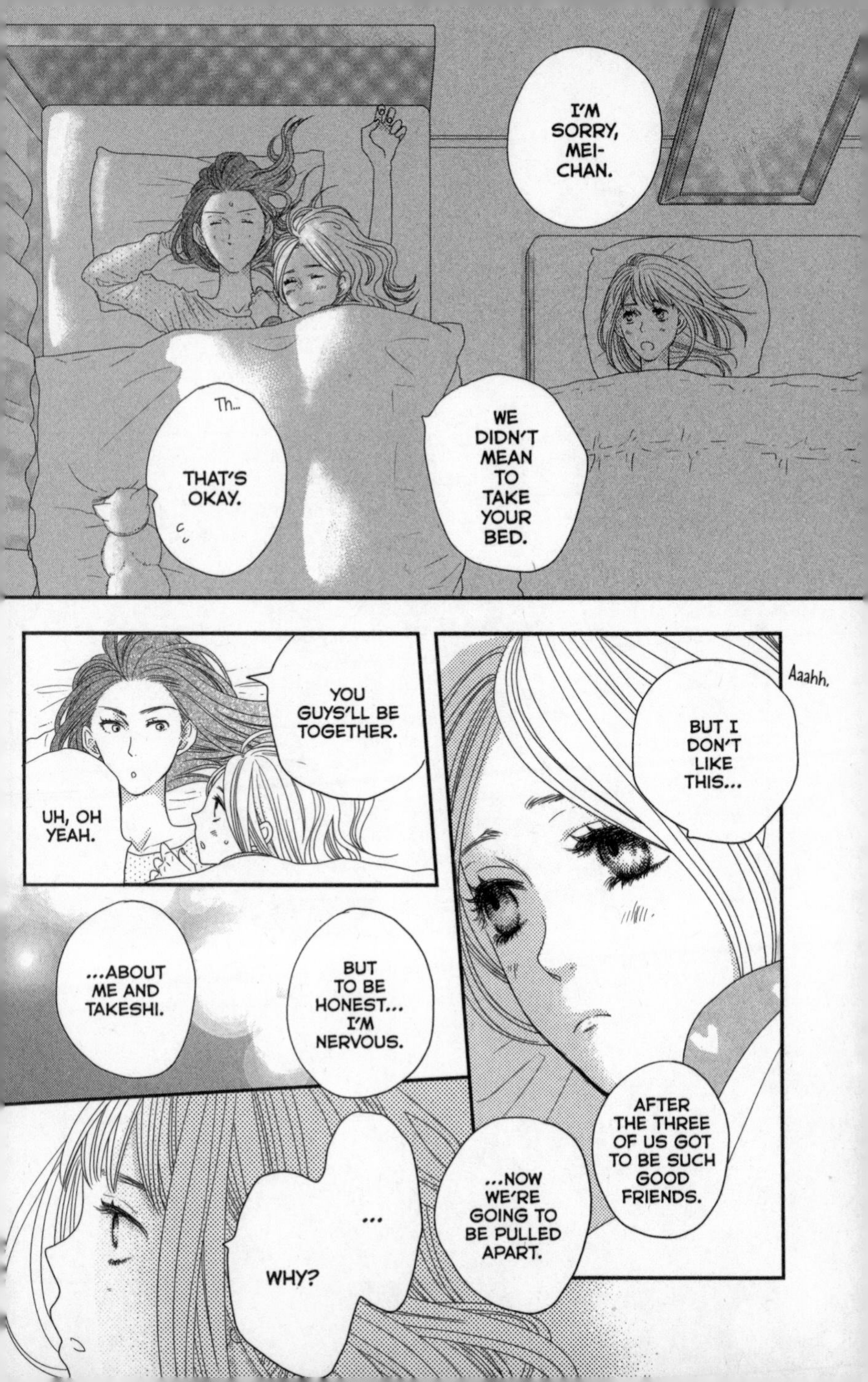
I'M SORRY, MEI-CHAN.
WE DIDN'T MEAN TO TAKE YOUR BED.
Th...
THAT'S OKAY.
Aaahh.
BUT I DON'T LIKE THIS...
AFTER THE THREE OF US GOT TO BE SUCH GOOD FRIENDS.
...NOW WE'RE GOING TO BE PULLED APART.
YOU GUYS'LL BE TOGETHER.
UH, OH YEAH.
BUT TO BE HONEST... I'M NERVOUS.
...ABOUT ME AND TAKESHI.
...
WHY?

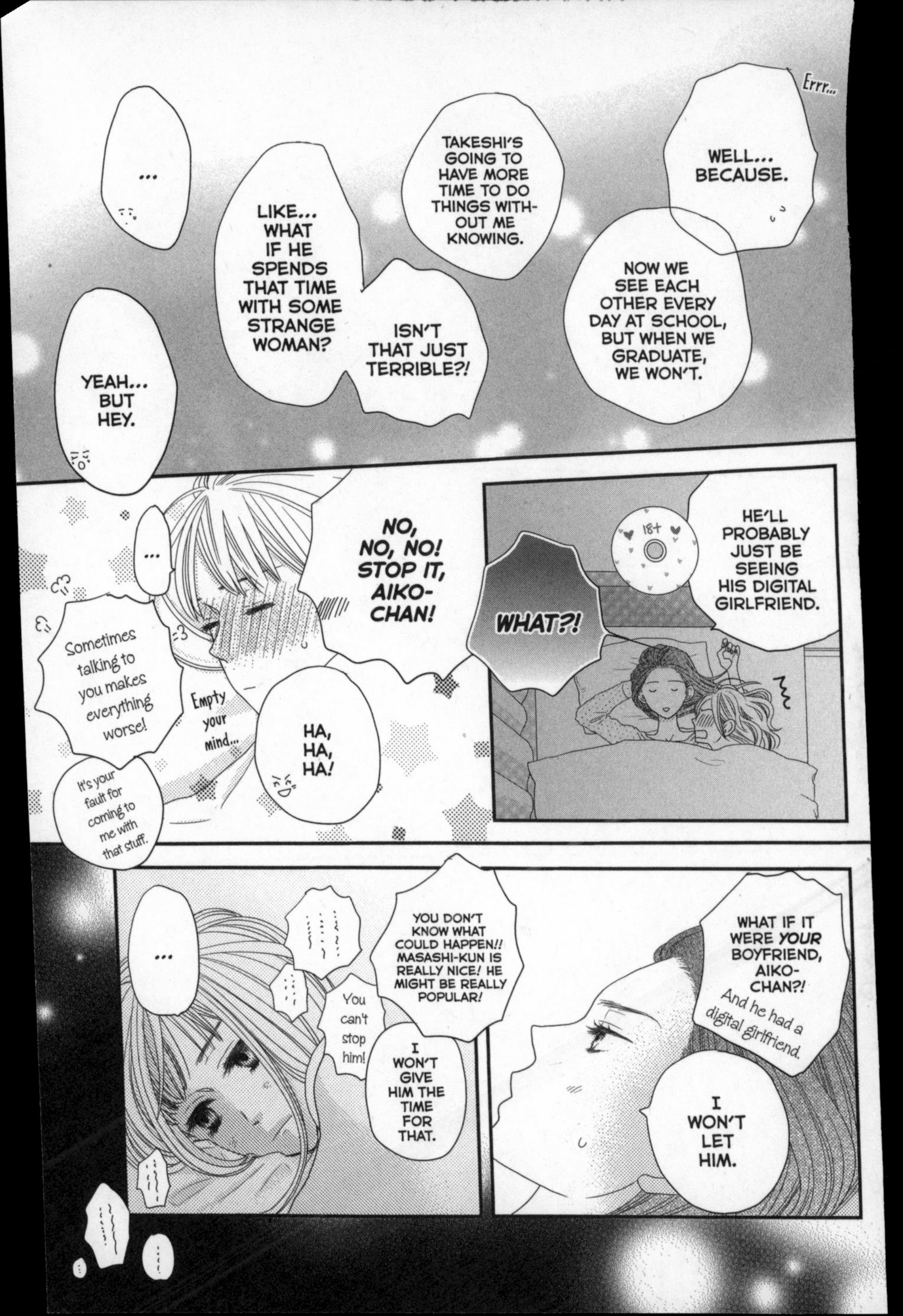
Errr...
WELL... BECAUSE.
NOW WE SEE EACH OTHER EVERY DAY AT SCHOOL, BUT WHEN WE GRADUATE, WE WON'T.
TAKESHI'S GOING TO HAVE MORE TIME TO DO THINGS WITH-OUT ME KNOWING.
LIKE... WHAT IF HE SPENDS THAT TIME WITH SOME STRANGE WOMAN?
ISN'T THAT JUST TERRIBLE?!
...
YEAH... BUT HEY.
HE'LL PROBABLY JUST BE SEEING HIS DIGITAL GIRLFRIEND.
18+
WHAT?!
NO, NO, NO! STOP IT, AIKO-CHAN!
...
HA, HA, HA!
Empty your mind...
Sometimes talking to you makes everything worse!
It's your fault for coming to me with that stuff.
WHAT IF IT WERE YOUR BOYFRIEND, AIKO-CHAN?!
And he had a digital girlfriend.
I WON'T LET HIM.
YOU DON'T KNOW WHAT COULD HAPPEN!! MASASHI-KUN IS REALLY NICE! HE MIGHT BE REALLY POPULAR!
I WON'T GIVE HIM THE TIME FOR THAT.
You can't stop him!
...

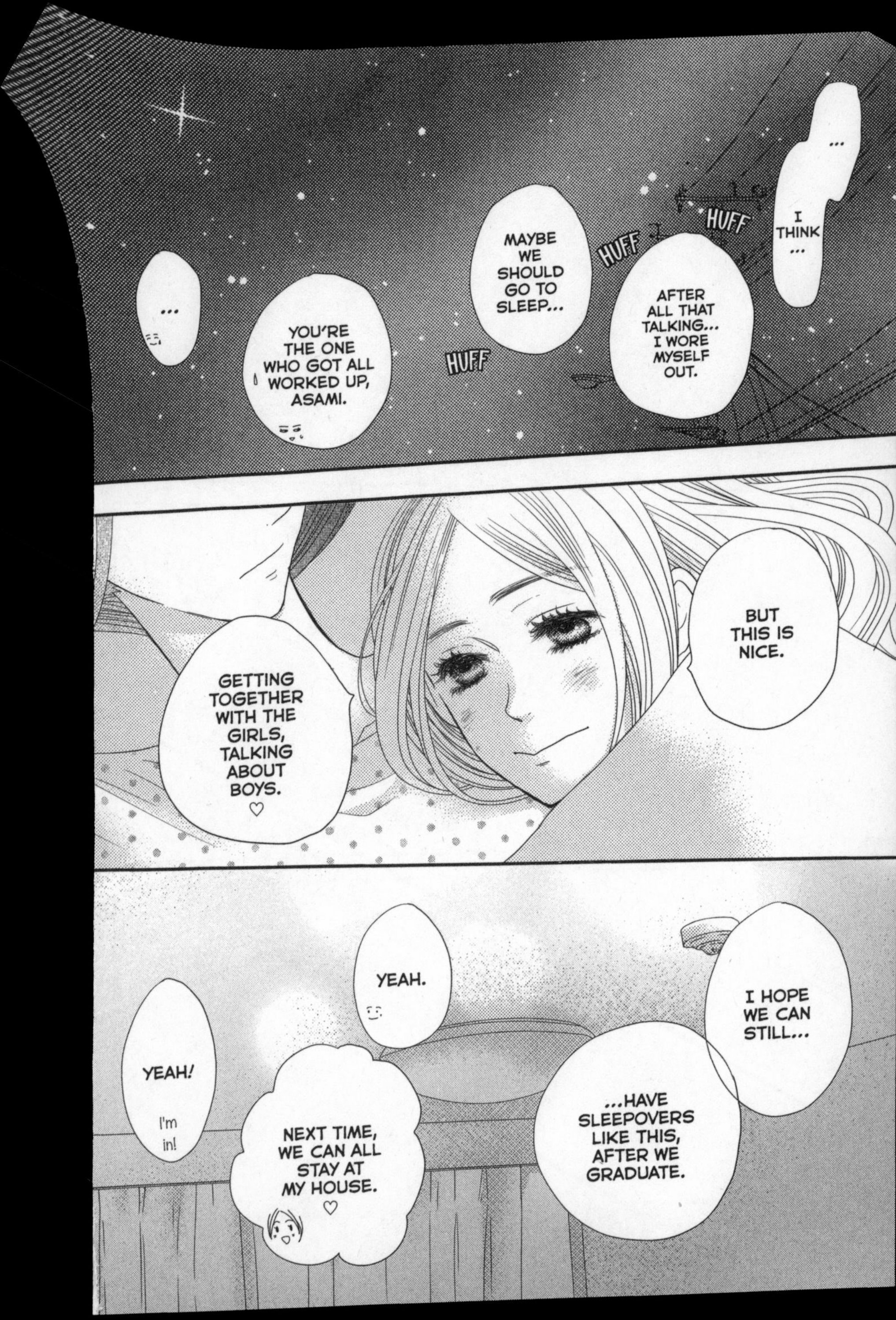
...
I THINK...
HUFF
AFTER ALL THAT TALKING... I WORE MYSELF OUT.
HUFF
MAYBE WE SHOULD GO TO SLEEP...
HUFF
YOU'RE THE ONE WHO GOT ALL WORKED UP, ASAMI.
...
BUT THIS IS NICE.
GETTING TOGETHER WITH THE GIRLS, TALKING ABOUT BOYS. ♡
I HOPE WE CAN STILL...
...HAVE SLEEPOVERS LIKE THIS, AFTER WE GRADUATE.
YEAH.
NEXT TIME, WE CAN ALL STAY AT MY HOUSE. ♡
YEAH!
I'm in!

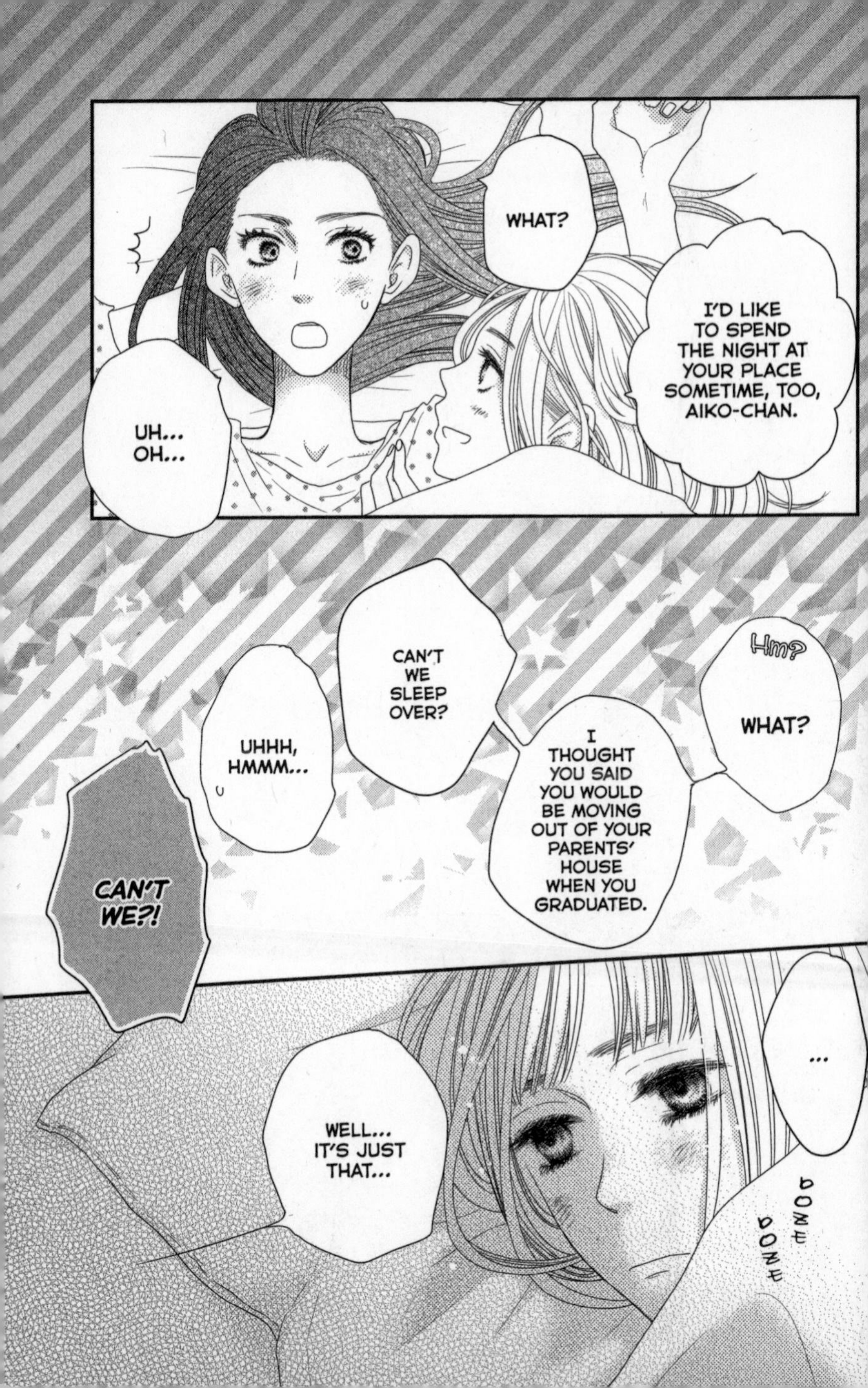
I'D LIKE TO SPEND THE NIGHT AT YOUR PLACE SOMETIME, TOO, AIKO-CHAN.
WHAT?
UH... OH...
Hm?
WHAT?
I THOUGHT YOU SAID YOU WOULD BE MOVING OUT OF YOUR PARENTS' HOUSE WHEN YOU GRADUATED.
CAN'T WE SLEEP OVER?
UHHH, HMMM...
CAN'T WE?!
...
DONG
DONG
WELL... IT'S JUST THAT...

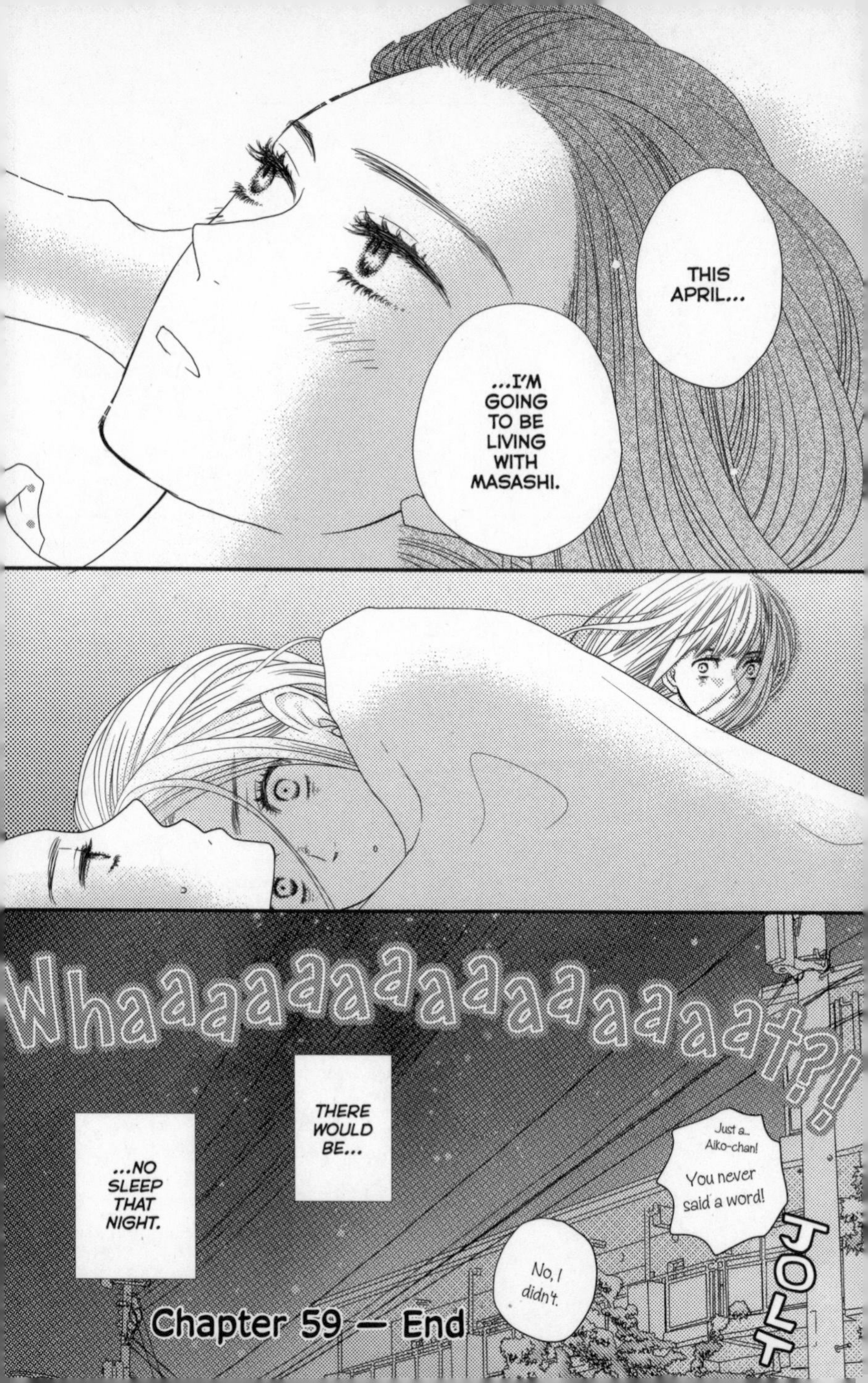
THIS APRIL...
...I'M GOING TO BE LIVING WITH MASASHI.
Whaaaaaaaaaaaaaaat?!
JOLT
Just a... Aiko-chan!
You never said a word!
No, I didn't.
THERE WOULD BE...
...NO SLEEP THAT NIGHT.
Chapter 59 — End

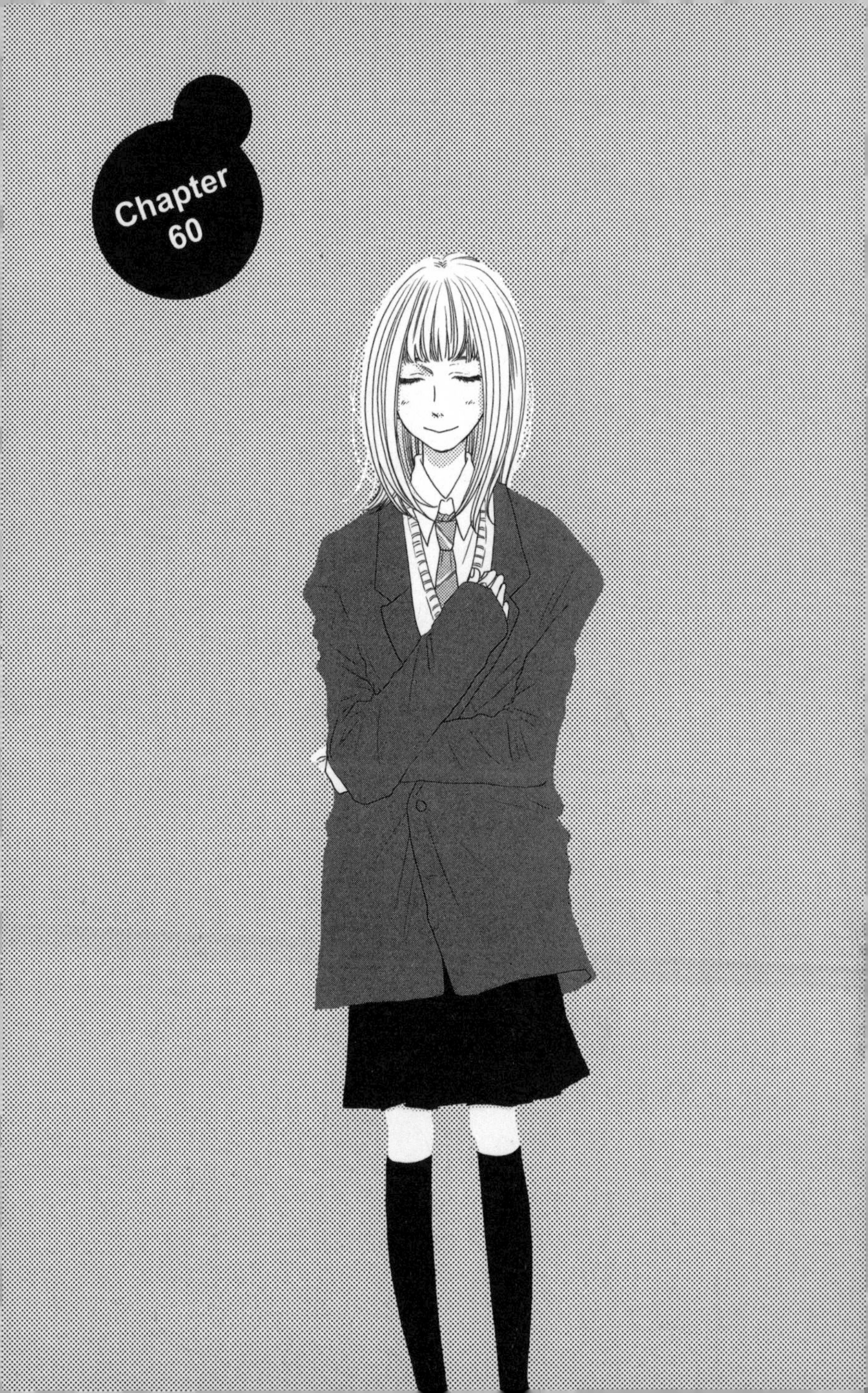
Chapter
60

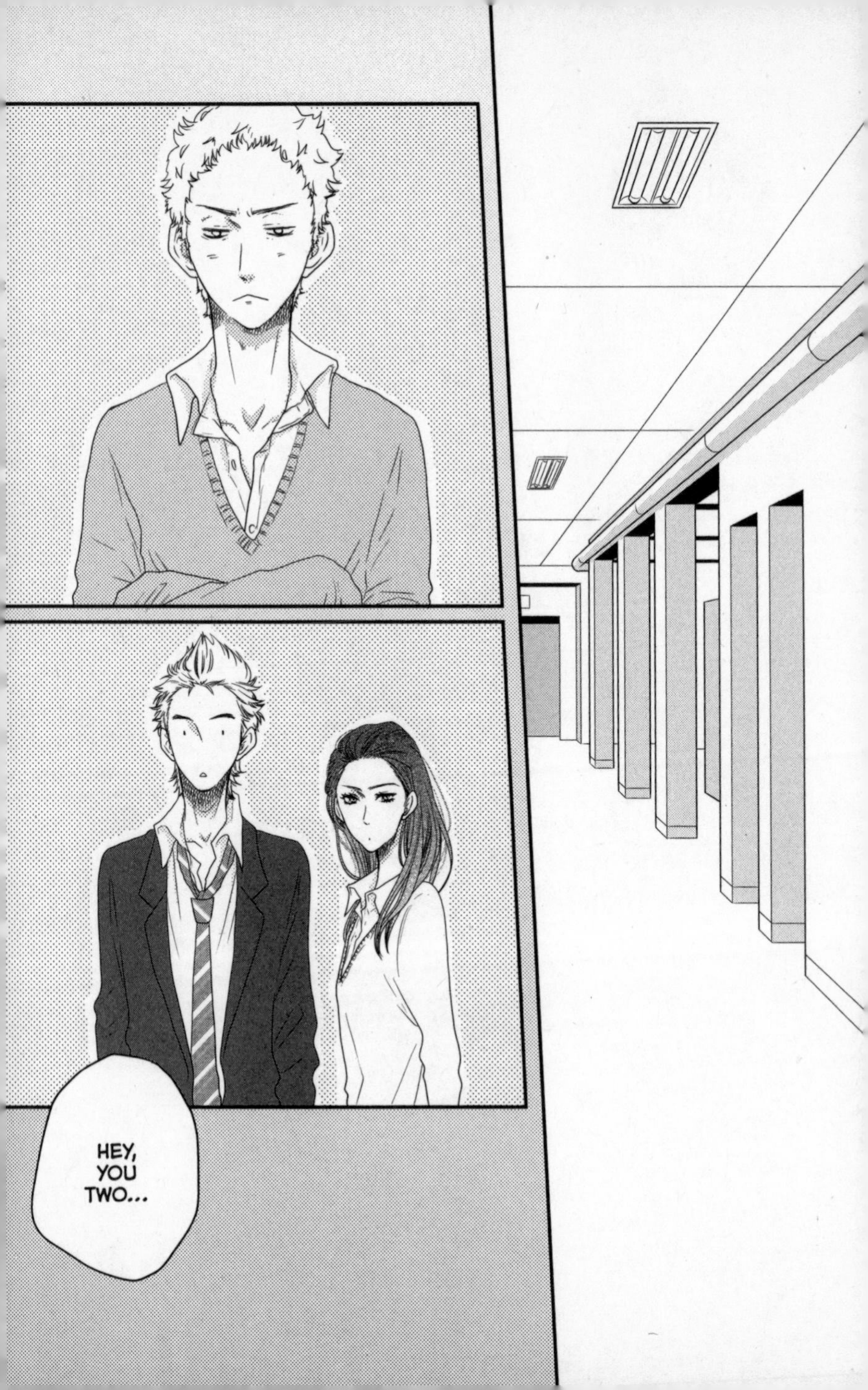
HEY, YOU TWO...

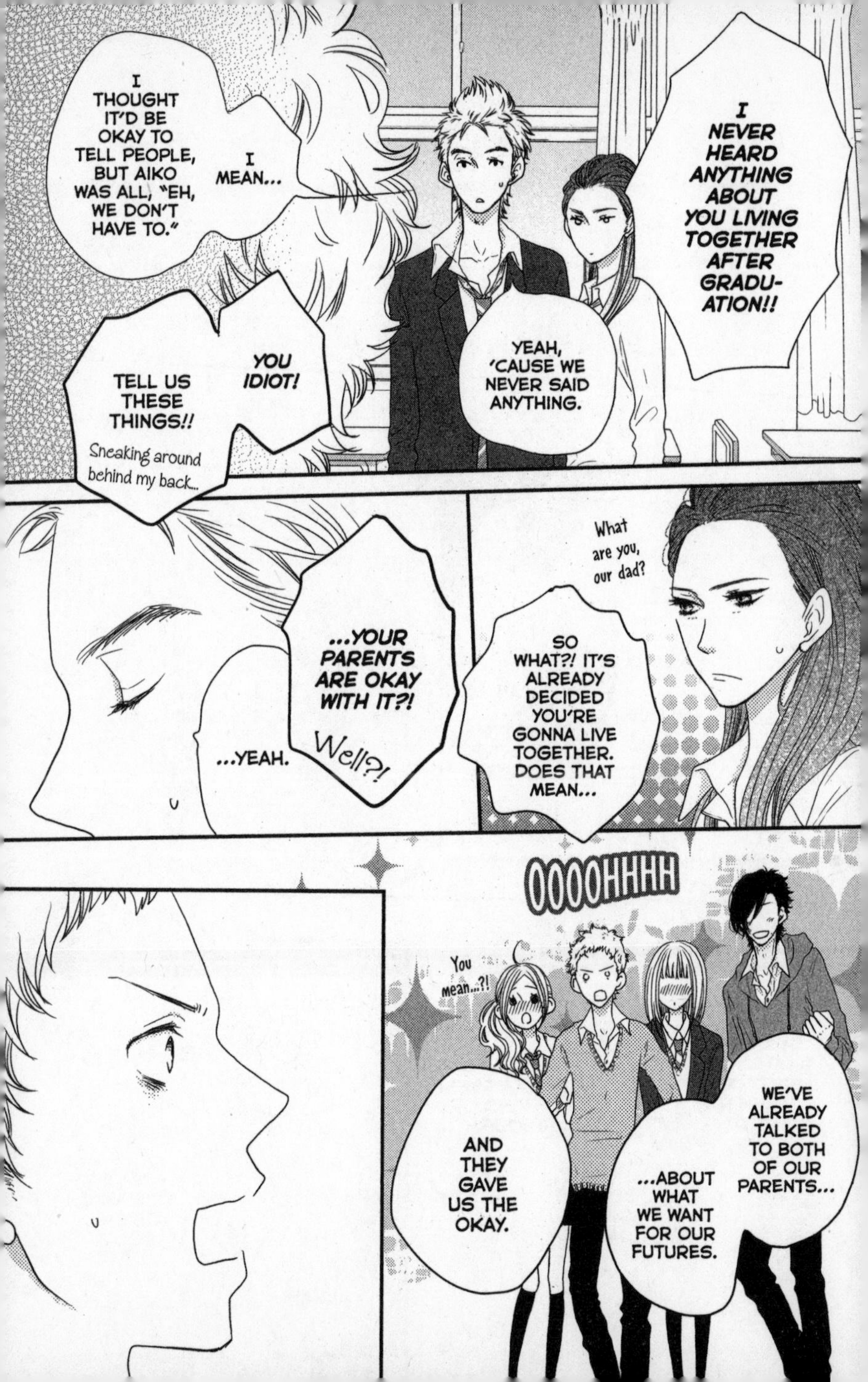
I NEVER HEARD ANYTHING ABOUT YOU LIVING TOGETHER AFTER GRADUATION!!
YEAH, 'CAUSE WE NEVER SAID ANYTHING.
I MEAN...
I THOUGHT IT'D BE OKAY TO TELL PEOPLE, BUT AIKO WAS ALL, "EH, WE DON'T HAVE TO."
YOU IDIOT!
TELL US THESE THINGS!!
Sneaking around behind my back...
What are you, our dad?
SO WHAT?! IT'S ALREADY DECIDED YOU'RE GONNA LIVE TOGETHER. DOES THAT MEAN...
...YOUR PARENTS ARE OKAY WITH IT?!
Well?!
...YEAH.
OOOOHHHH
You mean...?!
WE'VE ALREADY TALKED TO BOTH OF OUR PARENTS...
...ABOUT WHAT WE WANT FOR OUR FUTURES.
AND THEY GAVE US THE OKAY.

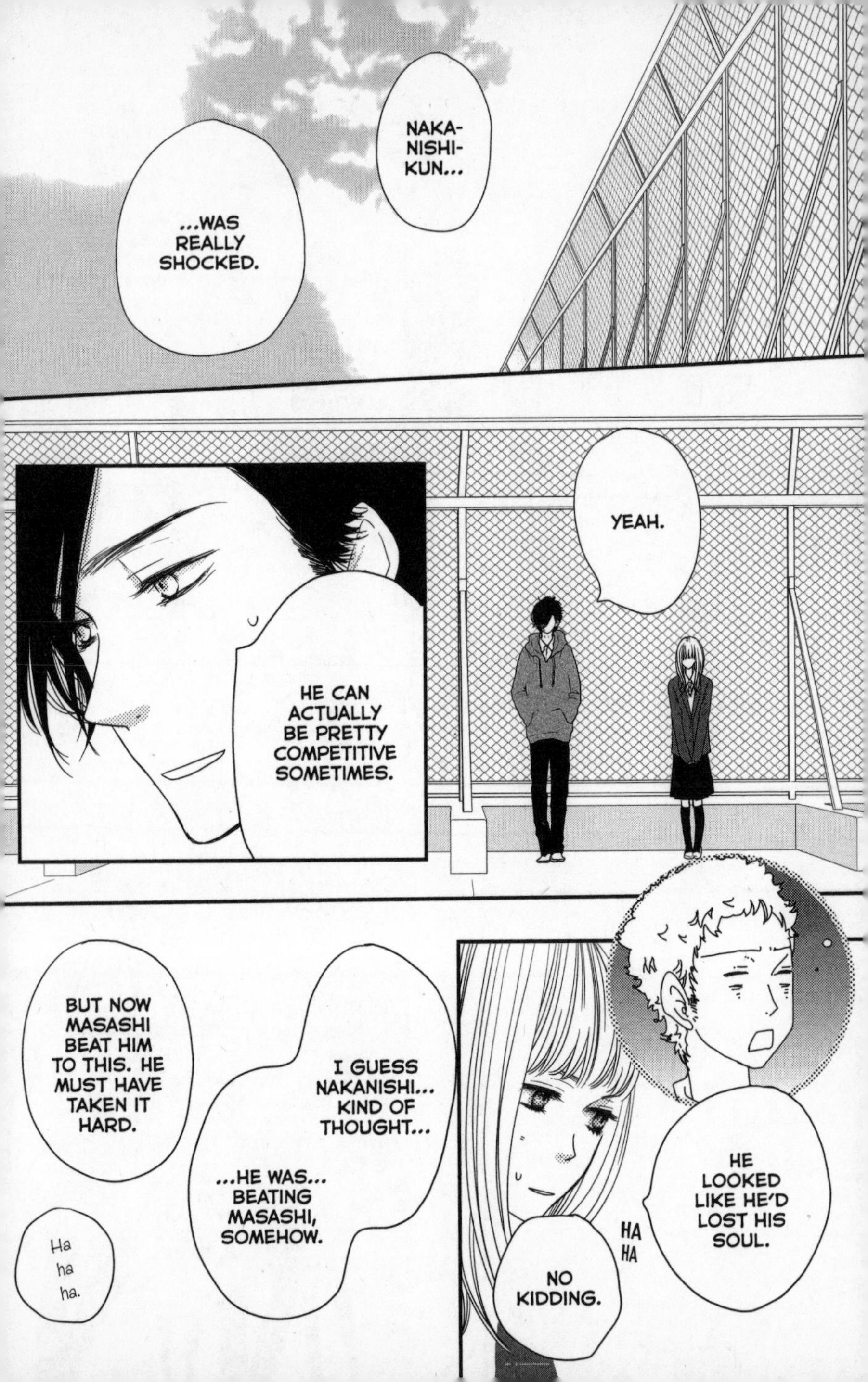
NAKA-NISHI-KUN...
...WAS REALLY SHOCKED.
YEAH.
HE CAN ACTUALLY BE PRETTY COMPETITIVE SOMETIMES.
HE LOOKED LIKE HE'D LOST HIS SOUL.
HA HA
NO KIDDING.
I GUESS NAKANISHI... KIND OF THOUGHT...
...HE WAS... BEATING MASASHI, SOMEHOW.
BUT NOW MASASHI BEAT HIM TO THIS. HE MUST HAVE TAKEN IT HARD.
Ha ha ha.

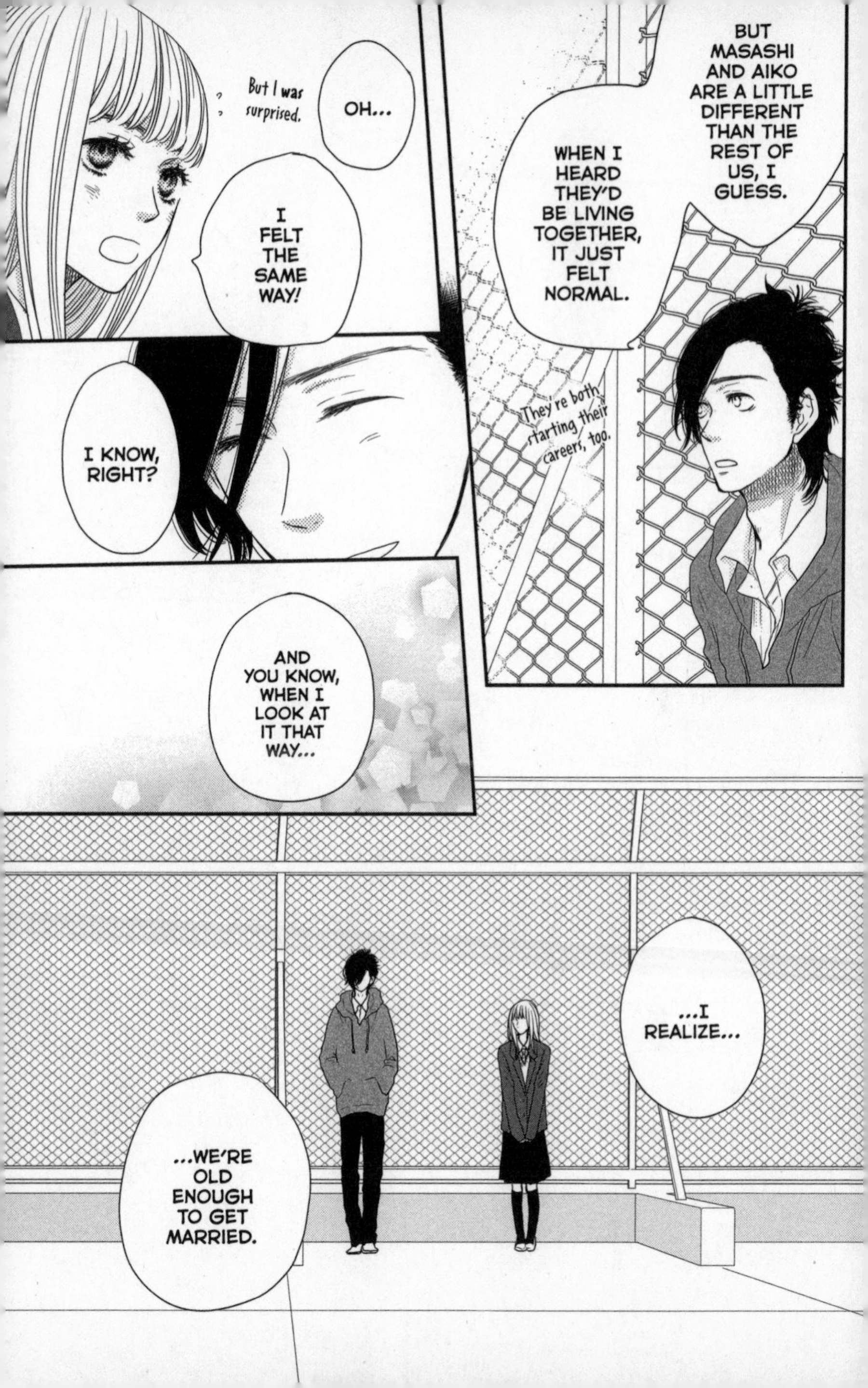
BUT MASASHI AND AIKO ARE A LITTLE DIFFERENT THAN THE REST OF US, I GUESS.
WHEN I HEARD THEY'D BE LIVING TOGETHER, IT JUST FELT NORMAL.
They're both starting their careers, too.
OH...
But I was surprised.
I FELT THE SAME WAY!
I KNOW, RIGHT?
AND YOU KNOW, WHEN I LOOK AT IT THAT WAY...
...I REALIZE...
...WE'RE OLD ENOUGH TO GET MARRIED.

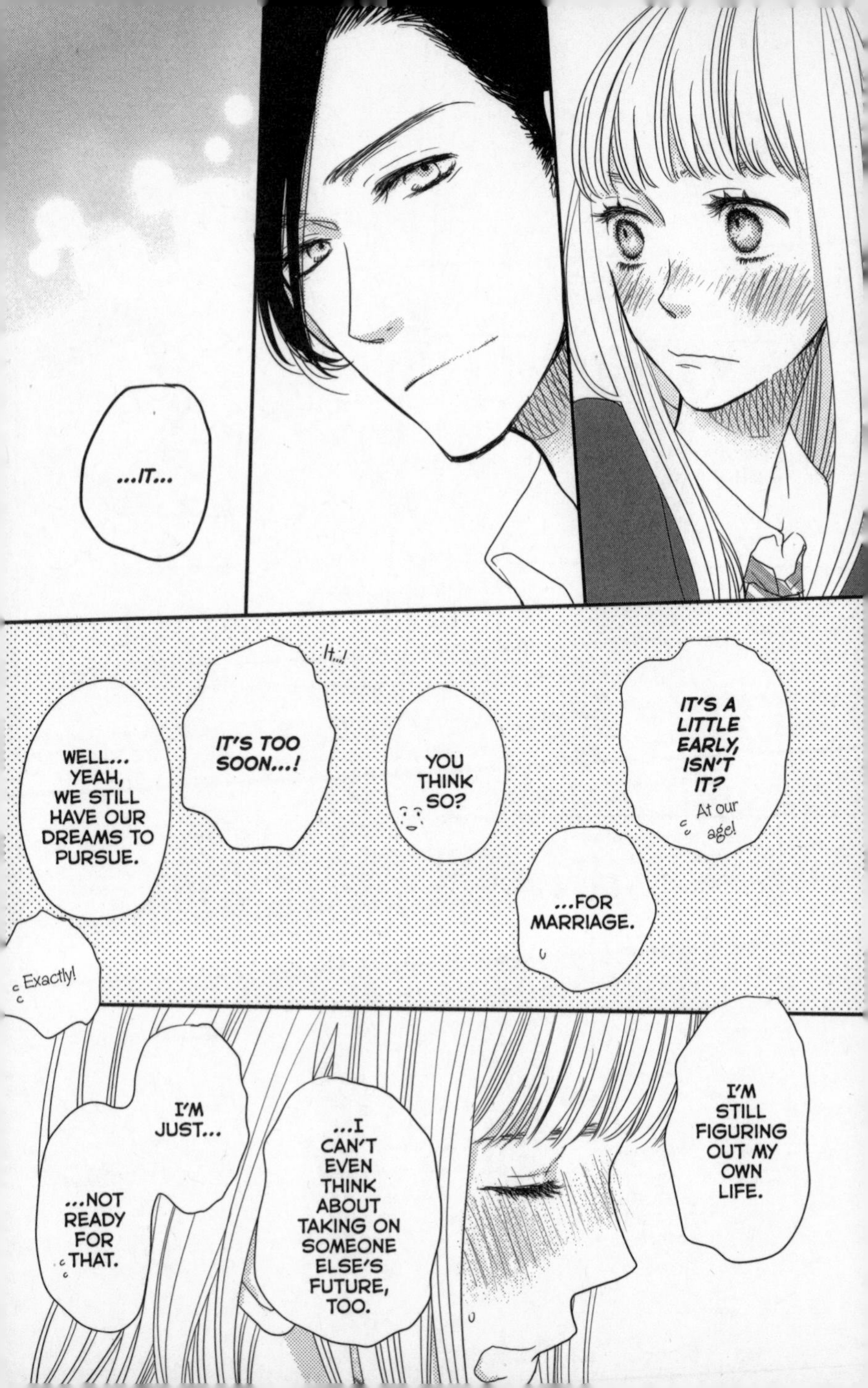
...IT...
IT'S A LITTLE EARLY, ISN'T IT?
At our age!
...FOR MARRIAGE.
YOU THINK SO?
It...!
IT'S TOO SOON...!
WELL... YEAH, WE STILL HAVE OUR DREAMS TO PURSUE.
Exactly!
I'M STILL FIGURING OUT MY OWN LIFE.
...I CAN'T EVEN THINK ABOUT TAKING ON SOMEONE ELSE'S FUTURE, TOO.
I'M JUST...
...NOT READY FOR THAT.

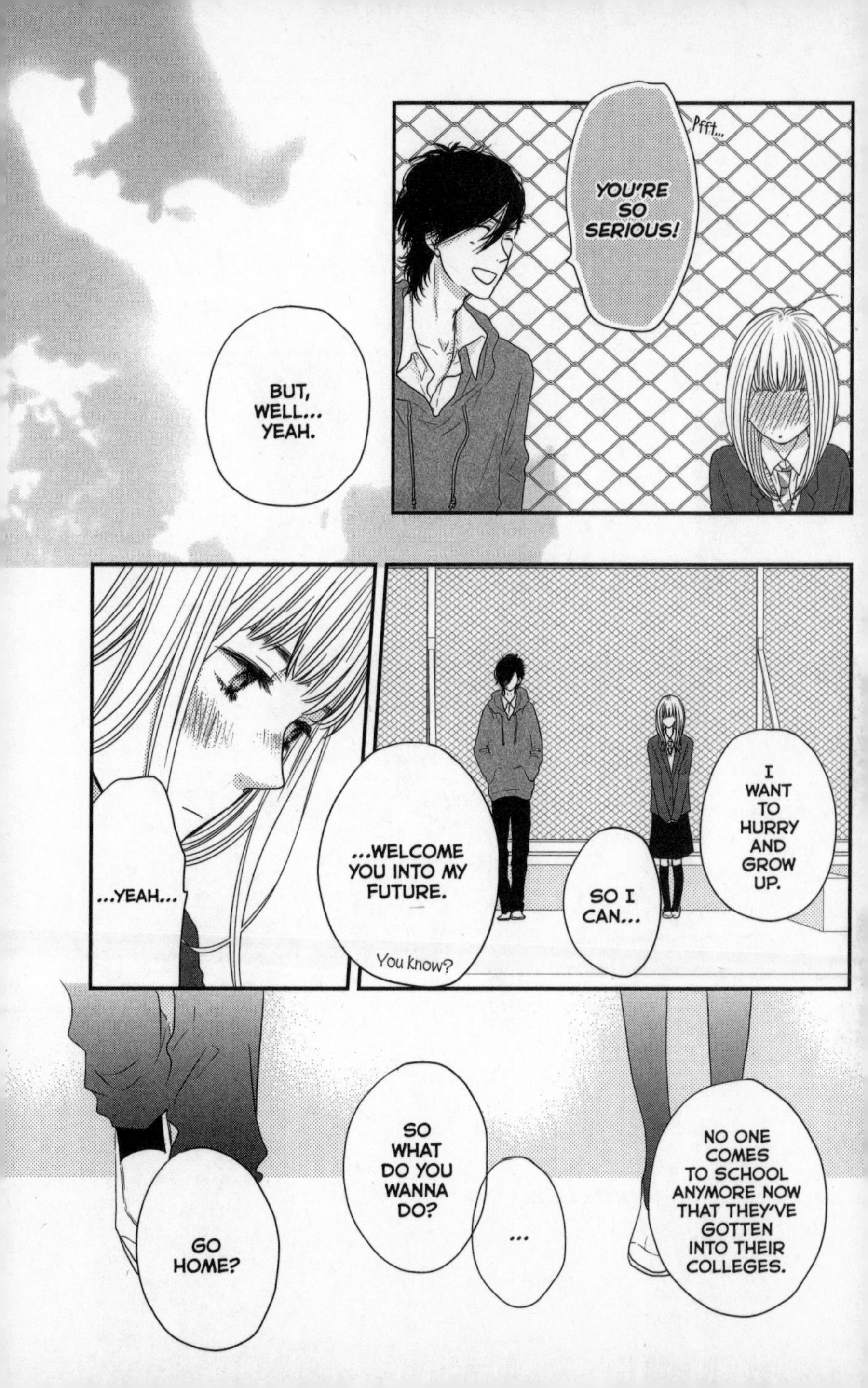
Pfft...
YOU'RE SO SERIOUS!
BUT, WELL... YEAH.
I WANT TO HURRY AND GROW UP.
SO I CAN...
...WELCOME YOU INTO MY FUTURE.
You know?
...YEAH...
NO ONE COMES TO SCHOOL ANYMORE NOW THAT THEY'VE GOTTEN INTO THEIR COLLEGES.
...
SO WHAT DO YOU WANNA DO?
GO HOME?

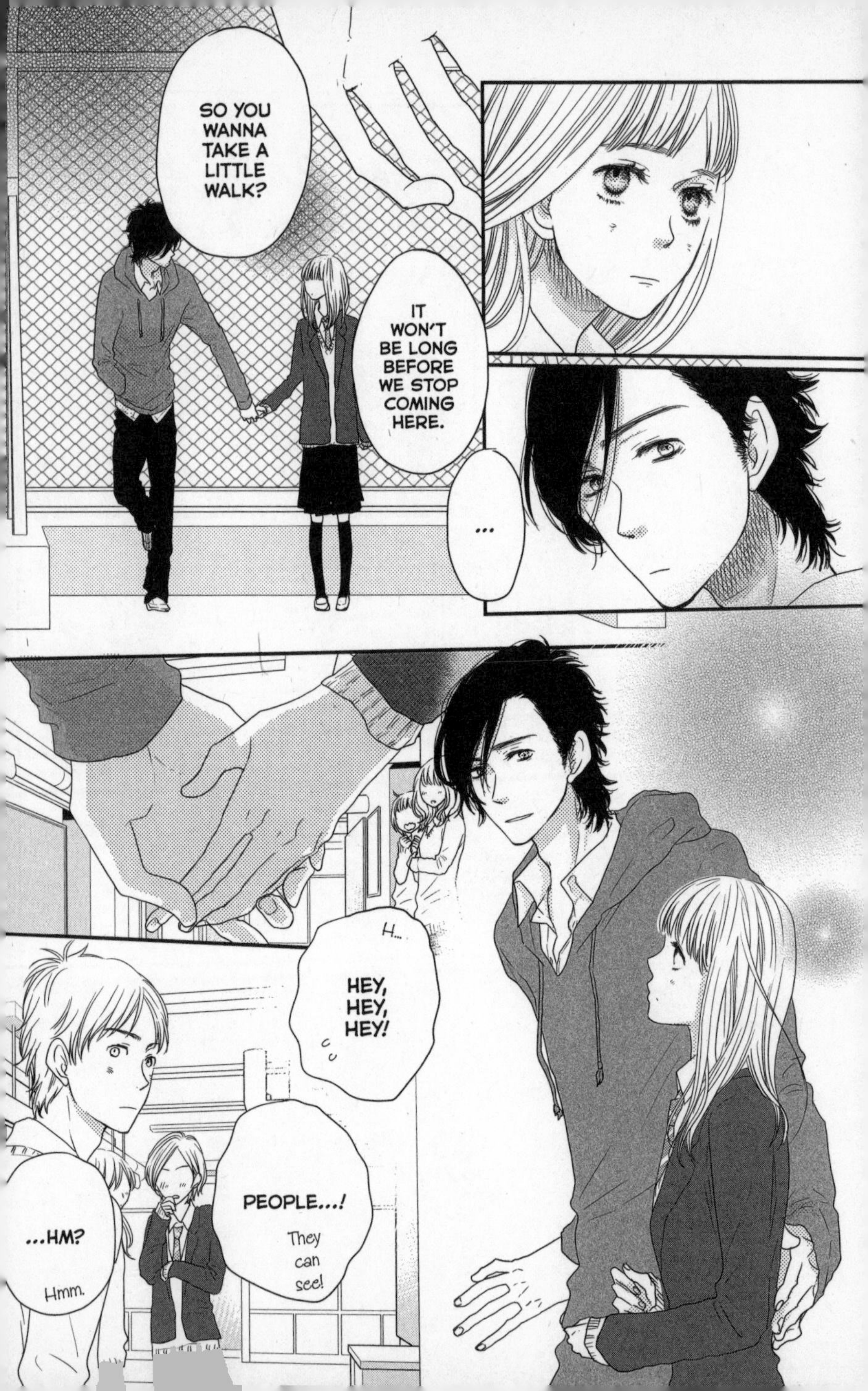
...
SO YOU WANNA TAKE A LITTLE WALK?
IT WON'T BE LONG BEFORE WE STOP COMING HERE.
H...
HEY, HEY, HEY!
PEOPLE...!
They can see!
...HM?
Hmm.

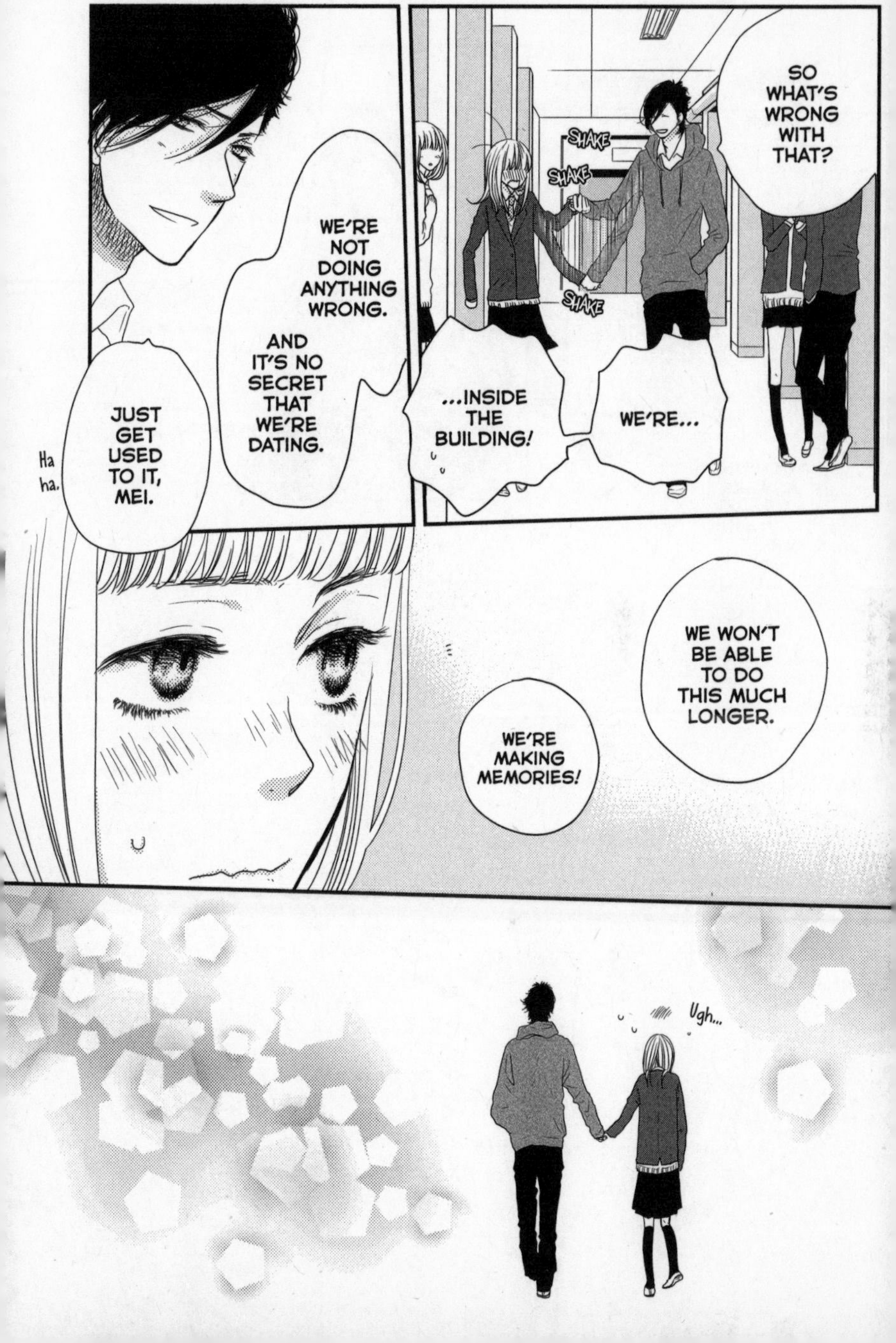
SO WHAT'S WRONG WITH THAT?
SHAKE
SHAKE
SHAKE
WE'RE...
...INSIDE THE BUILDING!
WE'RE NOT DOING ANYTHING WRONG.
AND IT'S NO SECRET THAT WE'RE DATING.
JUST GET USED TO IT, MEI.
Ha ha.
WE WON'T BE ABLE TO DO THIS MUCH LONGER.
WE'RE MAKING MEMORIES!
Ugh...

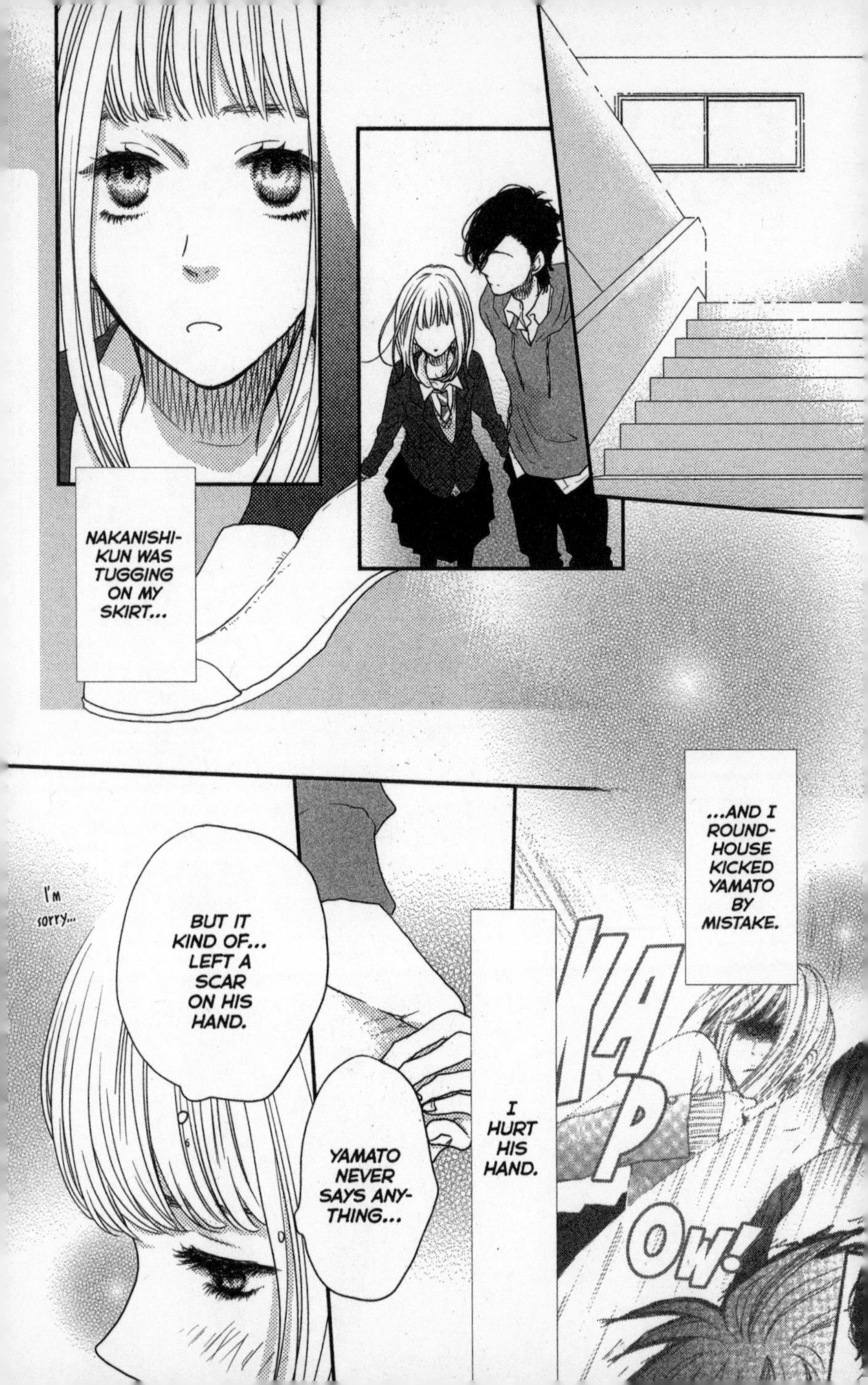
NAKANISHI-KUN WAS TUGGING ON MY SKIRT...
...AND I ROUND-HOUSE KICKED YAMATO BY MISTAKE.
OW!
I HURT HIS HAND.
BUT IT KIND OF... LEFT A SCAR ON HIS HAND.
I'm sorry...
YAMATO NEVER SAYS ANY-THING...

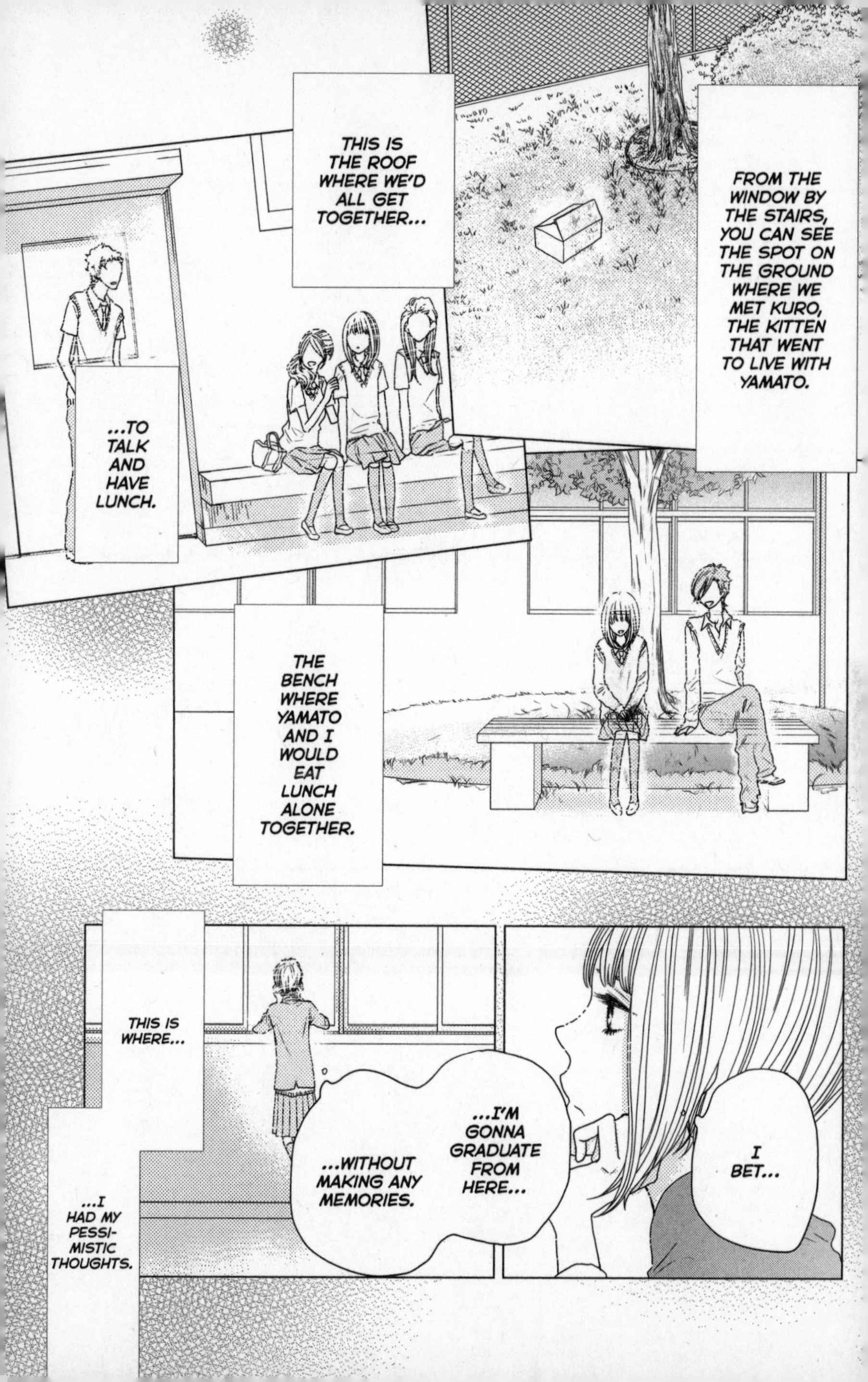
FROM THE WINDOW BY THE STAIRS, YOU CAN SEE THE SPOT ON THE GROUND WHERE WE MET KURO, THE KITTEN THAT WENT TO LIVE WITH YAMATO.
THIS IS THE ROOF WHERE WE'D ALL GET TOGETHER...
...TO TALK AND HAVE LUNCH.
THE BENCH WHERE YAMATO AND I WOULD EAT LUNCH ALONE TOGETHER.
I BET...
...I'M GONNA GRADUATE FROM HERE...
...WITHOUT MAKING ANY MEMORIES.
THIS IS WHERE...
...I HAD MY PESSI-MISTIC THOUGHTS.

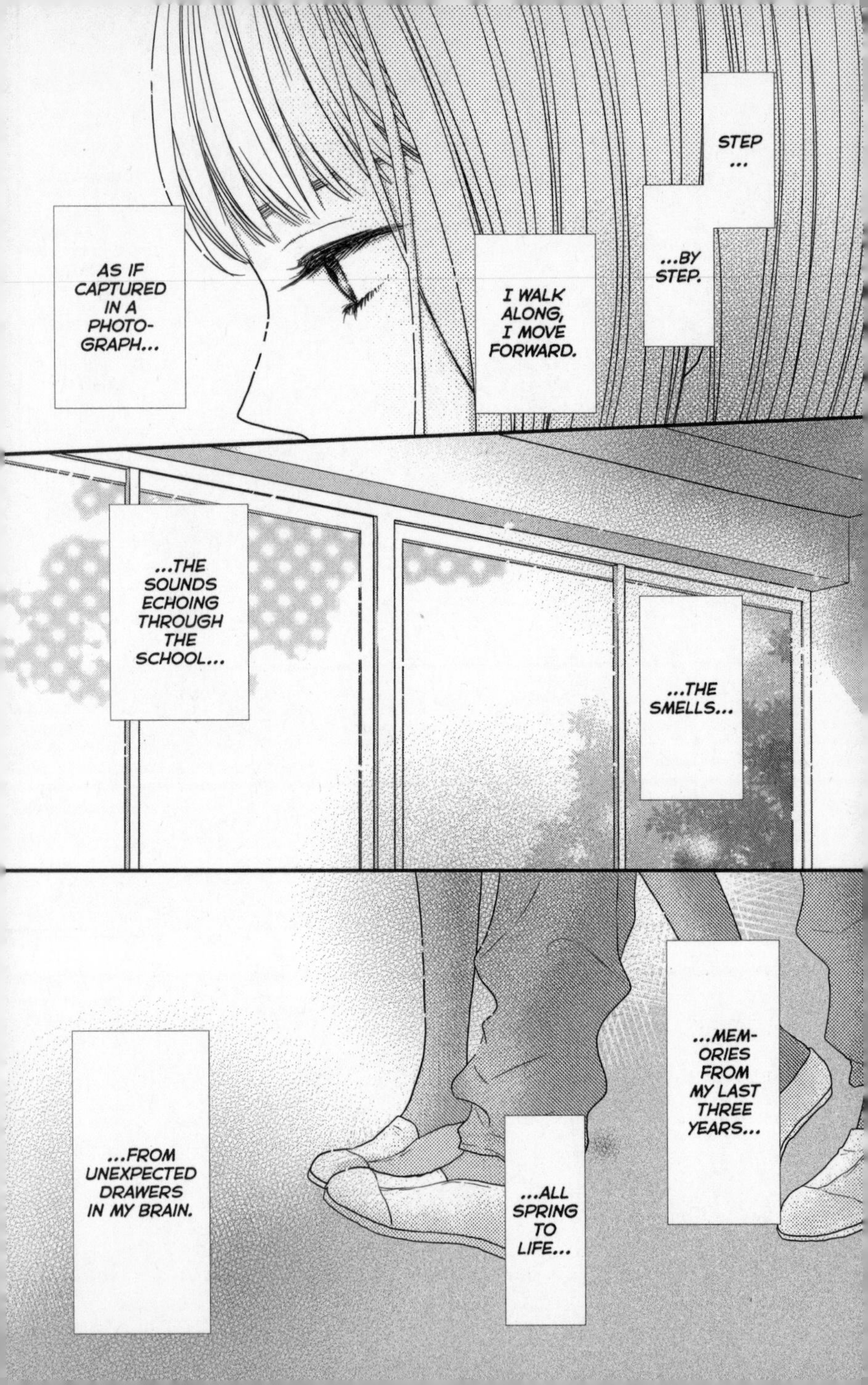
STEP...
...BY STEP.
I WALK ALONG, I MOVE FORWARD.
AS IF CAPTURED IN A PHOTOGRAPH...
...THE SMELLS...
...THE SOUNDS ECHOING THROUGH THE SCHOOL...
...MEMORIES FROM MY LAST THREE YEARS...
...ALL SPRING TO LIFE...
...FROM UNEXPECTED DRAWERS IN MY BRAIN.

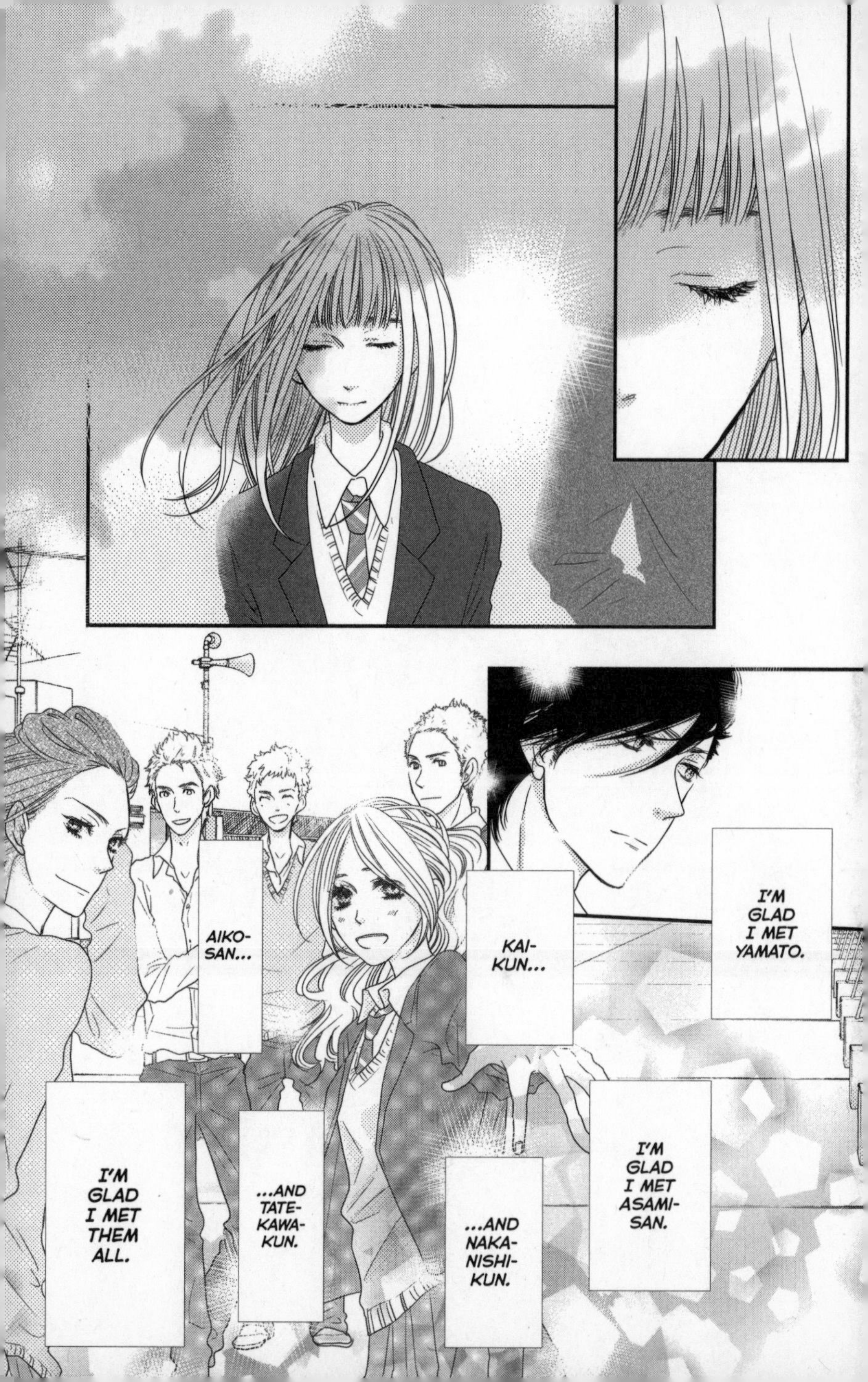
I'M GLAD I MET YAMATO.
I'M GLAD I MET ASAMI-SAN.
KAI-KUN...
...AND NAKA-NISHI-KUN.
AIKO-SAN...
...AND TATE-KAWA-KUN.
I'M GLAD I MET THEM ALL.

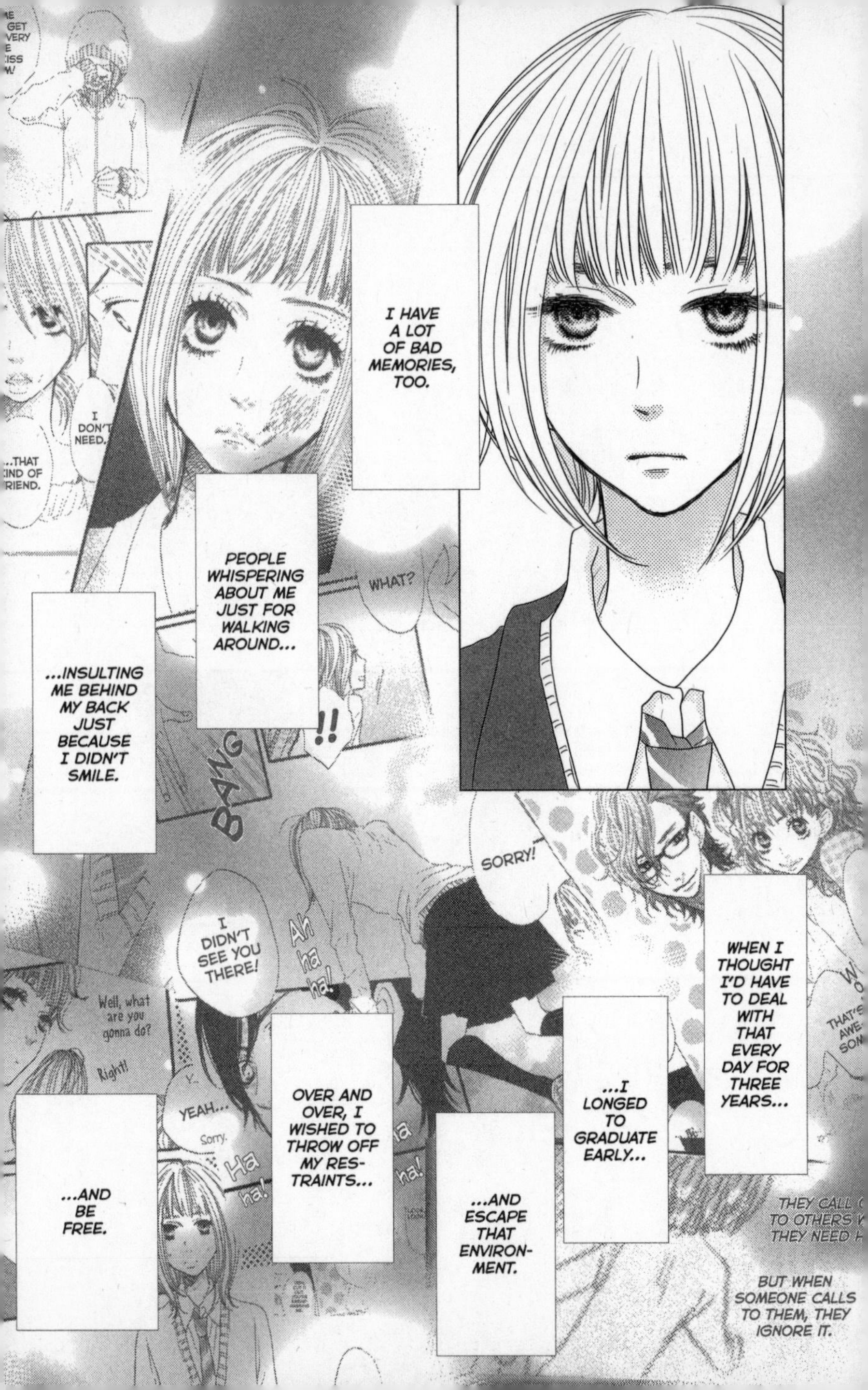
I HAVE A LOT OF BAD MEMORIES, TOO.
I DON'T NEED.
PEOPLE WHISPERING ABOUT ME JUST FOR WALKING AROUND...
WHAT?
!!
...INSULTING ME BEHIND MY BACK JUST BECAUSE I DIDN'T SMILE.
BANG
BUT WHEN SOMEONE CALLS TO THEM, THEY IGNORE IT.
WHEN I THOUGHT I'D HAVE TO DEAL WITH THAT EVERY DAY FOR THREE YEARS...
SORRY!
...I LONGED TO GRADUATE EARLY...
...AND ESCAPE THAT ENVIRONMENT.
I DIDN'T SEE YOU THERE!
Ah ha ha!
OVER AND OVER, I WISHED TO THROW OFF MY RES-TRAINTS...
Well, what are you gonna do?
Right!
YEAH...
Sorry.
Ha ha!
...AND BE FREE.

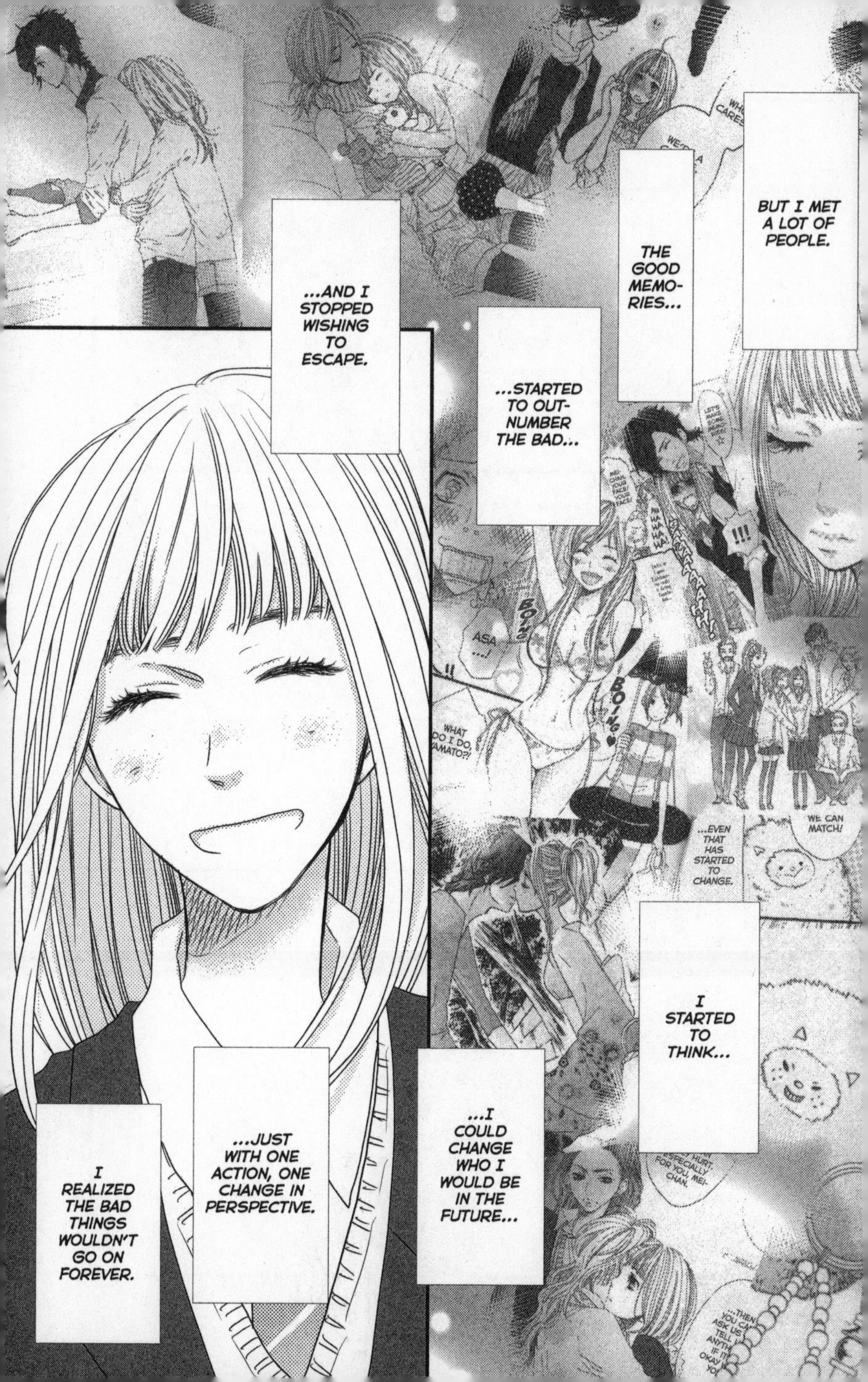
BUT I MET A LOT OF PEOPLE.
THE GOOD MEMORIES...
...STARTED TO OUT-NUMBER THE BAD...
...AND I STOPPED WISHING TO ESCAPE.
!!!
BOING
ASA ...
BOING
WHAT DO I DO, YAMATO?!
WE CAN MATCH!
...EVEN THAT HAS STARTED TO CHANGE.
I STARTED TO THINK...
...I COULD CHANGE WHO I WOULD BE IN THE FUTURE...
...JUST WITH ONE ACTION, ONE CHANGE IN PERSPECTIVE.
I REALIZED THE BAD THINGS WOULDN'T GO ON FOREVER.

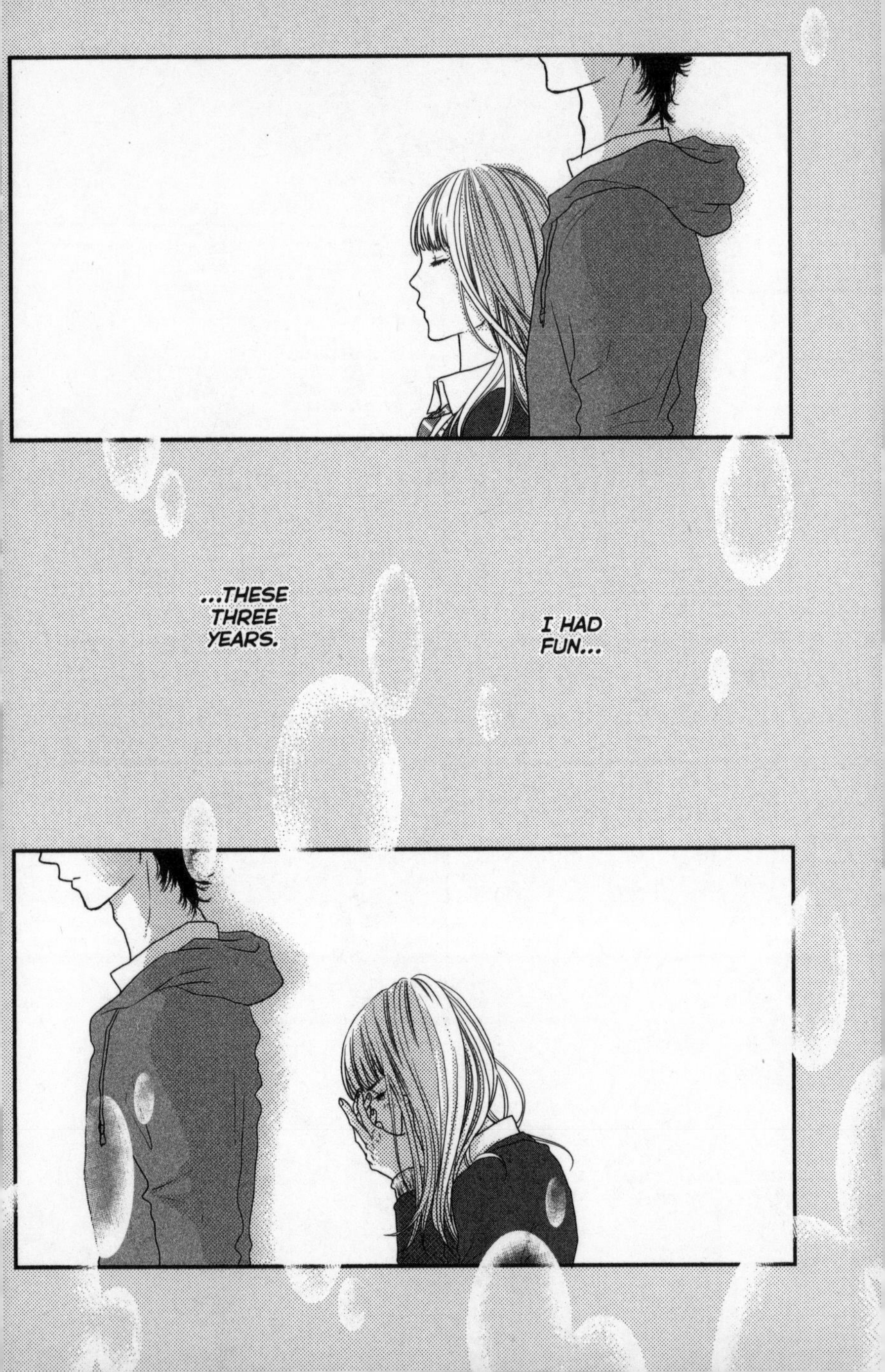
I HAD FUN...
...THESE THREE YEARS.

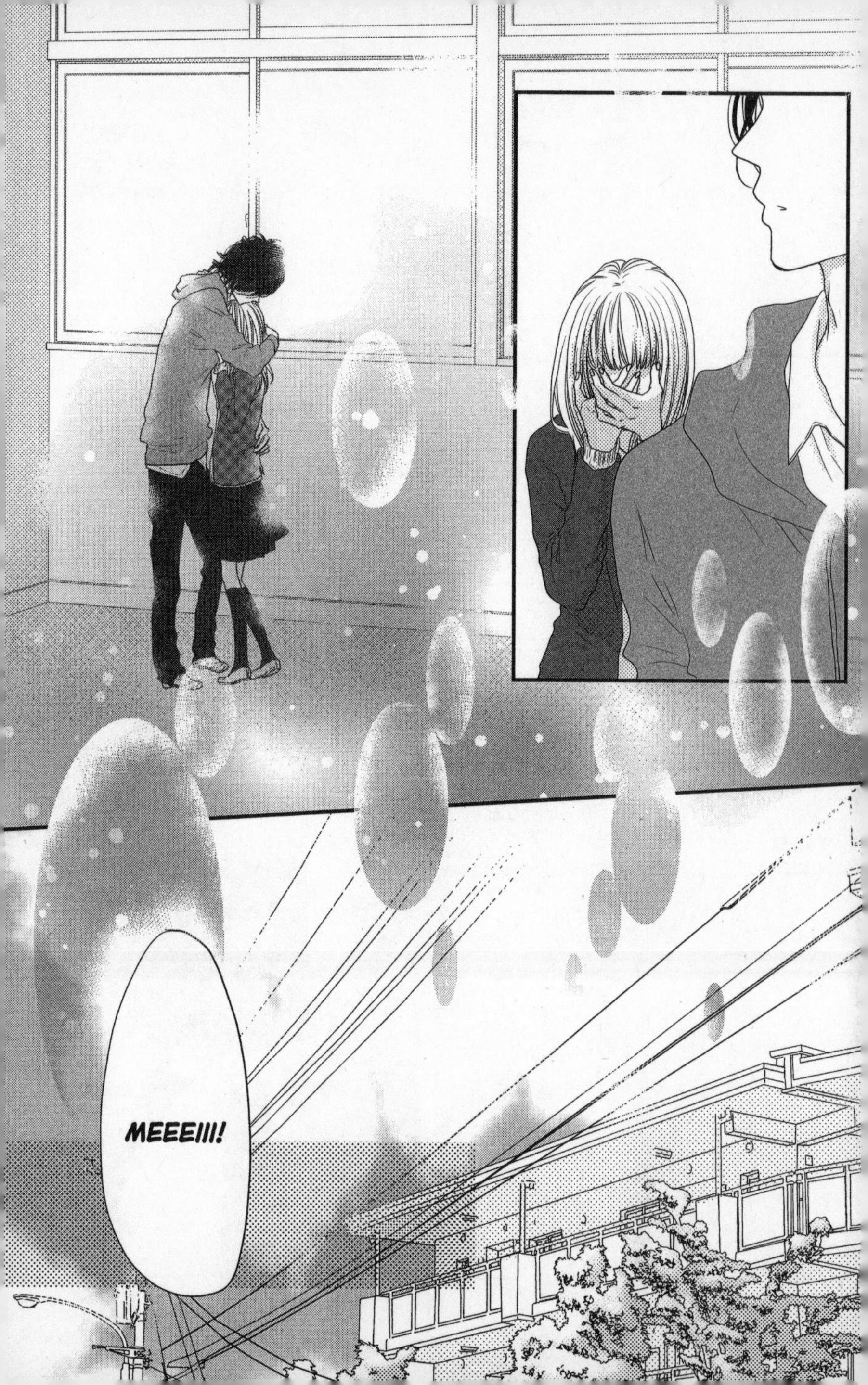
MEEEIII!

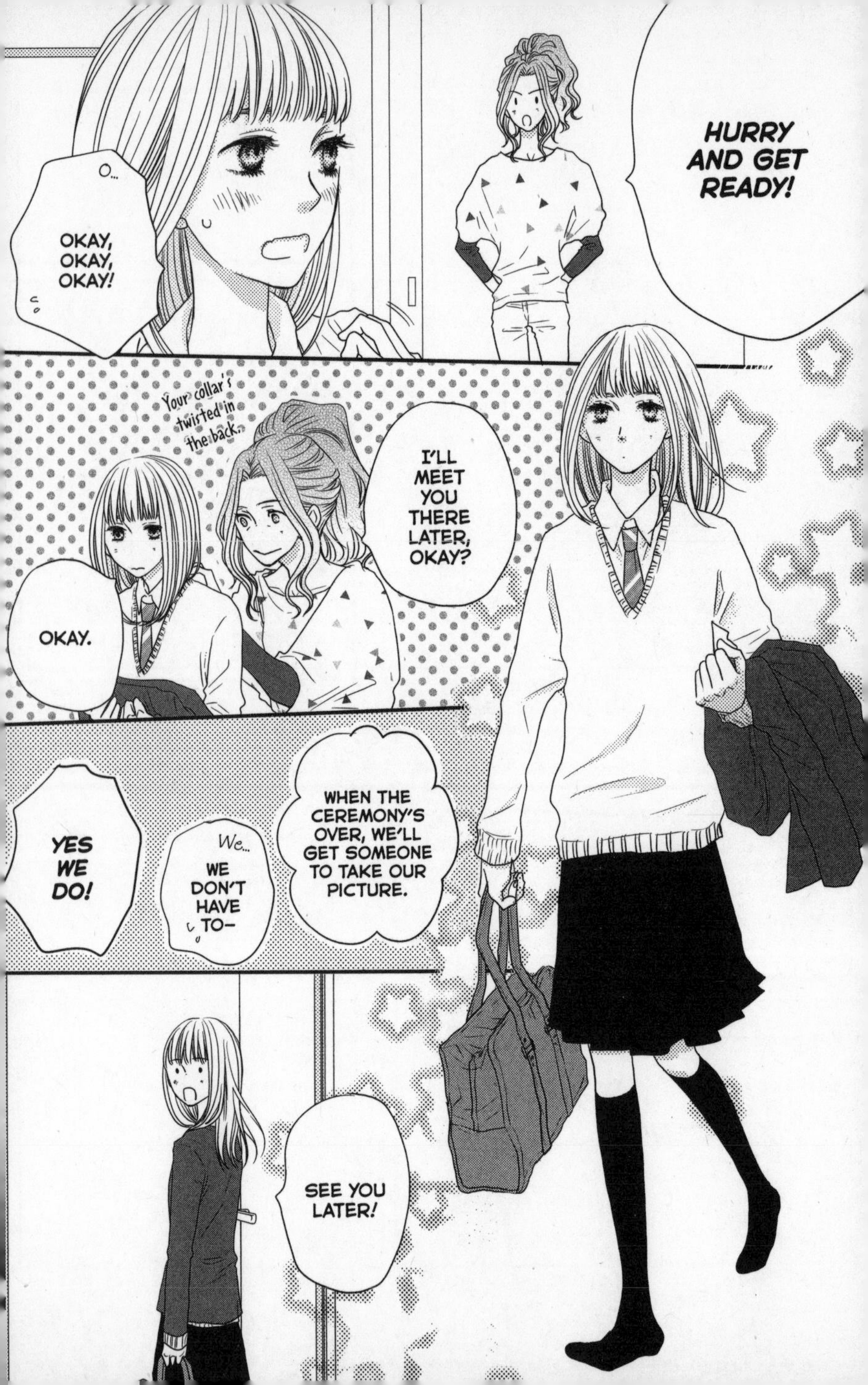
HURRY AND GET READY!
O... OKAY, OKAY, OKAY!
I'LL MEET YOU THERE LATER, OKAY?
Your collar's twisted in the back.
OKAY.
WHEN THE CEREMONY'S OVER, WE'LL GET SOMEONE TO TAKE OUR PICTURE.
We... WE DON'T HAVE TO—
YES WE DO!
SEE YOU LATER!

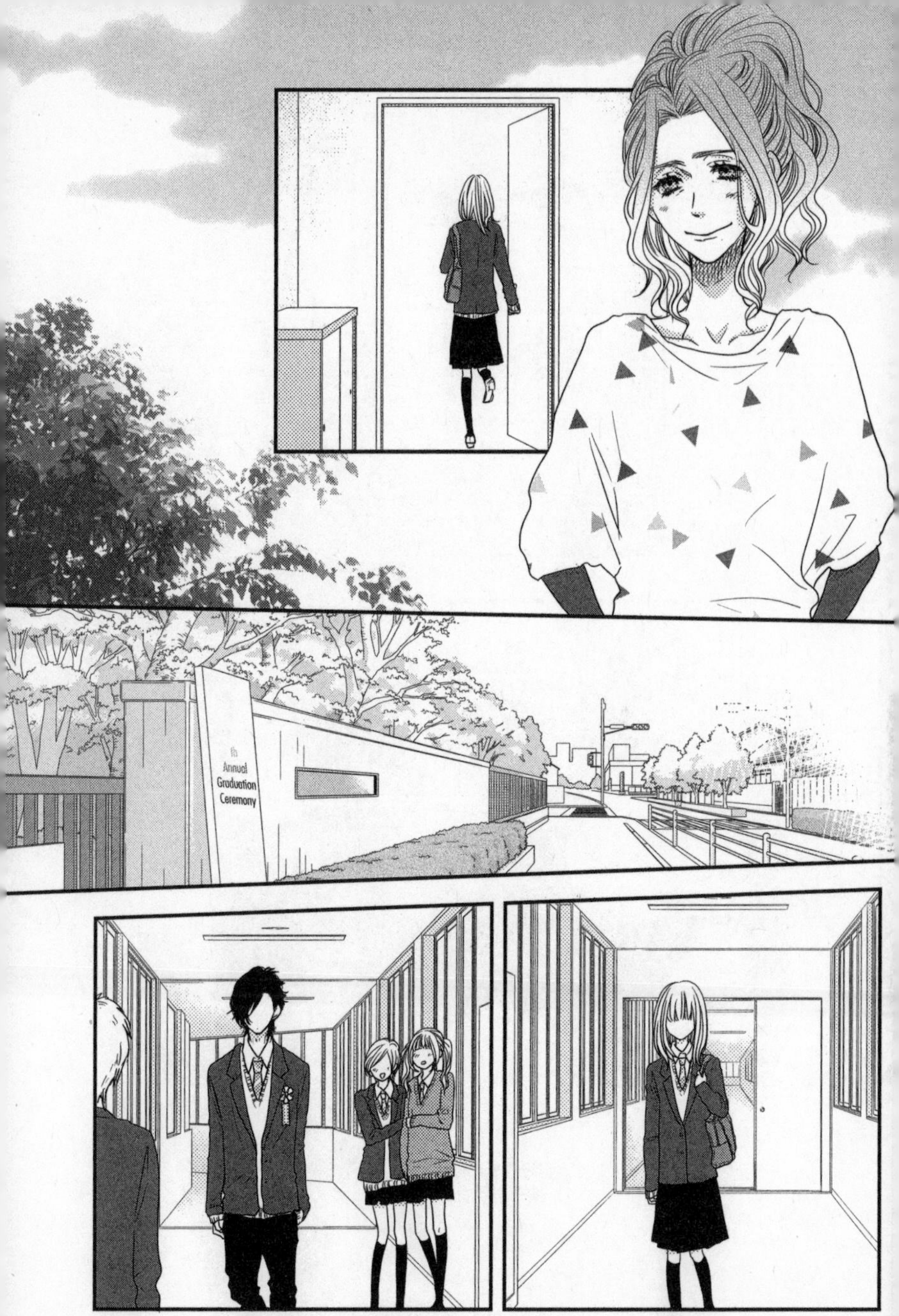
th
Annual
Graduation
Ceremony

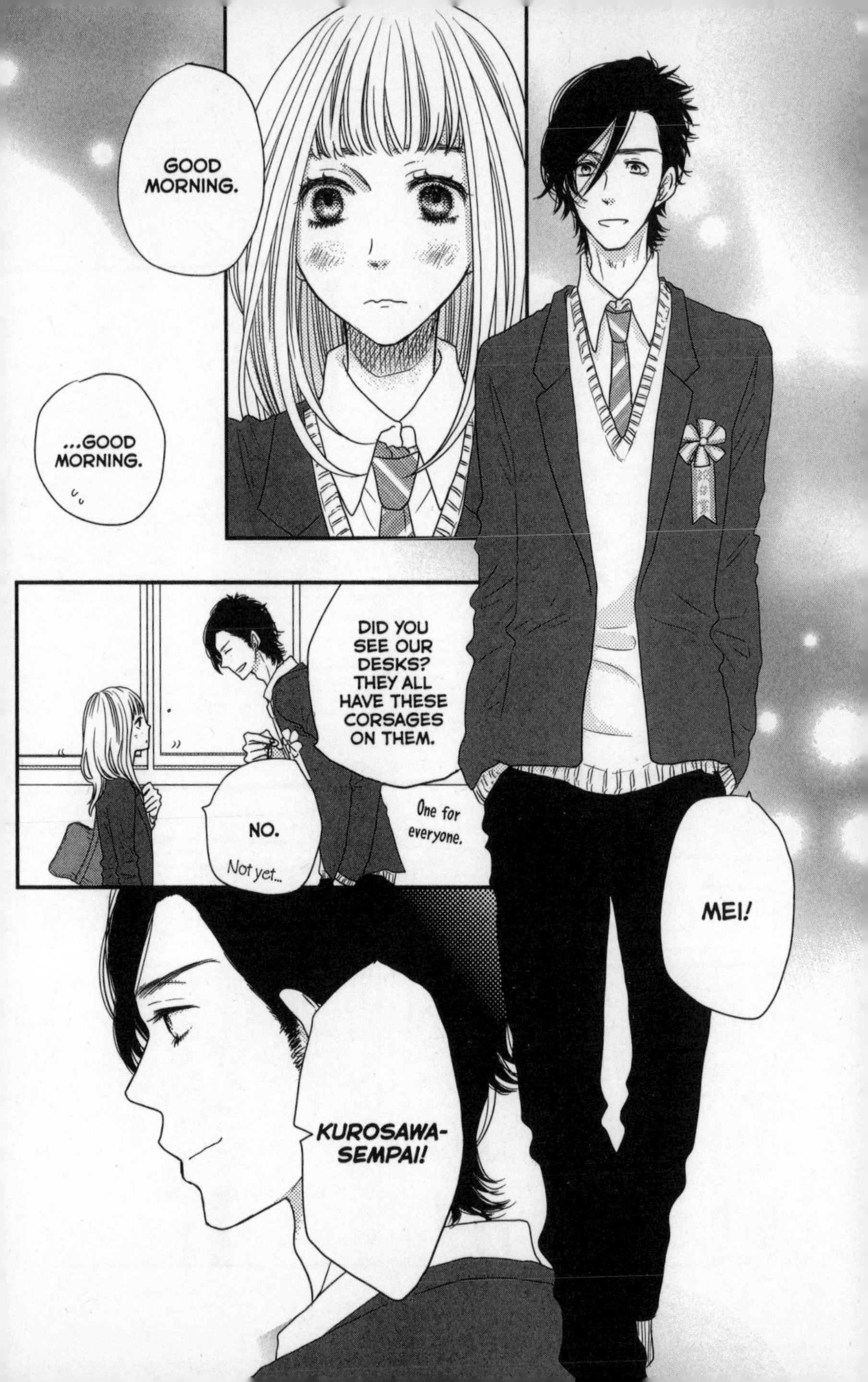
GOOD MORNING.
...GOOD MORNING.
DID YOU SEE OUR DESKS? THEY ALL HAVE THESE CORSAGES ON THEM.
One for everyone.
NO.
Not yet...
MEI!
KUROSAWA-SEMPAI!

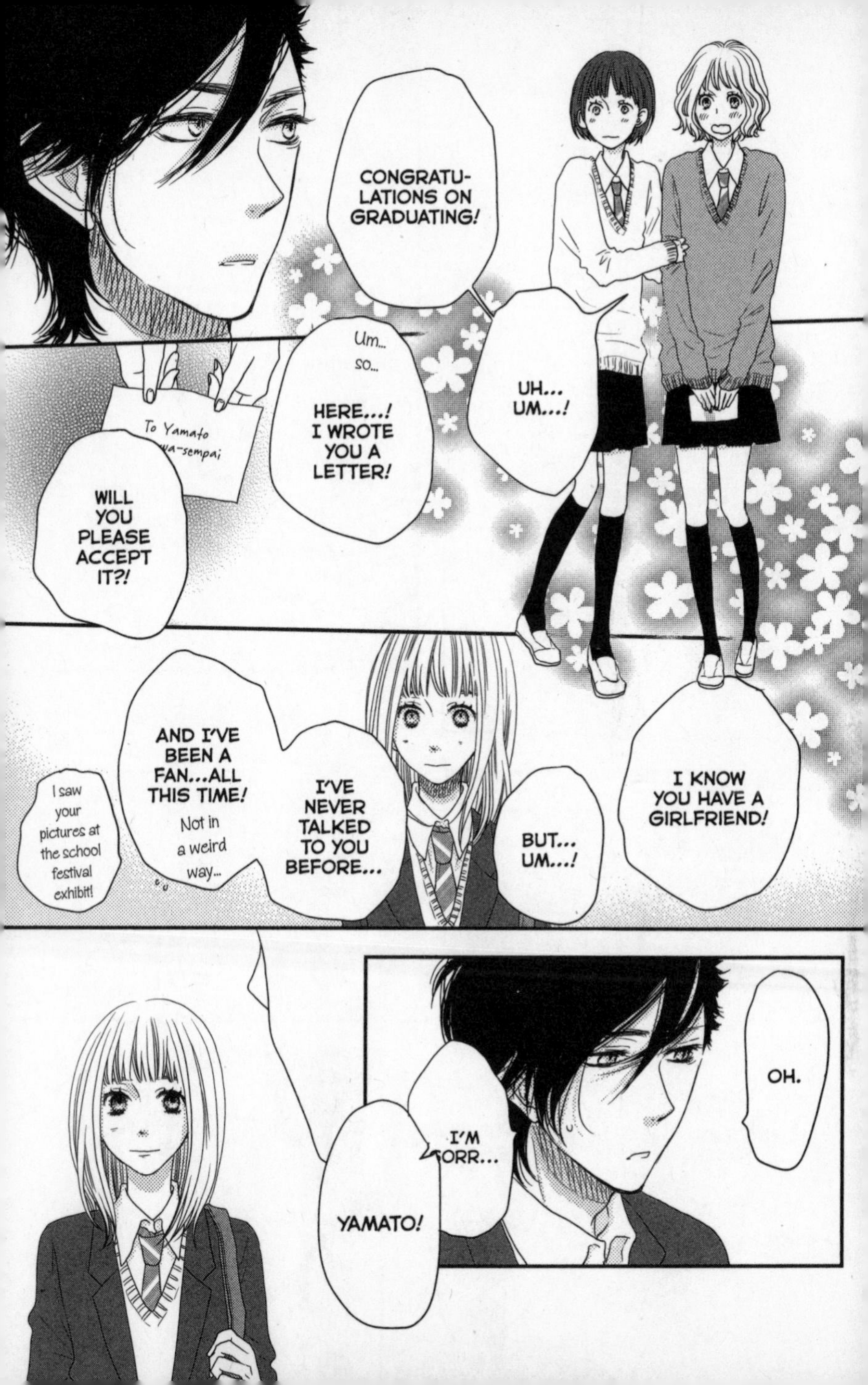
CONGRATULATIONS ON GRADUATING!
UH... UM...!
Um... so...
HERE...! I WROTE YOU A LETTER!
To Yamato
wa-sempai
WILL YOU PLEASE ACCEPT IT?!
I KNOW YOU HAVE A GIRLFRIEND!
BUT... UM...!
I'VE NEVER TALKED TO YOU BEFORE...
AND I'VE BEEN A FAN...ALL THIS TIME!
Not in a weird way...
I saw your pictures at the school festival exhibit!
OH.
I'M SORR...
YAMATO!

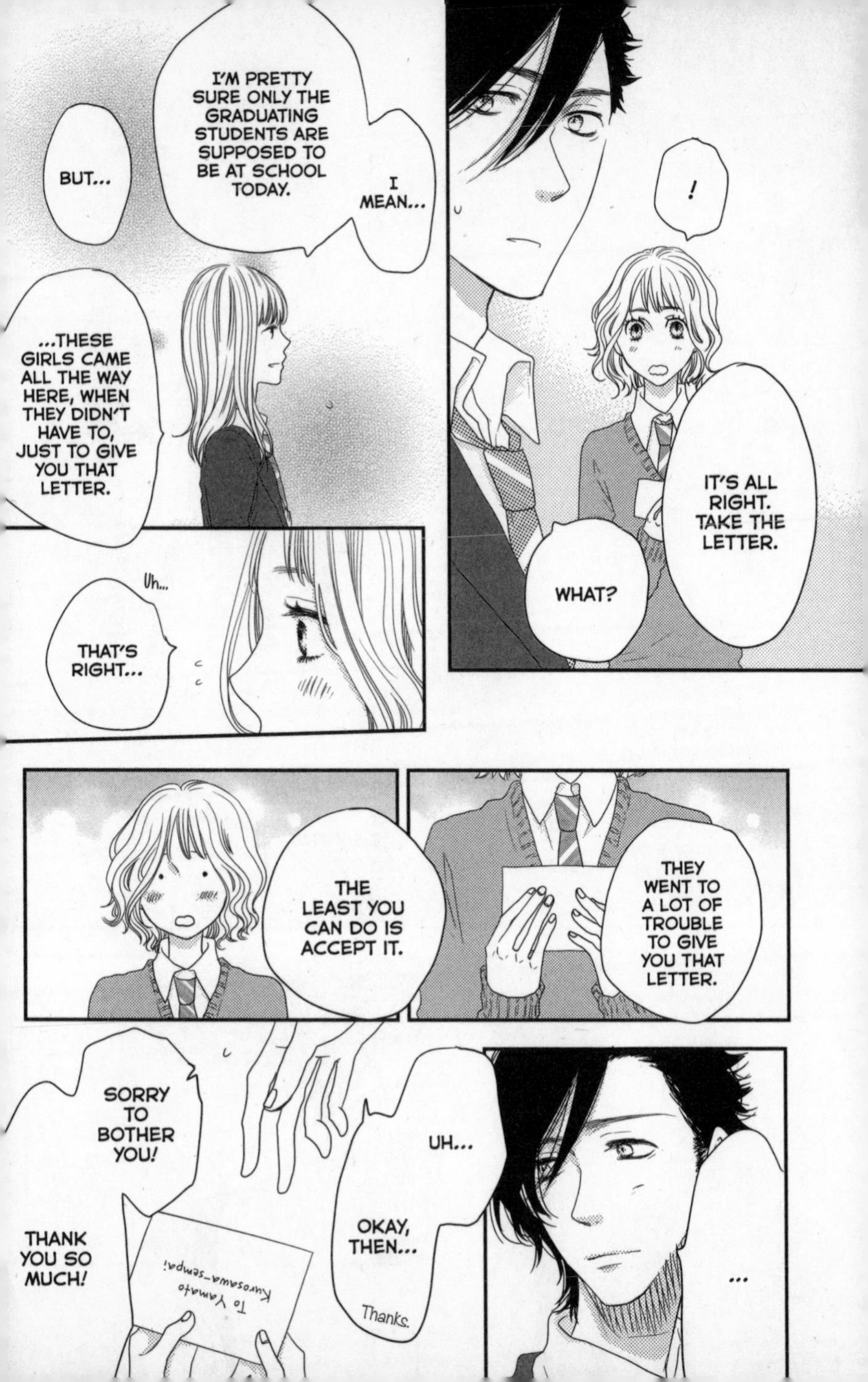
!
IT'S ALL RIGHT. TAKE THE LETTER.
WHAT?
I MEAN...
I'M PRETTY SURE ONLY THE GRADUATING STUDENTS ARE SUPPOSED TO BE AT SCHOOL TODAY.
BUT...
...THESE GIRLS CAME ALL THE WAY HERE, WHEN THEY DIDN'T HAVE TO, JUST TO GIVE YOU THAT LETTER.
Uh...
THAT'S RIGHT...
THEY WENT TO A LOT OF TROUBLE TO GIVE YOU THAT LETTER.
THE LEAST YOU CAN DO IS ACCEPT IT.
...
UH...
OKAY, THEN...
Thanks.
SORRY TO BOTHER YOU!
THANK YOU SO MUCH!
To Yamato Kurosawa-sempai

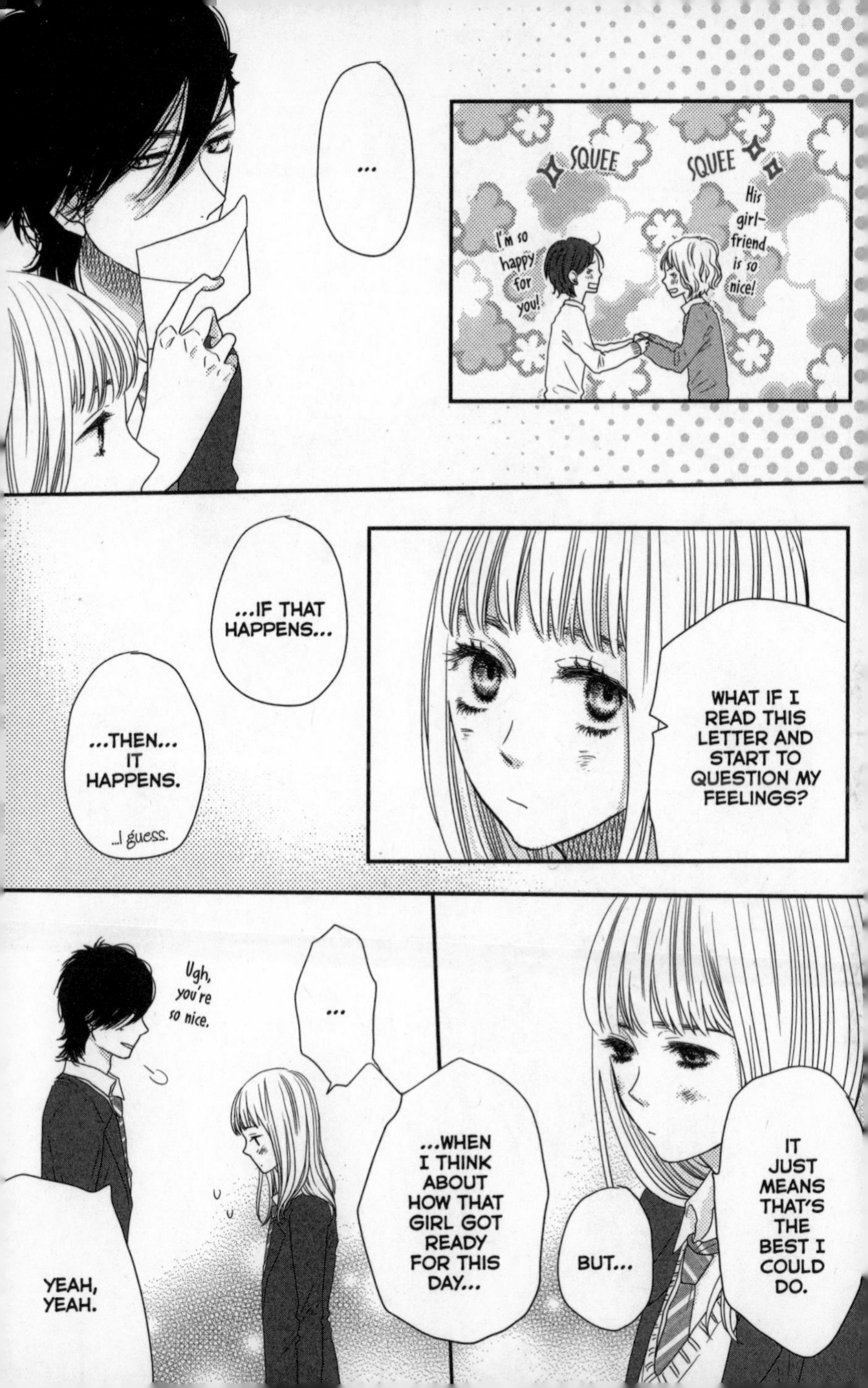
SQUEE
His girl-friend is so nice!
SQUEE
I'm so happy for you!
...
WHAT IF I READ THIS LETTER AND START TO QUESTION MY FEELINGS?
...IF THAT HAPPENS...
...THEN... IT HAPPENS.
...I guess.
IT JUST MEANS THAT'S THE BEST I COULD DO.
BUT...
...WHEN I THINK ABOUT HOW THAT GIRL GOT READY FOR THIS DAY...
...
Ugh, you're so nice.
YEAH, YEAH.

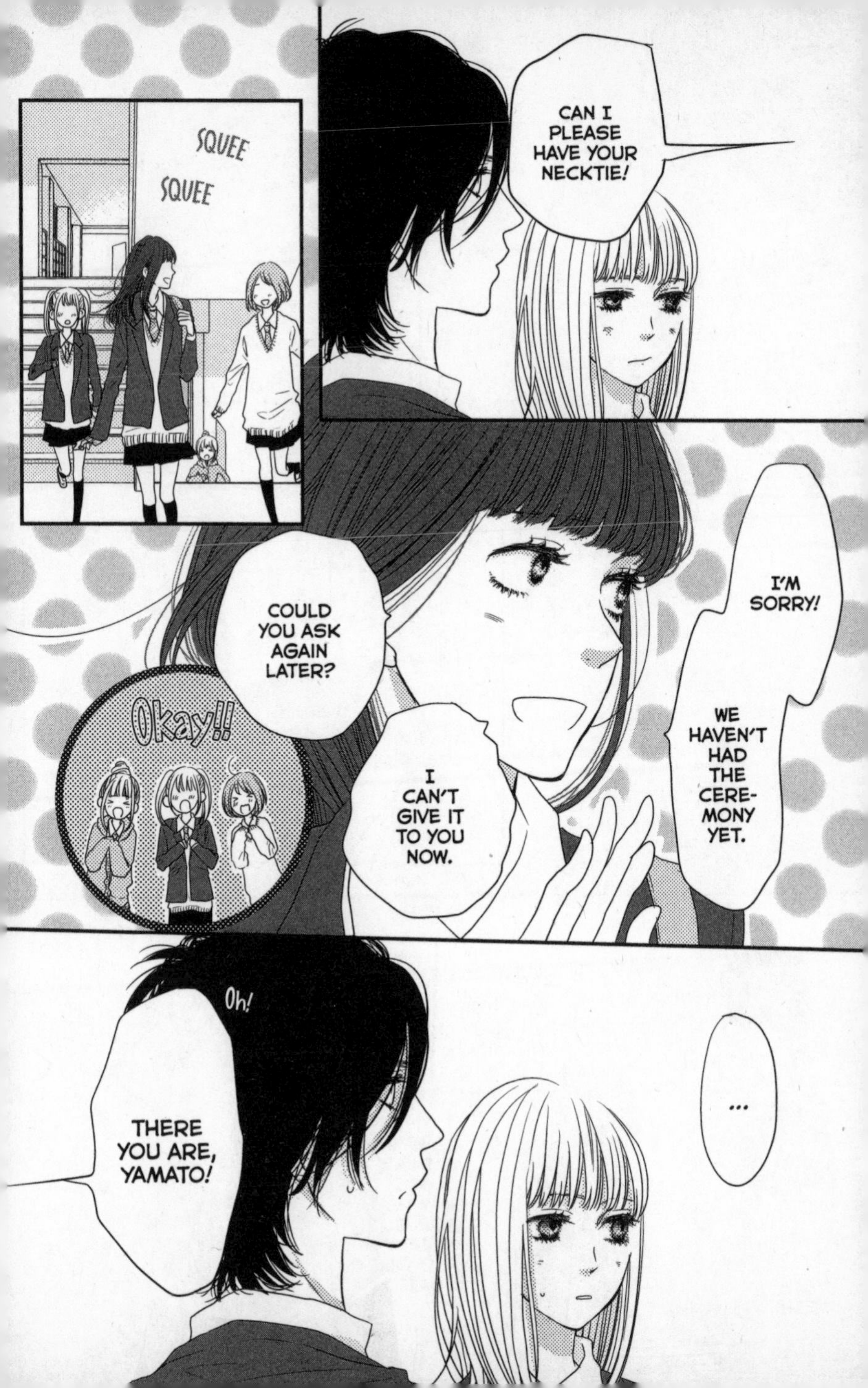
CAN I PLEASE HAVE YOUR NECKTIE!
SQUEE
SQUEE
I'M SORRY!
WE HAVEN'T HAD THE CERE-MONY YET.
I CAN'T GIVE IT TO YOU NOW.
COULD YOU ASK AGAIN LATER?
Okay!!
...
Oh!
THERE YOU ARE, YAMATO!

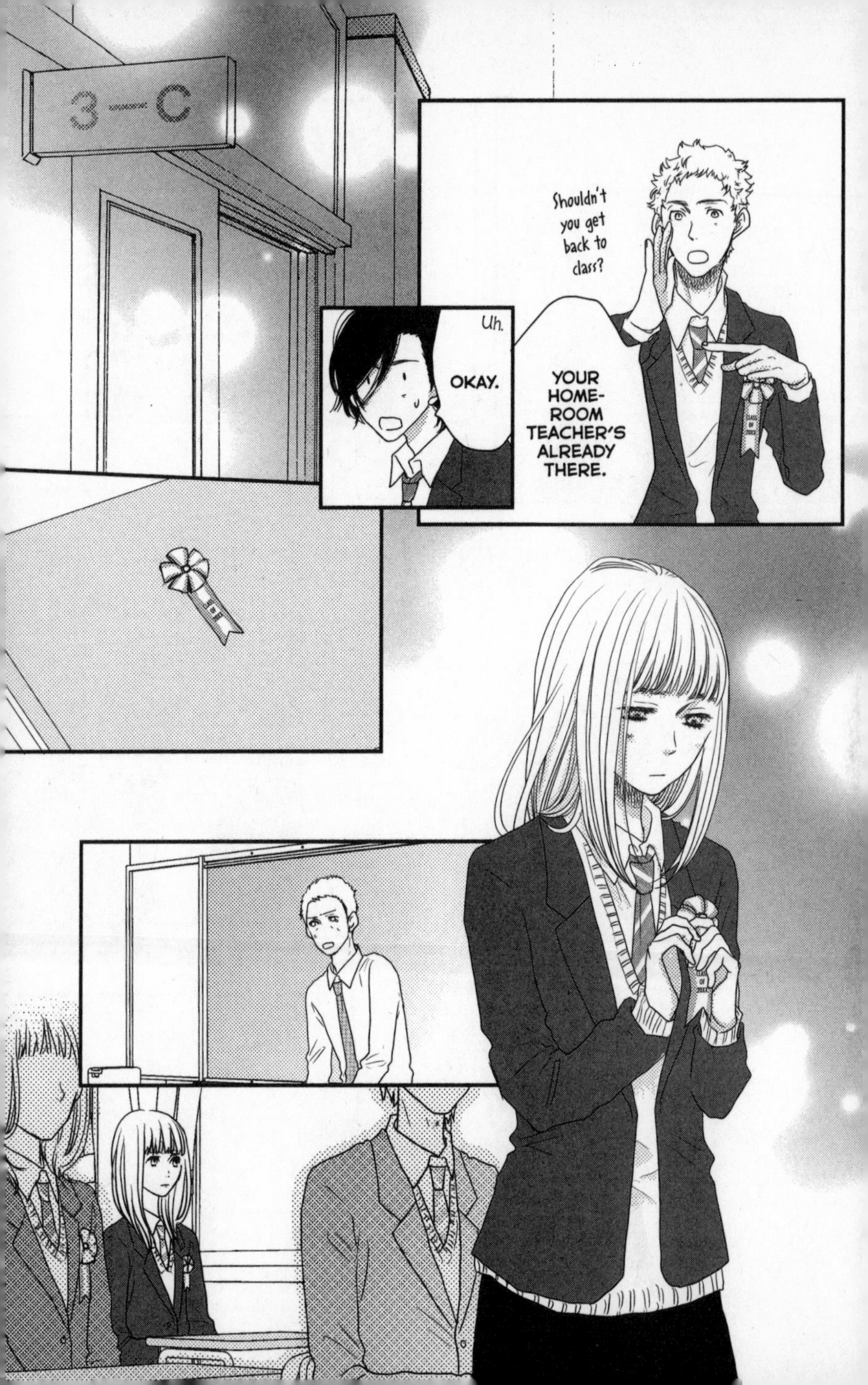
Shouldn't you get back to class?
YOUR HOME-ROOM TEACHER'S ALREADY THERE.
Uh.
OKAY.

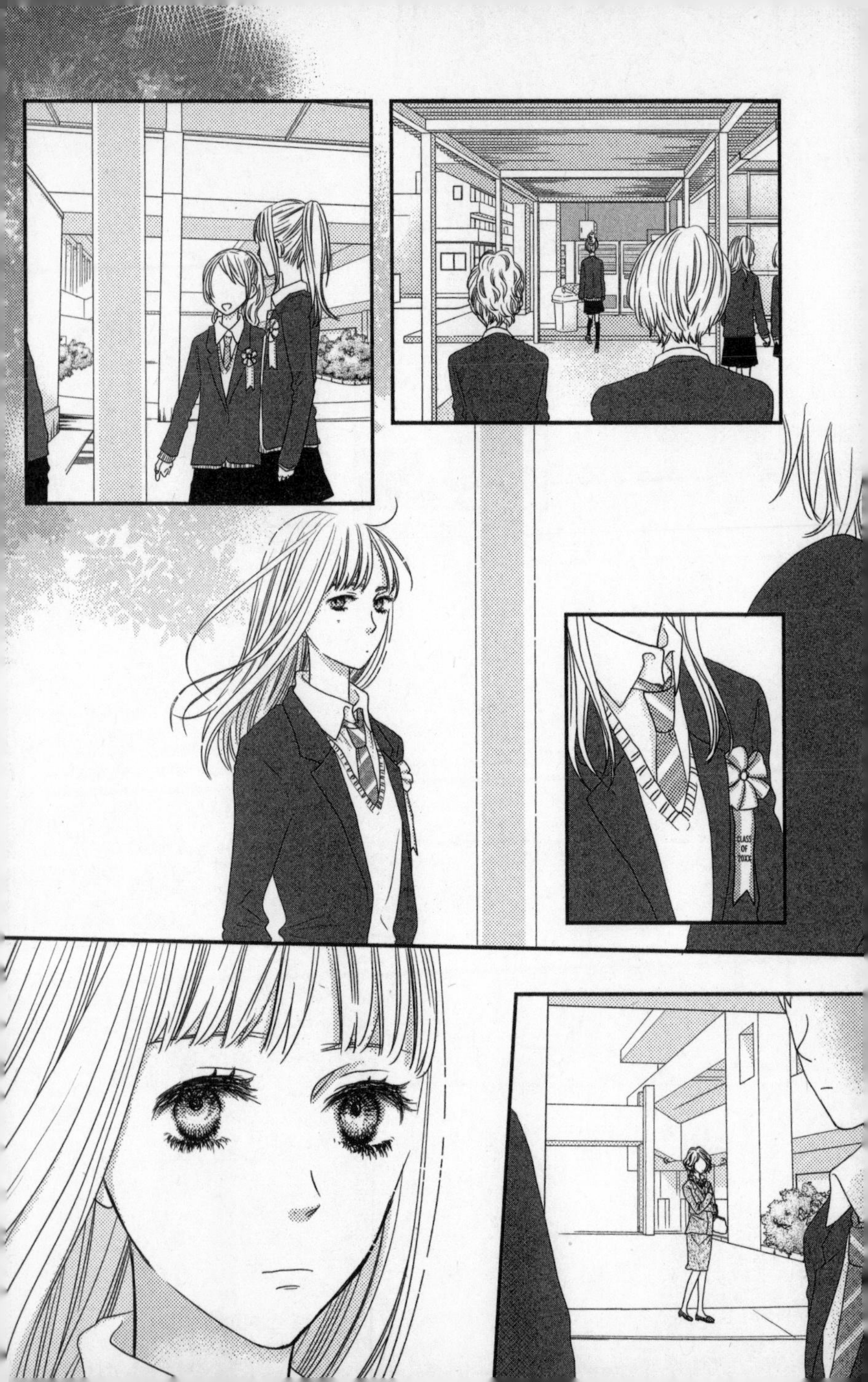
CLASS OF 20XX

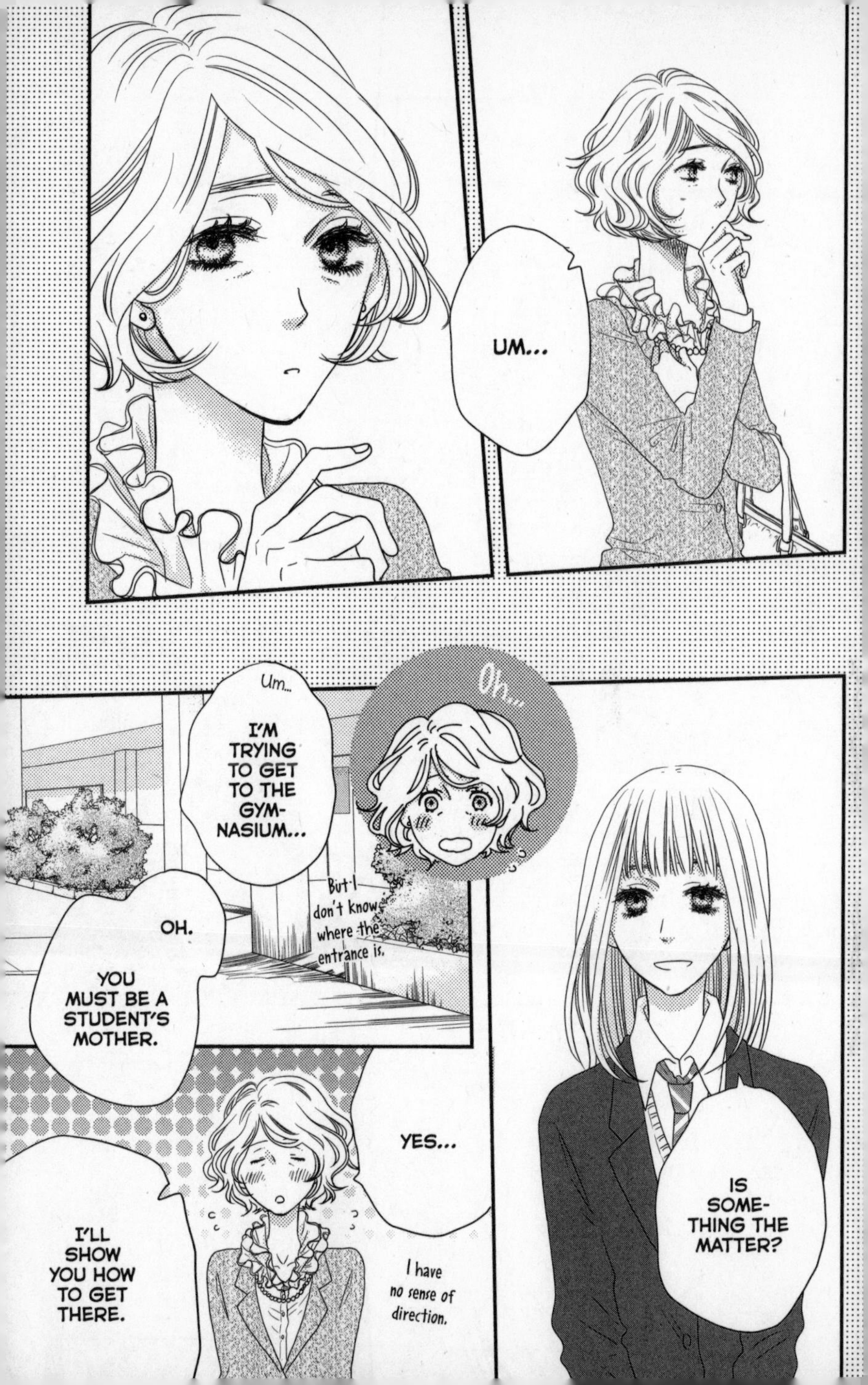
UM...
IS SOMETHING THE MATTER?
Oh...
Um...
I'M TRYING TO GET TO THE GYMNASIUM...
But I don't know where the entrance is.
OH.
YOU MUST BE A STUDENT'S MOTHER.
YES...
I have no sense of direction.
I'LL SHOW YOU HOW TO GET THERE.

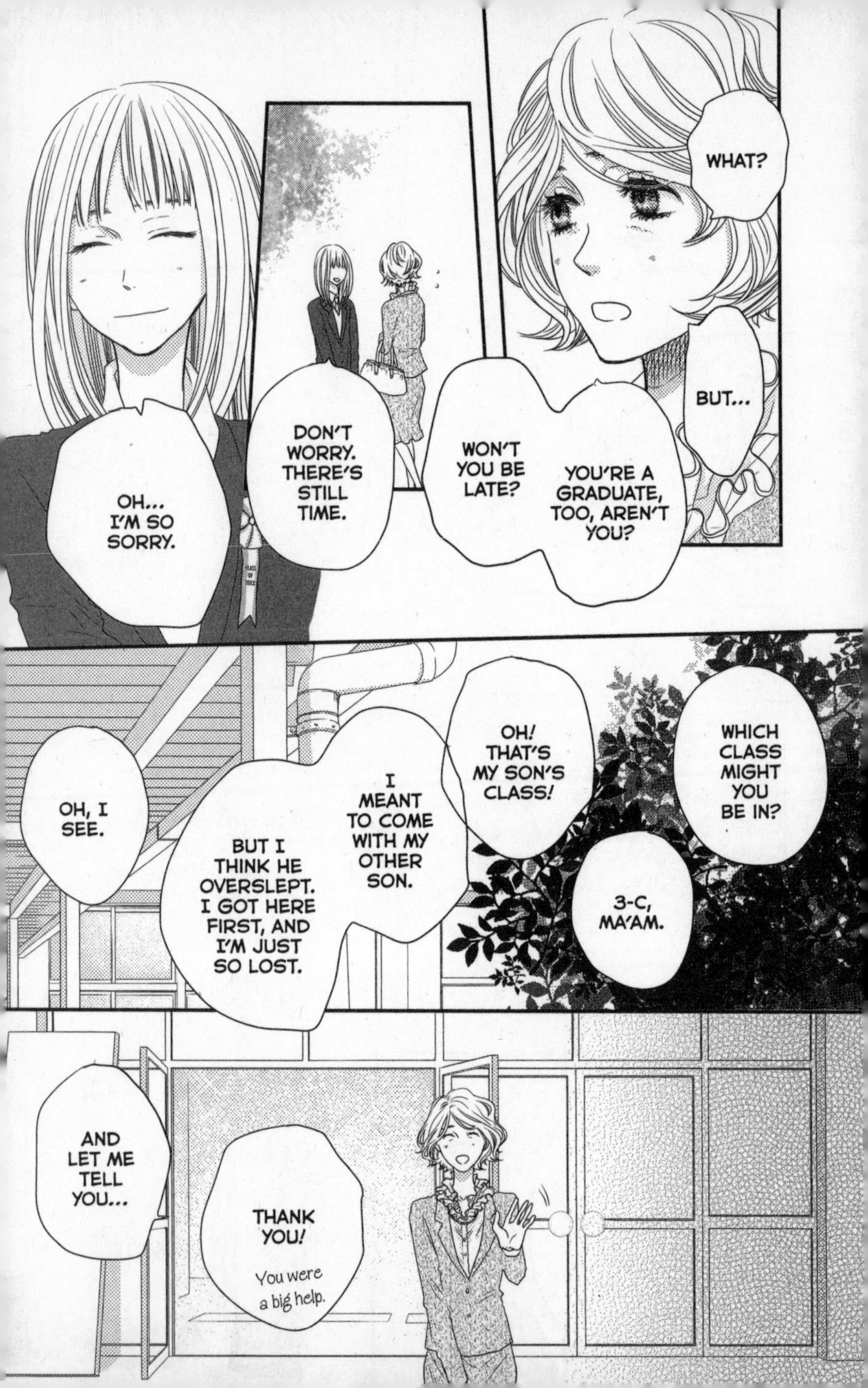
WHAT?
BUT...
YOU'RE A GRADUATE, TOO, AREN'T YOU?
WON'T YOU BE LATE?
DON'T WORRY. THERE'S STILL TIME.
OH... I'M SO SORRY.
WHICH CLASS MIGHT YOU BE IN?
3-C, MA'AM.
OH! THAT'S MY SON'S CLASS!
I MEANT TO COME WITH MY OTHER SON.
BUT I THINK HE OVERSLEPT. I GOT HERE FIRST, AND I'M JUST SO LOST.
OH, I SEE.
THANK YOU!
You were a big help.
AND LET ME TELL YOU...

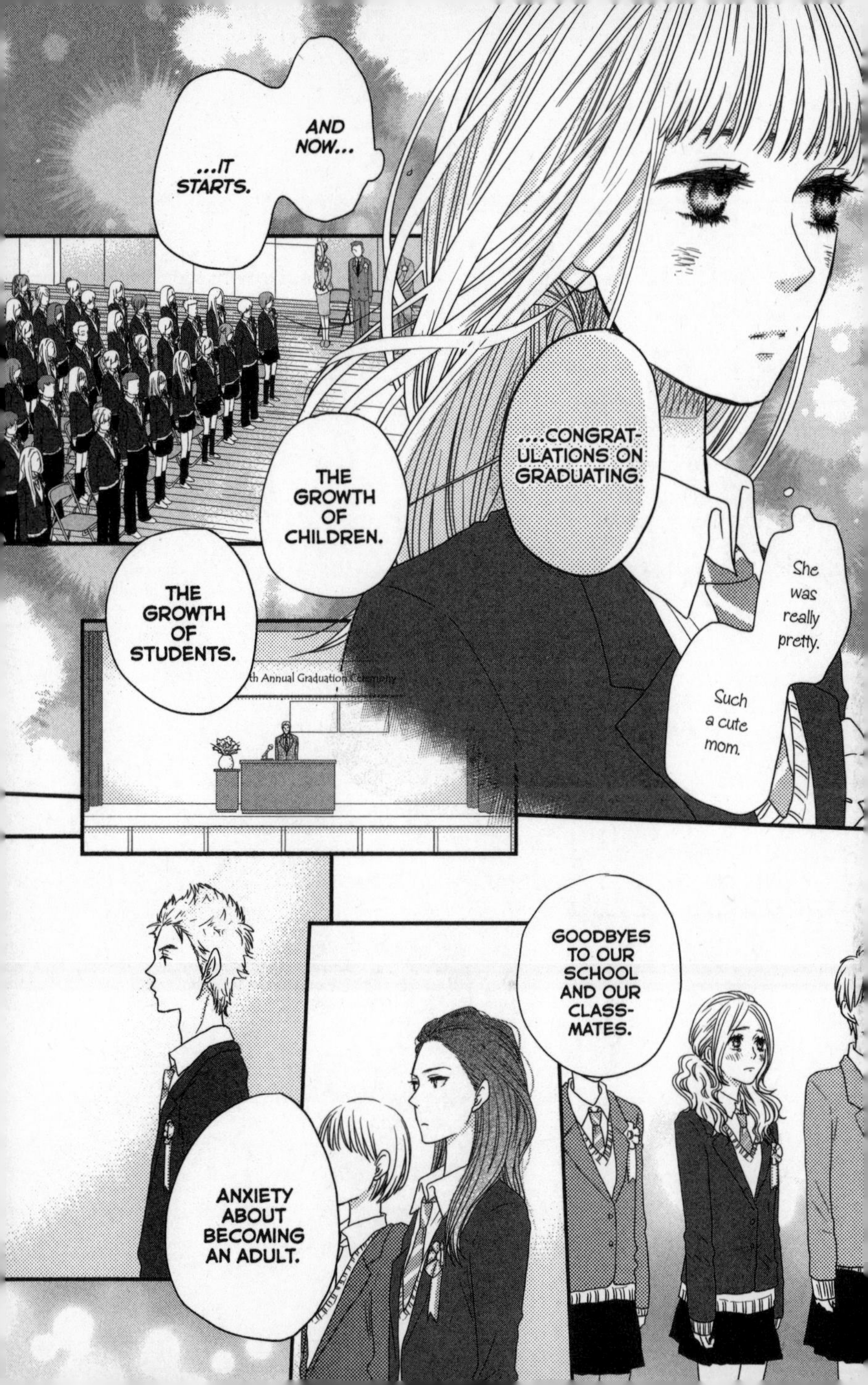
She was really pretty.
Such a cute mom.
....CONGRATULATIONS ON GRADUATING.
AND NOW...
...IT STARTS.
THE GROWTH OF CHILDREN.
THE GROWTH OF STUDENTS.
Annual Graduation
GOODBYES TO OUR SCHOOL AND OUR CLASSMATES.
ANXIETY ABOUT BECOMING AN ADULT.

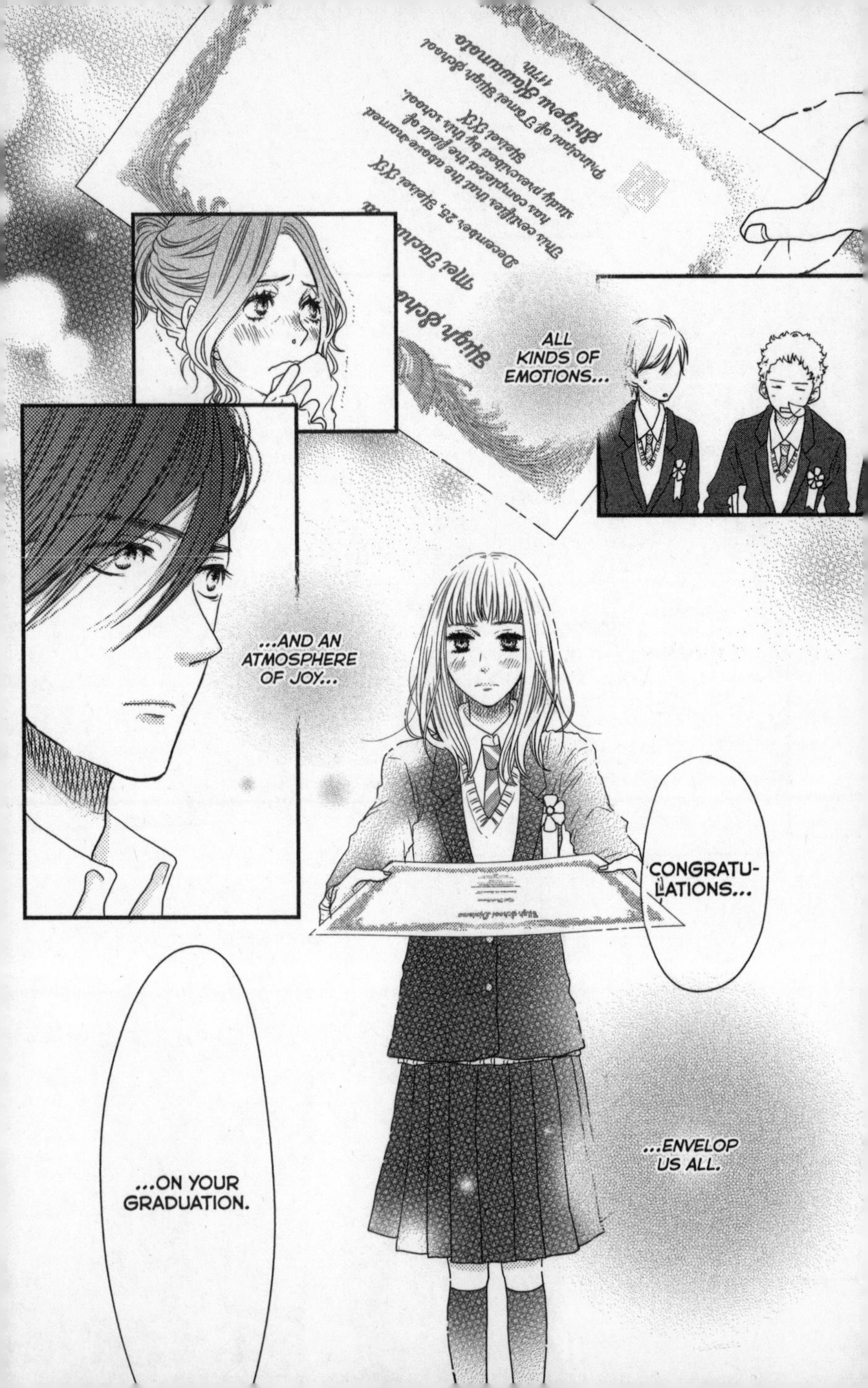
ALL KINDS OF EMOTIONS...
...AND AN ATMOSPHERE OF JOY...
CONGRATU-LATIONS...
...ENVELOP US ALL.
...ON YOUR GRADUATION.

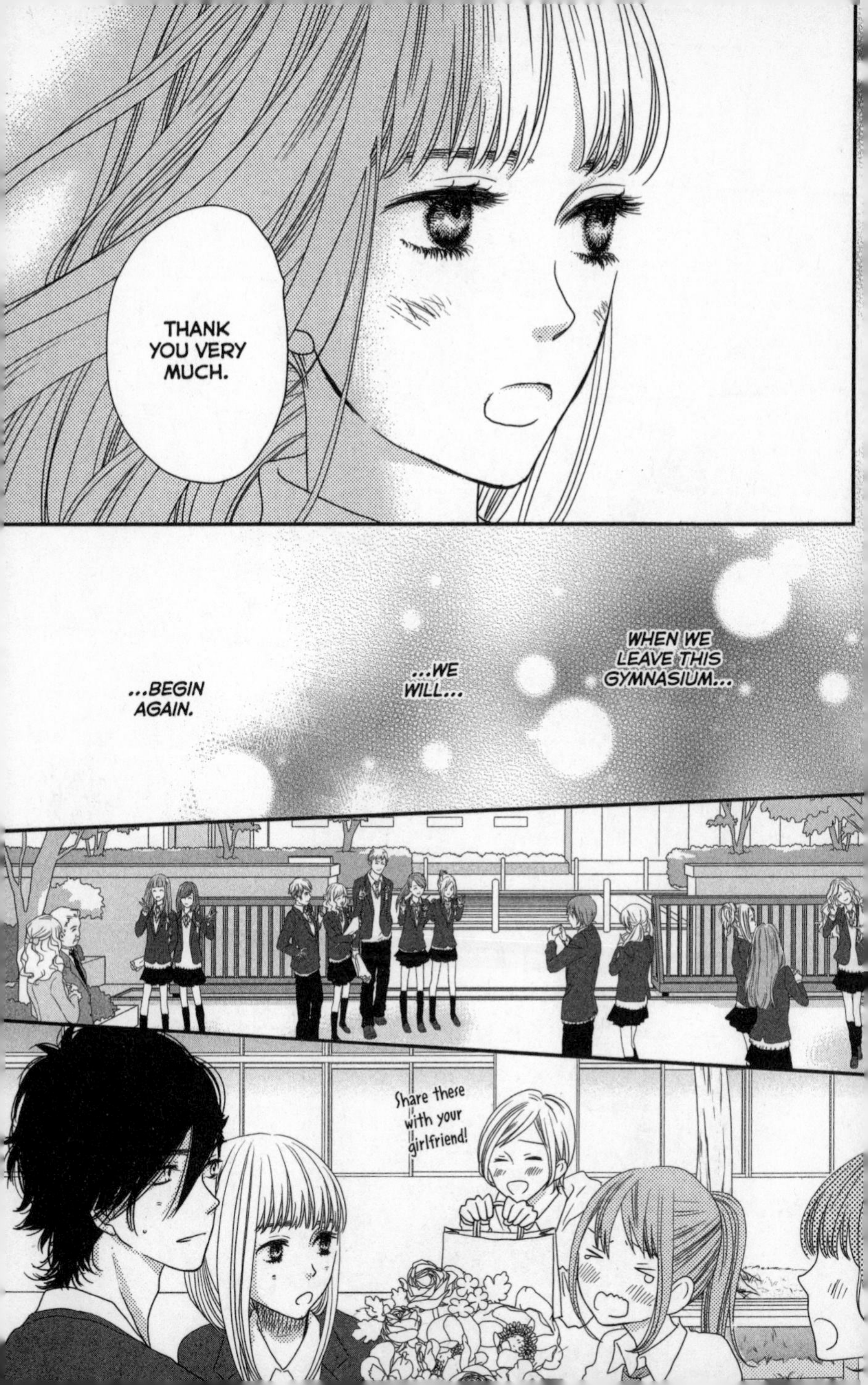
THANK YOU VERY MUCH.
WHEN WE LEAVE THIS GYMNASIUM...
...WE WILL...
...BEGIN AGAIN.
Share these with your girlfriend!

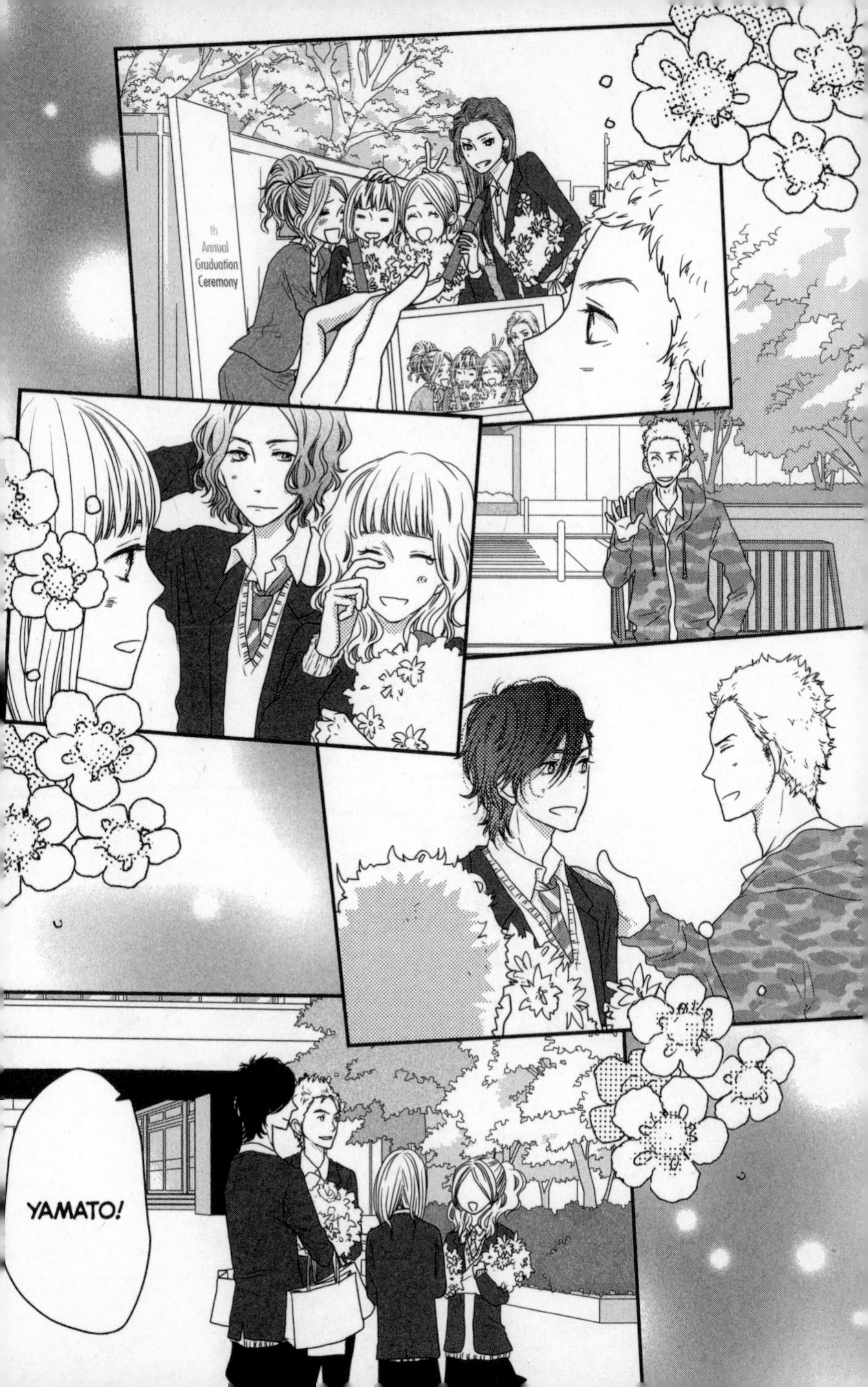
th Annual Graduation Ceremony
YAMATO!

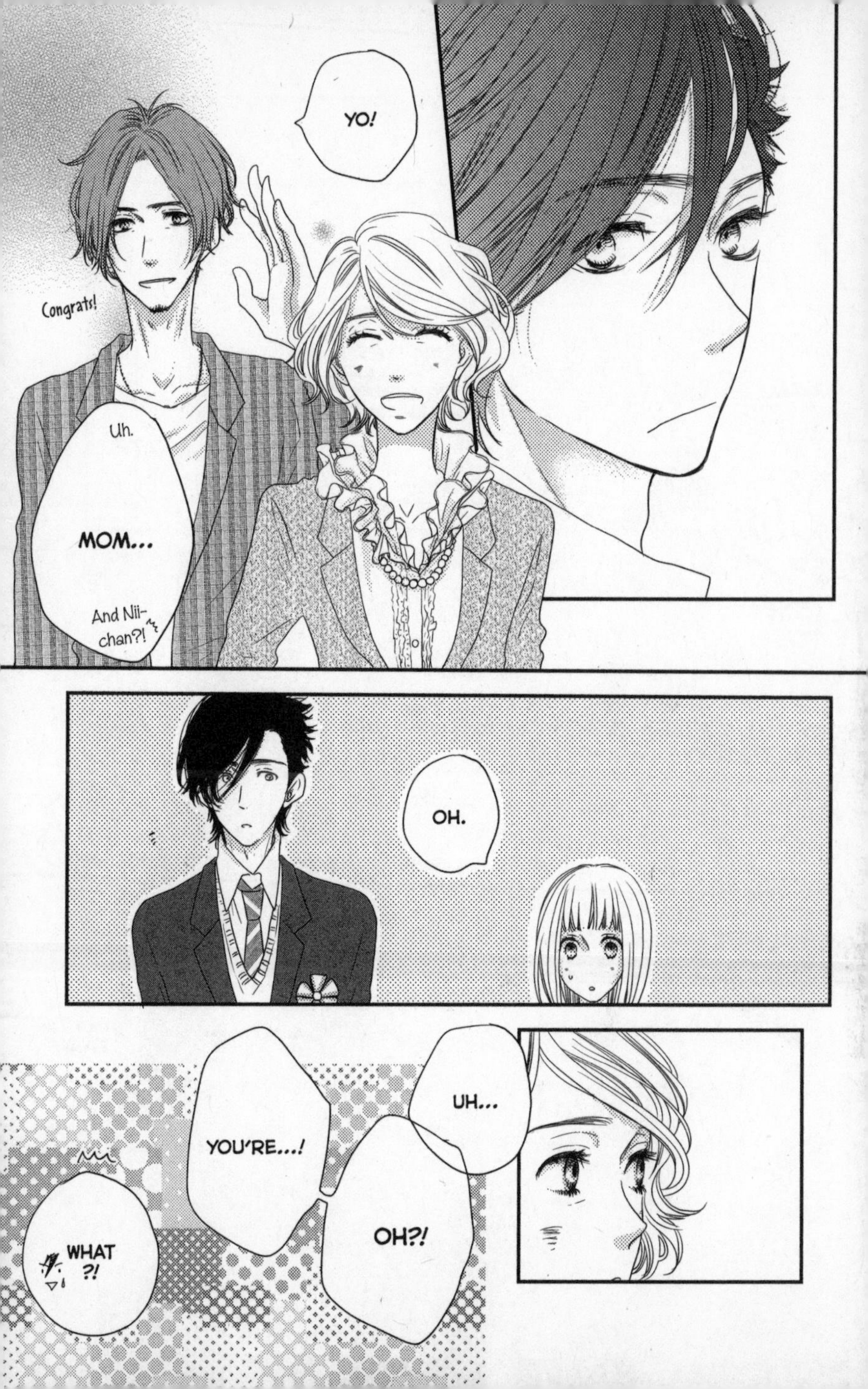
YO!
Congrats!
Uh.
MOM...
And Nii-chan?!
OH.
UH...
YOU'RE...!
OH?!
WHAT ?!

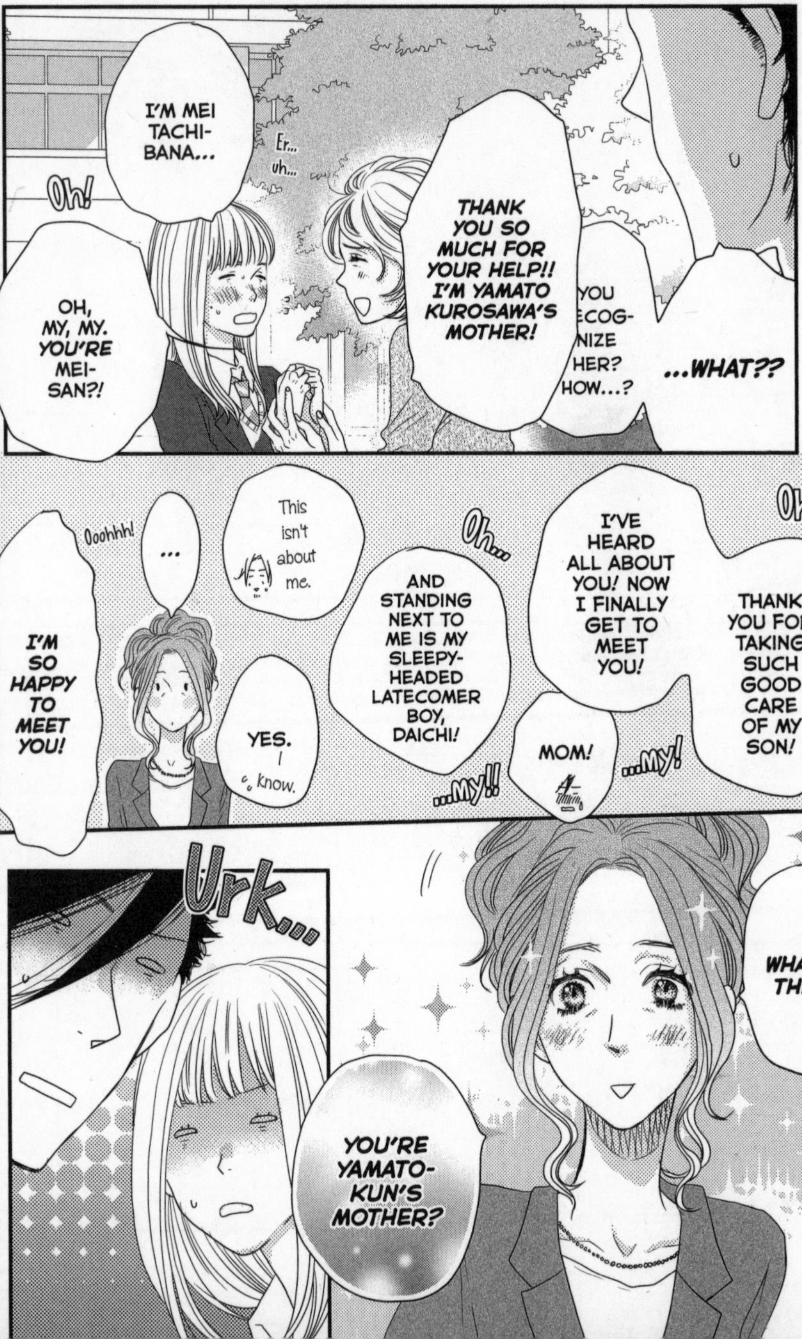
THANK YOU SO MUCH FOR YOUR HELP!! I'M YAMATO KUROSAWA'S MOTHER!
YOU RECOG-NIZE HER? HOW...?
...WHAT??
I'M MEI TACHI-BANA...
Er... uh...
Oh!
OH, MY, MY. YOU'RE MEI-SAN?!
Oh...
THANK YOU FOR TAKING SUCH GOOD CARE OF MY SON!
...My!
I'VE HEARD ALL ABOUT YOU! NOW I FINALLY GET TO MEET YOU!
MOM!
Oh...
AND STANDING NEXT TO ME IS MY SLEEPY-HEADED LATECOMER BOY, DAICHI!
...My!!
This isn't about me.
YES.
I know.
...
Ooohhh!
I'M SO HAPPY TO MEET YOU!
WHAT'S THIS?
YOU'RE YAMATO-KUN'S MOTHER?
Urk...

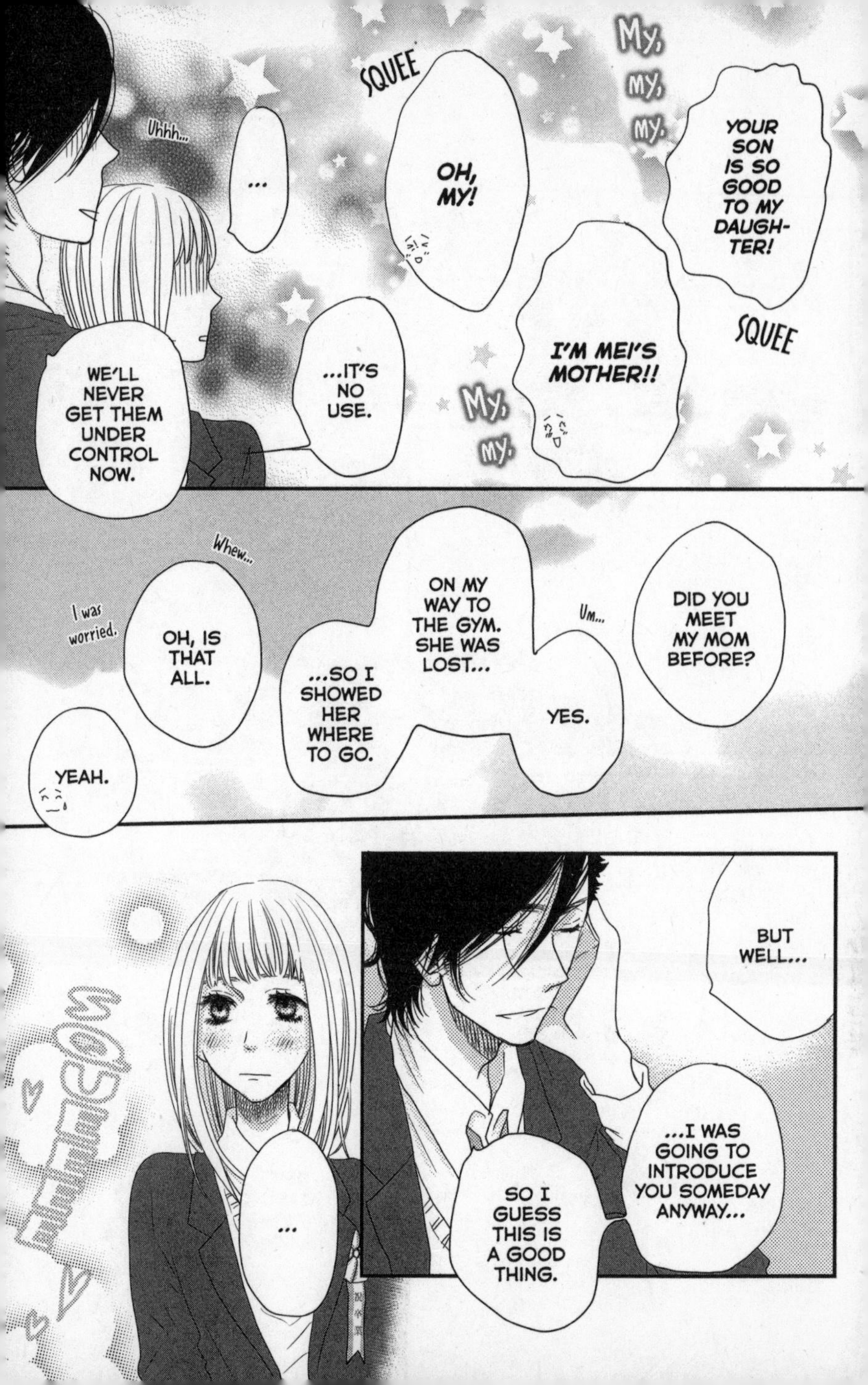
My, my, my.
YOUR SON IS SO GOOD TO MY DAUGHTER!
SQUEE
I'M MEI'S MOTHER!!
My, my.
OH, MY!
SQUEE
...
Uhhh...
...IT'S NO USE.
WE'LL NEVER GET THEM UNDER CONTROL NOW.
DID YOU MEET MY MOM BEFORE?
Um...
YES.
ON MY WAY TO THE GYM. SHE WAS LOST...
...SO I SHOWED HER WHERE TO GO.
Whew...
OH, IS THAT ALL.
I was worried.
YEAH.
BUT WELL...
...I WAS GOING TO INTRODUCE YOU SOMEDAY ANYWAY...
SO I GUESS THIS IS A GOOD THING.
...

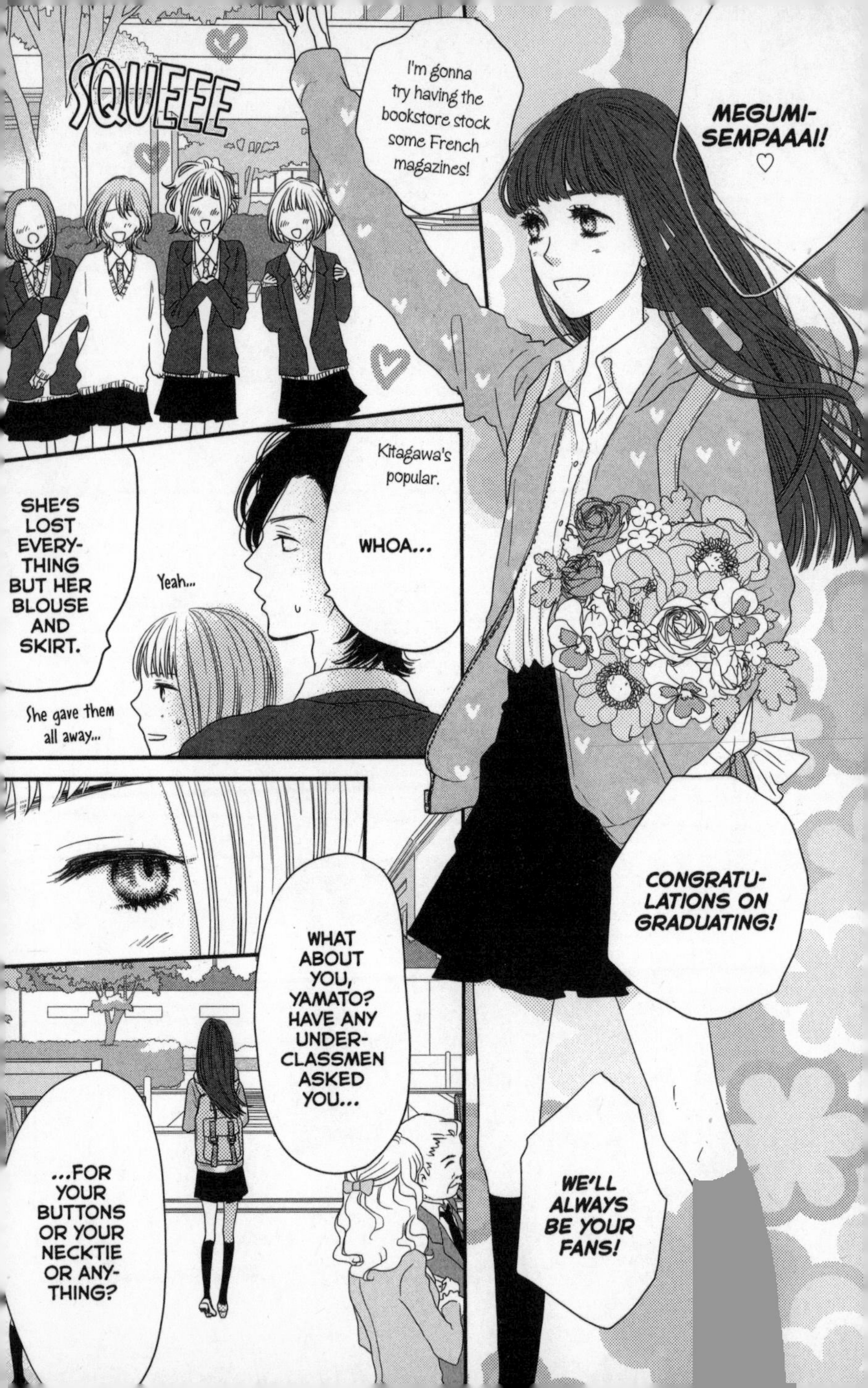
MEGUMI-SEMPAAAI! ♡
I'm gonna try having the bookstore stock some French magazines!
CONGRATULATIONS ON GRADUATING!
WE'LL ALWAYS BE YOUR FANS!
SQUEEE
Kitagawa's popular.
WHOA...
Yeah...
SHE'S LOST EVERYTHING BUT HER BLOUSE AND SKIRT.
She gave them all away...
WHAT ABOUT YOU, YAMATO? HAVE ANY UNDERCLASSMEN ASKED YOU...
...FOR YOUR BUTTONS OR YOUR NECKTIE OR ANYTHING?

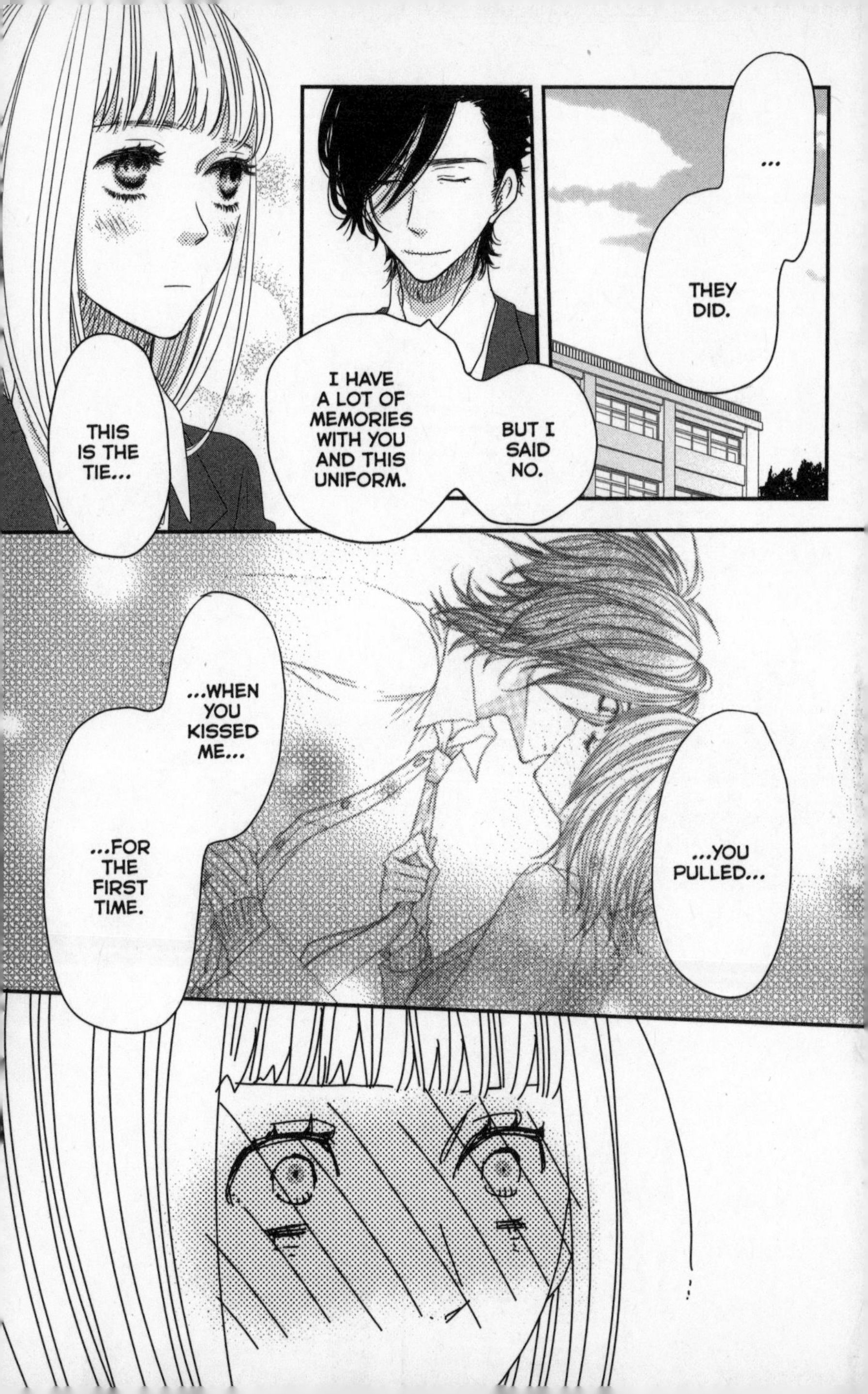
...
THEY DID.
BUT I SAID NO.
I HAVE A LOT OF MEMORIES WITH YOU AND THIS UNIFORM.
THIS IS THE TIE...
...YOU PULLED...
...WHEN YOU KISSED ME...
...FOR THE FIRST TIME.

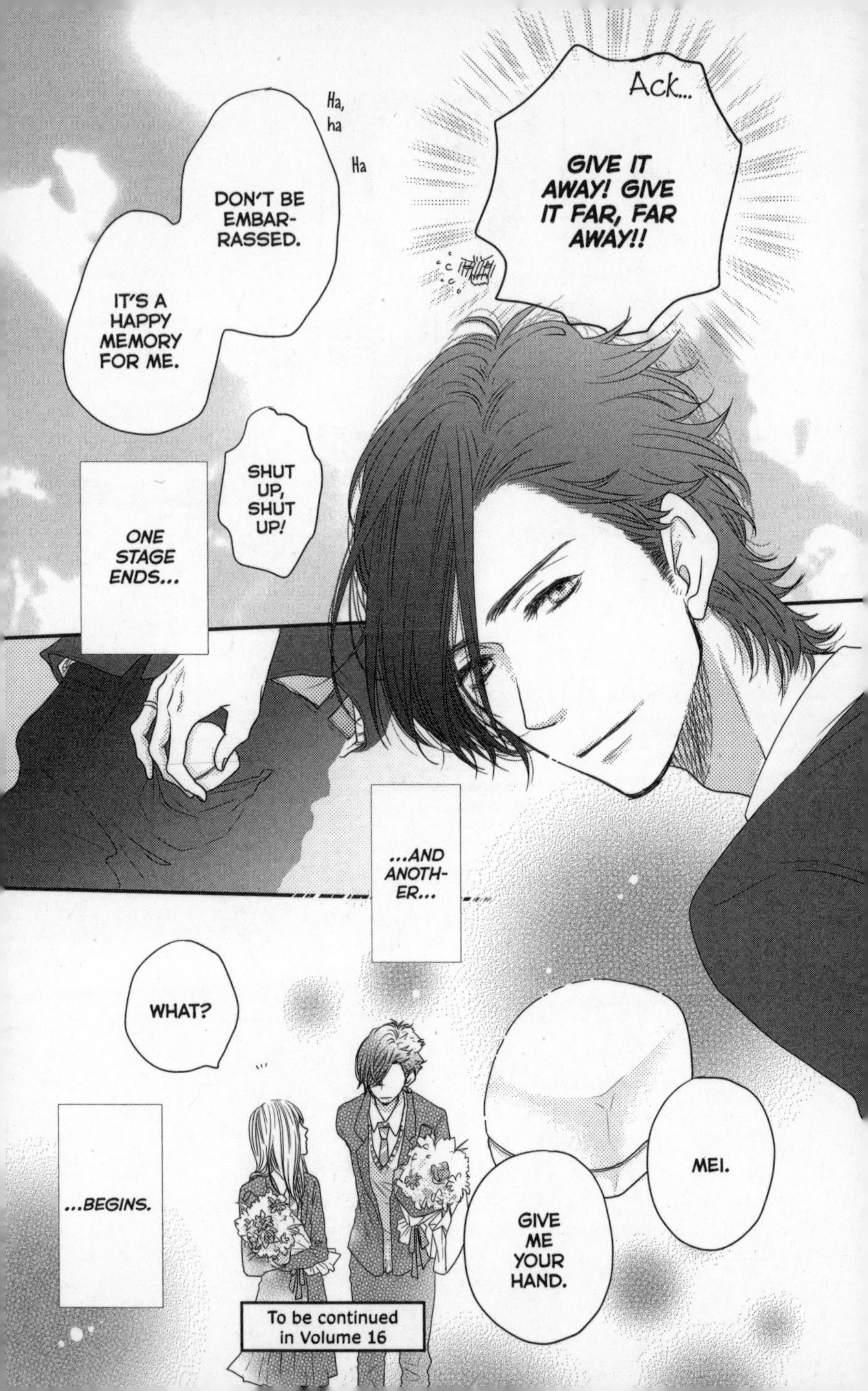

Ack...
GIVE IT AWAY! GIVE IT FAR, FAR AWAY!!
Ha, ha
Ha
DON'T BE EMBAR-RASSED.
IT'S A HAPPY MEMORY FOR ME.
SHUT UP, SHUT UP!
ONE STAGE ENDS...
...AND ANOTH-ER...
MEI.
GIVE ME YOUR HAND.
WHAT?
...BEGINS.
To be continued in Volume 16

Say "I love you".

Hello. I'm Kanae Hazuki. This is volume 15. It's been seven years since this series started, and we've finally made it to this point. As you can see, the high school arc ends in this volume. Mei and her friends have graduated. (But Kai still has one more year of high school life to go... (ha ha)) I feel like it went by so fast, but like it's also taken such a long time...

Oh yeah, there have been a few questions that I've been thinking I need to answer for a while but haven't been able to until now. So about Asami being in Mei's class for their third year... At first, I had decided that there were no class changes between second and third year, but as I was drawing, my world's rules got fuzzy... and the third-years ended up with a class change, too ; ;

I would like to apologize to anyone who got confused while reading. I'm sorry. Whew, I finally got that answered.

This is my first real series, and the first time I've drawn something for so long, so even as I draw it now, I'm more afraid than ever. I'm hopeless... ← Excuses, excuses...

But I love all of my characters, and so as a parent, I want to make sure all of them are happy.

Now then, all of these characters are graduating high school. When one stage ends, another begins. Everyone is standing at a new starting point. I think some of you will be thinking, "Wait, it's not over?" No, it's not over. I mean, they're just getting started. Their life drama is only beginning. They're only starting to add depth to their lives.

Thinking on it now, I enjoyed my high-school life well enough, but I have a lot more memories from my life now. I was wondering why that would be, and it might be because I started actually looking around me, and thinking and doing things for myself. When you become an adult, responsibilities are born into your life. But those responsibilities make you grow yourself. If you can get a good handle on those responsibilities as you move through life, then it will give your life more depth and create lots of memories. If you never become an adult, and always run from responsibilities, you'll never grow, and you can't make any memories, good or bad. And that's part of what I want Mei and her friends to work toward.

Let's say there are students in school right now with obstacles in their path, who are thinking, "Ugh, school is so boring." As someone who's experienced that, I can at least say, "Just wait a little longer." I've been saying this for a long time now, but high school isn't all there is to life. There are a lot of things that get more fun when you become an adult. I guess when you're in middle school and high school, you have adults and the law protecting you, so you don't have a lot of responsibilities. But I think there's only so much enjoyment to be had from that.

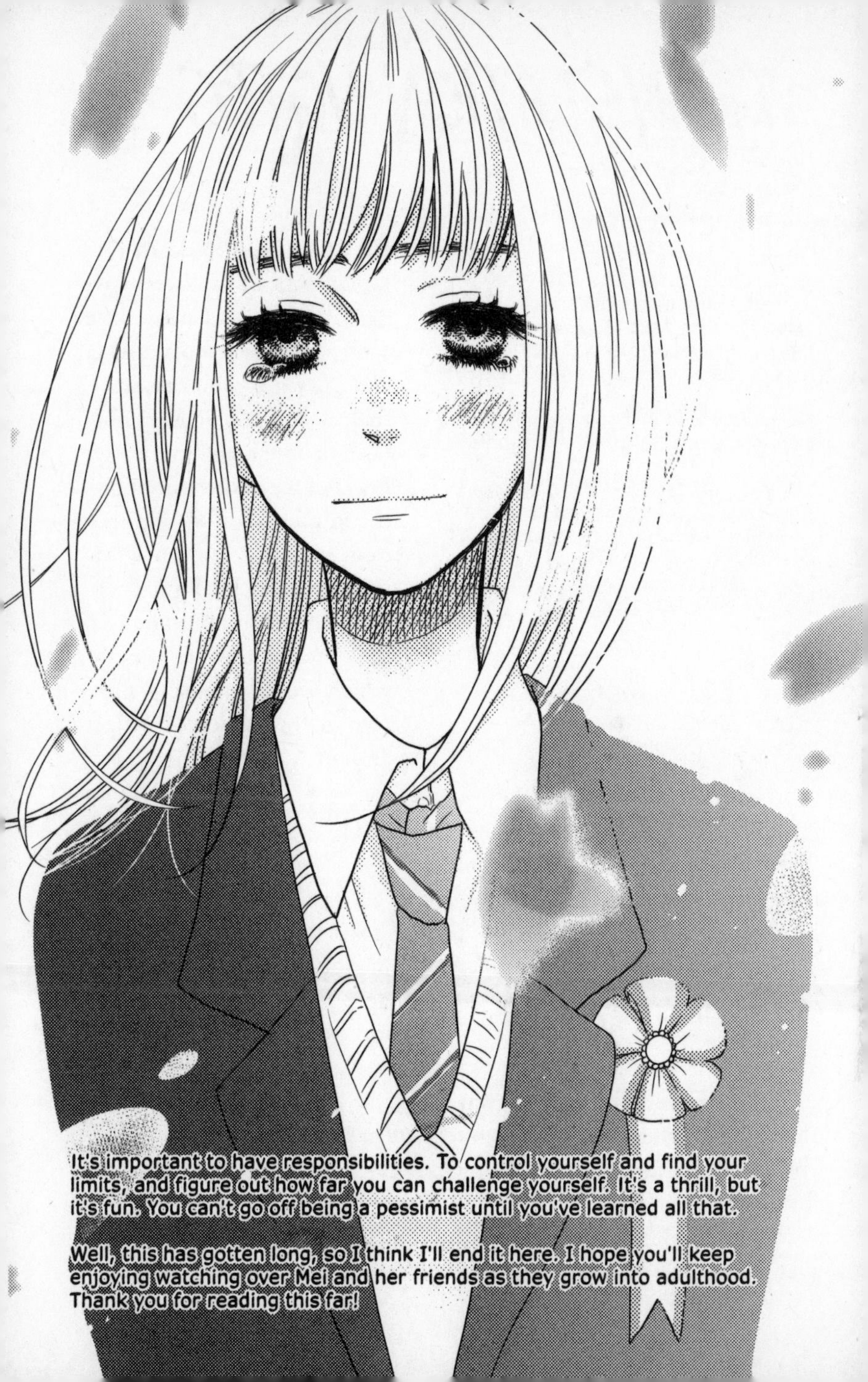

It's important to have responsibilities. To control yourself and find your limits, and figure out how far you can challenge yourself. It's a thrill, but it's fun. You can't go off being a pessimist until you've learned all that.

Well, this has gotten long, so I think I'll end it here. I hope you'll keep enjoying watching over Mei and her friends as they grow into adulthood. Thank you for reading this far!

TRANSLATION NOTES

Page 64: Kanmidokoro

Literally meaning "sweet flavor place" or "place of sweet flavor," a *kanmidokoro* is a place where you can eat Japanese sweets, such as *shiratama* and *gyūhi*, both of which are little cakes made of glutinous rice flour—the former is round, and the latter is often cut into squares but sometimes molded into shapes. Both are common toppings for the dessert known as *anmitsu*, which is a jelly made of algae (agar jelly) and served with fruit and other toppings.

Page 74: Japanese style Christmas

In Japan, the big winter holiday to spend with your family is New Year's, so Christmas is often celebrated as a romantic holiday. So Angelo is saying he wants to have a romantic Christmas with his girlfriend this year, like they do in Japan.

Page 158: Given everything away

In Japan, if someone you want to remember is graduating and you're afraid you may never see them again, it's traditional to ask for something to remember that person by, usually a piece of his or her school uniform, such as a button or necktie. Megumi is so popular that she doesn't have enough pieces of her uniform to go around.

a Silent Voice

KODANSHA COMICS

"The word heartwarming was made for manga like this." -Manga Bookshelf

"A harsh and biting social commentary... delivers in its depth of character and emotional strength." -Comics Bulletin

"A very powerful story about being different and the consequences of childhood bullying... Read it." –Anime News Network

Shoya is a bully. When Shoko, a girl who can't hear, enters his elementary school class, she becomes their favorite target, and Shoya and his friends goad each other into devising new tortures for her. But the children's cruelty goes too far. Shoko is forced to leave the school, and Shoya ends up shouldering all the blame. Six years later, the two meet again. Can Shoya make up for his past mistakes, or is it too late?

Available now in print and digitally!

Yamada-kun AND THE Seven Witches

KODANSHA COMICS

"A very funny manga with a lot of heart and character."
—Adventures in Poor Taste

SWAPPED WITH A KISS?!

Class troublemaker Ryu Yamada is already having a bad day when he stumbles down a staircase along with star student Urara Shiraishi. When he wakes up, he realizes they have switched bodies—and that Ryu has the power to trade places with anyone just by kissing them! Ryu and Urara take full advantage of the situation to improve their lives, but with such an oddly amazing power, just how long will they be able to keep their secret under wraps?

Available now in print and digitally!

Say I Love You. volume 15 is a work of fiction. Names, characters, places, and incidents are the products of the author's imagination or are used fictitiously. Any resemblance to actual events, locales, or persons, living or dead, is entirely coincidental.

A Kodansha Comics Trade Paperback Original

Published in the United States by Kodansha Comics, an imprint of Kodansha USA Publishing, LLC, New York.

Publication rights for this English edition arranged through Kodansha Ltd, Tokyo.

First published in Japan in 2015 by Kodansha Ltd., Tokyo as *Sukitte iinayo.* volume 15.

ISBN 978-1-63236-269-8

Printed in the United States of America.

www.kodanshacomics.com

9 8 7 6 5 4 3 2 1
Translation: Alethea and Athena Nibley
Lettering: Jennifer Skarupa
Editing: Ajani Oloye
Kodansha Comics edition cover design: Phil Balsman